Contents

Lists of Maps

GREEK ISLAND HOPPING is essential reading for the
independent traveller who wishes to discover the delights of
Greece and her islands for himself. This revised and updated
edition offers a fund of useful information on where to stay,
what to see, what to eat and drink, and what are the specialities
of a particular island. Dana Facaros has provided separate
chapters on Crete, the Cyclades, the Dodecanese, the Ionian
Islands, the North-Eastern Aegean Islands, the Saronic Islands,
the Sporades and Evia, together with clearly designed maps
which provide essential information at a glance.

Greek Island Hopping
A Handbook for the Independent Traveller
DANA FACAROS

SPHERE BOOKS LIMITED
30–32 Gray's Inn Road, London WC1X 8JL

First published in Great Britain by Gentry Books Limited
under the Wilton House Gentry imprint, 1979
Reprinted, revised and updated 1980
Copyright © Dana Facaros 1979
Published by Sphere Books Ltd,
in association with Gentry Books, 1981

To the memory of my great-uncle
Theologos Facaros
former mayor of Ikaria

Printed and bound in Great Britain by
Collins, Glasgow

Introduction

Thanks to an exquisite beauty, present political stability, the massive efforts of the National Tourist Organization of Greece, current fashion and a reputation for being cheap, Greece has become one of the greatest tourist centres of the world. The reasons to come are so many and so good that some people don't bother to use their return tickets home. In particular the islands of Greece, from Byron's time to our own, have been acclaimed the most enchanting of an enchanting country, "the butter on the bread," as it were. However, any traveller expecting to find this enchantment in rustic backwardness will find his road a bit difficult; he is much more likely to encounter the lukewarm cup of Nescafé or the ubiquitous, plastic-wrapped "tost".

The Greeks, for their part, regard the tremendous tourist trade in their country with mixed reactions. The growth of tourism has given many of them jobs, and in some cases, saved entire islands from depopulation. Liberal-minded Greeks praise the influence of western morality and free thought, which, brought by connections from abroad, have begun to change the lives of the people, especially the women, who were once raised only to be wed. On the negative side, the locals do not rejoice when their bus to the village is brimmed to the chrome with tourists who stick ruck sacks in their faces. Foreigners are also reported to carry lice, eat all the fish, and swim in the buff. Worst of all, many who come spend very little money.

These complaints, however, are very minor — except for the latter as it affects the national economy. The grumblers may be a little curt (for Greeks) when dealing with tourists but never worse. On the other hand, the kindness of the people is often overwhelming, most of all on the islands. The famous Greek hospitality has survived the invasion from the Occident: a *xenos* is still as much "guest" as "stranger," despite the new Greek word *touristas*. *Touristas* isloate themselves in luxury hotels and can be seen only through the windows of their air-conditioned buses. The *xenos* comes out to know and play with the Greeks. Friendly interest on the part of the visitor will invariably lead to a more than reciprocal response, no matter how many obituaries on Greek hospitality are written by those expecting all doors to open automatically.

7

Acknowledgements

I would like to thank the many members of the National Tourist Organization of Greece for their kind assistance in writing this guide, and the following people without whose moral, physical and financial assistance it would not have been possible: my parents and my grandmother, Mrs. Despina Facaros; Joseph Coniaris, Sotiros S. Kouvaras of Ithaki, Filia and Kosta Pattakos, Carolyn Steiner, and Julie Wegner.

Part 1
The Greeks of Today

History

Aristotle, the greatest Greek scholar of all time, proclaimed man a political animal, and the Greeks today take that word "political" in its most literal sense. As one could see after the recent death of Archbishop Makarios, the President of Cyprus, events of the past still burn deep in the hearts of the Greek people. In order to understand present attitudes one must know the historical developments that formed them, and for that reason the following outline of the last 130 years of Greek history is included. It is only an outline, and those with further interests can refer to the small collection of books in English on the subject or to the Greek people themselves. Ancient and Byzantine history, which touches Greece less closely today, is dealt with under Athens and the individual islands.

From Hellenistic times to the end of the Byzantine Empire, Greek people lived not only within the boundaries of modern-day Greece but throughout Asia Minor, in particular that part of Asia Minor which is now Turkey. Constantinople was their capital, and it was Greek. Not once during the 400-year Turkish Occupation did these people and their brethren in Europe stop considering themselves Greeks — and the Turks, for the most part, were content to let them be Greeks as long as they paid their taxes.

The revolutionary spirit that swept through Europe at the end of the 18th and beginning of the 19th centuries did not fail to catch hold in Greece, by now more than weary of the lethargic inactivity and sporadic cruelties of the Ottomans. The Greek War of Independence was begun in the Peloponnese in 1821, and it continued for more than six years in a series of bloody atrocities and political intrigues and divisions. In the end the Great Powers, namely Britain, Russia, and France, came to assist the Greek cause, especially in the decisive battle of Navarino (20 October 1827) which in effect gave the newly formed Greek government the Peloponnese. Count John Capodistria of Corfu, ex-secretary to the Tzar of Russia, became the first President of Greece, which included the Peloponnese and the peninsula up to a line between the cities of Arta and Volos. While a king was sought for the new state, Capodistria followed an independent policy which succeeded in offending the pro-British and pro-French factions in Greece — and also the powerful Mavromikhalis family who assassinated him in 1831. Before the subsequent anarchy spread too far, the Great Powers appointed Otto, son of King Ludwig I of Bavaria, as King of the Greeks.

Under Otto began the Great Idea, as it was called, of uniting all the lands of the Greek peoples with the motherland, although it made little advance at the time. Otto was peacibly ousted in 1862 and the Greeks elected William George, son of the King of Denmark, as "King of the Hellenes". By this they meant all the Greek people, and not merely those within the borders of Greece. The National Assembly drew up a constitution in 1864 which made the nation officially a democracy under a king, a system that began to work practically under Prime Minister Kharilaos Trikoupis in 1875. With the long reign of George I Greece began to develop with an economy based on sea trade. The Great Idea, always in the back of the Greek Mind, waited for an opportune moment to ripen.

In 1910 the great statesman from Crete, Eleftherios Venizelos, became Prime Minister of Greece for the first time. Under his direction the opportune moment came in the form of the two Balkan Wars of 1912-13, as a result of which Crete, Samos, Macedonia and southern Epirus were annexed to the Greek nation. Meantime King George was assassinated by a madman, and Constantine I ascended to the throne of Greece. Constantine married the sister of Kaiser Wilhelm and had a close relationship with Germany. When the First World War broke out, so did a dispute as to whose side Greece was on. Venizelos supported the Allies and Constantine the Central Powers, although he officially remained neutral until the Allies forced him to mobilize the Greek army. Meanwhile, in the north of Greece Venizelos had set up his own government with volunteers in support of the Allied cause. After the war the Great Idea still smouldered, and Greek forces were sent to occupy Smyrna (present-day Izmir) and advance on Ankara, the new Turkish capital. It was a disaster. The Turks, under Mustapha Kemal (later Ataturk) had grown far more powerful after their defeat in the Balkan War than the Greeks had imagined. In August 1922 the Greek army was completely routed from Smyrna, and many Greek residents who could not escape were slaughtered. Constantine immediately abdicated in favour of his son George II and died soon afterwards. The government fell and Colonel

Plastiras with his officers took over, ignobly executing the ministers of the previous government. Massive population exchanges were made between Greece and Turkey to destroy the main reason behind Greek expansionist claims, and the Greeks were confronted with the difficulties of a million Anatolian refugees.

In 1929 a republic was proclaimed which lasted for ten shaky years, during which the Greek communist party, or KKE, was formed and gained strength. After the brief Panglos dictatorship, the Greeks elected Venizelos back as President. He set the present borders of Greece (except for the Dodecanese islands, which belonged to Italy until 1945). During his term of office there was also an unsuccessful uprising by the Greek Cypriots, four-fifths of the population of what was then a British Crown Colony, who desired union with Greece.

The republic, beset with economic difficulties, collapsed in 1935, and King George II returned to Greece, with General Metaxas as his Prime Minister. Metaxas had dictatorial control of the county under the regime of the 4th of August, which crushed the trade unions and all leftist activities, exiling the leaders. Having prepared the Greek army long in advance for the coming war, Metaxas died in 1941 after his historic "No!" to Mussolini. Indeed, in 1940, with Italian troops on the Albanian border, Greece was the first Allied country to join Britain against the Axis voluntarily. The Greek army stopped the Italians and then pushed them back into Albania.

But by May 1941 all of Greece was in the hands of the Nazis, and George II was in exile in Egypt. As bad as the occupation was in Greece, political strife compounded it, fired by the uncertain constitutionality of a monarch who had been acting for so many years without parliamentary support. The Communist-organized EAM, the National Liberation Front, attacked all the competing resistance groups so rigorously that they came to support the monarchy as a lesser evil than the Communists. These Monarchists, as they were called, were supported in turn by the British. Nothing could be done, however, to prevent Civil War from breaking out three months after the liberation of Greece. The army of the EAM almost took Athens when the King finally agreed not to return to Greece without a plebiscite.

After the World War and the Civil War the country was in a shambles, economically and politically. Americans began to supersede the British in Greek affairs; Britain had her own difficulties. The elections of March 1946 were observed by the Americans and ran peaceably. A few months later the King was welcomed back to Greece, although he died a year later to be succeeded by his brother Paul.

Recovery, expecially in the sphere of economics, happened very slowly, despite American assistance. Stalin was also very interested in the strategic location of Greece. In a round about way this caused the second Civil War in 1947 between the communists and the government. The USA became deeply involved trying to defend the recent Truman Doctrine, and government forces finally won out in October 1949, allowing the country to return to the problems of reconstruction.

With the Korean War in 1951 Greece and Turkey became full members of NATO, although the Cyprus issue again divided the two lands. The Greek Cypriots, led by Archbishop Makarios in 1954, clamoured and rioted for union with Greece. Either for military reasons (so believe the Greeks) or to prevent a new conflict between Greece and Turkey, the Americans and British were hardly sympathetic to Cyprus' claims. Meanwhile Prime Minister Papagos died, and Karamanlis replaced him, staying in office for eight years. The stability and prosperity begun under Papagos increased, agriculture and tourism becoming the major industries. The opposition to Karamanlis at this time criticized him for his pro-Western policy, basically because of the Cyprus situation, which grew worse all the time. Because of the island's one-fifth Turkish population and its locality, the Turks would not agree on union for Cyprus — the independence or partitioning of the island was as far as they would go. Finally in 1960, after much discussion on all sides, Cyprus became an independent republic and elected Makarios its first President. The British and Americans were considered to be good friends again.

Then once more the economy began to plague the government. The royal family became unpopular, there were strikes, and in 1963 occurred the famous assassination of Deputy Lambrakis in Thessaloniki, for which police officers were tried and convicted. Anti-Greek government feelings rose in London, just when the King and Queen were about to visit. Karamanlis advised them not to go, and their insistence sparked off his resignation. George Papandreau of the opposition was eventually elected President. King Paul died and Constantine II became King of Greece.

In 1964 violence broke out in Cyprus again, owing to the disproportional representation in government of the Turkish minority, problems temporarily solved at the time. A quarrel with the King caused Papandreau's resignation, and there was much bitterness, leaving political allegiances between Monarchists and Republicans. The party system deteriorated and on 21 April, 1967 the colonels established their military dictatorship. George Papandreau and his son Andreas were imprisoned, the latter charged with treason. George Papadopoulos became dictator, imprisoning thousands without trial. In 1967 another grave incident occurred in Cyprus, almost leading to war. Shortly afterwards, Constantine II fled to Rome.

The proclaimed aim of the colonels' junta was a moral cleansing of Christian Greece. Democratic freedom was suppressed notoriously, and the secret police were guilty of the cruellest tortures. Yet the British and American governments tolerated the regime, the latter very actively for its NATO interests. The internal situation went from bad to worse, and in 1973 students of the Polytechnic school in Athens struck. Tanks were brought in and many were killed. After this incident popular feeling rose so high that Papadopoulos was arrested, only to be replaced by his arrester, the head of the military police and an even worse dictator, Ioannides. The nation was in turmoil. Attempting to save his position by resorting to the Great Idea appeal, Ioannides tried to launch a coup on Cyprus by assassinating Makarios, intending to replace him with a president who would declare the long-desired union of Cyprus with Greece. It was a fiasco. Makarios fled, and the Turkish army invaded Cyprus. The dictatorship resigned and Karamanlis returned to Athens from Paris where he had been living in self-exile. He immediately formed a new government, released the political prisoners and legalized the Communist Party. He then turned his attention to Cyprus, where Turkish forces had occupied 40 per cent of the island. But the Greek army was not strong enough to take on the Turks, nor did the British or Americans come to help.

On 17 November, 1974 an election was held, which Karamanlis easily won. The monarchy did less well and Greece became the republic it is today. In 1977 Archbishop Makarios died, leaving the Cyprus issue even more up in the air than before in the minds of the Greeks, although the Turks seem to consider it well nigh settled. This is still one of the major debating points in Greek politics, along with entrance into the European Common Market and continued connections with NATO (the Greeks are understandably slow to forgive the Americans for their support of the junta). Social reform is also a very important issue with the left.

The major political parties in Greece at this moment are the ND, or New Democratic, of Karamanlis; the Centre Union (Enosi kentrou) of Mavros; the Nees Dynamis, or Young Force, of Mangkakis; the Socialist Party, or PASOK, of Andreas Papandreau; and the communist parties KKE and KKE essoteriko (national) — the latter having no connections with the Soviet Union.

Religion

With the exception of some Roman Catholics in the Cyclades, nearly all Greeks belong to the Orthodox church; indeed, being Orthodox and speaking Greek were traditionally the two most important criteria in defining a Greek, no matter where he was born. The church has so much to do with being "Greek" that even the greatest doubters can hardly conceive of marrying outside the church, or neglecting to have their children baptized. Much emphasis is put on ceremony and decorum, which has changed very little since the foundation of the church in the 4th century by Constantine the Great, Emperor of Constantinople. As Constantinople took the place of Rome as the political and Christian capital of the world, the Greeks believe their church to be the only true successor to the original church of Rome. Therefore, a true Greek is called a *Romiós*, or Roman, and the Greek language of today is called *Romaíka*.

The Orthodox church is considered perfect and eternal; if not, its adherents cannot be saved. This explains the violence of the controversy over the icons in the 8th century, when iconoclasts, influenced by the mid-eastern religions, declared images of divine beings as sacrilegious. This debate served to sever the Roman Catholic church from the Orthodox, compounded by the crowning of Charlemagne as the Emperor of Rome, which had previously been subject to the Emperor of Constantinople. Further divisions arose over the celibacy of the clergy (Orthodox priests can marry before they are ordained) and the use of the phrase "and the son" in the Holy Creed, the issue which caused the final schism in 1054 when the Pope's representative Cardinal Humbert excommunicated the Patriarch of Constantinople.

After the fall of the Byzantine Empire, the Turks not only allowed the Orthodox church to exist, but imparted great powers to the Patriarch. The church was thus able to preserve many Greek traditions through the dark age of Ottoman rule, including education; on the other hand it often abused this power against its own flock, especially on a local scale. According to an old saying, priests, headmen, and Turks were the three curses of Greece; the priests haven't exonerated themselves from the list even today, which now includes the king and the cuckold. "See how many churches there are?" the people ask. "See how rich they are? And see how poor the people?"

The vast quantity of churches one sees on some islands has little to do with the priests, however, for they were built by families or individuals, especially by sailors, seeking the protection of a patron saint. Some were built to keep a promise, others are in simple thanksgiving. Architecturally there is an endless variety of styles, depending on the region, period and terrain, as well as the wealth and whim of the builder. All but the tiniest of chapels have an *iconstasis*, either of wood or stone, which separates the *heiron* or sanctuary where only the ordained are allowed from the rest of the church. When you visit a Greek church (almost all are closed during the mid-afternoon siesta) it is good form to dress discreetly and to leave a few drachmas for upkeep.

Almost all these churches have only one service a year, on the name day of the patron saint (name days are celebrated in Greece far more widely than birthdays. "Many years!" *(chrónia pollá!)* is how to greet people on their nameday). This annual celebration is called a *yiortí* or more frequently *panayiéri,* and is the cause for feasts and dancing after the church service. If feasible a *panayiéri* takes place in the church yard; otherwise you'll find them in neighbouring wooded areas or in tavernas. The food can be superb but is more often basic and plentiful; for a set price you receive more than your share and a doggy bag full, generally of goat. Occasionally a *panayiéri* is free, and it goes without saying that these are the most popular, no matter how long a walk is necessary to get to them. These parties are also the best places to hear Greek village music and to learn its dances. For that reason the major ones for each island are included in this book, although by no means all. In the case of Crete there are at least two or three every day. 15 August, the Assumption of the Virgin *(tis panayias)* is the largest *panayiéri* in Greece apart from Easter and perhaps Christmas. The faithful sail to Tinos, the

Lourdes of Greece, and other centres connected with Mary, and for that reason this is not the ideal time for travel among the islands, especially the Cyclades. Not only are the boats filled to over capacity, but the August Meltemi wind blows with vigour, and Greek matrons, the most ardent pilgrims of all, are also the worst sailors I have ever seen.

Greek weddings are another very interesting and lovely spectacle. The bride and groom stand solemnly before the chanting priest, while the surrounding family and friends often do everything but watch the proceedings. White crowns, bound together by a white ribbon, are placed on the heads of bride and groom and the *koumbáros,* or best man, exchanges them back and forth. The newlyweds are then led around the altar three times, which spurs the guests into action as they bombard the happy couple with fertility-bringing rice and flower petals. After congratulating the bride and groom one is given a small gift of sweetened almonds, a *boboniéra.* This is followed by the marriage feast and dancing, which lasted up to five days in the past. If you are in the vicinity of a wedding you will be offered a sweet cake, and if you are interested you'll probably be invited to come along as a special guest.

Baptisms are cause for similar celebration. The priest immerses the baby completely in the Holy Water three times (no vulnerable spots on modern Greeks!) and almost always gives the little one the name of a grandparent. For extra protection from the forces of evil, village babies often wear a *filaktó,* or amulet. Anyone who visits the baby at home must first be sprinkled with Holy Water, in case he has the evil eye.

Funerals in Greece, for reasons of climate, are carried out as soon as possible after death, and are announced by the village churchbells. The dead are placed in the earth for three to five years (longer if the family pays) after which time the bones are dug up and placed in the family box to make room for the next resident. It is curious that the *aforismós,* or Orthodox excommunication, is believed to prevent the body decaying after death. Ceremonies are performed in memory of the departed three, nine and 40 days after death, and on the first anniversary. They are sometimes repeated annually. Sweet buns and sugared wheat *koúliva* are given out after the ceremony.

Further Reading

Clogg, Richard and Yannopoulos, George, *Greece Under Military Rule* (London 1972)

Dakin, Douglas, *The Unification of Greece 1770-1923* (London 1972)

Heurtley, W. A., Darby, H. C., Crawley, C. W. and Woodhouse, C. M., *A Short History of Greece from Early Times to 1964* (Cambridge and New York 1966)

Kousoulas, George D., *Revolution and Defeat: The Story of the Greek Communist Party* (Oxford 1965)

Legg, Keith R., *Politics in Modern Greece* (Stanford, Calif. 1969)

Mavrogordato, J., *Modern Greece 1800-1921* (London 1931)

O'Ballance, Edgar, *The Greek Civil War, 1944-1949* (London and New York 1966)

Pallis, A. A., *Greece's Anatolian Adventure and After* (London 1937)

Papandreou, Andreas, *Democracy at Gunpoint* (New York 1970, London 1971)

Stephens, Robert, *Cyprus: A Place of Arms* (London and New York 1966)

Sweet-Escott, Bickham, *Greece: A Political and Economic Survey 1939-53* (London and New York 1954)

Ware, Timothy, *The Orthodox Church* (Baltimore, Ma. 1963, London 1964)

Woodhouse, C. M. *The Greek War of Independence* (London 1952, New York 1967)

Woodhouse, C. M., *Modern Greece: A Short History* (London 1977)

In London a likely place to find these books is at the Hellenistic Book Service, 122 Charing Cross Road, London WC2, tel. (01) 836 7071. In Athens the best bookstore for English books on Greek subjects can be found on 4 Nikis St., Syntagma Square, and is called Eseftheroudakis.

Language

Although modern Greek, or *Romaĺka,* is a minor language spoken by few non-Greeks, it has the special distinction of having caused riots and the fall of a government (in 1901). In Greece today there exist basically two languages, the purist or *katharevousa,* and the popular or *demotiki.* Both are developments of ancient Greek, but although the purist is consciously classical, the popular is as close to its ancient origins as French is to Latin. While many purist words are common in the speech of the people, the popular dominates, especially in the countryside.

Until the turn of the century all literature appeared in the purist language. What shook Athens with riots in 1901 was the appearance of the *Iliad* and the *New Testament* in the demotic. When the fury died down a bit, more and more writers were found to be turning their pens to the demotic. Cavafy, the first great modern Greek poet, wrote in both the popular and purist. In its "moral cleansing" of Greece the Papadopoulos government tried to revive the purist, but with little success.

Knowing the language of any country makes the stay twice as enjoyable; in Greece, especially, people spend much of the day talking. But modern Greek isn't a particularly easy language to pick up by ear, and it is often spoken at great velocity (if you speak slowly someone is sure to interrupt). If you buy a modern Greek grammar, check to see if it has the demotic and not just the purist. Even if you have no desire to learn Greek, it is helpful to know at least the alphabet — so that you can find your way around — and a few basic words and phrases.

The Greek Alphabet

A α	álfa	(short a as in father)
B β	víta	(v sound)
Γ γ	gámma	(slightly gutteral g or y sound)
Δ δ	thélta	(hard th as in though)
E ε	épsilon	(short e as in bet)
Z ζ	zíta	(z sound)
H η	íta	(long e as in bee)
Θ θ	thíta	(soft th as in thin)
I ι	yóta	(long e as in be sometimes like y)
K κ	káppa	(k sound)
Λ λ	lámtha	(l sound)
M μ	mi	(m sound)
N ν	ni	(n sound)
Ξ ξ	ksi	(x as in ox)
O o	omicron	(o as in open)
Π π	pi	(p sound)
P ρ	ro	(r sound)
Σ σ (ς)	sigma	(s sound)
T τ	taf	(t sound)
Y υ	ipsilon	(long e as in bee)
Φ φ	fi	(f sound)
X χ	chi	(German ch as in doch)
Ψ ψ	psi	(ps as in stops)
Ω ω	omega	(o as in open)

Note: i is as i in machine.

Dipthongs and consonant combinations

αι	(short e as in bet)
ει, οι, υι	(i as in machine)
ου	(oo as in too)
αυ	(av or af sound)
ευ	(ev or ef sound)
ηυ	(iv or if sound)
γγ	(ng as in angry)
γκ	(hard g; ng within word)
ντ	(d; nd within word)
μπ	(b; mp within word)

Yes	ne or ah me (This is accompanied by a short nod or tilt of the head)	Ναί

no	óchi, óxi	Όχι
	(This is accompanied by a backwards jerk of the head, with a click of the tongue, smack of the lips or raise of the eyebrows)	
yes	málista	Μάλιστα
	(This is the formal yes)	
I don't know	then xéro	Δèν ξέρω
	(An even greater throwing back of the head, or a display of empty hands)	
I don't understand (Greek)	then katalavéna (hellinika)	Δèν καταλαβαίνω ('Ελληνικά)
does someone speak English?	Iné kanés poo na milá anglika?	Είναι κανεις πoù νà μιλᾶ àγγλικά;
go away	fíyete	Φύγετε
help	voíthia	βοήθεια
my friend	o filos moo (m)	ò φίλος μου
	ee fíli mou (f)	ή φήλη μου
please	parakaló	Παρακαλῶ
thank you (very much)	evcharistó (parápolí)	Εὐχαριστῶ (παράπολύ)
you're welcome	parakaló	Παρακαλῶ
it doesn't matter	then pirázi	Δèν πηράζη
all right	ev táxi	Εν τάξει
excuse me	signómi	Συγγνώμην
pardon?	oríste?	'Ορήστε;
be careful	proséchte	Προσέξτε
nothing	típote	Τίποτε
what is your name?	pos sas léne?	Πῶς σᾶς λένε;
how are you?	ti kánete?	Τì κάνετε;
hello	yásou	Γείασου
goodbye	yásou, andio, hérete	Γείσου,'Αντίο, χαίρετε
good morning	kaliméra	Καλημέρα
good evening	kalispéra	Καλησπέρα
good night	kali níkta	Καληνύκτα
what is that?	ti íne aftó?	Τί εἶναι αὐτό;
what?	ti?	Τì
who?	piós? (m), piá? (f)	ποιός, ποιά
where?	poo	ποῦ
when?	póte?	πότε
why?	yiatí?	γιατί
how?	pos?	πῶς

18

I (am)	ego (íme)	ἐγώ (εἶμαι)
you (are) (sing)	isí (íse)	ἐσύ (εἶσαι)
he, she, it (is)	aftós, aftí, aftó (íne)	αὐτός, αὐτή, αὐτὸ (εἶναι)
we (are)	imés (ímaste)	ἐμεῖς (εἴμαστε)
you (are) (pl)	ísis (íste)	ἐσεις (εἶστε)
they (are)	aftí (m), aftés (f), aftá (n) (íne)	αὐτοί, αὐτὲσ, αὐτὰ (εἶναι)

I have	écho	ἔχω
You have (sing)	échis	ἔχεισ
he, she, it has	échi	ἔχει
we have	échomen	ἔχομε
you have (pl)	échete	ἔχετε
they have	échoon	ἔχουν

I am lost	échasa to thrómo	Ἔκασα τό δρόμο
I am hungry	pinó	Πεινῶ
I am thirsty	thipsó	Διψῶ
I am tired	íme kourasménos	Εἶμαι κουρασμένος
I am sleepy	nistázo	Νυστάζω
I am ill	íme árostos	Εἶμαι ἄρρωστος
I am poor	íme ftochós	Εἶμαι πτωχός
I love you	sagapóh	Σ'ἀγαπῶ

good	kalá	καλά
bad	kakó	κακό
so-so	étsi kétsi	ἔτσι κ'ἔτσι
slow	sigá sigá	σιγά σιγά
fast	grígora	γρήγορα
big	megálo	μεγάλο
small	mikró	μικρὸ
hot	zésti	ζέστη
cold	crío	κρύω

Shops, services, sightseeing

I would like	tha íthela	Θὰ ἤθελα
where is?	poo íne?	Ποῦ εἶναι;
how much is it?	póso káni?	Πόσο κάνει;

bakery	artopiton	Ἀρτοποιεῖον
bank	trápeza	Τράπεζα
beach	paralía	παραλία
bed	kreváti	κρεββάτι
bookshop	vivliopolío	Βιβλιοπολεῖο
book	vivlío	βιβλίο
butcher	kreopolíon	Κρεοπωλεῖον
church	eklisía	Ἐκκλησία
cinema	kinimatográfos	Κινηματογράφος

food (see also page 43)	fayíto	φαγίτο
hospital	nosokomío	Νοσοκομείω
hotel	xenodochío	Ξενοδοχείο
house	spíti	σπίτι
kiosk	períptero	Περίπτερο
money	leftá	λεφτά
museum	mooséo	Μουσείο
music	musikí	μουσική
newspaper (foreign)	efimerítha (xéni)	ἐφημερίδα (ξένη)
pharmacy	farmakío	Φαρμακείο
police station	astinomía	Αστινομία
policeman	astílaka	ἀστυφύλακα
post office	tachithromío	Ταχυδρομείο
restaurant	estiatório	Ἐστιατόριω
ruins	archéa	ἀρχαία
sea	thálassa	Θάλασσα
shoe store	papootsís	Παπουτσής
student	fititís	φοιτητής
telephone office	OTE	OTE
theatre	théatro	Θέατρο
toilet	tooaléta	τουαλέττα
tourist policeman	astifílaki toristiki	ἀστυφύλακα τουρηστηκι
a walk	vólta	βόλτα

Time

what time is it?	ti óra íne?	Τί ὥρα εἶναι;
month	mína	μήνα
week	evthomáda	ἐβδομάδα
day	méra	μέρα
morning	proí	πρωί
afternoon	apóyevma	ἀπόγευμα
evening	vráthi	βράδυ
yesterday	chthés	χθές
today	símera	σήμερα
tomorrow	ávrio	αὔριο
now	tóra	τώρα
later	metá	μετά
it is early	íne norís	Εἶναι νωρισ
it is late	íne argá	Εἶναι ἀργά

Numbers

one	évas (m), mía (f), éna (n)	Ἕνας, μία, ἕνα
two	theo	Δύο
three	tris (m, f), tría (n)	Τρεῖς, τρία
four	téseres (m, f), téssera (n)	Τέσσερεις, τέσσερα

five	pénde	Πέντε
six	éxi	Ἔξι
seven	eftá	Ἐφτά
eight	októ	Ὀκτώ
nine	ennéa	Ἐννέα
ten	théka	Δέκα
eleven	ántheka	Ἔντεκα
twelve	thótheka	Δώδεκα
thirteen	theka tría	Δεκατρία
fourteen	theka téssera	Δεκατέσσερα
twenty	íkosi	Εἴκοσι
twenty-one	íkosi enas/mía/éna	Εἴκοσι ἔνας/μία/ἔνα
thirty	triánda	Τριάντα
forty	saránda	Σαράντα
fifty	penínda	Πενήντα
sixty	exínda	Ἐξήντα
seventy	evthomínda	Ἑβδομήντα
eighty	ogthónda	Ὀγδόντα
ninety	enenínda	Ἐνενήντα
one hundred	ekató	Ἐκατό
one thousand	chília	Χίλια

Months/Days

January	Ianooários	Ἰανουάριοσ
February	Fevrooários	Φεβρουάριος
March	Mártios	Μάρτιος
April	Aprílios	Ἀπρίλιος
May	Máios	Μάϊοσ
June	Ioónios	Ἰούνιοσ
July	Ioólios	Ἰούλιοσ
August	Avgoostos	Αὔγουστος
September	Septémvrios	Σεπτέμβριος
October	Októvrios	Ὀκτώβριος
November	Noémvrios	Νοέμβριος
December	Thekémvrios	Δεκέμβριος
Sunday	Kiriakí	Κυριακή
Monday	Theftéra	Δευτέρα
Tuesday	Tríti	Τρίτη
Wednesday	Tetárti	Τετάρτη
Thursday	Pémpti	Πέμπτη
Friday	Paraskeví	Παρασκευή
Saturday	Sávato	Σάββατο

Transport

the airport	to arothrómio	τὸ ἀεροδρόμιο
the aeroplane	to aroplàno	τὸ ἀεροπλάνο

the bus station	ee stási ton leoforíon	ἡ στάση τῶν λεωφορείων
the bus	o leoforío	ὁ λεωφορεῖο
the railway station	o stathmós too tréno	ὁ σταθμὸς τοῦ τραίνου
the train	to trénou	τὸ τραῖνο
the port	to limáni	τὸ λιμάνι
the port authority	to limenarchion	τὸ λιμεναρχεῖον
the ship	to plíon *or* to karávi	τὸ πλοῖον/τὸ καράβι
the steamship	to vapóri	τὸ βαπόρι
the car	to aftokínito	τὸ αὐτοκίνητον
a ticket	ena isitírio	ἕνα εἰσιτήριο

Travel directions

I want to go to	thélo na páo sto (*m*), sti (*f*)	Θέλω νὰ πάω στὸ, στή..
how can I get to ...?	póso boró na páo sto (*m*), sti (*f*) ... ?	Πόσο μπορῶ νὰ πάω στὸ, στή ...
can you give me a ride to ...?	boréte na me páte sto (*m*), sti (*f*) ...?	Μπορεῖτε νὰ μὲ πάτε στὸ, στή ...;
where is ...?	poo íne ...?	Ποῦ εἶναι
how far is it?	póso makriá íne?	Πόσο μακρυὰ εἶναι;
when will the ... come?	póte thae 'erthi to (*n*), (*f*), o (*m*) ... ?	Πότε θὰ ἔρθει τὸ, ἡ, ὁ ...,
when will the ... leave?	póte tha févi to (*n*), ee (*f*), o (*m*) ...?	Πότε Θὰ φύγει τὸ, ἡ, ὁ ...;
from where do I catch...?	apó poo pérno	Ἀπὸ ποῦ παίρνω
how long does the trip take?	póso keró tha pári to taxíthi?	Πόσο καιρὸ θὰ πάρη τό ταξίδι;
please show me	parakaló thíkstemoo	Παρακαλῶ δεῖξτέμου
how much is it?	póso káni?	Πόσο κάνει;
the (nearest) town	o horió (o pió kondá)	ὁ χωριὸ (ὁ πιό κοντά)
good trip	kaló taxíthi	Καλὸ ταξίδι
here	ethó	ἐδῶ
there	ekí	ἐκεῖ
close	kondá	κοντά
far	makriá	μακρυὰ
full	yemáto	γεμάτο
left	aristerá	ἀριστερὰ
right	thexiá	δεξιά
forward	embrós	ἐμπρός
back	píso	πίσω
north	vória	Βόρεια
south	nótia	Νότια
east	anatoliká	Ἀνατολικά
west	thitiká	Δυτικά
corner	gonía	γωνία
square	platía	πλατεῖα

Driving

where can I rent ...?	poo boró na enikiáso ...?	Ποῦ μπορῶ νὰ ἐνοι-κιάσω ...;
a car	énan aftokínito	ἕνα αὐτοκίνητο
a motorbike	éna mechanáki	ἕνα μηχανάκι
a bicycle	éna pothílaton	ἕνα ποδήλατον
where may I buy petrol?	poo boró nagorázso venzíni?	Ποῦ μπορῶ ν' ἀγοράζω βενζίνη;
where is a garage?	poo íne éna garáz?	Ποῦ εἶναι ἕνα γκαράζ;
a mechanic	éna mikanikó	ἕνα μηχανικό;
a map	éva chárti	ἕνα χάρτη
where is the road to ...?	poo íne o thrómos yiá ...?	Ποῦ εἶναι ὁ δρόμοσ γιά ...;
where does this road lead?	poo pái aftós o thrómos?	Ποῦ πάει αὐτὸσ ὁ δρόμοσ;
is the road good?	íne kalós o thrómos?	Εἶναι καλόσ ὁ δρόμοσ;
exit	éxothos	ΕΞΟΔΟΣ
entrance	ísothos	ΕΙΣΟΔΟΣ
danger	kínthinos	ΚΙΝΔΥΝΟΣ
slow	argá	ΑΡΓΑ
no parking	apogorévete ee státhmevsis	ΑΠΟΓΟΡΕΥΕΤΑΙ Η ΣΤΑΘΜΕΥΣΙΣ
keep out	apagorévete ee ísothos	ΑΠΟΓΟΡΕΥΕΤΑΙ Η ΕΙΣΟΔΟΣ

Part 2
Getting To and Around Greece and the Islands

by air, p.24 by train, p.26 by bus, p.27 by ship, p.28 by yacht, p.33 by car, p.34 by motorbike or scooter, p.36 by bicycle, p.36 hitch hiking, p.37 customs and immigration, p.37 what you can bring into and take out of Greece duty-free, p.37

_____

By air
Charter flights to Athens and occasionally to the islands are frequent in the summer from European and North American capitals. Check the travel sections in newspapers, or get advice from travel agencies or the offices of the following airlines:

in Canada: Canadian Pacific Western Airlines, and Wardair

in Great Britain: Britannia, British Air-Tour, British Caledonian, British Midland Airways, Dan-Air, Laker Airways and Monarch Airlines

in Ireland: Aer Lingus

in the USA: Aeroamerican, Overseas National Airways, Overseas National Panamerican, Saturn Airways, Trans International Airlines and World Airways.

Regular flights are available direct to Athens on these airlines:

from Adelaide: Quantas

from Boston: TWA

from Brisbane: Quantas

from Chicago: Olympic, British Air and TWA

from Denver: TWA

from Detroit: TWA

from Indianapolis: TWA

from Johannesburg: Olympic, SAS, and SAA

from Kansas City: TWA

from London: British Air, Olympic, EAA, Singapore Air, Sabena and JAT
from Los Angeles: TWA
from Melbourne: Alitalia, Olympic, and Quantas
from Montreal: British Air, Olympic and Sabena
from New York: British Air, Olympic, Sabena, and TWA
from Nicosia: Olympic and Cyprus Airways
from Philadelphia: TWA
from Pittsburgh: TWA
from St. Louis: TWA
from San Francisco: TWA
from Sydney: Alitalia, Garuda, Olympic, Quantas, Singapore Air and UTA
from Washington: British Air and TWA

Direct flights on Olympic Airways are also available as follows:
to Corfu, from Dusseldorf, Frankfurt, London,Munich, Paris and Vienna
to Herakleon, from Frankfurt and London
to Rhodes, from Frankfurt and London
to Thessaloniki, from Dusseldorf, Frankfurt, London, Stuttgart, Vienna, Brussels and Zurich

Flights from Athens to the Islands are available on Olympic Airways. To be assured of a seat, especially in the summer, you should book your ticket as far in advance as possible. Groups of 15 or more receive a 5 per cent discount, infants up to two years old a 90 per cent discount, and children of two to twelve years a 50 per cent discount. The following fares, in drachmas, are correct at the time of writing:

Athens to	Frequency	Single fare in drachmas
Alexandroupolis (for Samothrace)	daily	1630
Chania (Crete)	daily	1310
Chios	daily	1190
Corfu	daily	1810
Herakleon (Crete)	daily	1560
Kavala (for Thassos)	daily	1690
Kephallonia	daily	1380
Kos	daily	1750
Kythera	4 a week	1880
Limnos	daily	1350
Milos	daily	1560
Mykonos	daily	1310
Mytilini (Lesbos)	daily	1380
Rhodes	daily	2060
Samos	daily	1380
Santorini	daily	1560

Skiathos	3 a week	1310
Thessaloniki (for		
N.E. Aegean Is.)	daily	1500
Zakynthos	3 a week	1380

Addresses and telephone numbers of airlines in Athens (area code 01) are as follows:

Aeroflot: 2 Karageorgi Servias; tel. 3220986

Air Canada: 10 Othonos; tel. 3235143

Alitalia: 9 El. Venizelou; tel 3229414. Airport tel. 9702502

Canadian Pacific: 4 Karageorgi Servias; tel. 3230344. Airport tel. 9702001

British Airways: 10 Othonos; tel. 3222521. Bookings tel. 3230476. Airport tel. 9704411

Cyprus Airways: 10 Philellinon; tel. 3246965. Airport tel. 9704411

JAT: 4 Voukourestiou; tel. 3223675. Airport tel. 9709382

Olympic: 6 Othonos; tel. 9292444. Also 122 Leoforos Syngrou; tel. 9292333. Airport tel. 9811211

Quantas: 5 Mitropoleos; tel. 3232792. Airport tel. 9703810

SAS: Sins & Vissarionos; tel. 3634444. Airport tel. 9703514

Sabena: 8 Othonos; tel. 3236821. Airport tel. 9702003

South African Airways: 2 Karageorgi Servias; tel. 3229007. Airport tel. 9009282 or 9718747

TWA: 8 Xenofondos; tel. 3236831. Airport tel. 9702211

UTA: 4 Karageorgi Servias; tel. 3230501

Getting to and from Ellinikon Airport, Athens: Ellinikon Airport is divided into two: East (international airlines) and West (Olympic Airlines, both international and domestic flights). A bus leaves for the West Airport from the Olympic Agency on Othonos St. and costs 21 dr. ILPAP and KTEL buses run every 15 minutes to the East Airport from Leoforos Amalias, in front of the National Garden and cost 21 dr. East Airport is connected to Piraeus by bus no. 185, which leaves from Theotoki and Sofokleous Streets in Piraeus.

By train

From London to Athens there are three daily trains, the Athenai Express, the Akropolis Express, and the Hellas Express, all of which take three days. And a hot, crowded, stuffy three days they are too, especially in Yugoslavia. First class from London via Paris is around £250 return, second class £160 return. Anyone under 26 years of age can obtain a reduction on these fares by purchasing tickets at Transalpino, located in Victoria Station, London.

    Hardy souls who deny themselves even one night in a couchette are advised to bring with them three days' provisions, including water, and some toilet paper. Those who intend to sleep in a prone position, beneath seats and feet, should also bring something to lie on. Wear the oldest and most comfortable clothes you own (and save yourself the trouble of washing them before you go).

Domestic train routes of possible interest to island hoppers are as follows:

	Frequency	Single fare in drachmas	
		1st class	2nd class
Athens — Thessaloniki (for N.E. Aegean Is.)	6 a day	627	418
Athens — Alexandroupolis (for Samothrace)	3 a day	969	646
Thessaloniki — Alexandroupolis	4 a day	315	200
Athens — Chalki (Evia)	9 a day	108	72
Athens — Patras (for Ionian Is.)	7 a day	318	212
Athens — Kalamata	9 a day	437	291
Athens — Volos (for Sporades)	3 a day	490	327

Students with valid identification can obtain a 50 per cent reduction on domestic train fares, and groups of more than ten people a 30 per cent discount.

In Athens, the railway station for northern Greece is Larissa Station, Delighianni St., tel. 8213882. The station for the Peloponnese is across the tracks; tel. 5131601. In Piraeus, the station for the Peloponnese is near the Piraeus-Athens metro on Akti Kalimassioti. The station for northern Greece lies further down the road on Akti Kondili. For further information, telephone the O.S.E. (Hellenic Railways Organization): 5222491 or 3624402/6.

By bus

Taking a bus from London to Athens is always a possible alternative for those who decide that a train trip is too expensive or too easy a route to travel. With three and a half days (or more) on the road, adventures are practically included in the ticket price.

Inquire at the Victoria Coach Station, in London. In Athens, two addresses are Economy Travel, 18 Panepistimou (El. Venizelou) St., and the famous Magic Bus, which has an office in Plaka on Kidathineon St. Look in the region of Filellion St. by Sintagma Square for further possibilities. There is a choice of routes, via France or Germany, and the cost of a return ticket will be approximately £60.

The domestic bus service in Greece is efficient and regular, if not always a bargain. Each bus is decorated at the whim of its driver, with pin ups, saints, wall paper, tinsel, tassels, and plastic hands which wave violently when the bus falls into a pot hole. Bus services from Athens relevant to this book are as follows:

From Athens to	No. per day	Terminal	Tel. No.	Single Fare (dr.)	Duration of Trip
Chalki (Evia)	30	Liossion	8317153	100	1.30 hrs.
Edipsos (Evia)	3-5	Liossion	8317153	185	3.30 hrs.
Gythion	4	Kifissou	5124913	405	6.30 hrs.
Igoumenitsa (for Corfu)	3	Kifissou	5125954	595	8.30 hrs.
Kavala (for N.E. Aegean Is.)	2	Kifissou	5129407	815	11.00 hrs.
Kephallonia	1	Kifissou	5129498	573	8.00 hrs.
Kerkyra (Corfu)	3	Kifissou	5129443	595	11.00 hrs.
Lefkas	3	Kifissou	5133583	475	7.00 hrs.
Patras (for Ionian Is.)	14	Kifissou	5124914	330	3.30 hrs.
Rafina (for Cyclades, and Evia)	frequent	Mavromateon	8210872	35	1.00 hrs.
Thessaloniki (for N.E. Aegean Is.)	11	Larissis Rlwy Sta.	5222491	540	8.00 hrs.
Volos (for Sporades)	9	Liossion	8317186	420	5.00 hrs.
Zakynthos	2	Kifissou	5129432	355	7.00 hrs.

To get to the terminal at 100 Kifissou St., take bus no. 62 from Omonia Square (Villara and Menadrou Sts.). For the terminal at 260 Liossion St. take bus no. 63/34 from Leoforos Amalias, by the National Garden. Take a bus or streetcar north, towards Areos Park on 28th Octovriou St. for the Mavromateon terminal.

During the summer, it is advisable to reserve seats in advance on the long distance buses. Tickets for these journeys must normally be bought before one boards the bus, although on short trips one pays in transit. (Handing the conductor a 1000 dr. note for a 15 dr. ride does not improve foreign relations.)

There are never enough buses on the islands in the summer, nor is it customary to queue. However, you will not be left behind if it is humanly possible for you to squeeze on. If you can wake up in time, you will find that buses are rarely crowded early in the morning.

By Ship

The most popular sea route in Greece is from Italy, with daily ferry services from Ancona, Bari, Brindisi and Venice. The most popular of these is the daily service from Brindisi, which leaves at 10 pm (connecting with the train from Rome) and arrives in Corfu the next morning. Passengers are allowed a free infinite stopover in Corfu if that island is not their ultimate destination, before continuing to Igoumenitsa or Patras. If you plan to sail during the summer season, try to arrive in Brindisi as early as possible, as the passage is occasionally overbooked. Students and young people are entitled to a 30 per cent reduction on most lines.

Steamer and ferry services of varying regularity also connect Piraeus to the following ports:

to/from Piraeus		Duration	
Alexandria, Egypt	steamer	1½ days	Stops at Herakleon, Crete, once a week
	ferry	3 days	
Barcelona, Spain	steamer	5 days	
Beirut, Lebanon	steamer	4 days	Often via Rhodes
	ferry	2 days	
Genoa, Italy	steamer	2½ days	
Haifa, Israel	steamer	2½ days	Often via Rhodes
	ferry	3 days	
Istanbul, Turkey	steamer	1 day	
Izmir, Turkey	steamer	1 day	
Larnaca, Cyprus	steamer	3 days	
Latakia, Syria	steamer	2½ days	
Limassol, Cyprus	steamer	1½ days	Often via Rhodes
	ferry	2 days	
Marseille, France	steamer	2 days	
	ferry	4 days	
Naples, Italy	steamer	1½ days	
	ferry	2 days	
Odessa, USSR	steamer	3 days in summer	
		2 days in winter	
Venice, Italy	steamer	1½ days	
	ferry	1½ days	

Tourist Offices or travel agents in the country of departure will advise you on fares for passengers and vehicles. These change frequently because of fluctuating exchange rates and inflation.

Less frequent services connect Piraeus with Constanta (Rumania), Bodrum (Turkey), Varna (Bulgaria), and Yalta (USSR). The George Papazoglou travel agency, in the arcade at 41 Stadiou St. (open 8.00-13.00 and 16.00-19.30; Sunday 10.00-12.00; tel. 3213075) can give you further information on these or any other ship or plane service, along with tickets. The daily newspaper *H Nay Temporikh* lists all the activities of the port at Piraeus and publishes weekly ship schedules. The National Tourist Office also publishes a weekly list of ship departures, both abroad and to the islands.

Boats to the islands: A little travelling through the islands will soon show you that each boat is as individual as a Greek bus. The many new ones are clean and comfortable and often air-conditioned. The older boats may lack some modern refinements but nevertheless they can be pleasant if you remain out on deck. The drinking water is never very good on the boats, but all sell beer, Coca Cola, and lemon or orange soda. Biscuits and cigarettes complete the fare on the smaller boats, while the larger ones offer sandwiches, cheese pies or even full meals.

All the boats are privately owned and although the Greek government controls the prices some will charge more for the same journey, depending on the facilities offered, speed, etc. If caiques relay you from shore to ship, you will pay 20 dr. more. Children under the age of four travel free, and between four and ten for half-fare. Over ten, they are charged the full fare. In the summer it is wise to buy tickets in advance, to guarantee a place and also because they are often 20 per cent more when bought on board. Refunds are rarely given unless the boat itself never arrives, stuck in Piraeus for tax delinquencies. Boats will arrive late or divert their course for innumerable reasons, so if you have to catch a flight home allow for the eccentricities of the system and leave a day early to be safe.

The following 1980 prices are in drachmas, and exclude the 19dr. embarkation tax from Piraeus. Note that all fares are subject to change without notice and should therefore by confirmed with the relevant authority in Greece.

Piraeus to	2nd Class (dr.)	Tourist Class (dr.)	3rd Class (dr.)	Duration of trip
Ag. Nikolaos, Crete	1149	865	653	
Amorgos	610	469	374	11.15 hrs.
Anafi	913	699	530	18.40 hrs.
Astypalaia	772	575	451	13.00 hrs.
Chania, Crete	880	642	469	11.00 hrs.
Chios	728	528	390	10.00 hrs.
Donoussa	—	657	506	10.30 hrs.
Elafonnissos	635	505	413	10.00 hrs.
Folegandros	728	553	430	12.00 hrs.
Halki	1284	946	703	
Herakleon, Crete	898	660	490	12.30 hrs.
Heraklia	—	657	506	15.40 hrs.
Ikaria	624	459	351	12.30 hrs.
Ios	657	520	430	10.00 hrs.
Kalymnos	771	577	451	14.00 hrs.
Karlovassi, Samos	763	595	439	14.30 hrs.
Karpathos	1292	954	725	
Kassos	1236	913	685	
Kimolos	535	415	348	6.00 hrs.
Kos	959	718	546	20.30 hrs.
Koufonissa-Skinoussa	—	657	506	14.30 hrs.
Kythera	731	578	470	
Kythnos	390	289	226	4.00 hrs.
Leros	771	577	451	11.30 hrs.
Milos	534	415	348	8.30 hrs.
Mykonos	525	407	335	6.15 hrs.
Mytilene	831	577	490	14.00 hrs.
Naxos	534	415	348	8.10 hrs.
Nissyros	959	720	546	22.30 hrs.

Piraeus to	2nd Class (dr.)	Tourist Class (dr.)	3rd Class (dr.)	Duration of trip
Paros	465	361	303	6.20 hrs.
Patmos	771	577	451	
Rhodes	1049	798	607	20.00 hrs.
Samos	831	610	468	16.00 hrs.
Santorini	657	520	430	12.00 hrs.
Serifos	441	330	256	5.10 hrs.
Sifnos	482	373	317	5.30 hrs.
Sikinos	—	657	506	10.30 hrs.
Sitia, Crete	1203	880	685	
Symi	827	718	546	26.30 hrs.
Syros	441	348	302	4.30 hrs.
Tilos	959	719	546	24.30 hrs.
Tinos	493	390	335	5.30 hrs.

Argosaronic Line (Tel. 4115801, 4511311)

Piraeus to	1st Class (dr.)	3rd Class (dr.)	Duration of trip
Aegina	141	107	1.30 hrs.
Hydra	230	171	4.10 hrs.
Poros	208	155	3.40 hrs.
Porto Heli	293	225	4.00 hrs.
Spetses	293	225	5.25 hrs.

Sporades Line (Tel. 4178084, 4172415)

Ag. Konstantinos to			
Alonissos	525	410	6.00 hrs.
Glossa	494	351	4.25 hrs.
Skiathos	473	305	3.15 hrs.
Skopelos	504	369	5.25 hrs.
Kymi, Evia to			
Ag. Efstratios	525	306	5.00 hrs.
Alonissos	575	434	2.45 hrs.
Glossa	630	493	5.00 hrs.
Limnos	525	365	7.10 hrs.
Samothrace	735	624	16.45 hrs.
Skiathos	683	534	5.30 hrs.
Skopelos	599	474	3.30 hrs.
Skyros	336	206	1.45 hrs.
Volos to			
Alonissos	473	328	5.00 hrs.
Glossa	322	269	3.30 hrs.
Skiathos	378	228	3.00 hrs.
Skopelos	420	288	4.30 hrs.

Evia and Cyclades Line (Tel. (0294) 23300)

Rafina to	3rd Class (dr.)	Duration of trip
Andros	249	2.30 hrs.
Karystos, Evia	167	2.00 hrs.
Marmari, Evia	116	1.15 hrs.
Tinos	292	4.00 hrs.

Kea-Kythnos Line (Tel. (0292) 25249)

Lavrion to	Tourist Class (dr.)	Duration of trip
Kea	148	1.30 hrs.
Kimolos	466	
Kythnos	219	
Milos	466	
Serifos	309	
Sifnos	466	
Syros	466	

Hydrofoil Line 'Flying Dolphins' (Tel. 4531716, 4529272)

Piraeus to	(dr.)	*P. Heli to*	(dr.)
Aegina	172	Piraeus	498
Poros	335	Poros	237
Hydra	413	Hydra	194
Spetses	458	Spetses	92
P. Heli	474	Nauplion	246
Nauplion	554		
Monemvassia	770	*Poros to*	(dr.)
		Piraeus	335
Hydra to	(dr.)	Hydra	125
Piraeus	434	Spetses	212
Poros	125	P. Heli	237
Spetses	176	Nauplion	422
P. Heli	194		
Nauplion	334	*Spetses to*	(dr.)
		Piraeus	481
Nauplion to	(dr.)	Poros	212
Piraeus	582	Hydra	176
Poros	422	P. Heli	92
Hydra	334	Nauplion	281
Spetses	281		
P. Heli	246		

Connections with other islands
Ag. Efstratos: ship once a week from Thessaloniki; also connections with Limnos.
Antiparos: the boat leaves Paroikia, Paros, 6 times a day; a caique will take you from Pounda if you open the Pounda church door.
Corfu: ferry boat 8 times a day from Igoumenitsa, 94 dr.; once a day from Patras, 420 dr.
Edipsos, Evia: ferry boat 6 times a day from Arkitsa, 58 dr.
Eretrea, Evia: ferry boat 35 times a day from Oropos, 35 dr.
Kephallonia: ferry boat twice a day from Patras, 277 dr.
Ithaka: ferry boat three times a week from Patras, 277 dr.
Limnos: ferry boat twice a week from Kavala, 419 dr.; twice a week from Thessaloniki; three times a week from Kymi, Evia.
Paxi: boat daily from Corfu; once a week from Patras, 420 dr.
Psara: small boat three times a week from Chios.
Salamis: ferry boat 50 times a day from Perama to Paloukia, 10 dr.; western ferry boat to Faneromeni; small boats from Piraeus to Paloukia, Kamateron, and Selinia.
Samothrace: small boat every morning from Alexandroupolis, 187 dr.; ferry boat twice a week from Kavala.
Thassos: ferry boat 30 times a day from Keramoti to Thassos capital, 37 dr.; 8 times a day from Kavala to Prinos, 74 dr.; 4 times a day from Kavala to Thassos capital, 88 dr.; once or twice a day from Kavala to Limenaria, 88 dr.
Zakynthos: ferry boat 4 times a day from Kyllini, 116 dr.; twice a week from Patras.

Connections with Turkey
Chios-Tsesme: twice a week, one way 600 dr.; return 1000 dr. Tel. Chios (0271) 24670.
Samos-Kusadasi: 3 a week, one way 600 dr.; return 850 dr. Tel. Samos (0273) 28295.

Note: all the above prices are tourist class.

Besides the regular steamers and ferry boats, there are a certain number of tourist boat services in the summer months. These can be very convenient but are usually more expensive than the year-round schedules. Free caique rides from island to island are more difficult to find nowadays, as most business is carried out between the individual islands and Athens. For transport to the more remote islands, ask about the mail boats or fishing boats. Friendly yachtsmen may also give you a lift — it never hurts to ask.

By Yacht
Yachting is by far the best way of seeing the Greek islands, and more and more people do it every year. A vast effort has been made by the

National Tourist Organization to construct marinas and yacht supply stations, and one is never very far from a safe anchorage. There are 27 official ports of entry and exit in Greece: Ag. Nikolaos, Alexandroupolis, Argostoli, Chania, Chios, Corfu, Ermoupolis, Herakleon, Itea, Kalamata, Katakolon, Kavala, Lavrion, Kos, Myrina, Mytilene, Nauplion, Patras, Pylos, Pythagorion, Preveza, Rhodes, Thessaloniki, Volos, Vouliagmeni Marina, Zakynthos, and Zea Marina. All these ports have yacht supply stations; others are noted in this book under the individual islands.

Yachts entering Greek waters must fly the code flag 'Q' until cleared by entry port authorities. Afterwards it is customary to fly a Greek courtesy flag. Upon arrival the **port authority** *(Limenarkion)* issues all yachts with a transit log, which entitles the yacht and crew to unlimited travel in Greek waters. It also allows crew members to buy fuel, alcohol and cigarettes duty free. The log should be renewed yearly, or after leaving and re-entering Greek waters. Yachtsmen who intend to spend a night ashore should first get their passports stamped.

Any boat smaller than a yacht is defined as a pleasure craft, whether it is a sailing, motor or rowing boat. These are noted down in the owner's passport upon entry to Greece and are allowed to circulate for four months, a period which is renewable at customs.

The greatest **navigational hazard** in the Aegean Sea is the Meltemi, the strong north wind. It generally peaks in August, and is also often encountered in July and September. The suffocating Sirocco from Africa blows occasionally in western Greek waters.

The Greek meteorological service issues warnings of any likely hazards on the radio telephone service (3 minutes after every hour and half hour in English). The Greek radio network transmits weather bulletins in English every day at 6.50 am-7.00 am in winter (6.30 am-6.50 am in summer), 1.10 pm-1.25 pm and 9.45 pm-10.00 pm.

More details on radio services and other information are given in the National Tourist Organization's handbook *Greece for the Yachtsman,* which can be found at any of the organization's offices abroad. Also helpful are H. M. Denham's books, *The Aegean — A Sea Guide to its Coasts and Islands* and *The Ionian Islands to Rhodes.*

By Car

Driving from London to Athens at a normal pace takes around 3½ days, which is why one sees so few British cars in Greece. Unless you are planning to spend a few weeks on one or two islands, a car is not really worth the expense and trouble of bringing it to Greece. If you do decide to bring one, the smaller the better: both for squeezing it on to the ferry boat, and for negotiating the sometimes very narrow village roads. You'll also save on the rather expensive petrol.

One of the best bets for **North Americans and Australians** who want to drive in Greece is to buy a car for the duration of your trip, with an agreement to sell it back to the company when you leave. Several companies in Paris can arrange this, though it is not possible in Greece itself. Alternatively, there are many rent-a-car companies on the mainland and the larger islands.

An **International Driving Licence** is not required by British, Austrian, Belgian or German citizens. Other nationals can obtain an international licence at home, or at one of the Automobile Club offices in Greece (ELPA), by presenting a national driving licence, passport, photograph and 300 dr. The minimum age is 18 years.

The Motor Insurance Bureau at 10 Xenofontos St., Athens, tel. (01) 3236733, can tell you which Greek insurance company represents your own, or provide you with additional cover for Greece.

There are five **frontier posts** for Greece, all open day and night:
   Yugoslavia: Evzoni and Niki
   Bulgaria: Promahon
   Turkey: Kastania and Kipi
Customs formalities are very easy and usually take very little time.
Current fuel prices are as follows:
   96 octane petrol (super) : 33 dr. a litre
   90-92 octane petrol (regular) : 29 dr. a litre
   diesel: 13 dr. a litre
Parking in the centre of Athens, or the Green Zone, is forbidden outside designated parking areas. The following streets form the borders of the Green zone: Sekeri, Botassi, Stournara, Marni, Menandrou, Pireos, Likourgou, Athinas, Mitropoleos, Philellinon, Amalias and Vassilissis Sophias.

While driving in the centre of Athens may be a hair-raising experience, the rest of Greece is easy and pleasant. There are very few cars on the roads, even in summer, and all signs have their Latin equivalents. Traffic regulations and signalling comply with standard practice on the European Continent (i.e. driving on the right). Crossroads and low visibility in the mountains are probably the greatest hazards. Where there are no right of way signs at a crossroads, give priority to traffic coming from the right, and always bleep your horn on blind corners. Take special care when approaching an unguarded railway level crossing. It is also advisable to take a spare container of petrol along with you, as petrol stations are inconsistent in their frequency. There is a speed limit of 50 kmh (30 mph) in inhabited areas: other speed limits are indicated by signposts in km. Horn blowing is prohibited in Athens and other big cities. The Greek Automobile Club (ELPA) operates a breakdown service within 60 kms. of Athens, Salonika, Larissa, Patras, and Herakleon: dial 104.

Greek Automobile Club (ELPA) Addresses:
Athens: 2-4 Messogion St., Tower of Athens. Tel. (01) 7791615. Telex: 215763
Chania: 6 R. Pacha & V. Constantinou. Tel. (0821) 26059

Herakleon: Ayiou Dimitriou Souare. Tel. (081) 289440
Corfu: 29 Dionysiou Dimoulitsa. Tel. (0661) 29504
Kavala: 9 Filikis Etairias. Tel. (051) 29778
Larissa: 10 Patroklou. Tel. (041) 228660
Rhodes: 38 Akti Miaouli. Tel. (0241) 25066
Patras: 30-32 Georgiou A Square. Tel. (061) 276920
Thessaloniki: 45 Mitropoleos. Tel. (031) 270972
Tripolis: 1b Vas. Konstantinou & Spetsopoulou. Tel. (071) 26714
Volos: Riga Feraiou Square. Tel. (0421) 25001

Car Repair Shops in Athens:
Alfa Romeo: Motor Hellas, 132-135 Sungrou Ave. Tel. 9221101
Audi NSU: Terma Kolokynthous. Tel. 5128817
Cadillac, Chevrolet, Opel: Elfinco, 362 Syngrou Ave.
Chrysler, Colt, Dodge, Oldsmobile, Plymouth, Vauxhall, Volvo: Sarakakis Bros. 137 Athinon Ave. Tel. 3553119
Citroen: 100 Syngrou Ave. Tel. 9220445
Fiat, Simca, Neckar: Fiat, 73 Evdoxou. Tel: 9223311
Hillman, Humber, Sunbeam, Singer: 28 Karpou. Tel: 911836
Jaguar, Standard, Triumph: Aveex SA, 9 Thisseus. Tel: 9515611
Mercedez Benz: Viamax Buildings, Athinon Ave. Tel. 5711901
Moskvitch, Volga: 138 Pireos St. Tel. 3451911
Peugeot: Impotex, 97 Syngrou Ave. Tel. 919415
Subaru, SAAB: 101 Syngrou Ave. Tel. 9221870
Volkswagen: Cosmocar, 51-53 Miliaraki St. Tel. 2024570

By Motorbike or Scooter

Scooters are ideal for the islands in the summer. It almost never rains, and what could be more pleasant than a gentle thyme-scented breeze freshening your journey over the mountains? Scooters are both more economical and more practical than cars. They can fit into almost any boat and travel paths where cars fear to tread. Many islands have scooter rentals which are not expensive. However, be warned that not a few beds in Greek hospitals are occupied every summer by careless tourists who couldn't manage their motorbikes.

It is illegal to run motor bikes, cycles and scooters from 2 pm to 6 pm and after 11 pm. You will be more popular with other tourists and locals if you ride your scooter as little as possible through the town.

By Bicycle

For 10-20 dr. an hour one can rent a slipshod bicycle on most of the popular islands. Cycling has not developed in Greece however, either as a sport or a means of transport. Trains and planes carry bicycles for small fees, and Greek boats generally take them along for nothing. Crete and Evia are the best islands for cycling enthusiasts, Crete being the more rugged by far. On both islands you will find fresh water, places to camp, and a warm and surprised welcome in the villages.

Hitch hiking

With the rarest of exceptions, hitch hiking, or autostop as it is known in Greece, is perfectly safe. However, the lack of cars makes it a not particularly speedy mode of transport. The Greek double standard produces the following percentages for hopeful hitch hikers:

Single woman: 99 per cent of the cars will stop. You hardly have to stick out your thumb.

Two women: 75 per cent of the cars will find room for you.

Woman and man: 50 per cent; more if the woman is pretty.

Single man: 25 per cent if you are well dressed with little luggage; less otherwise.

Two men: start walking.

The best time for soliciting a ride is when you disembark from a ship. Ask around your follow passengers, or better still write your destination on a piece of paper (in Greek if possible) and pin it to your shirt with a naive and friendly smile. What you lose in dignity you will generally gain in a lift.

Customs and Immigration

The formalities for foreign tourists entering Greece are very simple. Citizens of all English speaking countries (except Rhodesia and South Africa) can stay for up to three months in Greece, simply on presentation of a valid passport. Rhodesians and South Africans are permitted two months.

If you want to extend your stay in Greece, you must report to the police ten days before your visa runs out. (If you are staying in Athens, register at the Athens Alien Dept., 9 Chalkokondyli St). Take your passport, four photographs, and, if possible, the name of a reference in Greece. You will receive a slip of paper authorizing you to stay for a period of up to six months. This has to be stamped at the end of every three succeeding months that you remain in Greece.

What you can bring into Greece duty-free

Private cars and pleasure craft for four months without further documents

Trailers and caravans need additional documentation: contact the National Organization of Tourism or your automobile club for more information.

Books

Camera (still and/or movie) and film

Sporting equipment

Typewriter
Record player and up to 20 records
2 packs playing cards
Dogs and cats with a veterinary certificate
Bicycle
Binoculars
2 guns and 20 cartridges (must be declared)
Tape recorder
Portable radio
Portable musical instrument
25 grams perfume
¼ litre eau de Cologne
1 bottle spirits
150 grams tobacco
10 kilos sweets
New articles worth US$150, whether for personal use or gifts
1500 drachmas
Any amount of money in other currencies more than US$500-worth should be declared

What you can take out of Greece duty-free
1 container olive oil up to 18 kilos
Souvenirs worth up to 4500 drachma
Art objects made after 1830 (anything of previous date, either bought or found, must first be licensed by the Greek Archaeology Service, Section of Antiquity Sales, 13 Polygnotou St. Antique shop owners will give you further details, and an exportation tax must be paid. Those caught sneaking even the most innocent unlicensed potsherd in their baggage will be severely prosecuted)
£10-worth of duty free souvenirs can be brought into the UK from Greece, and US$150-worth into the USA.

Part 3
Where to Stay, Drinking, Dining and Dancing

hotels, p.39   rooms in private homes, p.40   youth hostels, p.40   camping out, p.41   renting a house, p.41   a note on the Greek toilet, p.41   dining, p.42   music and dancing, p.46

Hotels

All hotels in Greece are divided into six categories: Luxury, A, B, C, D, and E. Prices are set and strictly controlled by the Tourist Office. Off season you can generally get a discount, sometimes as much as 40 per cent. In the summer season prices can be increased by up to 15 per cent.

Price per day in drachmas	A	B	C	D
Single room & breakfast	946	730	524	376
Single room demi pension	1231	977	751	585
Single room full pension	1516	1224	978	794
Double room & breakfast	1371	1068	7700	578
Double room demi pension	1941	1562	1154	996
Double room full pension	2511	2056	1608	1414

The rates for Luxury hotels are fixed individually. Those for E hotels are not quoted officially, but should be about 20 per cent less than D rates. A 6 per cent government tax will be added to all these prices. The charge for air-conditioning (heating or cooling) is 90 dr. for a single room and 120 dr. for a double room.

In a Luxury, A, B, or C hotel, a single person will pay 80 per cent in a double room. To have a second or third bed brought into a single or twin room raises its price by 20 per cent. If you stay for less than three days, the hotel may charge 10 per cent more, although this is rare.

During the summer, hotels with restaurants may require guests to take their meals in the hotel, either full pension or demi pension, and there is no refund for an uneaten dinner. 12 o'clock noon is the official check-out time, although on the islands it is usually geared to the arrival of the next boat. Most Luxury and Class A, if not B, hotels, located far from the town or port, supply buses or cars to pick up guests.

Hotels down to Class B all have private bathrooms. In C some do and some don't. In D you will be lucky to find a hot shower, and in E forget it. In these hotels neither towel nor soap is supplied, although the bedding is clean.

The importance of reserving a room in advance, especially during July and August, cannot be overemphasized. Reservations can be made through:

The Hellenic Chamber of Hotels, 6 Aristidou St., Athens.
Tel. Athens 3237193 (from Athens: between 8.00 a.m. and 8 p.m.) or Athens 3236962 (from abroad: between 8.00 a.m. and 1 p.m.)
Telex 214269 XEPE GR. Cable EXENEPEL

Rooms in Private Homes

These are for the most part cheaper than hotels and often nicer. On the whole, Greek houses aren't much in comparison to other European homes, mainly because the Greeks spend so little time inside them; but they are clean, and the owner will often go out of his or her way to assure maximum comfort for the guest. In most houses you can also get an idea of Greek taste, which is sometimes simple and good, but far more often incredibly corny, from plastic cat pictures that squeak to lamps in the shape of ships made out of macaroni.

While room prices are generally fixed in the summer, out of season they are always negotiable with a little finesse, even in June. Speaking some Greek is the biggest asset in bargaining, although not strictly necessary. Claiming to be a poor student is generally effective. Always remember, however, that you are staying in someone's home, and do not waste more water or electricity than you need. The owner will generally give you a tub to wash your clothes in, and there is always a clothes line. Most homes offer a continental breakfast.

The Tourist Police on each island have all the information on rooms and will be able to find you one, if you do not meet a chorus of Greeks when you leave the boat, chanting "Rooms? Rooms?". Many houses also have signs.

Youth Hostels

These can be found at Corfu (2), Crete (6), Santorini, Samos, Myconos, Naxos, Ios, Zachynthos, and Athens (4). Although it's safest to have a card you don't often need one. Most youth hostels are about 80 dr. a night, extra for shower, sheets, breakfast and dinner, if available. Reservations can be made through:

The Greek Association of Youth Hostels,
4 Dragatsaniou St., Athens.
Tel. Athens 3234107

Camping Out

The climate of summertime Greece is perfect for sleeping out of doors. In most places sleeping on the beach is permitted. This is ideal for its soft sandy mattress and the sea breeze which keeps hopeful insects at bay. For anyone who comes to the islands in July and August without making a hotel reservation this should be an option, for there are times when even a room in a house can't be found for all the money in the world.

Those who want to pitch a tent should not count on renting either it or other camping materials in Greece. Stores carry some things but the prices are high. If you plan to cook out, a camp stove is a good thing to bring, for the dryness of Greece makes it highly susceptible to fire. Fires should be lit only in rocky areas void of vegetation.

Each island has a different attitude towards camping. On some islands like Samothrace one can pitch a tent in any likely spot, on islands like Alonissos it is officially forbidden, although only enforced when the policeman comes around every two weeks to pull out tent poles, on other islands such as Mykonos one is politely referred to the official camping sites. Official camping sites eliminate the problem of finding fresh water, and they usually have trees and a beach nearby.

Islands with official camp sites are Corfu (5), Thassos (3), Aegina, Moni, Ios Crete (2), Mykonos, and there are others being laid out. Official sites charge 15-30 dr. a night for tents or caravans; 20-40 dr. a night for adults, and 15-25 dr. a night for children.

Renting a House

On most islands it is possible to rent houses or villas, generally for a month or more at a time. Villas can often be reserved from abroad: contact a travel agent or the National Tourist Organization for names and addresses. Houses can be found on the spot with a little inquiry: begin with the Tourist Police. With a little luck you can find a house sleeping 6, 8, or even 10 people, and depending on its age and facilities you can pay as little as 100 dr. a day. Facilities normally include a refrigerator, hot water, plates and utensils, etc. Generally, the longer you stay the more economical it becomes. Things to check for are leaking roofs, water supply (the house may have a well) and a supply of lamps if there is no electricity.

A note on the Greek toilet

This is, of course, supposing you find one. They lurk in tavernas, restaurants, and sweet shops, and it is good manners to buy something before you excuse yourself. Public toilets are often located by the beach, where you might have to pay 3 dr. to enter.

Greek plumbing makes up in inventiveness for what it lack in efficiency. Do not tempt fate by disobeying the little notices "the papers they please to throw in the basket" — or it's bound to lead to trouble. Also, a second flush in immediate succession will gurgle and burp instead of swallow. Many places in Greece have only a ceramic hole. Women who confront this for the first time should take care not to wet their feet: squat about halfway and lean back as far as you can. Always have paper of some sort handy.

Showers, priced 10 dr. cold and 20 dr. hot, are either manual or often the Special Greek Squirt, where a quarter of the water trickles on your head and the rest ricochets off the ceiling and on to your towel. If the water stops, try jiggling the sink or toilet. Sinks in Greece rarely have rubber stoppers.

Never drink the water without asking first. On dry islands, remember to ask what time the water is turned off.

Dining

Eating establishments in Greece are categorized into Luxury, A, B, and C classes. Prices are controlled by the Tourist Police, who also enforce sanitary and health regulations.

The menu in Luxury restaurants is often international; in others you will rarely find more than the basic Greek cuisine. This is steeped in rich golden olive oil and the ingredients are fresh and often produced locally. You may go back into the kitchens to examine the offerings before making a choice. There is usually a menu posted on the door with an English translation, listing the prices. The availability and variety of fish depends on the catch; a lack of fish on the islands is due most often to direct marketing to Athens. Each type of fish has its own price and you can specify how many you want. A lobster is around 500 dr., depending on weight. Remember that the redder the gills, the fresher the fish.

Lamb is the most common meat in Greece, and the substance of *souvlaki*, the meat on a spit that you can find anywhere. Goat is served at village feasts, along with rice or *pilafi*. Meat and chicken are either stewed in a sauce of olive oil and tomato, or grilled, accompanied with fried potatoes, spaghetti, or rice. A Greek salad can be just tomatoes or just cucumbers, or village style with tomatoes, cucumbers, black olives, peppers, onions, and feta cheese — a small one for one person and a big one for two or three. You eat this during the meal, dipping your bread in the olive oil. In the summer dinner is generally followed by melon or watermelon.

Restaurants (*estiatórion*) serve baked dishes and often grills as well. Those serving just a grill and roasts are called *psistarid*. A taverna may serve baked dishes or a grill or both, and is less formal than a restaurant. A sweet shop, or *zacharoplasteíon*, sells honey pastries, cakes, puddings and drinks and sometimes home-made ice cream. Many also serve breakfast, along with the less common dairy shops, or *galaktopoléion,* which sell milk, coffee, bread, yoghurt, rice pudding, and custard pies. Cheese pies and our old friend "tost" can appear almost anywhere.

Prices on Greek menus are written first without, then including service and tax charges. If you are served by a young boy (*mikró*), give him something or leave it on the table — tips are generally all he earns.

Most restaurants and tavernas serve two or three kinds of beer (Fix and Amstel are the most common), red or white *demestiká* and a *retsina* (resined wine, usually white). These most basic choices are supplemented by any variety of local and Greek wines, which can be excellent or poison. The opinion of the waiter is helpful. Some good wines to be found everywhere are the Cretan Minos and Olympia, Patras, Achaia, Nikteri (from Santorini), dry white Samina, and sweet wines from Samos and Patras (Mavrodoplini).

More and more rare are the tavernas with huge wooden barrels lining the walls; in many, however, you can buy wine by the jug or glass. You can also come with your own container and have it filled with local wine — the cheapest way to buy it. Cafés, or *kafeneíons* serve Turkish coffee — now known more often as Greek coffee (*café hellinikó*). There are 40 different ways to make this, although *glykó* (sweet), *métrio* (medium) and *skéto* (no sugar) are the basic orders. It is always served with a glass of water. Nescafe' with milk can only be found at the sweet shops, while cafés will serve cold coffee or *frappé*. Soft drinks and ouzo complete the general fare. Ouzo (or raki in Crete) is a clear anise-flavoured aperitif which many dilute with water. It is usually served with a snack called *mezédes* of infinite variety.

Greek *kafeneíons* in small towns are frequented mostly by men, who discuss the latest news, and play cards or backgammon.

The following items appear frequently on Greek menus:

ΟΡΕΚΤΙΚΑ	Orektiká	Hors d'oeuvre
Τσατσάκι	tsatsaki	yogourt and cucumbers
Ἐληὲς	eliés	olives
Ντολμάδες	dolmáthes	stuffed vine leaves
Διάφορα ὀρεκτικά	thiáfora orektiká	diverse hors d'oeuvre
ΣΟΥΠΕΣ	Soupes	Soups
Αὐγολεμονο	avgolemono	egg and lemon soup
Σοῦπα ἀπο χόρτα	soúpa apó chórta	vegetable soup
Ψαρόσουπα	psarósoupa	fish soup
Μαγειρίτσα	magirítsa	giblets in egg and lemon soup
ΖΥΜΑΡΙΚΑ	Zimárika	Pasta and Rice
Πιλάφι σάλτσα	piláfi sáltsa	pilaf
Σπαγεττο	spagéto	spaghetti
Μακαρόνια	makarónia	macaroni

ΛΑΔΕΡΑ	**Lathéra**	**Vegetables**
Πατάτες	patátes	potatoes
Ντομάτεσ γεμιστές	tomátes yemistés	stuffed tomatoes
Μελιτζάνες γεμιστές	melitzánes yemistés	stuffed aubergines / eggplants
Πιπερίεσ γεμιστέσ	piperíes yemistés	stuffed peppers
Φασόλια	vasólia	beans
φακή	fakí	lentils
χόρτα	chórta	greens

ΨΑΡΙΑ	**Psaria**	**Fish**
Ἀστακὸς	astakós	lobsters
Καλαμαράκια	kalamarákia	little squids
Οκταπόδι	oktapóthi	octopus
Μπαρμπούνια	barboúnia	red mullet
Γαρίδες	garíthes	prawns (shrimps)
Μαρίδες	maríthes	whitebait
Συναγρίδα	sinagrítha	sea bream
Μπακαλιάρος (σκορδαλιά)	bakaliáros (skorthaliá)	fried cod (with garlic and vinegar sauce)
Στρείδια	stríthia	oysters
Λιθρίνια	lithrínia	bass

ΑΥΓΑ	**Avgá**	**Eggs**
Ὀμελέτα Ζαμπὸν	omeléta zambón	ham omelette
Ὀμελέτα μὲ τυρί	omeléta me tiri	cheese omelette
Αὐγὰ τηγαιτά (μπρουγὲ)	avga tigetá (brouyé)	fried (scrambled) eggs

ΕΝΤΡΑΔΕΣ	**Entráthes**	**Entrées**
Κοτόπουλο	kotópulo	chicken
Μπιφτέκια	biftékia	hamburgers
Κουνέλι	kounéli	rabbit
Παστίτσιο	pastítsio	meat and macaroni
Μουσακά	mousaká	meat and aubergine / eggplant with white sauce
Σκώτι	skóti	liver
Μοσχάρι	moskári	veal
Αρνάκι	arnáki	lamb
Κοτολέτες χοιρινὲς	kotolétes chirinés	pork chops
Σουτζουκάκια	tsoutsoukákia	meat balls in tomato sauce
Λουκάνικο	lukániko	sausage

ΣΧΑΡΑΣ	**Skáras**	**Grills**
Σουβλάκια	souvlákia	meat on a skewer
Μπριζόλες	brizóles	veal chops
κότα ψητή	kóta psití	roast chicken

Κεφτέδες	keftéthes	meat balls
ΣΑΛΑΤΕΣ	**Salátes**	**Salads**
Ντομάτες	tomátes	tomatoes
'Αγγουράκι	angouráki	cucumbers
Ρωσσική	rossikí	Russian salad
Χοριατικιά	choriatikiá	village salad with cheese
Κολοκυθάκια	kolokithákia	courgettes / zuchini
ΤΥΡΙΑ	**Tiria**	**Cheeses**
Τυρόπιττα	tirópitta	cheese pie
Φέτα	féta	goat cheese
Κασέρι	kaséri	hard buttery cheese
Ροκφόρ	rokfór	blue cheese
Γραβιέρα	graviéra	like gruyére
ΓΛΥΚΑ	**Glyká**	**Sweets**
Παγωτό	pagotó	ice cream
Κουραμπιέδες	kourabíethes	white Greek cookies
Λουκομάδες	loukomáthes	hot honey fritters
Χαλβά	halvá	sesame seed sweet
Μπακλαβά	baklavá	honey pastry
Γαλακτομπούρεκκον	galaktoboúrekkon	custard pastry
Γιαοῦρτι	yiaóurti	yogourt
'Ρυζόγαλο	rizógalo	rice pudding
Καταΐφι	kataḯfi	shredded wheat with nuts and honey
Μπουγάτσα	bougátsa	custard tart
'Αμογδαλωτά	amigthalotá	almond cookies
ΦΡΟΥΤΑ	**Frúta**	**Fruit**
'Αχλάδι	akláthi	pear
Πορτοκάλι	portokáli	orange
Μῆλο	mílo	apple
Ροδάκινο	rothákino	peach
Πεπόνι	pepóni	melon
Καρπούζι	karpoúzi	watermelon
Δαμάσκηνα	thamáskina	plum
Σύκα	síka	fig
Σταφύλια	stafília	grapes
Μπανάνα	banána	banana
Βερύκοκα	veríkoka	apricot
	Miscellaneous	
Νερό (βραστό)	neró (vrastó)	water (boiled)
Ψωμί	psomí	bread
Βούτυρο	voútiro	butter
Μέλι	méli	honey

Μαρμαλάδα	marmalátha	jam
Αλάτι	aláti	salt
Πιπέρι	pipéri	pepper
Ζάχαρι	zákari	sugar
Λάδι	láthi	oil
Ξείδι	xíthi	vinegar
Μουστάρδα	mustárda	mustard
Λεμόνι	lemóni	lemon
Γάλα	gála	milk
Τσάι	chái	tea
Σοκολάτα	sokoláta	chocolate
Λογαριασμό	logariasmó	the bill / check
Στὴν ἠγειά σασ!	stíniyásas	to your health!

If someone treats you to a drink in a cafe, restaurant, or at home, never forget to toast them. Complete strangers will buy you drinks if you've caught their fancy: the waiter will point out the treater for you to toast.

Music and dancing

Greek music is either city music or village music. The music of the city includes the popular jukebox tunes and most bazouki music, whereas village music is played on the bag pipes (tsamboúna), the clarinet (klarino) the violin and sometimes the dulcimer (sandoúri). Cretan music specializes in the lyre and is in a class by itself.

On the islands you can hear both city and village music, the former at the *bazoukia*, or Greek night clubs, which usually feature certain singers. Many play records or washed-out musak until midnight as the customers slowly arrive. One generally buys a bottle of white wine and fruit and dances until 4 in the morning. Be prepared to spend at least 300 dr. an evening. To hear the village, or folk music, you must go into the villages, to the festivals or weddings. In many places Sunday evening is an occasion for song and dance. The singing of village music is generally modest; with city music not only do the professional singers perform, but any local with a good voice will often get up to sing a few songs. After an hour of drinking, a particular favourite or a good dancer is liable to make the enthusiasts forget the new law against *spdsimo*, or plate breaking, whose supporters end up paying for missing place settings.

On a particularly energetic evening someone is bound to get up and dance holding a fully set table between his teeth, while others dance with wine glasses or bottles on their heads. When matrons begin to belly dance on the table, you know it's time to go.

In the tavernas one may hear either city or village music. Some put on permanent shows, and others have music only occasionally. Athens is awash with tourist shows and discotheques during the summer but starts swinging to all kinds of Greek music in November, when Plaka reverts back to the Athenians. Most musicians on the islands go to Athens in the winter.

The lyrics to most Greek songs deal with the ups and downs of love. Serious composers (Mikis Theodorakis is the best known) often put poetry to music, doing splendid renderings of the lyrics of George Seferis and Yannis Ritsos. The guerillas *(partizanis)* and the Communists have a monopoly of the best political songs, many by Theodorakis. Cretan songs are often very patriotic (for Crete) and many are drawn from the 17th-century epic poem the *Erotókritos,* written in the Cretan dialect by Vincento Kornaro.

Every island in Greece has its special dance, although today it is often only the young people's folk dance societies that keep them alive, along with the island's traditional costumes. The best time to find them dancing is on each island's Day of Liberation from the Turks or any other anniversary of local significance. Here are details of three excellent folk dance companies:

Athens:
Dora Stratou Greek Folk Dances, Dora Stratou Theatre, Philopapou Hill.
Tel. 3224861 mornings, 914650 afternoons.
From beginning of May to end of September.
Shows begin at 10.00 pm every day, with an additional show at 8.00 pm on Wednesday and Sunday.
Tickets: 130, 100 or 70 dr.; 50 dr. for students.
Corfu:
The Corfu Ballet in the Old Fortress.
Tel. (0661) 30520 and 30360.
15 May to the end of September.
Performances at 8.30 pm every day except Sunday, before the 'Sound and Light' show.
Tickets: 70 dr.; 50 dr. for students (entrance for both dancing and 'Sound and Light').
Rhodes:
Nelly Dimoglou Greek Dances, The Old City Theatre.
Tel. (0241) 20157 and 27524.
From June to October.
Performances at 9.00 pm every day except Saturday.
Tickets: 120 dr.; 60 dr. for students.

Although these shows are beautiful and interesting, there's nothing like getting up to dance yourself — a splendid way to work off the big dinner just consumed at a *panayiéri.* The one dance everyone knows is the basic one two three kick kickie, or Stae Tría, done in a circle with hands on shoulders. The circle is never complete, however: even in this simple dance someone leads, setting the pace and variation of the dance (for all know each dance a little differently) and generally supplying the special effects with leaps, foot slaps, kicks, little skips or whatever he or she likes. Cretans are the best leaders — some are almost contortionists.

Sta Tría often begins at a slow pace and picks up towards the end. The Sýrto, on the other hand, retains its slow graceful pace throughout. It has only six easy steps which are repeated until the end, but watch the leader for variations. This is considered the oldest Greek dance of all, dating back at least into Hellenistic times. The Kalamatíano, a twelve-step dance, is a little more difficult. If a Greek invites you to dance the Bállo, a couple's dance, follow your partner's lead. While there are certain set steps to the Tsíphte Téli, or belly dance, it has become a free spirited dance for the loose limbed.

The Zeybékiko is normally performed by men, although upon occasion women also dance it. This is the serious deliberate solo dance that inspires the most *spastico*, for everyone loves to watch a good Zeybékiko dancer with his friend before him on one knee, clapping out the rhythm. The Hasápiko, better known as the Zorba dance in the West and traditionally done by two men, will require some practice but is well worth learning. This is even more true of the Cretan dances with their small furious steps and hops, which have a habit of lasting until your adrenalin has pumped its last. The remedy for this is a glass of raki, and before you know it you'll be dancing another Pentozale or Pedekto.

Almost all Greeks love to dance and are never surprised when visitors want to join in the fun. People interested in learning Greek dancing can often find locals to teach them, or they can follow the steps in a book published by Lycabettus Press: *Greek Dances* by Ted Petrides. Folk music to practice by can be heard daily on Greek radio at 7 pm, on a programme called 'Musiki tou Laousmas' ('Music of our People').

Part 4
Wild Animals and Other Concerns

Animals

The only ferocious animal most tourists will meet is the wily mosquito, who is easily outsmarted with an insect coil (Katol and Moontigers are two brands) for 27 dr. As only a few islands provide breeding grounds for mosquitoes, it is not worth buying a coil until you see the whites of their eyes. Mules can be mean, but they are foiled by staying out of their back legs' kicking range. Pin cushiony sea urchins live by rocky beaches, and if you step on one with bare feet, you'll know it. The spines might break and imbed themselves even deeper if you try to force them out; olive oil and a lot of patience is recommended, to get the spine to slip out. Pale brown jellyfish (*médusas*) may drift in anywhere depending on winds and currents. Unless they find a tender spot, a jellyfish sting is not very painful, although they can leave scars on certain people.

The truly dangerous creatures are much more difficult to find. Poisonous snakes and scorpions live only in the wildest parts of the country. If you have the rare misfortune to be bit or stung, you should quickly tie a tourniquet between the wound and your heart, clean the wound and suck out the blood and poison. Most importantly, stay calm. Get to a doctor as soon as possible, but never run. Mountain sheep dogs are a more immediate danger in outer rural areas: by stooping as if to pick up a stone to throw at it, you might keep a dog at bay. If bitten, go immediately to a doctor.

Sharks are seldom found near the coastal regions of Greece. Blood attracts them, so if you are wounded, swim for shore without delay.

Underwater fishermen should ask their Greek confréres about other dangerous fish in the area, such as the Dracula, an unlikely delicacy, whose razor-sharp fins can kill.

Again, these dangers are very rare, and most people never hear of them, much less see them. However, if you do plan to camp in an out-of-the-way area, it never hurts to have a tetanus shot before coming.

The hunting season (mainly for hare and fowl) is from 25 August to 15 March. For further information contact the Greek Federation of Hunting Societies, 2 Korai Street, Athens; tel. 3231271.

Banks and money

The word for bank in Greek is *trdpeza*, derived from the word *trapezi*, or table, and thus from the days of the money changers. On all the islands with more than goats and a few shepherds there is some sort of banking establishment. If you plan to spend time on one of the more obscure islands, however, such as Antikythera or Kastellorizo, it is safest to bring enough drachmas with you. On the other hand, the small but popular islands often have only one bank, where exchanging money can take a long time to accomplish. Waiting can be avoided if you go at 8 in the morning, when the banks open (normal banking hours are 8 am to 1 pm). Most island banks are closed on both Saturday and Sunday.

Traveller's cheques are always good to bring, not only in case they are stolen, but because they command a better exchange rate than currency. The major brands of traveller's cheques and international banking cards are accepted everywhere. Athens is the easiest place for arranging to have money sent from abroad, but any island bank will advise you on the quickest methods elsewhere.

The **Greek drachma** is divided into 100 lepta, which nowadays is used only in the form of 50 lepta coins. Drachmas are circulated in coins of 20, 10, 5, 2 and 1. The variety of sizes can be very confusing, since coins from the monarchy, the republic, the junta and the present republic are all in circulation today. The notes are easier to follow: they come in 50, 100, 500, and 1000 drachmas, each with its own colour and size. You are allowed to bring 750 drachmas into Greece; this is a good idea if you intend to arrive on a Saturday or Sunday.

The main **banks in Athens** are:
American Express Bank, 15-17 Venizelou St. Tel. 3234781
Bank of America, 10 Stadiou St. Tel. 3234004
Bank of Attica, 19 El. Venizelou St. Tel. 3247415/3226205
Bank of Greece, 21 El. Venizelou St. Tel. 3230551
City Bank N.A., 8 Othonos St., Syntagma. Tel. 3227471
City Bank N.A., 2 Filikis Eterias Sq. Tel. 3618619
City Bank N.A., 47-49 Akti Miaouli, Piraeus. Tel. 4523511
Credit Bank, 10 Pesmazoglou St. Tel. 3245111
Credit Bank, 9 El. Venizelou St., Syntagma.
Credit Bank, 230 Kifisias Ave., Psychico.

Credit Bank, 224 Syngou Ave.
Continental Bank, 24 Stadiou St., Tel. 3241562
First National Bank of Chicago, 13 El. Venizelou St. Tel. 3602311
National Bank of Greece (open in the afternoon, 5.30 pm to 7.30 pm),
86 Aeolou St. Tel. 3210601
National Bank of Greece, 2 Karageorgi Servias, Syntagma. Tel.
3222730/3236481

If you run out of money in Greece, it usually isn't too difficult to find a **temporary job** on the islands, ranging from shining cucumbers to laying cement. The *kafenions* are good places to inquire. Work on yachts can sometimes be found by asking around at the Athenian Marinas. For tutoring and domestic work contact Miterna, 28 Ermou and 2 Kornarou Streets, Athens. Hotel work may be found at the Hellenic Chamber of Hotels, 6 Aristidou St., Athens. The theatre agents, for work as extras in films, are off Academias Ave. by Kanigos Square. English tutoring and work as a nanny might be found through the Social Services Station, Box 1038, Athens. Teachers may also apply to the American Community Schools of Athens Inc., 129 Ag. Paraskevis, Ano Neo Chalandri, Athens.

Conversion Tables

The **metric system** is used throughout Greece.

1 centimetre	= 0.39 ins	1 inch	= 2.54 centimetres
1 metre	= 3 ft 3½ ins	1 yard	= 91.44 centimetres
1 kilometre	= 0.621 miles	1 mile	= 1.61 kilometres
500 grams	= 1 lb 1¾ oz	½ lb	= 227 grams
1 kilogram	= 2 lb 3¼ oz	1 lb	= 454 grams
5 litres	= 1.1 Imp. gallons or	1 Imp. gallon	= 4.54 litres
	= 1.3 US gallons	1 US gallon	= 3.78 litres

To convert °Fahrenheit to °Centigrade:
°Centigrade = (°F - 32) ÷ 1.8 or
= (°F - 32) x ⅝
°Centigrade to °Fahrenheit
°Fahrenheit = (°C x 1.8) + 32 or
= (°C x ⅑) + 32

Two other Greek measurements you may come across are the *stemma*, a Greek land Measurement (1 stemma = ¼ acre), and the *oka*, an old fashioned weight standard, divided into 400 *drams* (1 *oka* = 3 lb; 35 *drams* = ¼ lb, 140 *drams* = 1 lb).

The **electric current** in Greece is mainly 220 volts or 50 AC. In more out of the way places you may find 110 volts. US 60 cycle appliances will function on 50 AC but will work more slowly than normal.

Greek time is Eastern European, or two hours ahead of Greenwich time.

Embassies and Consulates in Greece

Australia:	15 Mesogeion St., Athens. Tel. 8216800
Canada:	4 Ioannou Genadiou St., Athens. Tel. 739511
Great Britain:	1 Ploutarchou & Ypsilantou Sts., Athens. Tel. 736211
	24 Akti Possidonos, Piraeus. Tel. 4178345
	North Zabeli Rd., Corfu
	Polidou St., Rhodes. Tel. (0241) 27306
New Zealand:	29 Vas. Sofias Ave., Athens. Tel. 727515
South Africa:	69 Vas. Sophias Ave., Athens. Tel. 729050
U.S.A.:	91 Vas. Sophias Ave., Athens. Tel. 712951
United Nations Office:	36 Amalias Ave., Athens. Tel. 3229624

Health

There is at least one doctor on every island, whose office is open from 9 am to 1 pm and from 5 pm to 7 pm. On many islands there are hospitals which are open all day. Special emergencies are taken to Athens by helicopter, or occasionally a ship will divert its course to take the critically ill. The flat fee is 300 dr. for a doctor's consultation, although this is often waived or decreased for minor tourist ailments. Most doctors pride themselves on their English, as do their friends the pharmacists, whose advice on minor ailments is also good although their medicine is not particularly cheap.

Coca cola or retsina cuts down the oil in Greek foods. Lemon juice can also help stomach upsets. The sea quickly cures cuts and abrasions. If anything else goes wrong, the Greek villagers will advise you to pee on it.

Holidays

1 January	New Year's Day	*Protochroniá*
6 January	Epiphany	*Ton Theofaníon*
25 March	Greek Independence Day	*Ikosi pémpti martíou*
	Shrove Tuesday	*Kathari Théftera* (follows a three-week carnival)
	Good Friday	*Megáli Paraskeví*
	Easter	*Páscha*
	Easter Monday	*Théftera tou Páscha*
1 May	May Day (International Labour Day)	*Protomayíou*
15 August	Assumption of the Virgin	*Kołmisis tis Theotókou*
28 October	*"Ochi"* Day (in celebration of Metaxas' "no" to Mussolini)	*Ekosi októ oktovríou*
25 December	Christmas	*Kristoúyena*
26 December	St. Stephen's Day	*Théfteri i méra ton Kristoúyena*

Note that most businesses and shops also close down for the afternoon

52

before and the morning after a religious holiday. If a national holiday falls on a Sunday, the following Monday is observed. The Orthodox Easter is generally a week or so after the Roman Easter.

Mountain Climbing and Skiing

Crete is the island queen of Greek mountain sport, with three mountain refuges. A fourth is on the island of Evia. In all, you can expect to pay about 50 dr. per bed per night.

Lefka Ori (White Mountain), Crete:
Kallergi, alt. 1680 m. (5510 ft.); 40 beds. Tel. Chania (0821) 24647.
Volikas, alt. 1480 m. (4860 ft.); 30 beds. Tel. as above.
Psiloritis (Mount Ida), Crete:
Prinias, alt. 1100 m. (3610 ft.); 16 beds. Tel. Herakleon (081) 287110.
Mount Dirfys, Evia:
Liri, alt. 1100 m. (3610 ft.); 36 beds. Tel. Chalki (0221) 25230.
There is skiing from December to March at both Kallergi and Liri.
Three important addresses in Athens for mountaineers and skiers are:
The Hellenic Alpine Club, 7 Karageorgi Servias. Tel. 3234555.
The Hellenic Touring Club, 12 Polytechniou St. Tel. 548601.
The Hellenic Federation of Excursion Societies, 4 Dragatsaniou. Tel. 3234107.

The National Tourist Organization of Greece

The National Tourist Organization can answer almost any question about Greece. When they don't know the answer, they can usually refer you to someone who does.

There are three offices in Athens:
Syntagma Square, 2 Karageorgi Servias (same building as National Bank of Greece). Tel. 3233545.
East Airport, Ellinikon. Tel. 9799500.
4 Stadiou, Stoa Spyromiliou (head office). Tel. 3223111.
There are also branches in Corfu, Chania, Herakleon, Kos and Rhodes.
Abroad there are offices in:
Australia: Greek National Tourist Organization,
                c/o Consulate General of Greece,
                National Building, 250 Pitt Street, Sydney, NSW.
                Tel. 619514; telex 52-8126.
Canada: National Tourist Organization,
                c/o Consulate General of Greece,
                1350 W. Sherbrook Street, Suite 620, Montreal, Quebec H3G IJI.
                Tel. 8449464.

Great Britain: National Tourist Organization of Greece,
195 Regent Street, London W1R 8DL.
Tel. 734 5997; telex 21-122.
United States: Greek National Tourist Organization, 168 N. Michigan
Avenue, Chicago, Ill. 60601.
Tel. 6416600/7821084.
Greek National Tourist Organization,
627 West 6th Street, Los Angeles, Calif. 90017.
Tel. 6266696.
Greek National Tourist Organization, Olympic Tower,
645 Fifth Avenue, New York, NY 10022.
Tel. 42157778; telex 66489.

Islands with no branch office of the National Tourist Organization have **tourist policemen** who offer the same assistance, besides helping tourists find accommodation. In Athens there are three tourist police stations, and a magic telephone number — 171. 171 not only speaks good English, but can tell you everything from ship departures to where to spend the night. Tourist Police stations in Athens are at:

7 Syngrou St. (the home of 171).
Larissa Train Station. Tel. 8213574.
East Airport. Tel. 9819730.

At Piraeus the Tourist Police are on the Akti Miaouli. Tel. 4523670.

You can always tell a tourist policeman from other policeman by the little flags he wears on his pocket, showing which languages he speaks.

Photography

Greece lends herself freely to beautiful photography, but charges a fee in her museums. For an 8 to 16 mm still camera, without tripod, one buys a ticket for the camera. For a still camera with tripod, the following scales apply:

each picture without flash: 80 dr. for amateurs, 120 dr. for professionals
each picture with flash: 100 dr. for amateurs, 150 dr. for professionals
opening the glass case or displacing objects — each picture without flash: 100 dr. for amateurs, 150 dr. for professionals; each picture with flash: 120 dr. for amateurs, 180 dr. for professionals
on archaeological sites, a flat fee of 150 dr. for amateurs, 120 dr. for professionals

For short movie films of unanimated scenes in museums, the fee is 1000 dr. a day for amateurs and 2000 dr. for professionals. On archaeological sites, the fees are 600 dr. a day for amateurs and 1250 dr. for professionals. These fees are greatly reduced if more than five archaeological sites are to be filmed. Long films of unanimated scenes, by either amateurs or professionals, must be licensed by the Inspector General of Antiquities, 14 Aristidou and Pesmazoglou Streets, Athens.

The fee will be at least 10,000 dr.

For underwater photography, see "Underwater Activities," page 56.

While film for an instamatic can be found on most islands, other films can be found only in the larger towns. It is not cheap. The light in Greece in the summer is a lot stronger than it seems and is the most common cause of ruined photographs. Greeks invariably love to have their pictures taken, and although it's more polite to ask first, you should just go ahead and take the photo if you don't want them to rush off to beautify themselves and strike a pose. You should avoid taking pictures of the communications systems on the mountain tops.

If you bring an expensive camera to Greece, it never hurts to insure it. Above all, never leave it alone "for just a few minutes." Although Greeks themselves very rarely steal anything, other tourists are not so honest.

Post Offices

Signs for post offices (*tachidromío*) as well as post boxes are bright yellow and easy to find. Many post office employees speak English. Stamps can also be bought at the kiosks, although they charge a small tax. A stamp is a *grammatósima*.

If you do not have an address in Greece, mail can be sent to you Poste Restante to any post office in Greece, and can be picked up with proof of identity. After three months all unretrieved letters are returned to sender. If someone has sent you a parcel, you will receive a notice of its arrival, and you must go to the post office to collect it. You will often have to pay some handling fee, if not customs charges and duties if dutiable articles are contained. Fragile stickers attract little attention. In small villages, particularly on the islands, mail is not delivered to the house but to the village centre, either a café or bakery. Its arrival coincides with that of a ship from Athens.

If you want to mail a package, any shop selling paper items will wrap it sturdily for you for a small fee.

Telephones

The Organismos Telephikinonion Ellathos, better known as OTE, has offices in the larger towns and at least one on every island that has a telephone service. One can call both direct and collect (reverse charges) although the latter usually takes at least half an hour to put through. On the larger islands one may dial abroad direct (for Great Britain dial 0044, and for the USA 001 before the area code). You should also use OTE for calling other places in Greece. Telegrams can be sent from either OTE or the post office.

Local calls cost 2 dr. and can be made from many kiosks, *kafeníons*, and shops (always ask first).

It is often impossible to call Athens from the islands by mid-morning; the chances are far better in the evening. To defeat the beeps, whirrs, and buzzes you often get instead of a connection, try dialling as fast as you can. This somehow seems to work the best.

Underwater Activities

Underwater fishing with compressed air equipment is permitted only in certain areas in Greece, and authorization must be given by the naval authorities or captain of the port. You must be at least 20 years old, pay a small tax, and not fish within 100 m. (330 ft.) of public beaches or professional fishing areas. It is illegal to catch a fish weighing less than 150 grams (4 oz.) with a spear gun. Archaeological remains under water should not be interfered with, and any discoveries should be reported to the authorities.

Decompression chambers are available at:
The Hellenic Federation of Underwater Activities, Ag. Kosmos, Ellinikon. Tel. (Athens) 9819961.
The Naval Hospital of Piraeus, 66 Akti Moutsopoulou. Tel. 4512466.

Service stations for **compressed air** are available at:
The Hellenic Federation of Underwater Activities (address above).
Kartelia School, 4 Karageorgi Servias, Kastella. Tel. 422047.
Softoniadis Michail, 15 Paprigopoulou. Tel. 3236598.
Nautical Club of Corfu. Tel. (0661) 28470.
Nautical Athletism Club of Kalamaria, Thessaloniki. Tel. (031) 412068.
Nautical Association of Rhodes. Tel. (0241) 71359/23287.

Underwater diving schools operate from the Hellenic Federation of Underwater Activities, and in Piraeus at the Kartelia School and the P. Liami School, 1 Zanni Rd., Akti Moutsopoulou; tel. 451047. In Rhodes is the D. Koulia School, tel. (0241) 22296; and in Corfu, for Germans only, the Barakounta School at Paleokastritsa.

The following islands permit **underwater fishing and photography:** Hydra, Mykonos, Spetses, Zachynthos, Paxi (except in the region of Voutsi), Kephalonia (outside of the gulf of Sami to Ag. Ephimia), Levkada (except the south-west coast, between Rouda and Afteli bays), and Corfu (except south of cape Lefkimi and Arkoudila at Kountouri, near the islets Vido and Lazaretto, from cape Agni to Roda, or between Mathraki, Cape Taxiarchis and Cape Drastis).

Average sea temperatures

Jan	Feb	Mar	Apr	May	June	July	Aug	Sep	Oct	Nov	Dec
59°F	59°F	59°F	61°F	64°F	72°F	75°F	77°F	75°F	72°F	64°F	63°F
15°C	15°C	15°C	16°C	18°C	22°C	24°C	25°C	24°C	22°C	18°C	17°C

What to Bring to Greece

Even in the height of summer, evenings can be chilly in Greece, especially when the Meltemi wind is blowing. Always bring at least one warm sweater, if not a pair of long trousers. Those who venture off the beaten track into the thorns and rocks should bring sturdy and comfortable shoes — tennis shoes are very good. They should cover the ankles if you really like the wilderness, where scorpions and harmful snakes still exist. Plastic swim shoes are recommended for rocky beaches, where there are often sea urchins.

Summer travellers following whim rather than a pre-determined programme should bring a sleeping bag for sure, as lodgings of any sort are often full to capacity. Serious sleeping baggers should also bring an airmattress to cushion them from the gravelly Greek ground. Torches are very handy for moonless nights and caves.

On the pharmaceutical side, sea sickness pills, insect bite remedies, tablets for stomach upsets and aspirin will deal with most difficulties encountered. Soap, washing powder, a clothes line and especially a towel are necessary for those staying in Class C hotels or less. Bring a sink plug if you like sinks full of water. A knife is a good idea if you like *panayiéria*, where you are often given a slab of goat meat with only a spoon or fork to control it. A photo of the family and home is always appreciated by new Greek friends.

On all the Greek islands except for the most remote of the remote you can buy whatever you forgot to bring. Toilet paper and mosquito coils are the two most popular purchases on arrival. However, special needs such as artificial sweeteners, contact lens products, and so on can generally be found only in Athens and never on the islands.

Let common sense and the maxim "bring as little as possible and never more than you can carry" dictate your packing.

How much money you bring depends, of course, on what you do and how much you travel. A student with a card and sleeping bag and a normal appetite can survive and sight see for 150 dr. or $4.00 a day without deprivations. Long distant travelling will cost more.

Women

Greece is a perfect destination for women travelling on their own. Not only is it safe, but because they fundamentally respect them, Greeks refrain from annoying women as other Mediterranean men are known to do. Yet they remain friendly and easy to meet. While some have a difficult time believing that women are their equals, imagining that for a woman a night without company is unbearable mortification of the flesh, they are ever courteous and will rarely allow even the most liberated female (or male) guest to pay for anything. Any Greek who tries to take advantage of a woman earns himself a very bad reputation indeed.

On the other hand, Greek women of marriageable age will seldom travel alone, and grandmother teaches them that foreign women who do so are loose and wild creatures. A good Greek girl traditionally stays at home and helps mother. In the evening she may take a walk with the family — known as *volta* in Greek, or sometimes as "the bride market".

A young man, generally in his late twenties or early thirties, will find a likely girl there or through certain inquiries. He will then approach the father, to discover the girl's dowry — low wages and high housing costs demand that it contains some sort of living quarters from the woman's father, often added on top of the family house. The suitor must have a steady job. If both parties are satisfied, the young man is officially introduced to the daughter, who can be as young as 13 or 14 in the villages. If they get along together well, the marriage date is set. The woman who never marries and has children is sincerely pitied in Greece. The inordinate quantity of Greek widows (and not all wear the traditional black) is due to the 10 to 20 year age difference which often occurs between husband and wife.

Because foreign men don't follow the Greek customs, their interest in a Greek woman will often be regarded with suspicion by her family. Although the brother probably won't knife a man for glancing at his sister (still a custom in the backwaters of Crete), he is likely to tell him to look elsewhere.

Part 5
Athens and Piraeus

As most travellers to the Greek islands eventually find themselves in Athens and Piraeus, they are included in this book; those making their first journey to Greece will particularly want to spend two or three days in the capital. Although hot in the summertime, Athens does her best by tourists, offering them the memorials of a glorious past and almost unlimited wine, song and dance festivals for their entertainment.

Historical outline of Athens
Traces found by archaeologists prove that Athens was inhabited from the Neolithic age, c. 3500 BC. In the second millennium Ionians from Asia Minor invaded these pre-Hellenic people and established small city states throughout Attica, the main one being Kekropia (from the serpent god Kekrops, who later became connected with the real or mythical King Erechtheus, considered to be half snake and the original founder of Athens). The owl was sacred to Kekropia — as it was to the goddess Athena, and her worship and name gradually came to preside in the city.

In the 14th century BC Athens as part of the Mycenean empire of the Acheans invaded Crete, fought Thebes,and conquered Troy, but escaped the subsequent Dorian invasion which brought chaos into the Mycenean world. The Ionians and the Aeolians went back to the lands in Asia Minor and settled many of the Aegean islands. Two hundred years later Attica was conquered, and the Greek Dark Ages began, which lasted until the 8th century BC.

Sometime during the 8th century all the towns of Attica were peaceably united, an accomplishment attributed to the mythical King Theseus. Athens was then ruled by a king (the chief priest), the polemarch (or general), and the archon (or civil authority), positions that by the 6th century became annually elective. The continued conflict between the landed aristocracy and lower and rising commercial classes gradually brought about the solution of democratic government, specially under the reforms of Solon and Kleisthenes. In between these two rulers the tyrant Pisistratos, head of the popular party, began to make Athenian naval might a force to be feared by the other independent city states of Greece.

Kleisthenes' reforms broke down the old unsatisfactory political classifications by dividing the population into ten tribes. Each selected by lot 50 members for the people's assembly, from which a further lot was drawn to select an archon, creating ten archons in all, one from each tribe. The head archon gave his name to the Athenian year. Meanwhile as Persian strength grew in the east, Ionian intellectuals and artists settled in Athens and the roots of Attic tragedy were formed.

After the fall of Ionia to the Persians (Athens had briefly assisted the Ionian case), Darius, the King of Kings, turned to subdue Greece, and in particular Athens, who posed the only threat to his fleet. In 490 BC his vast army landed at Marathon only to be defeated by a much smaller Athenian army, led by Miltiades. Powerful Sparta and the other states then recognized the eastern threat but the defence of Greece was left primarily in the hands of the Athenians and their fleet, which grew in strength under Themostokles. In 480 BC Xerxes, the new Persian king, invaded Greece with a massive fleet and army. The Athenians fled and their city was destroyed, yet the Persian navy floundered against the Greeks at Salamis, and the whole issue of the invasion was finally settled by the Athenians and Spartans at the battle of Plataea.

Having proved her naval might, Athens set about creating a maritime empire for the stability of her internal politics. She ruled the confederacy at Delos, demanding contributions (later tributes) from the islands in return for protection from the Persians. Sea trade also became necessary to support the city's population, whose agriculture was based on the olive and the vine, and colonization ensured a continual food supply to Athens. The democracy became truly imperialistic under Perikles, who had the Delian treasury brought to Athens for safe keeping and also in order to beautify the city. This was the golden age of Athens, during which she led the world in art, architecture, theatre, and philosophy. Phidias, Herodotos, Sophocles, Aristophanes, and Socrates are just a few names from that age.

The Peloponnesian War (431-404 BC) was caused in part by Athenian expansion in the west. Sparta, Athens' great foe, had superiority on land, Athens on the seas. Back and forth the struggle went, exhausting each side with little benefit to either, until Lysander captured Athens, razed the walls, and set up the brief rule of the Thirty Tyrants.

Democracy was restored but Athen's imperialist ideas were not, although she built up a second maritime hegemony. The Peloponnesian War, however, had struck a blow from which Athens could not totally recover; the population grew dissatisfied with public life, and refused to tolerate innovators and critics such as Socrates, whom they put to death. Economically Athens also had trouble keeping a balance of trade, which she so desperately needed. Yet her intellectual tradition held true in the 4th century, bringing forth such as Demosthenes, Praxiteles, Menander, Plato, and later Aristotle.

Philip II of Macedon took advantage of this turmoil to bring the city states together under Macedon, for an expedition against Persia, whose ruler, Artaxeres Ochus was threatening the Greek states. A last torch of patriotic independence was held up against the Macedonians by Demosthenes, the Athenian orator, but with little success. Philip subdued Athens and had begun to plan his campaign against Persia when he was assassinated, leaving his son Alexander to conquer the East. When Alexander died, Athens had to defend herself against his striving generals. In 294 BC Dimitrios Poliorketes (the Besieger) took the city, followed by Antigonas Gonatas. Alexandria and Pergamon became Athen's intellectual rivals, although Athens continued to be honoured by them.

In 168 BC the Romans took Athens and gave her Delos. Eighty years later Athens betrayed Roman favour by siding with Rome's enemy, Mithridates of Pontos, for which Sulla destroyed Piraeus and the walls of the city. But Rome always remembered her cultural debt to Athens, and many leading Romans attended Athens' schools and gave the city great gifts. Conversely many Greek treasures ended up in Rome. St. Paul preached to the Athenians in 44 AD, and they gradually became converted to Christianity. In the 3rd century AD Goths and barbarians sacked Athens, but were eventually driven away, leaving the city to join the growing Byzantine Empire.

The Byzantine Emperors closed the philosophy schools and changed the temples to churches, including the Parthenon which became a cathedral. By now Athens had lost almost all of her former importance. She became the plaything of the Franks after they pillaged Constantinople at the beginning of the 13th century. St. Louis appointed Guy de la Roche as Duke of Athens, a dukedom which passed through many outstretched hands, including the Catalans', the Neapolitans' and the Venetians'. In 1456 the Turks took Athens, turning the Parthenon into a mosque and the once sacred Erechtheion into a harem. The Venetians under Morosini attacked the Turks in 1687 and accidently blew up part of the Parthenon with a bomb. A year later the Venetians left, unsuccessful, and the citizens who had fled returned to Athens. In 1800 Lord Elgin began the torrent of monument removal from Athens to European museums.

During the War of Independence, the Greeks under Gouras took the Akropolis and were besieged by the Turks, who succeeded in retaking the heights although their blockade was broken by the French. But finally, by 1833 all of Athens was free again, and in 1834 she was declared the capital of the new Greek state.

The few hundred war-scarred houses deteriorating under the Akropolis hardly fitted the bill as a capital city, however. When Otto of Bavaria, the first King of the Greeks arrived, he brought his own architects with him. The new city was laid out on the lines of Stadiou and El. Venezelou streets which boast most of Otto's neoclassical public buildings. The rest of the city's architecture was abandoned to unimaginative white and grey concrete structures, spared monotony only by the hilly Attic terrain.

Modern Athens, with more than two million inhabitants, has a busy life of its own during the day. The depopulation of the villages for the suburbs has produced the woes common to many a great city, and Athens spreads out further and further. Transportation is a big problem. But at night, especially in the winter, things begin to cook, and not only in the egg-lemon soup pots of Plaka. Athenians rarely eat before 10 or 11 at night, and they want to be entertained afterwards. If a day of sightseeing hasn't numbed the tourist to further delights, he or she should make every effort to come along and join in.

Museums and Sites in Athens

Agora Museum: open daily 7.30 am-7.30 pm; Sunday and holidays 10 am-6 pm. Closed Tuesday. 25 dr. entrance; 2.5 dr. with student card (includes the Theseum and ancient agora); Thursday and Sunday free. Tel. 3210185.

The **stoa of Attalos,** in which the museum is housed, was reconstructed by John D. Rockefeller from the original 2nd century BC stoa or gallery built by King Attalos II of Pergamon. The items inside are finds from the Agora.

The **Theseum,** actually dedicated to Hephaistos, the god of metals and smiths, was built in the middle of the 5th century BC and is the best preserved Greek temple in existence. Architecturally it belongs to the Doric order, and was perhaps designed by the architect of the temple at Sounion. It is constructed almost entirely of Pentalic marble. Metopes with scenes from the lives of Heracles and Theseus (for whom the temple was named) decorate the temple. It became a church in the 5th century and English protestants were buried there during the last century. In 1834 the government declared it a national monument.

The **Agora,** excavated by the American School of Archaeology, was the centre of Athenian civic and social life. Here the citizens spent much of their day; here Socrates questioned their basic conceptions of life and law. In 480 BC the Persians destroyed all the buildings of the Agora, which were then rebuilt in a newer and grander style. Most suffered greatly from the Roman and barbarian destructions. Only the foundations are left of the **Bouleuterion** or council house, and the neighbouring Temple of the Mother of the Gods or **Metroon,** built by the Athenians in reparation for their slaying of a priest from the cult. The round **Tholos** or administration centre is where the administrators or *prytanes* worked, and as some had to be on call all hours of the day, kitchens and sleeping quarters were included. Its final reconstruction took place after Sulla's rampage in 88 BC. Only a wall remains of the **Sanctuary of the Eponymous heroes of Athens,** the ten who gave their names to Kleisthenes' ten tribes. The **altar of Zeus Agoraios** received the oaths of the new archons, a practice initiated by Solon.

The 4th century **Temple of Apollo** was dedicated to the mythical father of the Ionians, who believed themselves descended from Ion, son of Apollo. In the museum is the huge statue which once stood inside the temple, representing the god. Almost nothing remains of the **Stoa Basileios,** or of Zeus Eleutherios, which played a major role in Athenian history as the court of the annual archon, where trials concerning the security of the state took place. By the Stoa of Zeus stood the **Altar of the Twelve Gods,** from which all distances in Attica were measured. Besides it ran the **Panathenaic Way,** of which some Roman signs remain by the Church of the Holy Apostles. It went to the Akropolis, crossing the Agora, from which the population would watch the ceremonial procession that celebrated the union of Attica. South of the Altar of Twelve Gods was a **Temple to Ares,** built in the Doric style in the 5th century BC, perhaps by the Theseum architect. The **Three Giants** stood before a 5th century AD **gymnasium** that had been built in the same place as the **Odeon of Agrippa,** of which parts of the orchestra remain further on. This had been built in 15 BC and collapsed 200 years later. The later gymnasium was a part of the University of Athens which Justinian closed in the 6th century AD. By the **Middle Stoa** (2nd century BC) one finds the ruins of a **Roman temple** and the ancient shops and booths. On the other side of the Middle Stoa is the popular court, or **Heliaia** organized by Solon and built in the 6th century BC. The Heliaia was the largest court of Athens which heard questions dealing with politics well into Roman times.

Between the **South and East Stoas** (2nd century BC) is the **Holy Apostles Church** (Ag. Apostoli) originating from the 11th century. When St. Paul visited Athens, he spoke in the Agora, and the church commemorates the event. In 1956 the American School of Classical Studies restored it and the many fine Byzantine paintings within. Across the Panathenaic Way are some remains of **Valerain's Wall** thrown up in 257 AD against the Barbarian threat, and created out of the ruins of the Agora which remained outside its protection. The ruins between Valerian's Wall and the Stoa of Attalos belong to the **Library of Pantainos,** built by Flavius Pantainos in 100 AD and destroyed 167 years later.

Akropolis: open daily 7.30 am-7.30 pm; Sundays and holidays 10 am-6pm; closed on Tuesdays. Entrance for the Akropolis and the Akropolis museum is 50 dr.; 5 dr. with student card. Tel. 3236665.

Two nights before and two nights after a full moon the Akropolis is open from 9 pm to 11.45 pm. On nights without a full moon there is a **sound and light show**, 1 April-31 October, presented daily in English 9 pm-9.45 pm. Tickets are 50 dr. or 25 dr. for students. They can be obtained at the Athens Festival Box Office, 4 Stadiou St. (in the arcade), tel. 3221459 or 3223111 extension 240; or at the entrance gate at Ag. Dimitriou, Loumbardis Hill before the performance, tel. 9226210.

The **Akropolis,** supplied by the spring Klepsydra, was inhabited from the end of the Neolithic Age, the people being attracted by its natural fortified position. The Myceneans added a Cyclopean wall and built the palace of their king by the present Erechtheion. This palace was replaced by a temple to the god of the spring, Poseidon, and to Athena. In mythology, these two gods took part in a contest to decide who would be the patron of the new city. With his trident Poseidon struck a spring out of the rock of the Akropolis, while Athena invented the olive tree, which the Athenians judged the best.

Under the tyrant Pisistratos a great gate was constructed in the wall, but the Athenians later dismantled it and Delphi cursed it. When the Persians arrived in 480 BC the cult statue of Athena was hurried to the protection of Salamis and in good time, for the Persians burnt the Akropolis. Themostokles built a new rampart out of the old Parthenon,and under Perikles the present plan of the Akropolis buildings was laid out.

The path to the Akropolis follows the Panathenaic way, built at the consecration of the Panathenaic Festival in 566 BC. Following it one comes first to the **Beulé Gate** (named after its discoverer Ernest Beulé) which includes monumental stairways built by the Romans and two Venetian lions. Up the reconstructed Panathenaic ramp one enters the **Propylaia,** the massive gateway built in the same place as Pisistratos' gate by the architect Mnesikles under Perikles. This was considered the architectural equal of the Parthenon by the ancient Greeks, but was damaged when a Turkish powder magazine inside blew up in the 17th century. Now the Propylaia has been carefully restored.

On either side of the actual entrance are the north and the south wings. The north wing held a picture gallery (Pinakotheke); the smaller south wing consisted of only one room of an unusual shape, because the priests of the neighbouring Nike temple didn't want the wing in their territory. The actual entrance had five doors, the middle one opening on the Panathenaic Way. Of the Doric and Ionic orders, it was never finished because of the Peloponnesian War.

The **Temple of Athena Nike,** or Wingless Victory was built by the architect Kallikrates in 478 BC of Pentelic marble. Inside was kept a statue of Athena, a copy of a much older wooden statue. Its lack of wings, unlike later victory statues, gave it its second name. In 1687 the Turks destroyed the temple to build a tower. It was rebuilt in 1835 and again in 1936 as the bastion beneath it was crumbling. It is of the Ionic order, and decorated with friezes, although the north and western ones were taken to England by Lord Elgin and are now replaced by cement casts. From the temple of Athena Nike one can see the whole Saronic golf, as Aegeus could when watching for the return of his son Theseus from his Cretan adventure with the Minotaur. Theseus was to have signalled his victory with a white sail but forgot. Seeing the black sail, the king threw himself off the precipice in despair.

The **Parthenon,** the glory of the Akropolis and probably the most famous building in the world, if not the most imitated, was constructed between 447 and 432 BC under the direction of Perikles' artist Phidias, the 5th century's greatest sculptor. The name Parthenon, which means the Chamber of Virgins, was first used only a hundred years after its construction; before that it was called the Great Temple. It is constructed entirely of Pentelic marble, of the Doric order. Inside it once stood the famous statue of Athena Parthenos by Phidias, more than 36 feet high and made of ivory and gold. In the National Museum one can see a small copy of it.

The genius of the Parthenon may be observed in its foundation, which is curved slightly to prevent an illusion of drooping caused by straight horizontals. To make the columns appear straight the architect bent them a few centimetres inward. Corner columns were made wider to complete the illusion of perfect form.

The outer colonnade consists of 46 columns and above them are the remains of the Doric frieze: on the east was portrayed the battle of giants and gods, on the south the Lapiths and Centaurs (much of this is in the British Museum today), on the west the Greeks and the Amazons, and on the north the battle of Troy. Little remains of the pediment sculptures which represented the gods. The Ionic frieze above the interior colonnade depicts the Panathenaic Procession and was designed by Phidias. This representation of the quadrennial procession bringing Athena a golden crown and sacred garment, or *peplos,* is considered one of the masterpieces of Greek art.

As previously mentioned, the Parthenon was severely damaged in 1687 when a Venetian bomb hit the Turks' powder stores inside; the destruction was continued in 1894 by an earthquake, after which reconstruction began. Today air pollution threatens to give the kiss of death to this graceful prototype of bulky bank buildings. Entrance within the Parthenon itself is forbidden and a conference has been planned with the aim of saving the building. Suggestions already offered include coating the marble with clear plastic, building a dome over it, or sending it off to complete the Akropolis collection in the British Museum.

The last great monument on the Akropolis is the **Erechtheion,** a peculiar building of the Ionic order, owing its idiosyncrasies to the various cult items and older sanctuary it had to encompass. Beneath it stood the Mycenean House of Erechtheus, mentioned in Homer, and the primitive cult sanctuary of Athena; on one side of this was the Sacred Olive Tree which Athena created, and under the north porch the mark formed by Poseidon's trident when he brought forth his sea spring in their contest. The tomb of Kekrops, the legendary founder of Athens, is in the Porch of the Maidens or Karyatids; there Erechtheus died at the hand of either Zeus or Poseidon. Within the temple stood the cult statue of Athena Polias, who received the sacred *peplos* and crown of the Panathenaic Procession. It was she whom the Athenians hid during the Persian offensive.

The sanctuary was quickly restored after the Persian fire, but the marble temple, which had been planned by Perikles, was not started until 421 BC. It became a church in the 7th century and a harem under the Turks, the sacred place of the trident marks being used as a toilet. Lord Elgin took parts of the temple, including one of the maidens. In 1909 reconstruction work on the Erechtheion was finished.

Basically the Erechtheion is a rectangular building with three porches. Inside were two cellas or chambers, the largest East Cella dedicated to Athena Polias, the smaller cella to Poseidon-Erechtheus. The north porch consists of six tall Ionic columns; and an opening was made in the roof and floor to reveal the trident marks, for it was considered sacrilegious to hide something so sacred from the view of the gods. The six famous maidens gracefully supporting the roof on their heads are also an Ionian motif. To escape pollution, the originals are now in the Akropolis Museum and have been replaced by casts.

The **Akropolis Museum** houses a collection of sculptures and reliefs from the temples, in particular of maidens, or Kores.

Beside the Akropolis is the **Areopagos,** or hill of Ares, the god of war. There sat the High Council, who figured so predominantly in Aeschylos' play *The Eumenides* where mercy defeated vengeance for the first time in history during the trial of the matricide Orestes. Although Perikles removed much of the original power of the High Council, under the control of the ex-archons it continued to advise on the Athenian constitution into the Roman period.

On the south side of the Akropolis are two theatres. The older, the **Theatre of Dionysos,** was used from the 6th century BC when Thespis created the first true drama, and was often modified up to the time of Nero. In this theatre the annual Greater Dionysia was held, in honour of the god of wine and patron divinity of the theatre, Dionysos. The dramatic competitions included in the festival led to the staging of some of the world's most perfect tragedies, which were premiered here. Beside the theatre stood two temples to Dionysos Eleutherios, and the stage that remains is from the 4th century BC. The area before the stage, the **proskenion,** is decorated with scenes from the life of Dionysos, made in the 1st century AD.

Above the theatre is an **Asklepieion,** a sanctuary to the god of healing. The stoa which remains is from the second sanctuary. The first and oldest to the west originally belonged to the water goddess, but very little of it remains. Both Asklepieions were connected with the parent cult at Epidauros.

The **Theatre of Herodes Atticus** was built by a private citizen, Atticus, in 161 AD and was partially covered. Now it hosts the annual **Festival of Athens,** which combines the modern European with the ancient Greek in presenting theatre, ballet, and concerts of classical music by companies and orchestras from all over the world. Performances are given from mid-May until the end of September. Prices vary greatly and there are always student tickets. Children under 10 are not admitted. Advance booking begins 10 to 15 days before the start of each programme, and further information and tickets may be obtained from:

The Athens Festival Box Office, 4 Stadiou St. (in the arcade). Tel. 3221459 or 3223111 ex. 240.

Open daily 8.30 am-1.30 pm and 6pm-8.30 pm; Sunday 9 am-12 am.

The Herod Atticus Theatre. Tel. 3232771 or 3223111 ex. 137.

Open 6.30 pm-9 pm before each performance (performances begin at 9 pm).

Tickets for the **National Theatre** can be bought at the National Theatre Box Office, at the corner of Ag. Konstantinou and Menandrou Sts, tel. 5223242; and tickets for the **State Opera** at Olympia Box Office, 57 Akedemiou St,, tel. 3612461.

Benaki Museum: on the corner of Vasilis Sophias and Koumbari St. Tel. 3611617. Open daily 8.30 am-2 pm. Sundays and holidays 10 am-6pm. Closed Tuesdays. Admission 40 dr. This museum holds the collection of Antonios Benaki, who spent 35 years of his life amassing objects from Europe and Asia, Byzantine and Islamic. It holds the finest Greek folk costume collection, and other objects of interest ranging from letters of Venizelos, a wooden Macedonian library and paintings attributed to El Greco, to George Seferis' Nobel Prize.

National Archaeology Museum: Patission & Tossitsa Sts. Tel. 8217717. Open daily 7.30 am-7.30 pm. Sunday 10 am-6 pm. Closed Monday. Admission 50 dr., 5 dr. with student card; free Thursday and Sunday. The National Museum contains some of the most spectacular finds made in Greece including the frescoes from Santorini, gold from Mycenae, statues, reliefs, tomb stelai, and a superb pottery collection from all periods. The ancient art of Cyprus is also on display, until it is deemed safe to send it back home.

National Gallery: Across from the Athens Hilton. Tel. 711010. Open 9 am-4 pm. Sunday 10 am-2 pm. Closed Monday. Entrance 20 dr., free Wednesday and Sunday. Also called the Alexander Soustou Museum, the National Gallery contains works by modern Greek artists and other contemporary exhibits.

Historical-Ethnological Museum: at the Palea Vouli (Old Parliament), Stadiou St. Tel. 3237617. Open 9 am-1 pm. Contains memorabilia from the War of Independence, including Lord Byron's sword, and portraits of the heroes.

Popular Art Museum: 17 Kydathinaion St. Tel. 3213018. Open 9 am-2 pm. Closed Monday. The museum has a collection of Greek folk art, both religious and secular, along with paintings by primitive artists.

The Pnyx: on the hill west of the Akropolis. Nowadays the setting for the Akropolis Sound and Light Show, the Pnyx once hosted the General Assembly of Athens and the great speeches of Perikles and Demosthenes. On assembly days citizens were literally rounded up to fill the minimum attendance quota of 5000, but they were paid for their services to the state. Later the assembly was transferred to the theatre of Dionysos. On the summit of the nearby Hill of the Muses is the **Philopappos Monument,** the tomb of Caius Julius Antiochos Philopapos, a Syrian Prince and citizen of Athens. The monument was built for him by the Athenians in 114 AD in gratitude for his beneficence to the city.

Roman Agora: located between the Agora and the Akropolis. Entrance 25 dr. Dating from the end of the Hellenistic age, the Roman Agora contains the **Tower of the Winds,** or Clock of Andronikos, built in the 1st century BC. Run by a hydraulic mechanism, it stayed open day and night so that the citizens could know the time. The name Tower of the Winds derives from the frieze of the eight winds that decorate its eight sides. The Roman Agora also contains the **Gate of Athena Archegetis,** dating from the 1st century BC and built with funds from Julius and Augustus Caesar; there is also a court and the ruins of stoas. Beside the Agora is the Fehiye Djamii, the Victory or Corn Market Mosque.

Byzantine Museum: 22 Vasilis Sophias Ave. Tel. 711027. Open daily 7.30 am-7.30 pm. Sunday 10 am-6pm. Closed Monday. Entrance 50 dr., 5 dr. with student card; free Thursday and Sunday. The museum includes some examples of Early Christian art,and a fine collection of Byzantine sculpture, icons, gospels and other objects from the Byzantine Empire.

Keramikos Museum: 148 Hermou St. Tel. 3463552. Open daily 7.30 am-7.30 pm. Sunday 10 am-6pm. Closed Tuesday. Entrance 25dr., 2.5 dr. with student cards. Thursday and Sunday free. The Keramikos Museum contains the most interesting finds from the ancient cemetery, the Keramikos. The site was used for burials from the 12th century BC and continued to be used into Roman times. Roads to the academy, the Agora, and the Sacred Way passed through the Keramikos, which was just outside the city walls and thus to the Sacred Gate and the Dipylon Gate.

Following the Streets of the Tombs the visitor can see the rich private tombs built by the Athenians in the 4th century BC. Those with large stone vases are for the unmarried dead, others are in the form of miniature temples and stelai, the best of which are now in the National Museum.

Temple of Olympian Zeus: open 7.30 am-7.30 pm. Small admission fee. Fifteen columns remain of one of the hugest temples of the ancient world, begun under the tyrant Pisistratos but stopped when the tyrants fell from power. Work was continued in 175 BC under a Roman architect, Cossutius, in Pentelic marble, but again halted when the temple was half finished by the death of Cossutius' patron, Antiochos IV, Epiphanes of Syria. Hadrian had the temple finished in 131 AD. Nearby are the ruins of ancient houses and a bath, and at the far end stands **Hadrian's Arch**, which divided the city of Theseus from the city of Hadrian. It was built in the 2nd century AD. It is in the area of the Temple of Zeus that the Athenians celebrate the Easter Resurrection.

War Museum: Located at Vasilis Sophias and Rizari Sts. Tel. 739560. Open 9.30 am-1 pm. Wednesday 2 pm-5 pm. Sunday 10 am-2 pm. Closed Tuesday. Inside are weapons from various periods, uniforms, models etc.

Wine Festival at Dafni: 10km (6 miles) outside Athens. Take bus 100/67 from Eleftherias Square. 9 July-11 September, every day 7 pm-1 am. Admission 50 dr. at the gate. A variety of Greek wines and foods, music, singing, and dancing make up a Greek wine festival and Greeks attend as much as foreigners. Wine is free once the admission price is paid.

Byzantine Churches and Monasteries in Athens

Agii Apostoli: see under Agora (page 63).

Agii Theodori: This 11th century church is at Klathmonos Sq. at the end of Dragatsaniou St. It has a beautiful door; the bell tower and some of the decorations inside are more recent additions.

Kapnikarea Church: a few blocks from Agii Theodori, on Ermou St. It is from the late 11th century and built in the shape of a cross, its cupola sustained by four large columns. Kapnikarea is the church of the University of Athens.

Panayia Gorgoepikoos, or Ag. Eleftherios, on Mitropoleos Sq. Also known as the little Metropolitan Church to distinguish it from the nearby cathedral, this is considered the loveliest church in Athens. Built in the 12th century and restored in the 19th, it still contains the marbles placed inside at its construction, including an ancient calendar.

Dafni Monastery: Take bus 100/67 from Eleftherias Sq. for the 10 km. (6 mile trip), both to the wine festival and to this, one of the finest Byzantine monuments in Greece. The name Dafni derives from the temple of Apollo Dafneios, upon which the monastery was founded in the 6th century, near the Sacred Way. The monastery church dates back to the 11th century, and contains some of the most wonderful mosaics in Greece, especially of Christ Pantokrator, considered a masterpiece of the mosaic art.

Dining and Drinking in Athens

Lykavitos (mt. Lycabettus): The name of this hill, which Athena dropped from the sky, comes from the pack of wolves which once haunted its slopes. A funicular makes the trip to the top easy, or one can walk which takes about an hour. The view of Athens from the summit is fantastic, and one can eat and drink while enjoying it. The small chapel there is dedicated to Ag. Georgios.

Monastraki: On Athinas St. and Monastraki Sq. This is the best place to buy souvenirs in Athens, from the many small shops selling handicrafts and antiques. Every Sunday morning a flea market takes place in the square.

Plaka: Plaka, the "flat land", is the centre of Athenian night life, although rather expensive of late. Basically undeveloped after the War of Independence, it is the oldest district of Athens. Most of the houses date from before 1875, and now serve as tavernas, some authentic with their wine barrels and folk music, others more modern.

Sintagma: Athens' Constitution Sq. or Sintagma is the centre of town and sports shady cafés surrounded by tourist offices, agencies, banks and hotels. It is Athens' prime spot for drinking coffee at a dollar a cup in order to watch the other tourists walk by; it is also where the Casanovas come "spearing" for women. Restaurants in the area, especially in the grand hotels, are considered the "best", meaning that they offer the same food, service and prices one finds in other large restaurants in Europe.

Plaka and northern Athens up to Kifissia have good Greek food and entertainment, as do the sea resort areas such as Glyfada, although these are also expensive. Cheap Greek dishes can be had everywhere, and generally, the smaller the restaurant, the better quality the food.

Low priced accommodation in Athens: area code 01

Youth Hostel Number One, 57 Kypselis and Ag. Meletiou Sts.; tel. 8225860. Breakfast, meals offered.

Youth Hostel Number Two, 1 Drossi St. and 87-89 Alexandros Ave.; tel. 6463669/6426529/6442421. No meals.

Youth Hostel Number Four, 3 Hamilton St. and 97 B. Patission St.; tel. 8220328/8226425. Breakfast offered.

Lord Byron Youth Hostel, 20 Kallipoeos St., tel. 7664889. Breakfast and meals.

YMCA, 28 Omirou St.; tel. 626970. Men only.

YWCA, 11 Amerikis St.; tel. 624294. Women only.

International, 46 Nikis St.; tel. 3229567. Dormitory.

Interline, 42 Nikis St.; tel. 3235342. Breakfast available.

Frantis' House, 39 A Nikis St. Dormitory and rooms.

Lakis' House, 11 Parthenons St.; tel. 9226440. Breakfast available.

John's House, 5 Patroou St.; tel. 3222697. Dormitory.

Pericles, 39 Kapnikareas St.; tel. 3248805. Dormitory and rooms. Breakfast available.

Clair's House, 16 Frynichou St.; tel. 3229284. Breakfast available.

Diogenes' House, 12 Herefondos St.; tel. 3224560/3247142. On the roof, dormitory, and rooms.

Piraeus

The port of Athens, Piraeus — pronounced "Pirefs", was the greatest port of the antique world and today is one of the busiest in the Mediterranean. Especially in the case of island travellers, it is best to come and go and not really to stay, as symbolized by its singular lack of benches. One must be a very special tourist to find much charm in the tall grey buildings and hurly-burly of the streets, although Marina Zea with its multitudes of yachts makes a pretty scene, as do the neon kinetics of the advertisements when one sails from Piraeus in the evening. The tall, half-finished building on the waterfront was built and abandoned by the junta when they found that the foundations were mixed with sea water. Somehow its useless silhouette makes a fitting monument to that ignorant and often cruel government.

Historical Outline of Piraeus

Piraeus was inhabited from pre-Hellenic times by an Artemis-worshipping people who left only the Serangeion (also called the cave of Paraskevas or Zeno) to their memory. The Serangeion can be found at Kastelli, by Mikrolimani, and was used as baths into Roman times. When Phaliron, the old port of Athens, could no longer cater for the growing needs of the city, Themostocles founded the port of Piraeus (in the 5th century BC) and his work was finished by Kimon and Perikles. The Miletian geometrician Hippodamos planned the city in the straight right-angled weave of streets which still exists today. At this time the famous Long Walls were built, connecting Athens to Piraeus, of which a few vestiges remain at Marina Zea.

The Piraeus of antiquity was a progressive, cosmopolitan centre, its heart at the huge agora in the middle of the city. In its stoas were held the world's first commercial fairs and trade expositions, some on an international scale. All religions were tolerated, and women were allowed for the first time to work outside the home.

As Piraeus was so crucial to Athens' power, the conquering Spartan Lysander destroyed the Long Walls in 404, at the end of the Peloponnesian War. Piraeus made a brief comeback under Konon and Lykurgos, who rebuilt the port's arsenals. After the hundred-year Macedonian occupation and a period of peace, General Sulla decimated the city to prevent any anti-Roman resistance, and for 1900 years Piraeus remained an insignificant village with a population as low as 20. A huge lion at the entrance of the port, placed there in 1040 by the Viking Harold Haardrada, gave Piraeus the Venetian names Porto Leone or Porto Draco. With the selection of Athens as the capital of free Greece after the War of Independence, Piraeus has regained some of its former glory as the reigning port of a sea going nation.

Piraeus Today

In recent years the port of Piraeus has been simplified and should pose
no problems to those who want to leave it as quickly as possible.

Ships are grouped according to their destination and almost anyone
you ask will be able to tell you the precise location of any particular
vessel. There is no lack of ticket agents in the port area. They are all very
competitive, but the prices are the same no matter where you go. 'Where
do you want to go — Naxos? Crete?' they call out, as you walk by with a
suitcase. For information on boat schedules, it is best to visit the **Tourist
Police** on Akti Miaouli by Skouze St. Ticket agents often don't know or
won't tell you information on lines other than their own.

There are three main **railway stations.** The electric train service
serves Athens, as far north as Kifissia, the most beautiful suburb of the
city. The terminal is right across the street from the quay and frequent
trains run from 6 am to 1.30 am. The railway stations for northern
Greece and for the Peloponnese are a bit further down the road.

Buses to Athens run throughout the day and night (no. 70 to Om-
monia from Themostocles Sq. and no. 165 to Sintagma from H.
Trikoupi). The no. 185 bus service to the East Airport leaves from
Theotoki and Sofokleous Sts.

The quickest route to a **youth hostel** from Piraeus is to take the train
or bus to Ommonia, and walk down Stadiou St. to Pragastaniou Rd. Here
you will find Youth Hostel no. 4. In Piraeus itself there are many **hotels,**
but unless you move away from the business district they are generally
noisy. Some people sleep out in the squares, particularly in Karaiskaki,
but they have to put up with lights, noise, and the neighbouring dis-
cothèques.

If you find yourself in Piraeus with time on your hands, you could visit
the new **Archaeology Museum** at H. Trikoupi and Alkiviadou Sts.:
open daily 9 am - 1 pm and 4 pm - 6 pm. Sunday 10 am - 2 pm. Closed
Tuesday. Entrance 24 dr.; 2.5 dr. with student card; free Thursday
and Sunday. The **Marine Museum** on Akti Themostocles by
Freatidos St. is also very interesting: open daily 9 am - 12.30 pm. Sunday
and holidays 10 am - 1 pm and 6 pm - 9 pm. Entrance free. It has plans
from the great Greek naval battles, ship models and mementoes from the
War of Independence. You could also visit the **Hellenistic Theatre** at
Zea, which occasionally has performances in the summer.

Beaches are not far away, although on most you must pay to enter.
Kastella is the closest, followed by New Phaliron which is free. Bus 1A
leaves for Ag. Kosmos, by the airport, where you can play tennis or
volleyball; at Glyfada, further down the road (bus 125), you can swim
and play golf.

Piraeus' **restaurants** range from small souvlaki places (Steki tou
Xadzi, by Zea is a good, average-priced restaurant) to the delicious but
not cheap fish restaurants at Microlimani. The Piraeus region also
swings at night, and one can hear bazouki music at Microlimani, Tzit-
zifies, and numerous places along the shore all the way to Vouliagmeni.

Zea, Glyfada and Vouliagmenı are the three **marinas** organized by the National Tourist Organization. Prices are comparable to other European marinas. Piraeus is also the place to charter yachts or sail boats, from 12-foot dinghies to deluxe twin-screw yachts. Write to the Association of Boat and Yacht Rental Agents, Post Office Box 341, Piraeus, for information and prices. You must have a diploma from a sailing club to rent a boat without a crew.

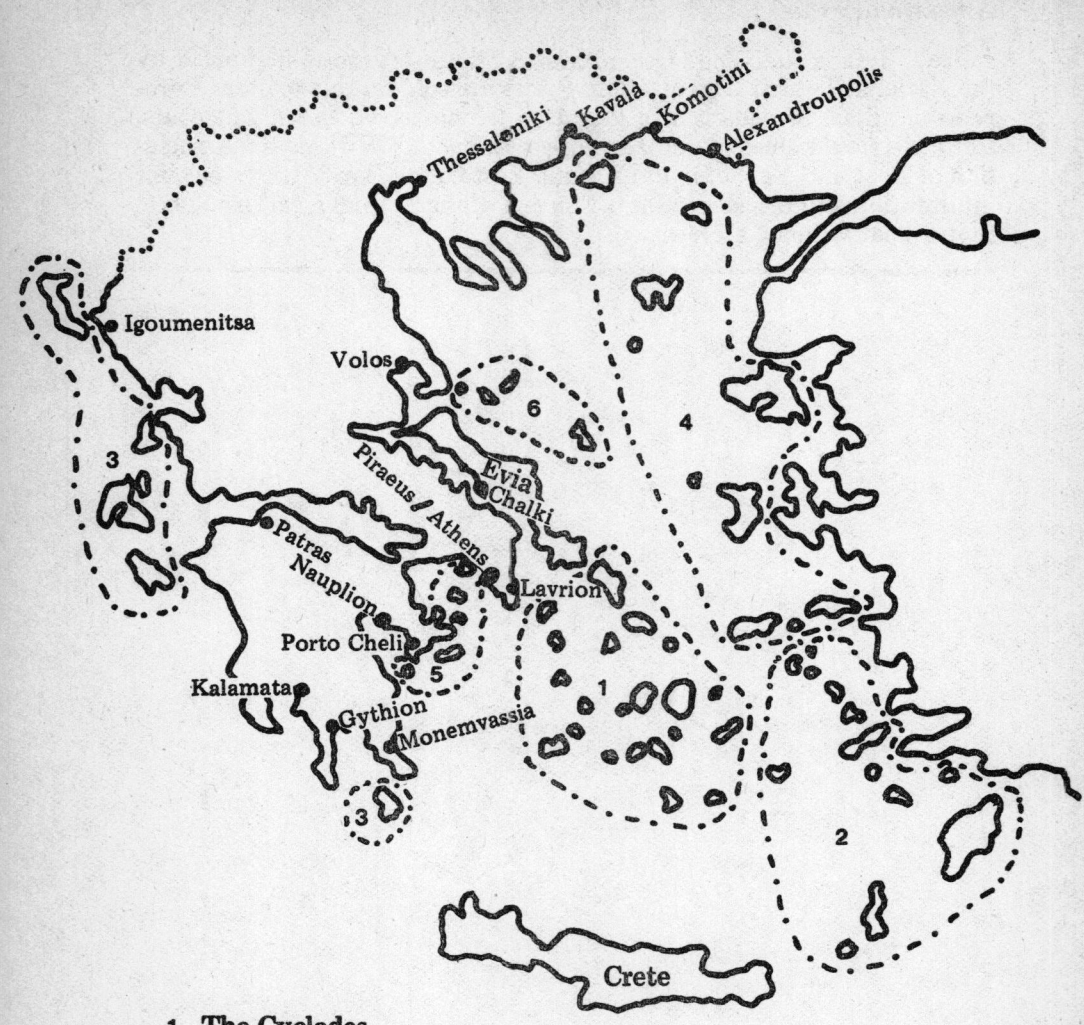

1 **The Cyclades**

2 **The Dodecanese**

3 **The Ionian Islands**

4 **The North-East Aegean Islands**

5 **The Saronic Islands**

6 **The Sporades**

Greece and the Islands

74

THE ISLANDS

For all practical purposes the islands of Greece have been divided into seven major groupings: the Cyclades, the Aegean islands surrounding Delos; the Dodecanese, the thirteen islands lying off the south-west coast of Asia Minor; the north-eastern Aegean islands, stretching from Thassos to Ikaria; the Ionian islands between Greece and Italy; the Saronic islands, in the Saronic Gulf; the Sporades, spread off the coast of Thessaly and Evia; and Crete, the largest island in Greece.

This wealth of islands (over 3000 all told, although a mere hundred or so are inhabited) has created a great variety of cultural nuances, besides a thriving business for Greek ships. Islands by their very nature are the individualists of the geographic world, and the Greek islands are not only different from the mainland and from one another, but every islander has a sneaking suspicion if not a burning belief that his or her island is the best in Greece; debates between two islanders as to whose homeland is preferable are always highly inconclusive. One island may have more resources, but on the poorer island the people are better because they must work harder. On an island with tourists the people make money, but islands without tourists have peace and quiet. And so on. Thus the visitor must also choose, according to his own taste, where to spend a holiday, a few months, or perhaps a lifetime. Each island has its own special charm, and the only general rule that can be made in "doing the islands" is to do them leisurely so as not to miss it.

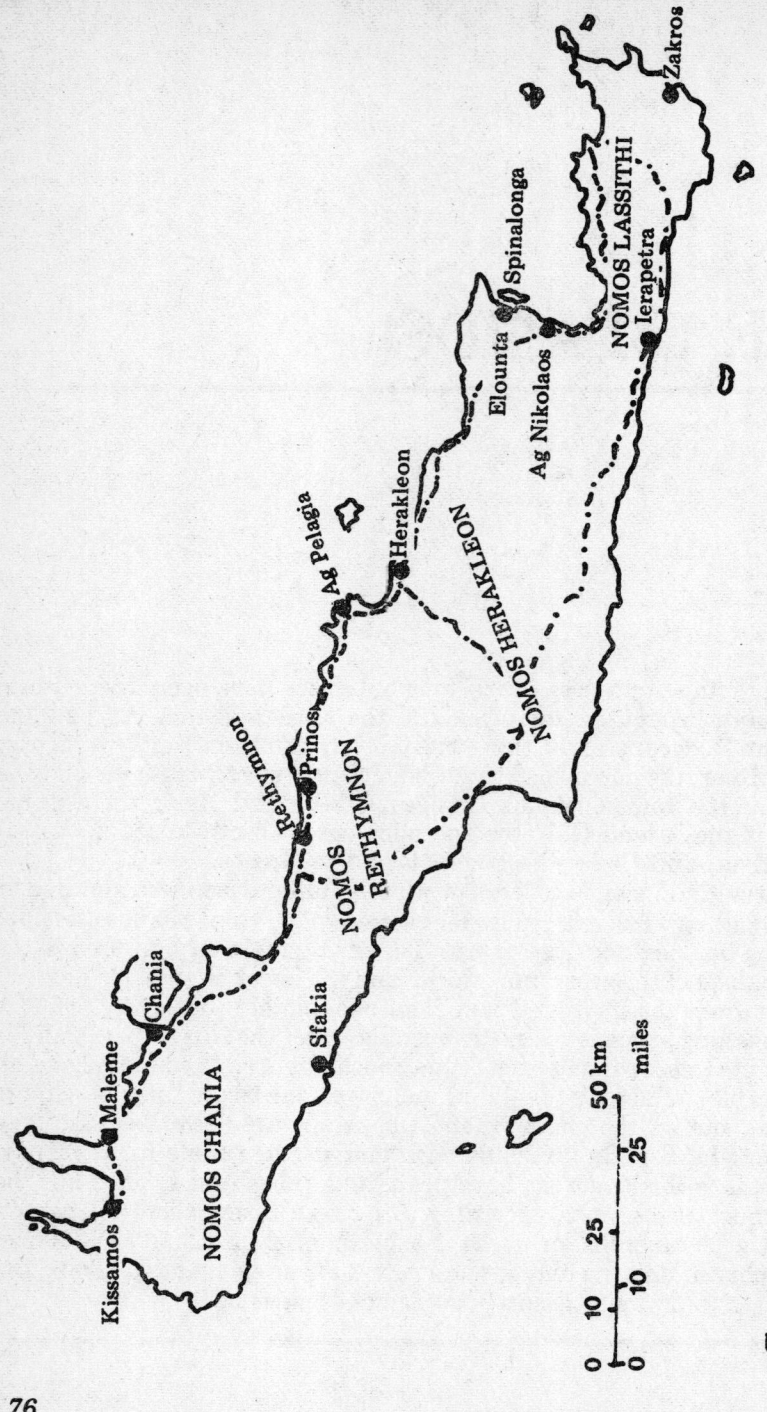

Zakros

NOMOS LASSITHI

Spinalonga

Ierapetra

Elounta

Ag Nikolaos

NOMOS HERAKLEON

Herakleon

Ag Pelagia

Rethymnon

Prinos

NOMOS
RETHYMNON

Chania

Maleme

Sfakia

Kissamos

NOMOS CHANIA

50 km

25

25

10

10

0

0

miles

Crete

Part 6
Crete

Crete, the home of the great Minoan civilization, is the largest, most
varied and yet most distinct island in Greece, and has produced such
brilliant sons as El Greco, Eleftherios Venizelos, Nikos Kazanzakis,
Mikis Theodorakis, and father Zeus himself. The island has 250 species
of native vegetation, besides its own dialect, music, dances, and dress.
Between the most remote mountain villages and international resort
areas, the Gorge of Samaria and the Palace of Knossos, there is something on Crete for everyone. Most wonderful of all are the Cretan people
themselves.

Connections: By air, two flights a day from Athens to Chania, and on
to Rethymnon; three to six flights daily from Athens to Herakleon; three
flights a week from Rhodes in the summer; two flights a week from Lon-
don to Herakleon; three flights a week from Frankfurt. By ship from
Piraeus every evening (6:30 pm or 7:00 pm) to both Chania and
Herakleon. On Mondays a boat leaves Piraeus at 9:00 am, arriving in
Chania at 8:00 pm; on Sundays there is a late evening boat to Chania.
Three connections weekly with Santorini; once a week with Oia, Naxos,
Paros, Syros, Ios. A new service connects Kasteli to Kapsali (Kythera),
Gythion, Ag. Pelagia (Kythera), Elafonissos, Neopolis, Monemvassia,
Kiparission, Piraeus. Another service connects Ag. Nikolaos, Sitia,
Kassos, Karpathos, Halki, and Rhodes twice a week. Ship from Alexan-
dria to Herakleon once a week.

History

Crete was settled sometime around 6000 BC by a people probably from Asia Minor, who built their small houses in Knossos and other future Minoan capitals. In 3000 BC, the end of the Neolithic period, a new population arrived, inspiring new forms in pottery and a move from stone tools to copper. This period is called the Early Minoan. The Middle Minoan (1900 BC) saw the advent of palaces, towns, and a system of writing, but in 1700 BC an earthquake (probably) devasted the buildings, forcing the people to start afresh.

From 1700-1450 BC is the height of the Minoan Civilization. The palaces were rebuilt and decorated with frescoes, and equipped with water and drainage systems. Colonies were settled on the islands, and the Minoans, ruling the seas, made contact with cities in Africa, Asia Minor, and on the Greek mainland, inspiring the myths of the great King Minos, which was probably the dynastic name of the Knossos kings. Linear A, the as yet undeciphered system of writing, was developed. But disaster struck Crete again in 1450 BC, thought to have been caused by a volcanic eruption, tidal waves, and earthquakes from nearby Santorini. The magnificent Minoan kingdoms were left in ruins.

Many believe that at this time Myceneans from the mainland invaded Crete, taking advantage of its now fallen state. In this late Minoan period (1550-1050 BC) only Knossos was built up again, and Linear B writing, also found at Mycenae and Thebes, predominated. Other towns began to be repopulated, and Chania prospered in particular, although Crete no longer exerted external influence. By 1100 BC and the beginning of the Iron Age the civilization had slowed down into a dark age, and the people took to the hills.

The Dorians invaded Crete, and by the Geometric period (8th century BC) Crete thrived. It is thought that the invaders coexisted peacefully with the native Minoans; inscriptions in Greek letters have been found that spell non-Greek words. As on the mainland small city states were gradually formed by the 5th century BC, fighting among themselves, building walls, and minting their own coins, ruled by a powerful aristocracy. Romans under Q. Metellus Creticus conquered Crete in 67 BC, and Gortyn, inhabited since Minoan times, became the capital of the province of Crete and Cyrenaica.

Rich churches were constructed in Crete in the early Byzantine period, but in 823 AD Saracen Arabs conquered the island and stayed until its liberation in 961 by the Emperor Nikephoros Phokas. In the 13th century, the Genoese ruled Crete, but later sold it to Venice, who occupied the island from 1210 to 1669. The so-called Cretan school of artists flourished in the 15th and 16th centuries working both at home and in the rest of Greece. The epic romance *Erotokritos* was written by Kornaros. Great fortifications and public buildings were built by the Venetians.

When the Turks finally took Herakleon in 1669, after a 21-year siege, Crete fell into a new dark age, spiritually and economically. The Cretans rose up against the Turks more than 400 times, especially in 1821, but were inevitably the losers to the superior Moslem forces. In 1898 the Great Powers appointed Prince George High Commissioner of an independent Crete, and with the work of Venizelos the island became part of Greece in 1913. A major campaign of World War II saw the capture of Crete by the Germans in 1941, to which the Cretans, along with the British and New Zealanders who stayed, organized a heroic resistance.

Mythology

As Cronus, the ruler of the world, had been warned that a child of his would usurp his place, he swallowed every baby his wife Rhea, daughter of the Earth, presented to him. After this occurred five times, Rhea determined a different fate for her sixth child, Zeus. When he was born, she smuggled him to Crete and gave Cronus a stone instead, which the god duly swallowed. Mother Earth hid the baby in the Diktean Cave and set the Kouretes to guard him, to shout and beat their shields should the baby cry and wake Cronus' suspicions.

After Zeus grew up and had indeed taken his father's place by the simple expedient of castrating him, a girl named Europa caught his fancy. To avoid making his wife Hera jealous, Zeus abducted the maiden in the form of a beautiful bull and took her to Crete, where she bore him three sons: Minos, Rhadamanthys, and Sarpedon. Minos became the King of Crete at Knossos. When he was requested to prove that his claim to the throne was sanctioned by the gods, he remembered the form his father had taken and asked Poseidon to give him a bull from the sea to sacrifice. However, the bull of Poseidon was so magnificent that instead of killing it, Minos sent it to service his herds.

The kingdom of Minos prospered, ruling the seas and exacting tribute from all over the Mediterranean. But Poseidon never forgot Minos' lack of piety in not sacrificing the bull. In revenge he made Minos' wife Pasiphae (daughter of the sun and the nymph Crete, who gave the island its name) fall in love with it. Poor Pasiphae confided this problem to the great inventor Daedalus, who had been banished from Athens for murder and was now living in Minos' court. Daedalus responded by making her a hollow wooden cow, which she entered and with which the bull mated. This resulted in the birth of a monster with the head of a bull and body of a man, the Minotaur.

Naturally revolted by this new member of his household, Minos asked Daedalus to hide it. Obediently Daedalus built the Labyrinth, an impossible maze of corridors, and there he put the Minotaur. As this strange beast also showed a great liking for human meat, Minos took advantage of an Athenian insult to order that city to pay a tribute of seven maidens and seven youths in reparation, whom he would feed to the Minotaur.

Two tributes had been paid when Theseus, the son of Aegeus, King of Athens, showed up and demanded to be one of the victims. With great reluctance his father agreed, and Theseus went to Crete as part of the tribute. But Ariadne, daughter of Minos, fell in love with him : at first sight, and turned to Daedalus for help in saving in his life. Daedalus gave her a ball of thread. Theseus slew the Minotaur with his bare hands, retraced his way out of the labyrinth with Ariadne's ball of thread, and escaped, taking the Cretan princess along with him and the other Athenians. Although he left Ariadne on Naxos, he later married her younger sister Phaedra.

Minos was furious when he discovered the part Daedalus had played in the business and threw the inventor and his young son Ikaros into the Labyrinth. Although they managed to find their way out, escape from Crete itself was impossible, as Minos controlled the seas and was on the lookout for them. But Daedalus was never at a loss, and decided that what they couldn't accomplish by sea they would do by air. He made wings of wax for himself and Ikaros, and on the first fine day they flew towards Asia Minor. All went well until an exhilarated Ikaros disobeyed his father's command not to fly too close to the sun. The wax in his little wings melted, plunging him down to drown in what is now the Ikarian sea. The island on which Daedalus buried him also took on the name Ikaria.

After this the stories of Minos, the once great master of the sea and thus Greece, portray him as a bit of a dodderer, if indeed they refer to the same Minos. He is said to have chased Daedalus all over the world, taking with him a nautilus shell and a thread. In this way he hoped to trap him, as he knew that only the inventor could thread the shell. He later grew the ears of an ass which he hid under a hat, telling only his barber who was sworn to secrecy. When the wretched barber couldn't bear to keep such a secret any longer, he ran out to the fields and cried: "Minos has ass's ears!" If you listen closely, you can hear this echoed in the windblown grasses, even today. When Minos died, however, his father Zeus re-established his good name by making him one of the dread judges of the dead, along with his brother Rhadamanthys and his enemy Aeacus.

Crete Today

Crete is a rich island, and one of the few that hasn't known a drastic drop in population in recent years. Oranges, chestnuts, apples, carobs, potatoes, olive oil and wine are only a few of the agricultural products of the island, and many factories have been built, particularly near Herakleon, the largest city in Crete. A new highway has been constructed all along the north coast, speeding up traffic if not enhancing the scenic splendour. There are many fine beaches with many new hotels on the north and south coasts, and a growing number in the east.

Folk traditions are still a part of everyday life in Crete. Men in the villages often wear the baggy Cretan trousers, the salvaria, with boots, sashes, vests and black head bands, although they no longer carry the equally renowned Cretan daggers. Old mountain feuds have withered away while the old mountain-village generosity survives. Cretan weddings and gatherings are among the liveliest in Greece. The music is generally played on the lyra and laouto, often to lyrics from the *Erotokritos*, Crete's national epic, or to Matinades, rhymed couplets dealing with anything Cretan.

The mountain ranges of Crete naturally divide the island into four major areas, and these have also become Crete's political divisions. West of the White Mountains is the nomos (county) of Chania; between the White Mountains and Psilorites (Mt. Ida) is the nomos of Rethymnon; between Psilorites and the Lassithi Mountains lies the nomos of Herakleon; and east of the Lassithi Mountains is the nomos of Lassithi, of which Ag. Nikolaos is the capital.

Chania

Chania, the beautiful capital of Crete, is built on the site of ancient Kydonia, named for a certain King Kydon. After the disaster of 1450 BC it became one of the major cities of Crete, and prospered up to the Byzantine era, when it was ruined. Parts of the wall of ancient Kydonia can still be seen in the Kastelli district of town. In 1252 AD the Venetians set about rebuilding Kydonia, naming it La Canea. On the site of the ancient acropolis they constructed the fortress Kastelli, in which were built the lovely homes of the Venetian noblemen. This fortress was surrounded by a wall. In the late 15th century, alarmed by the threat of the pirate admiral Barbarossa, who had struck in neighbouring Rethymnon, the Venetians created a wall around the entire town and surrounded it with a moat more than 45 metres (150 ft.) wide and 9 metres (30 ft.) deep. A long jetty divided the harbour in two.

All these precautions did not keep out the Turks, however, and in 1645, less than 60 years after the completion of the city walls, they besieged and took Chania, installing pashas and beys at Kastelli and raising further fortifications. In 1850 they transferred the capital of Crete from Herakleon to Chania, where it remained during independence and after the island's annexation to Greece.

On 20 May, 1941, while General Student's parachutists invaded Crete, the Nazis bombed Chania, demolishing a good portion of the old walls and houses. While on paper, this, the Battle of Crete was a victory for the Nazis, their specially trained parachutists were almost all destroyed. Chania celebrates the anniversary of the Battle of Crete during the **Chania Festival,** which runs from mid-May to mid-June and includes folk dancing on the waterfront.

The centre of daily life in Chania is the **marketplace,** which looks like a train depot; the buses from Chania's harbour Souda drop one off in front of it. To go to the **Youth Hostel** walk a few feet to the Ag. Ioannis bus which takes about five minutes to reach its destination. The **Chania tourist office** on 6 Akti Tombazi can be found by a mosque on the waterfront (go down Mousouron St.).

Night life in Chania takes place in the tavernas and restaurants by the harbour, which is now used only for small fishing and pleasure craft. Cretan music can be heard every night, especially in a small austere cafe called **Lyraki,** where the locals go to hear their friends play to a glass of Cretan raki. Outside of town, towards Akrotiri and Galatas, there are also many popular places.

What to see in Chania: The Archaeology Museum is located in the Venetian church of San Francesco on Khalidon St.: open daily 9 am - 1 pm and 4 pm - 6 pm. Sunday 10.30 am - 2.30 pm. Closed Tuesday. Entrance 25 dr., 2.5 dr. with student card. Inside are local finds dating from the Early Minoan period, including pottery from Cyprus, with whom ancient Kydonia traded. There are also some fine classical finds.

The Historical Museum and Archives is on Sfakianaki St.: open 8 am-1 pm. It contains the second largest collection of historical material in Greece, dating from the Venetian Occupation down to the Independence of Crete.

One can still see parts of the **Inner Venetian Wall** around Kastelli, made out of stone from ancient Kydonia. Most of the houses inside were ruined in the bombing. However, a **Venetian quarter** still exists off Zambeliou St. and it has now become fashionable to repair the old crumbling houses. In the quarter, by the **Bastion San Salvatore,** lies a church of the same name, converted into the mosque Ser Topou Hassan Aga by the Turks. A gate on Theophnous St. is inscribed with the coat of arms of the Venieri, dating from 1608. Not far away, the **Experimental Café** has programmes of eastern music and ancient shadow plays; the **Aposperila,** a restaurant built in a huge medieval soapworks, has excellent Greek and Chinese cuisine.

On the other side of Kastelli is another charming part of town, the **Topana Quarter,** with a maze of tiny streets and old houses. On one side of it is the large church **Ag. Nikolaos,** built by the Venetians, used by the Turks to shelter a magical, healing sword when they converted it into a mosque, and claimed by the Orthodox church in 1918. A smaller church in the vicinity is **San Rocco** (1630). **Ag. Anargyrii,** built in the 16th century, was the only church to have continual Orthodox services through the Venetian and Turkish Occupations, and contains some very old icons.

In the Chalepa quarter stands the **house and statue of Eleftherios Venizelou,** the greatest statesman of modern Greece, and the **residence of the High Commissioner** Prince George. Walking towards the centre of town one passes many 19th century mansions and the public gardens. To see the **outer Venetian walls,** finished in 1590 (inscribed on the Koum Kapissi gate on Minos St.), turn to the east or west side of town where they are intact. By the east wall seven archs remain from the original 23 of the **Venetian Arsenali,** where a large ship building yard once stood. Continuing down the water front one finds the customs house, the Port Authority, and the **Tourist Information Pavilion,** located by the **Mosque of the Janissaries** (1645). The Janissaries were crack Ottoman troops supplied by the tribute of children; every fifth son of a Christian family had to join.

A **yacht marina** will soon be ready in the harbour: Chania is an official port of entry and supplies general provisioning. The **Naval Museum of Crete** (open 10 am - 12 am and 5 pm - 8 pm) is located across the harbour.

For a **swim** head to the west side of town, the further out the better. At Neo Chora, a five-minute bus ride from the centre of town, the beach is sandy, the sea clean, and there are tavernas along the water for a leisurely lunch. Further west towards the monument of the diving eagle, a German memorial to the 2nd Parachute regiment, are Glaros Beach and Kalamaki Beach. Aptera beach has a bungalow hotel.

The **post office** and **OTE** are on Stratigou Tzanakaki.

Restaurants: Aposperila, Kalamaki Almarida by the beach, Ta Kavouria, Faros, and Delfini on the harbour, Kipos in the gardens. Places with **food and music** are Arathousa, Kato Taratso, Estorial, KriKri, Kato Galatas and Trifonas. Annitsakis has good wines. In **Galatas,** 6 km. (4 miles) away, there are three good restaurants: Nykterida, Kalamaki, and Glaros. This is the home town of Mikis Theodorakis.

Discotheques in the region are Paparona (considered very good), Blow Up, Honolulu, Bola, and Kentro Vrachofori.

Panayiéria: On 15 August Chania hosts the Pan Cretan Festival. The Chania festival runs from mid-May to mid-June. In the neighbouring village of Chryssopigi there is a festival on Good Friday at Zoodochos Pigi.

The **specialities** of the town are hand-carved wooden chairs, shoes made to order, and daggers. Good doughnuts and bougatsa (custard pies) are made in the pastry shops. The Chaniotiko Syrto is Chania's special dance.

Chania Tourist Police: 23 Karaiskaki St. Tel. 24477.

The city of Chania is the best point of departure for **the rest of the nomos,** the land of the White Mountains. Geographically this west side of Crete is peculiar as it is slowly rising out of the sea, while eastern Crete is subject to a gradual sink, noticeable through the centuries. Chania nomos is the home of the longest gorge in Europe, Samaria, the last place in the world where the Cretan wild goat, the kri kri, lives in its natural habitat. The Chaniotes are known in Crete as the best musicians and warriors, especially those from Chora Sfakion. Excellent oranges, honey and olive oil are produced and west Chania is Crete's big chestnut producer. Kastelli and Kissamos wines are well known throughout Greece.

Buses for the nomos leave from Platia 1866 in Chania town; those for Rethymnon and Herakleon leave from the market. The Canea Travel

Nomos Chania, Crete

84

Bureau, 46 Karaiskaki St. runs tours to Samaria Gorge, Herakleon, Paliochora, Akrotiri, Kastelli-Phalassarna and Phaistos which in some cases may be preferable if one is pressed for time.

Akrotiri, one of the three "heads" of Crete, is directly east of Chania. Eleftherios Venizelos is buried there. By Profitis Elias church the Cretans raised the Greek flag in 1897 in the midst of a bombardment of international navies. The story runs that the admirals were so impressed by the courage of the Cretans, who at the risk of their lives held up the flag that had fallen from its pole during the battle, that they stopped fighting and applauded them. A Russian shell destroyed the church, but it is said that Prophet Elija avenged himself by blowing up part of the Russian ship the next day, killing many sailors.

There are two monasteries on Akrotiri. **Ag. Triada,** near Kabani, was founded by the Venetian Tzangarol at the beginning of the 17th century and has a lovely Renaissance church. On 8th October many pilgrims come to celebrate a large *panayiéri* held at the Monastery of **Ag. Ioannes Gouvernetou,** located by the stalactic cave Kimisios or Katholikon, where St. John the Hermit lived and died. At Spiliani another cave, **Anemospilia** (Cave of the Wind), has a pond and stalactites, and Arkoudia (Bear) cave has a rock bear inside and also an ancient church. A pretty beach can be found at the small village of Stavros. For good cheap fish the restaurant at **Aroni** is recommended; others are Nykterida and Asteria at **Korakies,** and Neraida at Ag. Matheos which has Cretan music.

Souda, at the crotch of Akrotiri, is Chania's port and wins no votes for charm, but it has a restaurant and hotels. Frequent buses connect it with the capital. A major NATO base is located at Souda, and its air force exercises can be rather obnoxious. But NATO is not the first to appreciate the superb harbour of Souda Bay, one of the best in the Mediterranean Sea. The Venetians fortified the bay's islet **Nea Souda,** and it was the last place on Crete to hold out against the Turks, despite their repeated attempts to capture it. At one time they tried to disarm the defenders psychologically by piling 5000 Christian heads around the walls. The fort, however, remained in the hands of the Venetians and Greek rebels, who took shelter there, until 1715 when Venice surrendered it to Turkey. The Turks built another fort, **Idzeddin,** at the south end of the bay by the ancient city Aptera, whose ruins supplied the stone for its construction. Together with Nea Souda, Idzeddin guarded the bay of Souda. South-west of the fort is the village **Malaxa,** an ancient mining centre. Ruins of two Byzantine churches, Agii Saranta and Agia Eleousa remain, but most spectacular is the ravine to the south, said to be 400 meters (1300 ft) deep, ridden with caves. The neighbouring village of **Mournies** was the birthplace of Venizelos.

Heading towards the middle "head" of Crete, called Rodopou on the map but known locally by its cape, **Spatha,** one comes to **Ag. Marina** with its old Venetian and Turkish houses. The islet facing Ag. Marina is **Ag. Theodoro,** and it, too, attracted the Venetian fortification architects. Its cave with its wide open mouth originally belonged to a hungry sea monster, with an appetite as big as Crete; Zeus, however, couldn't bear to see his home island devoured, and petrified the monster with a thunder bolt. Ag. Theodoro today is a refuge for the wild Cretan goat, the kri kri.

Close to Ag. Marinas is **Platanias** with a sandy beach and bamboo forest. Another beach is near **Maleme,** further west, where much of the Battle of Crete took place. The village of **Kolimbario** at the foot of Spatha is the point of departure for excursions on the 'head'. Its church Ag. Georgios celebrates its panayiéri on 23 April, but its monastery **Gonias,** also known as Hodegetria, is much better known. Founded in the early 17th century, it is a rich monastery with many lovely icons from the 17th century. Its panayiéri is on 15 August. The **Church of St. John of the hermit Gionas** is a two-hour walk north of Rodopou and is host to one of the largest panayiéria in Chania on 29 August. A tiny village north-east of Rodofou, **Afrata,** the last village on the head which is attainable by car, has a huge cave, Hellenospilios, with corridors 90 metres (300 ft) long containing stalactites and stalagmites and other geographic wonders. From Afranta it is a few hours by foot (or 1½ hours by caique from Kolimbario) to **Menias,** the port of ancient **Diktyna,** the most famous shrine to Artemis in Greece. Menias has a rocky beach juxtaposed by shady caves, and there are some ruins of the ancient port. Diktean Artemis had a popular following up to the end of the Roman Empire. The Diktean mountains in Lassithi were named for her, and Agamemnon stopped by to offer a sacrifice at her shrine in Polyrenia on his return home from Troy.

Polyrenia is south of Kastelli (the ancient port Kissamos) and more of it remains than of Diktyna. Founded by the Achaeans and Dorians, Polyrenia (meaning many flocks) supported a large population, supplied by a still visible aqueduct. Parts of the ancient walls remain, added to by the Romans and perhaps the Turks. The church of the 99 Holy Fathers was built on the site from temple material, and the cemetery lies in a temple's foundations. There are also ruins of roads and houses. The road leading to Polyrenia from Kastelli is again a ruin. Buses attempt it twice a day from Kastelli.

Kastelli is situated on a plain surrounded by hobbity hills which produce olives and grapes. To distinguish it from the various other Kastellis of Crete, the town's proper name is Kastelli Kissamou, a most proper name as Kastelli's castle was Kissamos' temple and theatre refashioned by the Venetians in 1550. This castle has a long and at times most melodramatic history. When the Cretan Kantanoleo captured it from the Venetians, they, as if recognizing Kantanoleo's authority, offered a highborn Venetian girl as his son's bride. At the wedding feast the Cretans were given drugged wine and the Venetians murdered them, taking the fort once more.

In the Kastelli post office is a small museum with a few discoveries from ancient Kissamos. Wine is the major product of the town, and there are panayiéria on 30 May, 27 June (Ag. Pandeliemenon), and 29 August (Ag. Ioannes). Thekthia by the sea is Kastelli's "romantic" restaurant, while Xirochakis in the square is also good. There is a rocky beach with a taverna.

Up at the ancient city of **Phalassarna** the beach is big and sandy — a bus goes there from Kastelli. There is a café and a stone throne, and a marker to show where Phalassarna once stood; some walls also remain by Koutri. Further north on the **Grambousa head** lies the famous Venetian fort, taken during the War of Independence by Greek refugees, in particular those from the two small islands of Psara and Kassos, which had been devastated by the Turks. Forced to make a living in troubled times, these refugees took to pirating so successfully that Capodistria had to intervene personally to stop them, and Grambousa fort became Turkish once more. It can still be seen today at Agriagrambousa. A trip by caique is by far the easiest way of getting there.

Once a day a bus leaves Kastelli for **Topolia,** with its pretty stalactic cave of Ag. Sophia, used since Neolothic times and still the shelter for a little church. At the nearby church of Ag. Kyryianni (960) are the remains of a Bishop Psaromilingos, who was martyred in the cave. We are now in Chania's chestnut region; in the village **Elos,** further south, there is a chestnut harvest festival (Yiorti tou Kastanas) on the second Sunday of October. Eight other villages in the area claim the chestnut as their major product; in July they also produce some of the best weddings in Crete.

Kouneni is the next large village, containing three Byzantine chapels, in particular Ag. Georgios, constructed in 1284, and Michail Archangelos (14th century), both with frescoes. Further down the road on the Libyan Sea is the **Monastery Chrysoskalitissa** (the Lady of the Golden Stair, but only the faithful can see the steps of gold), which hosts a *panayiéri* on 14-15 August. The islet **Elafonision** off the coast is a lovely place, popular with Chaniotes who want to escape from the cares of the world.

East of Kouneni lies the village of **Kandanos,** inhabited from ancient times and known for its freedom-loving inhabitants. The Nazis destroyed it after its brilliant resistance, and now the village is all new. Ruins of the ancient walls remain on the hill, and there are many Byzantine churches in the area with frescoes. **Kakodiki** to the south-west has a hundred springs with soft mineral waters known for curing kidney stones. Kali Keratai is the most famous. Michail Archangelos church (1387) contains frescoes. The springs at Temenia, Dzanoudianon and Limbinari are also known for their curative properties. Muscat-producing **Temenia** was built on the site of ancient Yrtakina, near the far grander Elyros, one of the largest Doric settlements on Crete. According to legend two sons of Apollo, Philakides and Philandros, founded the town, which worshipped them. Arrows, bows and bronze were exports of the pugnacious town of **Elyros,** which prospered until the Saracens destroyed it in the 9th century. Walls from the town and acropolis still exist.

In 1279 the Venetian conquerors built **Castel Selino,** more with the aim of subduing the rebellious Greeks than protecting their new territory. The castle did not last, however; the terror of the islands, Khair Eddin Barbarossa, arrived in 1539 and destroyed it on his pillaging path. Below the ruins of its walls is a lovely sandy beach. The small town Selino, now known as **Paliochora,** is called the Bride of the Lybian Sea. On 25 March a large *panayiéri* is held there. Among its Byzantine churches is Ag. Georgios of 1323, and there is a monastery dedicated to the 99 Holy Fathers.

From Paliochora it is an hour's caique ride to the ancient city of **Lissos,** another victim of the Saracen conquest and perhaps once the port of both Elyros and Yrtakina. A theatre, baths, houses, and temples can still be seen of this once-prosperous Doric-Roman-Byzantine town. Very close to Lissos was ancient Syia, modern **Sougia,** also a harbour of Elyros. Many signs of ancient times remain, including walls, an aqueduct, and a bath. On the floor of the 6th century church are lovely mosaics, both geometrical and scenic. Ag. Antonios (1382) is painted with frescoes. A cave by Sougia, Spyliara, is one of a multitude considered to have housed the Cyclopse Polythemos. On 8 September Sougia has a *panayiéri.*

The next village going eastwards down the Lybian sea coast is Ag. Roumeli, which also boasts a frescoed church, Panayia, built on a temple of Artemis by the Venetians. The town itself was constructed on the site of ancient Tarra with its sanctuary of Tarranean Apollo. Tarra was known for its fine glass made in the Roman period.

There are two ways to go to Ag. Roumeli: either take a boat from Chora Sfakion or walk through the **Gorge of Samaria,** mother nature's spectacular creation in Crete, and at 18 km. (11 miles) long the longest gorge in Europe. The customary approach is to take a bus from Chania to **Omalos,** the small village on a high mountain plain at the head of the gorge. To make sure that your trip lasts one day instead of two, take the early bus to Omalos. The caique from Ag. Roumeli to Chora Sfakion, from whence the bus leaves for Chania, is often a little late, while the bus goes on time, forcing visitors to support Sfakion's hotel industry. From Omalos one descends the Wooden Stair, the Xiloskala, into the gorge, which has footpaths and is easy to walk through. Four guards inside assure the life and well-being of the visitor, who should bring his own provisions. The walk down from Omalos averages 6 hours, while the walk up from Ag. Roumeli is 16-18 hours. Good walking shoes are highly recommended for the trip.

Lucky walkers may see a wild Cretan kri kri on the walls of the gorge, which rise to a sheer 3000 metres (1000 ft.), and in some places stand only 3 metres (10 feet) apart. The ruined town inside, Samaria, gave its name to the gorge and has a Venetian church dedicated to the Virgin Mary (1379). A caique (110 dr.) leaves Ag. Roumeli at 2 pm and 5 pm. For those staying in Ag. Roumeli or Chora Sfakia there are hotels, rooms, and restaurants as well as beaches (there is a nudist one between Loutro and Sfakia). Of these southern towns, Sougia is the least tourist oriented.

South of Ag. Roumeli is the triangular islet **Gavdos,** the southern most point of Greece and reputed to be the Island of Calypso. Boats leave twice a week from Paliochora for this place of charming beaches and shepherds but little tourist accommodation. The castle, Gozzo, is Venetian.

Ag. Ioannes is a three-hour mule ride east of Ag. Roumeli. An autonomous ancient city, Aradin, once inhabited the site of which a few vestiges remain. The old church of Archistratigos Michail was built from the stones of ancient Aradin. The region surrounding it is full of caves. Drakolakki cave is noteworthy — an underground labyrinth with a bottomless lake that requires both torch and string to explore.

Chora Sfakion in the wild mountains is the capital of the fiercest and bravest Cretans. Located by the sea, it supplied the Cretan revolutions. The many churches were built to enable the people to gather at seemingly harmless *panayieria,* to plot the next moves of a revolt. Villages in the province of Sfaka are often fortified on small hills, as the independent Sfakians also fought great feuds among themselves. The Venetians constructed a castle on the hill after the revolt of 1570, while a little further down the coast stood their fortress Ag. Nikitas, known today as **Frangokastello,** built in 1317, and used mainly to keep the Cretans under control. During the War of Independence a great massacre took place there. An Epirot insurgent, Khatzimichalis Dalianis, held Frangokastello with 650 Cretans until 8000 Turkish troops arrived to wrench them out. The Turks took the fort, and all of the Greeks inside were slain, including Dalianis, although sections of Cretans who had remained outside the fort quickly recaptured it. Meanwhile other Cretan chieftains captured the mountain passes and caused havoc when the remainder of the Turkish army turned to the north, winning guns and much needed supplies.

This event, the Massacre of Frangokastello, has given rise to the most authenticated of the million or so Greek ghost stories that exist. On 17 May, the anniversary of the massacre, the phantoms of the Cretan dead rise up at dawn, fully armed, and march silently towards the fortress to disappear into the sea. These are the famous Drosoulites, still ready to fight the enemy Turk. They have been seen so often that scientific explanations have been attempted, although as yet none can match the legend. A less spooky *panayiéri* of the Virgin takes place at Frangokastello on 15 August.

North of Frangokastello one finds the village of **Astendos** among the trees, with a brook of roaring water; **Askyfou,** the village with the ravine that spelt doom to enemy armies trapped inside; and pretty little **Asigonia,** with a large *panayiéri* on 23 August at the church Ag. Georgios, a site surrounded by plane trees and springs. Mountain villages such as these are rarely visited by foreign tourists, and are ideal for those who want to experience Cretan rural life. Closer to civilization is **Alikampos,** whose frescoed Church of the Virgin (1315) celebrates 15

August.

Georgioupolis on the coast was named in honour of Prince George and has a long sandy beach, part of the stretch which continues off and on all the way to Rethymnon and is a favourite area for big hotel builders. In the nearby village of **Mathe** is a church of Ag. Antonios with a carob tree for its roof.

Crete's largest lake, **Lake Kournas,** is also in the region, known for its eels. There are many good restaurants and rooms to rent in Georgioupolis.

Inland is **Vryses,** a popular destination for picnics; Greeks swim in its creek. In the Evangelistria church of **Fre** an icon works wonders, and a large *panayiéri* is held on 25 March. **Neo Chori** with its vast citrus orchards has a *panayiéri* on the Sunday following Easter Sunday, and there are a few remains of ancient habitations. Little **Kokkino Chora** on Cape Drapanon was the location for the film *Zorba the Greek,* and all the pictures of Anthony Quinn in the cafés will let no one forget it.

West of Kokkino Chora is **Kalyves** with a long beach, near the fortress Apokorona, built by the Genoese before they turned Crete over to the Venetians. The famous ancient city of **Aptera** is a few miles to the west, and many ruins remain on the site, also known as Paliokastro. The name Aptera, which means "wingless" comes from a music contest once held there between the Sirens and the Muses. When the Muses won, the enraged Sirens pulled out their own feathers, dived into the sea and drowned. They can be seen today in the form of the small white Leucae islets in Souda Bay. Huge cyclopean walls remain, along with an archaic temple to Apollo, a Hellenistic temple to the corn goddess Demeter, a Roman theatre and underground cisterns. Aptera remained inhabited until the Byzantine era.

In the heart of the nomos of Chania some of the best oranges in Crete are grown, and Cretan oranges have a reputation as being the best in the world. These citric superlatives are celebrated annually at **Skine** on 26 April during the Orange Festival. On 6 August the same village has a *panayiéri* of the Transfiguration. Neighbouring **Fournes** claims to have more than 120,000 orange trees; it also boasts the Cave of the Pig, and has a large *panayiéri* to Ag. Panteleimon on 27 July. At **Alikianou** the wedding massacre of Kantanoleon's Cretans took place, at the Venetian tower of Da Molin. Besides more bright green orange groves, Alikianou has a church of Ag. Georgiou (1243) with exceptional frescoes. Another orange growing village, **Meskla,** is a lovely little place. One church has mosaics from a temple of Aphrodite, left by the ancient city of Rizinia; another, the Transfiguration of the Saviour has lovely frescoes dating back to 1303. Byzantine frescoes can also be seen in the church of Christ the Saviour. **Lakoi** is yet another picturesque village, situated on a mountainside near the Plain of Omalos.

Beside these villages runs the majestic Therisson ravine, traversed by a road. It is known in Cretan history for the 1905 Revolution of Therisso, when the Cretans rose for union with Greece. Prassa to the west has a smaller ravine beside it and unusual rock formations and caves. There is a *panayiéri* on 25 March. Omalos to the south has a celebration on 27 July, and nearby is the path for one of the two refuges in the White Mountains run by the Hellenistic Alpine Club. (See mountain climbing, page 53).

Rethymnon

The modern **capital of Rethymnon** nomos is built on the ancient city of Rithymna, its classical name, although Late Minoan tombs in the city have been discovered proving previous inhabitation. A fortress was built where the ancient acropolis stood, and the Venetians reinforced it with a further wall upon their arrival. Below by the sea the town began to grow unprotected. It was thrice raided by pirates, beginning with the wily Barbarossa in 1538, and followed by Uluch Ali in 1562 and 1571, when Rethymnon was burnt. The Venetians finally decided something should be done, and walled in the city. They also made the Fortezza, one of the best preserved Venetian castles in Greece, although it was captured by the Turks in 1645. For a vivid account of Rethymnon as it existed under the Turks at Independence and during the exchange of populations, read *The Tale of a Town* by Pandelis Prevelakis, a native son. (The English translation can be found in any large town in Greece).

Despite gradual repairs, Rethymnon has retained its distinctive crumbling Venetian houses. Wooden balconies from Turkish times project over head, and the streets are narrow and often dark. This medieval atmosphere and a huge stretch of sandy beach in front of the town are Rethymnon's major attractions. Many people prefer it to the larger Chania and Herakleon. Another exceptional feature of Rethymnon can be found in the person of Kostas Palierakis, who runs the little glass **tourist office** by the post office on Leoforos Koundouri. He displays great zeal and love for his town. If, like most people, you arrive in Rethymnon by bus, you can easily find Kostas by simply walking up the hill to the first street and then turning right.

Nightlife in Rethymnon centres on the harbour where the small fish restaurants fill up every night with hungry customers. There are also discotheques in the area, one owned by a certain Vassilis whom everyone seems to meet. Vassilis owns about half of Rethymnon and is determined to make it prosper before he retires at the age of 35.

What to see in Rethymnon: The **Fortezza** is open daily from 7 am to 3 pm and is very interesting to stroll through. The mosque in particular is well preserved. You should also see the governor's house. In the Venetian Loggia, or club, a museum has been installed (closed from 1 pm to 5 pm and on Mondays) which contains a particularly good coin collection and other archaeological finds from the nomos. After the exchange of populations the Turkish cemetery was dug up to become a **public garden** and a small zoo for a few cramped animals. The Dradakis mansion is one of the more splendid houses in Rethymnon. Tall minarets recall the Turkish occupation. The big holiday of Rethymnon is the

Cretan Wine Festival, 15-30 July, which takes place in the public garden. The **yacht supply station** at the harbour (note the unusual lighthouse) provides fuel, water and provisions.

Restaurants: Lemonakis, Apostolis, Zambetakis, Frangoulatzis, Kyrianitakis, Makedonia and Demotikon. As the Bay of Souda and waters north of Rethymnon are Crete's best fishing grounds, fish in Rethymnon costs about half as much as in Ag. Nikolaos.

Music: Discotheques by the port; Barbarossa for Cretan music, and Limeri just outside the town. Many good tavernas and restaurants with music can also be found in the neighbouring village of **Misiria** (frequent buses), among them Skarveli, Plasari, Anamnissis, Gavala, and Karavasisis.

Tourist police: 52 Vas. Georgiou B. Tel: 22589.

The **nomos of Rethymnon** is rugged and the least visited of the Cretan *nomosi,* dominated in the east by Mt. Ida, or Psiloritis with its sacred cave. While Chania is known for producing Crete's fighters and musicians, Rethymnon, especially the town, is the home of intellectuals, and has produced some fine writers. Two dances from the nomos, the Pentozale and Sousta are danced all over Crete and names such as Arkadiou, Anogia, Preveli and Melidoni are engraved in Cretan history.

A small road south of Episkopi leads to the ancient city of **Lappa,** also called Phoenix in the past, and Lambe during the Byzantine period. Ruins remain dating from the still standing classical wall. To the tiny southern village of the peach **(Rodakinon)** the only public transport is from Frangokastello in nomos Chania. Rodakinon has a lovely beach and sun sheltering caves. As there are no restaurants someone will probably invite you in for dinner.

Further east along the Lybian sea is the village of **Plakias,** near another lovely beach. Plakias is a little more ready for tourists than Rodakinon and even has rooms for rent. From there one can visit **Preveli Monastery.**

Beautifully situated between the coast and Kouraliotiko ravine, this monastery was a great resistance centre during the Turkish and German occupations. In gratitude for its assistance to the Allies in 1941, the British gave Preveli two silver candlesticks.

Another route south of Rethymnon leads to **Armeni,** where a late Minoan cemetery has been discovered. Almost the entire Armeni population between the ages of 20 and 40 works in Germany now. **Spili** is a large mountain village on the way south. It is known for its crystal and has a long fountain of lion heads. Rooms are available and there are *panayiéria* on 29 June (Monastery Apostolos Paulos) and on 27 May at Ag. Pnevma. Continuing on the same road south one comes to **Ag. Galini,** a small fishing village turned tourist attraction; every house in town has a big sign before it advertising rooms. There is a beach and tavernas and transport to Phaistos in nomos Herakleon.

On the west slopes of Mt. Ida in the heart of the nomos are a group of

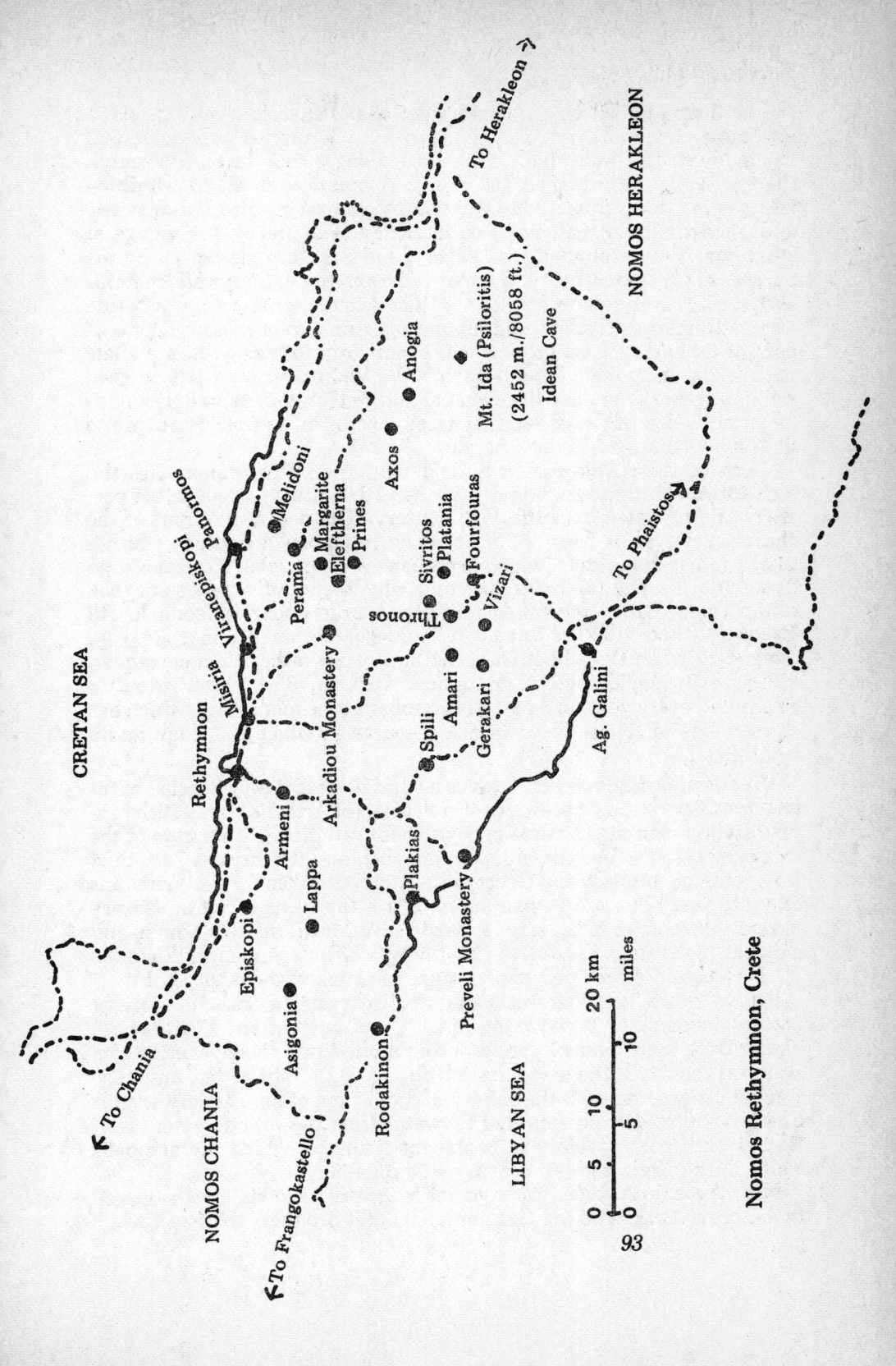

CRETAN SEA

NOMOS HERAKLEON

To Herakleon →

Mt. Ida (Psiloritis)
(2452 m./8058 ft.)
Idean Cave

Anogia

Axos

Melidoni

Margarite
Eleftherna
Prines

Sivritos
Platania
Fourfouras

Panormos
Viranepiskopi
Misiria

Perama

Thro/nos

Vizari

To Phaistos →

Rethymnon

Arkadiou Monastery

Amari
Gerakari

Ag. Galini

Spili

Armeni

Lappa

Plakias

Episkopi

Asigonia

Rodakinon

Preveli Monastery

NOMOS CHANIA

← To Chania

← To Frangokastello

LIBYAN SEA

20 km
miles
10
10
5
5
0
0

93

Nomos Rethymnon, Crete

small villages famed for their resistance. **Gerakari,** east of Spili, stood unconquered under Venetian, Turkish and German occupations, and has many houses from the Middle Ages, along with a tower. At **Amari,** the capital of the province, the church Asomatos has the oldest dated frescoes in Crete, from 1225. The nearby monastery also has frescoes, and an agricultural college. Two ancient towns are by the village of **Thronos: Vene,** founded by Ptolemy, and **Sivritos,** destroyed by the Saracens in the 9th century. A remarkable amount of their walls remains and Sivritos even retains a gateway. **Vizari** to the south was built beside a later Roman settlement and among the ruins are a mosaic floor and part of an early Christian basilica. From **Fourfouras** village a shale path leads up to one of the peaks of Mt. Ida, a five-hour trip in good walking shoes. There is a little chapel and well on top, as well as an unforgettable view of Crete. Another ascent can be made from **Platania** to the Cave of Pan (about two hours).

North of these villages, on a good road from Rethymnon, lies the **Arkadiou Monastery,** founded in the 11th century, although the present building dates from the 17th century. The decorative front of the church, however, is from 1587. Arkadiou resembles a small fort rather than a religious building, which is perhaps why the rebel Koroneos used it to hide his powder magazine, and why surrounding villagers took refuge there. On 7 November 1866, the Turks under Mustafa Kyrtil Pasha attacked Arkadi. After a two-day siege they had begun to enter the monastery when the Abbot Gaberiel blew it up rather than surrender, killing 829 people, both Cretan and Turkish. The heroic event is celebrated every year on 8 and 9 November at the monastery, which has three rooms of relics. There is also a tourist pavilion at Arkadi and a small hotel.

Viranepiskopi is on the north coast and possesses two churches of interest: a 10th century basilica by a sanctuary of Artemis, and a 16th century Italian church. The area is popular for camping. **Panormos** to the east is by the mouth of the Milopotamos river and the fortress Castelli of Milopotamos, built by the Genoese in 1206, but taken by the Venetians only six years later. Also in Panormos are the ruins of a 5th century basilica. Just south in the large stalactic cave **Melidoni,** 370 women and children took refuge in 1824, during the War of Independence. When the Turk Houssein discovered their refuge, he smoked them to death.

From Perama another road leads to **Margarite** with its thriving pottery industry and Maranthospilios Cave and ancient **Eleftherna,** dating from the Classical period and inhabited into the Byzantine age. Ruins of the walls, the acropolis, a bridge, a Byzantine tower, and huge Roman cisterns remain, the latter handy in time of siege. Eleftherna is built on a plateau and supplied by water from the Milopotamos river. Higher and more precipitous is ancient **Axos,** of which the acropolis walls, dating from the 8th century BC, remain.

Near Axos, is **Anogia,** a major resistance centre, which was burned by both the Turks and the Germans. Today it produces some of Crete's finest woven clothes with 700 traditional weaves in all, and also Crete's' best raki, ouzo's stronger cousin, also known as *tsikoutha*. On 6 August there is a fair. From Anogia a path leads to the **Idean Cave,** considered by some to have been the birthplace of Zeus, although the Diktean cave is the more popular candidate. Nevertheless the Idean Cave was very sacred to the ancients as proved by finds from the 9th century BC discovered inside it.

An ascent to the summit of **Mount Ida** can be made from Anogia, taking more than 12 hours. Other approaches begin from nomos **Herakleon.**

Herakleon

The city of Herakleon, the largest in Crete and fifth largest in Greece, was used as a port of Knossos up into Roman times. The invading Saracens built a new town over it and called it 'Kandak' for the moat they dug around its walls. As their base of piracy, Kandak also became a leading slave trade centre for the world. When Nickephoros Phokas liberated Crete in 961, the Byzantines called Kandak 'Kandax'. This turned into Candia or Candy when the Venetians made the town their Cretan capital in 1210, and the whole island became known as Candia or Candy. The Greeks called it Megalo Kastro, or just Kastro, for the huge fortifications constructed there by the Venetians from the 15th to 17th centuries. During the 16th century Michele Sammicheli, the greatest defence expert of his era, worked on Candia's walls, and the city, the seat of the Venetian-appointed Duke of Crete, became one of the leading Mediterranean sea ports.

The Turkish siege of Candia lasted for 21 years, from 1648 to 1669. Louis XIV sent the French to assist the Venetians towards the end of the struggle although the venture ended in disaster for his forces. By the time Francesco Morosini surrendered the city to the Turks on 5 September, 30,000 Christian defenders and 117,000 Turks had perished. The Venetians were allowed to leave in safety, Morosini eventually to blow up the Parthenon. Candia remained the capital of Crete under the Turks until 1850 when they transferred it to Chania. After independence the Greeks rechristened the city Herakleon, and it has since prospered due to its central location.

Herakleon (also Iraklion among other variations) is the least attractive city of Crete, but its position as an ideal departure point for visiting the Minoan cities, and its possession of the second most important archaeological museum in Greece, make its charm a minor consideration. The many hotels can accommodate a large flow of visitors. There is also a Youth Hostel, but suffice to say that it is a hot contender for the golden toilet seat award. A branch of the **National Tourist Organization** is next door to the archaeology museum on Xanthididou St.

What to see in Herakleon: The **Archaeology Museum:** open 8 am - 7 pm June through October; other months 9 am - 1 pm and 3 pm - 6

pm. Closed Tuesday. Entrance 50 dr.; 5 dr. with student card; free
Thursday and Sunday. The museum contains a truly fabulous collection
of items from Crete, from prehistoric to Roman times, including vases,
jewellery, weapons, statues, sealstones, carbonized food and magnificent
frescoes.

The Historical Museum of Crete: open 9 am - 1 pm and 3 pm - 6
pm. Closed Sunday. Entrance 25 dr.; 2.5 dr. with student card. Located
on Akti Makariou, across from the Xenia Hotel, the museum has many
beautiful Venetian relics, along with items from the Early Christian,
Byzantine, and Turkish periods. The library of Nikos Kazantzakis has
also been reconstructed inside.

Walking through the city one continually meets the great **Venetian
Walls,** more than 4,300 metres (14,000 ft) in total length, and in some
places 29 metres (95 ft) thick, with 12 small fort-like bastions. Tunnels
have been made through the old gates to adapt to modern traffic needs,
and on one of these bastions, Martinengo, the furthest to the south-west,
is the **grave of Kazantzakis.** This great Cretan author, who died in
1957, has inscribed on his tombstone, "I believe in nothing. I hope for
nothing. I am free." Another famous Cretan, Daskaloyiannis, a
resistance leader against the Turks, was flayed to death by the latter in a
square by the harbour where the arched Venetian ship shelters stand, the
16th century **Arsenals.** On the west jetty is the restored Rocca al Mare,
better known as **Megalos Koules,** built by the Venetians in 1523-1540.
It is open to visitors from 9 am - 1 pm and 4 pm - 7 pm daily, but closed
in the afternoon on Sunday.

From the harbour runs 25 Augostou St., where besides the many ticket
offices, tourist agencies, and banks is a reconstruction of the **Venetian
Loggia** (military club) built in the 1500s. The lionhead fountain in the
small but central **Platia Venizelou** is a 17th century Venetian work,
and very close to it is a small café selling superb peach and apricot
slushes. There are many shops in the vicinity along with the Venetian
church of St. Mark, now used as a concert hall. Reproductions of
paintings from Cretan churches are on display inside, and can be seen
for a small fee. Another church nearby is **Ag. Titos,** founded in the
Byzantine era and reconstructed after various earthquakes; the Turks
made it a mosque, and the Greeks now use it to house St. Titus' head,
which was sent back to Greece in 1966 from St. Mark's in Venice. **OTE**
is in the small green square.

The main square of Herakleon is **Platia Elevtherias,** where the
tourist office and **Archaeology Museum** are to be found, along with
shade and many sweet shops that cater to the evening strollers. The **post
office** is a block away on Platia Daskalyiannis and from there it is a
short walk to the **Tourist Police** on Vas. Konstantinou. Platia
Elevtherias is a junction of many streets, the real heart of the city: 1866
St. bustles with the market, 1821 has shops, and in front of the El Greco
hotel is the **bus stop for Knossos** (no. 2). Kalokairinou is the long main
shopping street of the city and 25 Augostou leads to Platia Venizelou and

the harbour. Continuing down Kalokairinou St. one passes the square of the huge **Ag. Minas** to the left, the cathedral of Herakleon built in the last century. Far more interesting, however, is the small **Ag. Aikaterini** to its right on the same square. Built in 1555, this houses an icon collection, six of them painted by the Cretan artist Mikalis Damaskinos, the 16th century master. They can be seen from 10 pm to 1 am and from 5 pm to 7 pm for 10 dr. Continuing down Kalokairinou St., one passes through the gate Porta Chanion, from where **buses to Phaistos and Anogia** leave. **Buses to Eastern Crete, Malia and Chania** leave from exactly the opposite side of town, by the harbour. A little way up the road is the **Herakleon Tennis Club** (non-members admitted, tel. 212934 / 24010).

The cleanest and closest beach to Herakleon is Amnissos and buses leave Herakleon every half hour from the bus station by the harbour. There are two hotels there. Amnissos was the harbour of Minoan Knossos, and there are ruins from that time and the archaic period (the Sanctuary of Zeus Thenatas). From here Idomeneus left for the Trojan War. Further down the coast **Hani Kokkini** or Kokkini Hani is also popular with the locals, and there are places to eat. Large hotels dot the long sandy beach all along the road to Malia.

Restaurants: Dionysos, Minos and Klimataria on Daidalou St., Ionia on Evans St., the Glass house on the quay (expensive), Maxim on Kondilaki, Caprice and Knossos by Platia Venizelou, Pas Psaria on 25 Augusto. On Evans and 1866 Sts. there are small tavernas. **Cretan music** can be heard at Arethousa, Erotokritos (very good), Kastro, Zamania, and Risitika, most of these places being located outside the city walls.

Discotheques: Near the centre of town are Blow Up (the best), Why Not?, Estorial, Stroboli, and Esperia.

Panayiéria: Herakleon Flower Festival 2-6 June; Grape Festival 11-19 September; and a huge panayiéri for the patron saint Ag. Minas on 11 November.

Tourist Police: Vas. Konstantinou St. Tel. 283190.

Nomos Herakleon contains almost all of the major Minoan sites, which one can visit independently (buses leave from the Herakleon harbour) or on coach excursions (Creta Tours) which pick visitors up at the beach hotels along the road from Malia to Herakleon. There are also excursions to popular sites in the other nomosi for those pressed for time. Besides the long stretch of sandy shore on the north, there are occasional small beaches to the south, the most famous of all being Matala. The Cretans from this nomos are known as the best singers, and their hopping Pedekto is Herakleon's contribution to the pan-Cretan dances.

Knossos, the powerful palace of King Minos, is one of the greatest archaeological finds of all time. Discovered and excavated by Sir Arthur Evans in 1900 onwards, it has been partly reconstructed unlike the other Minoan sites, thus affording the visitor an idea of past Minoan grandeur.

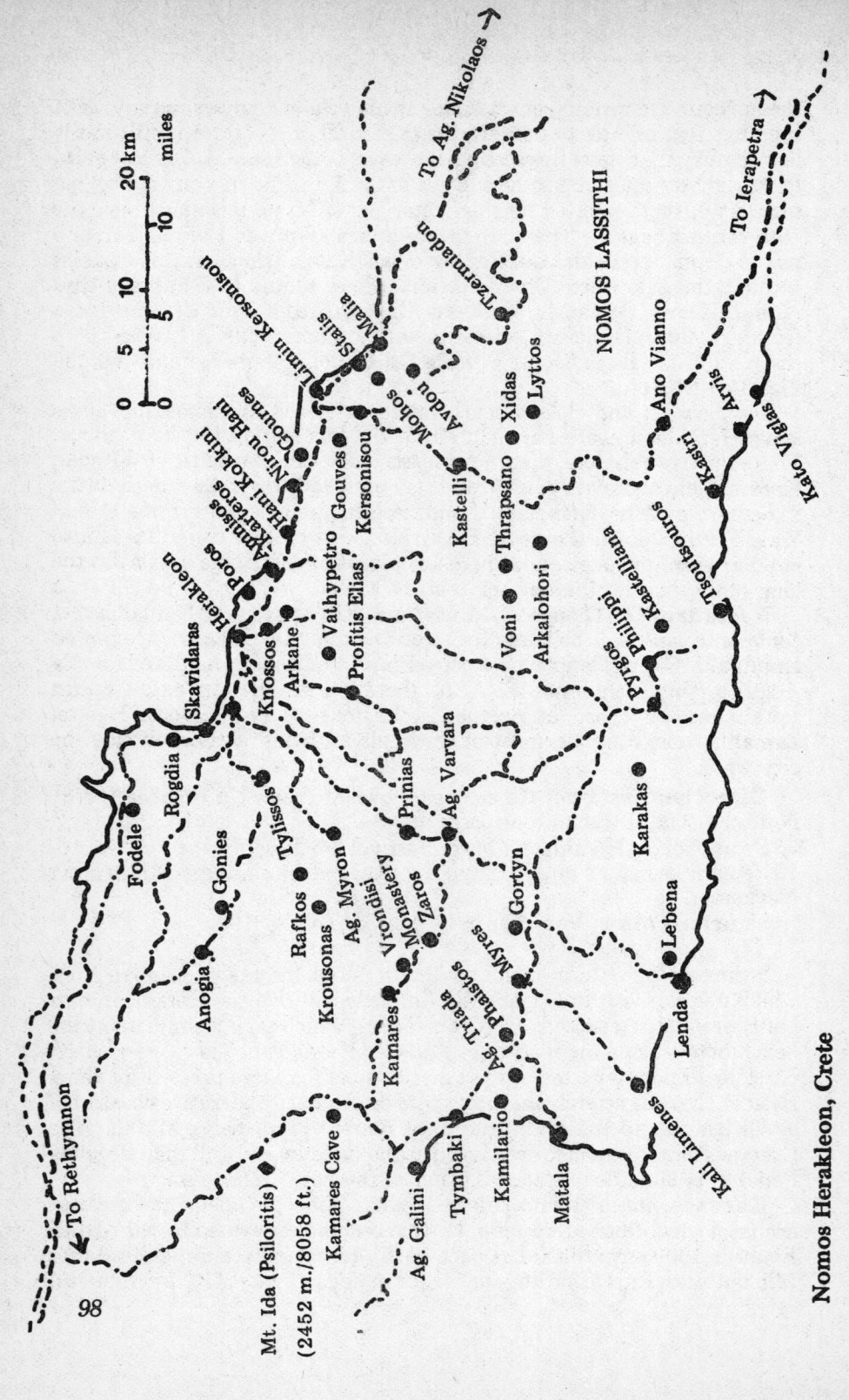

To Rethymnon

98

Fodele
Rogdia
Skavidaras
Anogia
Gonies
Hecakleon
Poros
Amnisos
Karteros
Hani Kokkini
Nirou Hani
Gournes
Limin Kersonisou
Stalis
Malia
To Ag. Nikolaos

Tylissos
Knossos
Arkane
Vathypetro
Profitis Elias
Gouves
Kersonisou
Mohos
Avdou
Tzermiadon

Rafkos
Ag. Myron
Vrondisi
Monastery
Prinias
Ag. Varvara
Kastelli
Voni
Thrapsano
Xidas
Lyttos

NOMOS LASSITHI

Krousonas
Zaros
Arkalohori
Ano Vianno

Kamares
Ag. Triada
Phaistos
Gortyn
Myrtes
Panagia
Pyrgos
Kato Kastellianna
Tsoutsouros
Kasteli
Arvis
Kato Vianno
To Ierapetra

Mt. Ida (Psiloritis)
(2452 m./8058 ft.)
Kamares Cave
Ag. Galini
Tymbaki
Kamilario
Matala
Kali Limenes
Lenda
Lebena
Karakas

0 5 10
0 5 10 20 km
          miles

Nomos Herakleon, Crete

The bus to Knossos leaves Herakleon from the harbour or the El Greco Hotel (no. 2) every 15 minutes; by the site and in the village of Knossos there are cafés, tavernas and restaurants. The site is open from 7.30 am to sunset in summer, and from 9 am to sunset in winter. Entrance 50 dr.; 5 dr. with student card; free Thursday and Sunday. Detailed guides are available at the excavations.

Remains prove that the first inhabitants of Knossos came during the 7th millennium BC. Circa 1950 BC they built a palace, which fell in the earthquake of 1700. Construction of a new palace followed, and it is the remains of this that one sees today. In 1400 BC it was destroyed by a great fire. The inhabitants at the time were probably Mycenean, as shown by the finds of Linear B tablets. The lack of later construction on the immediate palace site and the discovery of coins depicting the Minotaur are thought to prove the subsequent sacredness of the spot as the ancient labyrinth. Indeed the still present maze of stairways and floors, corridors, and rooms of the reconstructed palace show how the idea of the labyrinth could have formed in the imaginative mind.

After the destruction of the palace, a Geometric community flourished which was to become one of the leading cities of Crete in the 3rd century BC, although a war with Lyttos made it lose its supremacy to Gortyn. The Romans built a large city in the area, and inhabitation lasted until the early Byzantine period. The bishop of Knossos is mentioned in the annals of the church.

The excavations at Knossos are entered at the west court of the palace. If one continues directly to the left, one finds the oldest road in Europe, the Royal Road, used for religious processions and dances to the theatre, also the oldest in Europe. The idea of the amphitheatre was then undeveloped, and it looks more like a large stairway. To the right of the west court is a porch leading to the Corridor of the Procession and the south entrance, Propylaeum, of the palace with frescoes on the wall. A staircase from the Propylaeum leads to an upper floor of storage rooms and others; a descending staircase brings one to the Throne Room and Lustral Basin. From the large central court back up the stairs one can enter a series of rooms including huge storage pithois and rooms with their frescoes recopied on the walls. On the north side of the palace one sees the brightly painted charging bull. As is the case throughout Knossos, the columns are peculiar to the Minoan, thickening at the top. These are thought to be in imitation of a certain cyprus tree native to the gorge of Samaria.

On the east side of the palace one can see the huge pithoi from the first palace, and the excellent water system that supplied Knossos, also visible under the floor in the Queen's Megaron and its bathroom, another European first. Also in this area are the upper and main Halls of the Double Axes, the Grand stairway, the Corridor of the Draught-board, the separate House of the Chancel Screen and others, most labelled in English. A path to the south leads to the House of the High Priest and the Royal Temple tomb, although these can only be visited with special authorization. The same is true of the Little Palace across the highway.

West of Herakleon, along the road to Rethymnon, is the village **Rogdia,** with a Venetian fort, Kastro of Rogdia, located by the shore. **Fodele,** further north, is considered the birthplace of El Greco. To the south of it lies the **Minoan Tylissos** by a pretty village of the same name. There are three large villas from the Late Minoan Period, destroyed in 1400 BC. These can be seen throughout the day for a 5 dr. entrance fee. Another Minoan country house exists at **Sklavokambos** along the road towards Gonies. **Ag. Myron** is a large village south of Tylissos with a panayiéri on 8 August. Ancient **Rafkos** with scanty ruins is to the north; **Krousonas,** a small village in the afternoon shadow of Mt. Ida, celebrates Ag. Charalambos' Day with a big fete on 10 February.

Prinias further south has the ruins of ancient Ryzenia on its acropolis, with two archaic temples and a later Hellenistic fort. In **Ag. Varvara** a small church marks the centre of Crete, and a road leads to **Kamares,** from whence one can climb to the Kamares Cave on Mt. Ida. Kamares cave is famous for the discovery of fine Minoan pottery there, called Kamares Ware. By mule the trip takes 4 hours, and one can travel all the way to the top of Mt. Ida from Kamares in 10 hours. (For information on the Hellenic Alpine Club shelter, see Mountain Climbing [page 53]).

Vrondisi Monastery lies between Kamares and Zaros. Its church has 14th century frescoes, while the nearby Ag. Fanourios, the church of Valsamonero, has 15th century frescoes considered to be some of the finest in Crete.

South of Ag. Varvara is the ancient city of **Gortyn,** excavated by the Italians in 1880 and 1961. Although inhabited from Neolithic times, its fame began after the fall of Knossos, when it became one of the ruling cities of Crete, with ports at Matala and Lebena. In 189 BC Hannibal passed through Gortyn, and later the Romans made it their capital of the province of Crete and Cyrenaica. Although in the *Iliad* Homer describes Gortyn as walled, the walls that remain were begun by Ptolemy Philopator but left unfinished. St. Paul sent St. Titus to convert Gortyn, and Titus was its first bishop. In 828 the Saracens destroyed the city.

The most remarkable of the vast remains at Gortyn is the Law Code of Gortyn, which was inscribed at the beginning of the 5th century BC and built into the Roman Odeum in 100 AD. It is written in boustrophedon, or as the ox plows, left to right and right to left. The laws encompass criminal offences including adultery. Other remains include a theatre, a temple on the acropolis, the residence of the Roman governor (Praetorium), and temples of Pythian Apollo and of Isis and Serapis. There are also the remains of a 6th century basilica of Ag. Titos.

The port of Gortyn, **Lebena,** by modern Leanda on the Lybian sea, is known for its healing waters. In late Classical times an Asklepieion, a temple to Asklepios, the god of healing, was built here. Both it and the Hellenistic floor of the treasury have mosaics and there are also two large bath tubs. West of Gortyn is the large market town **Myres,** from which a road runs to **Matala** with its gorgeous beach and ancient tomb caves. These are still inhabited occasionally, although most people now sleep on the beach. The swimming is safe for children.

West of Myres lies the ancient city of **Phaistos,** also excavated by the Italian School of Archaeology, starting in 1900. It was one of the earliest inhabited places in Crete, dating from the same time as Malia and Knossos and mentioned by Homer. It was destroyed in Hellenistic-Roman times by the more powerful Gortyn. Its first palace was constructed in the Middle Minoan period, 2100 BC, and destroyed in 1700 BC; the second palace was built on top of the first and destroyed in 1400 BC. Below the palace, 50,000 people lived and worked for the king, and one can see the ruins of the villages surrounded by the rich and lovely Mesara Plain. The palace was three stories high, and the grand stairway leading to it has traces of the sacred snakes carved in it. Below it in the West Court lies the theatre. In the palace one can see the rooms of the king and queen, with bathrooms, the cisterns for storing rain water and one of the oldest metal forges in the world. By the excavations is a tourist pavilion with a café and food.

Neighbouring **Ag. Triada** (connected to Phaistos by a dirt road) supplied much of the gypsum and alabaster for the building of Phaistos. It was a Late Minoan settlement in its own right, where many people lived after the great destruction of 1400. The name Ag. Triada is derived from a small Venetian church near the site; the other church at the excavations is Ag. Georgios Galatas, 1302, which contains some frescoes. A small palace remains at Ag. Triada.

Pyrgos is the largest village east of Gortyn, and east of it, at **Philippi,** is a Byzantine fortress renovated by the Genoese, called Castel Belvedere for its remarkable view. This region of small villages and the monastery Foundadon is called the Kastelliana. East of this is Ano Viannos, or ancient Vienna, the inhabitants of which might have founded Vienne in France. On the old acropolis are the ruins of a Venetian castle and Turkish tower. Ag. Pelagia (1360) has frescoes. There is a castle near **Kastri** (of Mt. Kairatos), and a Venetian fortification at **Vigla** which is very well preserved, called Vigla of Kairatokambos. It was here that the Saracens entered Crete in 823. Down the coast is the **Monastery Avri,** and a pretty beach.

North from Ano Vianno is **Arkalohori** with a large panayiéri on 21 May. Minoan tombs and a sacred cave have been found there. In the small village of **Voni,** on the way to Kastelli, a folk festival takes place from 17 to 20 July. **Kastelli** is the chief village of the Pethiada, and is topped by the ruins of a Venetian castle; the 15th century church Eisodia Theotokon has very interesting frescoes. To the east is the ancient city of **Lyttos,** or Lyktos, the enemy of Knossos in Doric times. High up on the foothills of Mt. Dikti, Lyttos was wealthy and minted its own coins in Classical times, but in 220 BC Knossos destroyed it to put an end to the rivalry. Hellenistic walls remain, as does a Christian basilica with mosaics. Another ancient city, **Kersonisou,** to the north of Kastelli, was the port of Lyttos, but independent. It had a famous temple to Artemis. There is a later fort on the islet across from it.

West along the coast as far as Amnisos lies a long sandy beach, with hotels and many good but rather expensive restaurants. **Gouves,** a small village on the way, has a panayiéri on 26 July. At **Limin Kersonisou** there is an official camping area near the beach. **Gournes** is the home of an American Air Force Base; **Nirou Hani** has a Minoan Villa. Near Amnisos, in the direction of Eskopi, is the Cave of Eileithia, the protectress of childbirth, which originally held many Minoan ritual objects and today contains stalactites.

Towards the Eastern border of the nomos Herakleon is the Minoan city of **Malia.** The village of the same name has a nice youth hostel and beach. Excavated by the French School of Archaeology since the 1920s, the history of the palace of Malia follows the same pattern as that of the other sites: built in 1900 BC it was devastated by the earthquake 200 years later, and the second palace, built over the first, was ruined in the mysterious catastrophe of the 15th century BC. From the west court is the entrance to a long rectangular central court with a pit in the middle. In the Pillar Crypt to the left one can discern symbols carved in the pillars. Another little room further north is set at an oblique angle to the others, and might have been used for moon study or worship. On the same side are the Megaron, Lustral Basin and archives. Outside the palace a paved Minoan road still exists, and the sunken Hypostyle Crypt. By the sea is the cemetery, and to the west are the remains of a 6th century basilica.

Last of all, in the centre of the nomos is **Arkane,** where most of the island's table grapes are produced. There are actually two villages, Kato Arkanes and Epano Arkanes, the larger. In the Asomatos church (1315) are good frescoes of the same period as those in Ag. Triada. There are many Minoan remains in this region, including the walls in the village, a well, tombs, and other buildings. Arkanes is thought to have supplied water to Knossos. In nearby **Vathypetro** a Minoan villa has been found. Kanli Castelli, or the Bloody Fortress is also in the Arkanes region, and is believed to have been built by Nikephoros Phokas when he liberated Crete from the Saracens in 961. It later sheltered a harried Duke of Crete, much tried by the Duke of Naxos, Marcos Sanudo, who captured towns in Crete in defiance of Venice.

Lassithi

Ag. Nikolaos, the capital of the nomos Lassithi, was the ancient port of Lato, with the name of Lato Pros Kamara. Mandraki, a later name, lasted into Venetian times. The Genoese built the fortress of Mirabello above the bay of the same name, but the Turks demolished it and now the administration building of Lassithi occupies its place. When Ag. Nikolaos (named for a 9th century church) became capital of the nomos only 95 people lived there, although today its summertime population reaches 10,000. Of all the Cretan capitals, Ag. Nikolaos caters most obviously to the cosmopolitan crowd, which provide the major income for the town. For that reason it tends to be rather expensive; its often extolled smallness, charm, and quaintness is its business.

A small lake, more than 60 metres (200 ft.) deep, occupies the centre of town. In 1907 it was connected to the sea, and the channel is crossed by a small bridge. The **tourist police** station is easily found by the lake, in a stone building beside the peacocks. Restaurants and sweet shops line the lake, and continue along the sea in between the large hotels. The **youth hostel** lies on the hill over the bridge as does the **museum** (closed on Tuesday and in the afternoon) with finds from the region and a room devoted to folklore. The Akti Koundourou follows the sea shore, past rocky places where you can swim. There is a beach at the very end and a church, Ag. Nikolaos, patron of sailors, with 9th and 14th-century frescoes (the tourist police have the key). In the town, off Platia El. Venizelou, is the 12th century **Panayia** by the cathedral Ag. Triada. The **post office** can be found on 28th Octovriou St., and the **OTE** is a couple of blocks to the east. The **bus station** is by a rocky beach at the end of Sof. Venizelou St. where cheap souvlaki can be had.

From Ag. Nikolaos **steamers** go to Santorini, Karpathos, Kassos, Halki and Rhodes. Many companies offer excursions to popular sites.

Restaurants: Creta, Windmills, Charis, Lato by the harbour; less expensive are Vassilis, Zerfiros, Kallithea, Trata and Delta; those with music are Ikaros, Dilina, Aly Almyros. There are no places with real Cretan music.

Discotheques: Scorpios, Galaxy, Kastello (in the Mirabello Hotel, and one of the best in Greece), Studio, Romeos (taverna-disco) and 7-7.

Panayiéria: 6 December, Ag. Nikolaos; 29 May, Ag. Triada. Nautical week 27 June-3 July, with fireworks on the last day.

Beaches within bus range of Ag. Nikolaos are Elounda (buses 6 times a day), Kalo Chorio Beach, on the road to Sitia, Ammoudi by the Minos Beach Hotel, and Aly Almyros, 2km. (1¼ miles) east.

Tourist Police: on the lake. Tel. 22321.

Nomos Lassithi is the most varied of Crete: on its western border the high mountain plain, too cold for olives, grows wheat, apples and potatoes, while Vai on the east coast is a luxuriant, palm-lined beach in top tropical form. Lassithians claim to be the best lovers of Crete, although this is not unanimously agreed upon by other Cretans by any means, although they do give credit to the nomos for its potatoes and pigs. The Erotokritos poet Kornaro is from Lassithi, as well as a pope and Zeus himself, and a church near Ag. Nikolaos, Panayia Kera, has the best fresco paintings in Crete.

Directly off the coast of the city of Ag. Nikolaos is the islet **Ag. Pandes,** a refuge for the kri kri and site of a church of the same name, drawing pilgrims on 20 June. Otherwise one needs special permission to visit the goats. Other islets in Mirambelou Bay are **Psira** and **Mohlos,** both with Minoan ruins, dug by the American school of Archaeology.

One can hire caiques from Ag. Nikolaos or the village of Mohlos to visit them. North of Ag. Nikolaos is **Elounda,** on the site of the unexcavated port of Dreros, **Olous.** Inscriptions from the 2nd century BC prove a treaty between Rhodes and Olous and the walls of the port can still be observed in the sea. Artemis Britomartis was worshipped at the city, which was reported to have a wooden statue of the goddess made by Daedalus. Salt works of the Venetians exist in the area as well as a windmill, and a basilica with mosaics. In the village (once the location for a Disney film) the Stefanakis fish restaurant is good, and there is a discotheque called Milos.

Spinalonga, a half-hour caique ride from Elounda (the journey can also be made from Ag. Nikolaos) is a small islet formed by Venetian engineers when they dug a canal separating it from the Kolokytha (squash) peninsula. In 1579 they built a huge fortress on Spinalonga, on the ruins of the ancient fort of Olous. During the Turkish occupation Spinalonga held out like the other small island forts of Nea Souda and Grambousa, until a Venetian treaty handed it over to the Ottomans in 1715. The Turks settled it with soldiers and civilians. When they evacuated in 1904, it became a leper colony until 1952. The walls, houses, and cisterns make very impressive remains. **Plaka,** opposite the islet, was the supply centre for the lepers and is popular today with those seeking rest and relaxation.

West of Elounda a road leads to ancient **Dreros,** on a saddle between two hills, and discovered at the beginning of this century. Its remains include walls, a cistern, an archaic agora and a Geometric temple to Apollo Delphinios built in the 7th century BC, which produced the oldest hammered bronze statues to be found in Greece. **Milatos** to the north of Dreros was considered an enemy. Tradition has it that Sarpedon, one of Minos' brothers, won the affections of a certain boy the brothers quarelled over and left Crete for Asia Minor. He took with him not only the boy but people from Milatos, and they founded the great city of Miletus. In the 3rd century BC the Lyttians destroyed Milatos. The **Cave of Milatos** served as a refuge during the War of Independence for 2,700 people. Upon their discovery the Turks besieged them, and after two battles the refugees surrendered as the Turks had previously promised them safe conduct. However, the Turks massacred all the old men and children, and enslaved the women.

West of Milatos, on the highway from Herakleon, many Greek buses and cars stop at the shrine of **Ag. Georgios Selinaris** with its miraculous icon. **Neapolis** is the largest village en route to Ag. Nikolaos; the old village it was built on, Kares, witnessed the birth of Petros Filagros in 1340. Raised by Catholics, he became a professor of theology and was elected Pope Alexander V in 1409, during the schism. A year later, however, he died. Kares was destroyed in a rebellion in 1347 against the Venetians, and renamed new town, or Neapolis. There is a small museum with items from Elounda and Dreros, and on 14-15 August a large *panayiéri* celebrates the Assumption.

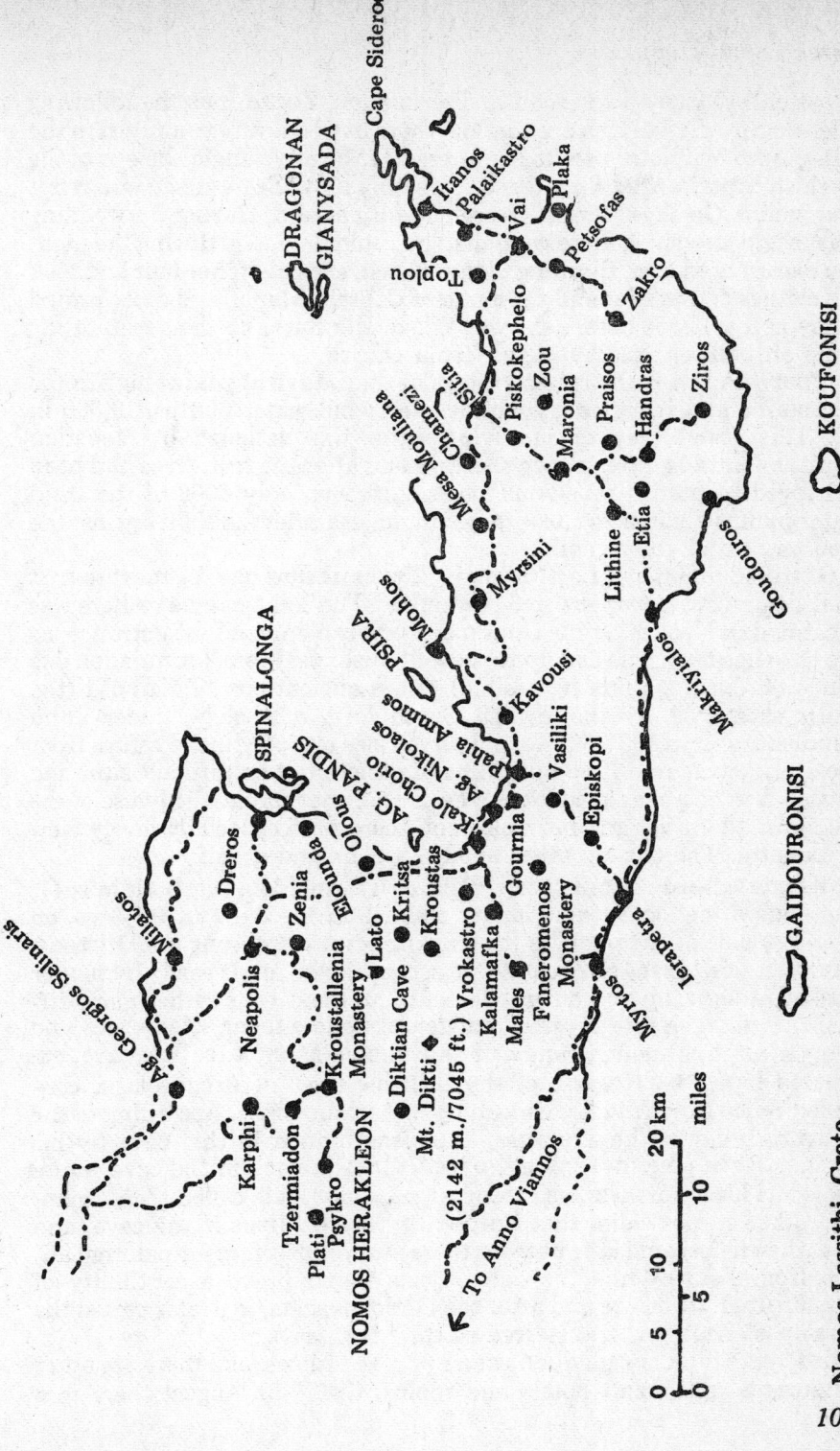

Nomos Lassithi, Crete

105

A small village on the road to Tzermiadon, **Zenia,** has the following tale: During the Turkish occupation, thére lived a lovely young girl in the village who had hair down to her knees. Her beauty caught the eye of the Turkish captain, who threatened to destroy all of Zenia if she would not marry him. On those terms, she reluctantly agreed. During the wedding feast she poured him more wine than he could hold, and during the night she decapitated him. Running to the church, she cut off her hair and took the clothes of a soldier and the name of Captain Manolis. She performed many heroic deeds before she was killed. Her hair and the decapitating knife are still on display in the Zenia church.

Tzermiadon is the largest village of the **Lassithi plain,** high in the mountains and irrigated by white-sailed wind water pumps, 10,000 in all. This scenic way of supplying water was designed by Venetian engineers in 1464, after a crop shortage and after the fruit trees had been destroyed to punish rebellious locals. Although only 6000 of the wind water pumps are in use today, they still make a splendid sight against the mountains and green plain.

Of the 18 villages of Lassithi plain, **Tzermiadon** has the most tourist facilities, with a *panayiéri* on 6 November. The **Trapeza cave** here was inhabited in Neolithic times, but today one can only see the entrance, as the cave has been boarded up to prevent mishaps. From Tzermiadon one can walk (with a guide if possible) to the ancient city of **Karphi** (the nail), excavated by the British School of Archaeology under John Pendlebury from 1937-39. Karphi served as a city of Minoan refuge from the Doric invaders in the Sub-Minoan period, but its difficult situation caused it to be abandoned later. One can see the temple, the house of the chieftain, the tower and barracks, and there is an especially lovely view of Lassithi. The trip up takes about an hour and a half.

Kroustallenia Monastery, right by Tzermiadon, was built in 1541, and housed the local revolutionary council during the war. **Psykro,** on the other side of the plain, is the starting point for visiting the **Diktean cave,** the birthplace of Zeus. While ascent can be made easily by foot or donkey (100 dr. up and down), descent into the cave is rather more difficult. It is advisable to wear old trousers and rubber-soled shoes and bring a torch, although candles are available at the site. The cave, excavated by D. G. Hogarth of the British School of Archaeology, contained relics from Middle Minoan up to Archaic times. According to the ancient Hymn of the Kouretes, Zeus was hidden in this cave by his mother Rhea (see mythology, page 79). A crevice in the cave wall is known as his cradle while a row of large stalactites is called 'Zeus' mantle'. Other stories claim that Europa conceived Minos in the cave, and that when he became king he went there every nine years for paternal advice from Zeus. While the cult objects found prove a continuity of worship at Dikti before and after the Doric invasion, in a later period the worship of Zeus was transferred to the Idean cave.

In Psykro a tourist pavilion caters to cave visitors, and there are other restaurants and small hotels and rooms. On 29-31 August there is a three-day *panayiéri* in the village; nearby **Ag. Georgios** celebrates the saint of the same name on 23 April, and **Magoula** has a *panayiéri* for Ag. Spyridon on 12 December. A village on the nomos border, **Plati,** contains the remains of a Minoan settlement, inhabited before and after the Doric invasion.

Lovely **Kritsa** village a few miles above Ag. Nikolaos is the "authentic" Cretan village visited by tourists from Ag. Nikolaos. It is indeed worthy of a visit for its architecture (although destroyed by the Saracens, it was reconstructed after the liberation of Crete by Nikephoros Phokas), for the view of the bay below, and for excursions to ancient Lato, and particularly to the church **Kera Panayia.** Built in the early part of the Venetian period, this church is open from 9 am to 12 am and from 2 pm to 5 pm. Almost the entire wall surface is covered with magnificent frescoes, depicting the life of Mary's mother St. Anne, of Mary herself, and other scenes from the New Testament. On 15 August a *panayiéri* is held at the church, and around this time traditional Cretan weddings take place with food and dancing in which one can participate for an entrance fee. Ancient **Lato,** also known as Goulas, is an hour's walk from Kritsa or a rough drive. It was excavated by the French School of Archaeology and is splendidly situated in a depression between two hills which formed its acropolises. It is an Archaic town, built in the 7th century BC and influences from Minoan palaces have been noted in the agora and stairway. The streets are paved with flagstones, and the walls have a double gateway. There are remains of temples, houses, a cistern, and a Hellenic prytaneion, or meeting place of the town elders. Goulas is the fortified part of the town.

From Krista one can also visit **Kroustas,** a village untouched by the tourism further down the road. Kroustas has some very old frescoed churches and a huge festival on 25 June, the feast of St. John, with bonfires and dances. The bus to Krista goes to Kroustas occasionally. More frequent buses from Ag. Nikolaos go south to the popular beach at **Kalo Chorio;** from Kalo Chorio's model farm one can visit **Vrokastro,** inhabited from 1000 BC and used as a refuge settlement during the Doric invasion. A Geometric fort stands on the hill. Close to the east is **Gournia,** a site excavated by Harriet Boyd Hawes in the early part of this century. It is the best preserved Minoan town on Crete, reaching its peak in 1600 BC, and many workshops, storerooms, houses and a small palace remain, as well as signs of a mine near the shore.

From Gournia one can take a path to **Pahia Ammos,** a growing resort with a good beach. To the south (the road turns by Gournia) is the late Byzantine monastery **Faneromenos,** high on the hill and the site of many resistance activities during the Turkish Occupation. South of Pahia Ammos lies **Vasilikis,** where an Early Minoan settlement was discovered at the beginning of this century by two Americans, Boyd and Seager. Mottled pottery produced from the site has been given the name Vasiliki Ware. Red plastered rooms, corridors and a courtyard of the palace remain among other ruins.

Ierapetra at the end of the road is the largest town on the Lybian sea, and the furthest south in Greece, only 370 km. (230 miles) from Egypt. In mythology Ierapetra was founded by the Telchines from Rhodes, who had the heads of dogs and the flippers of seals. The name they gave Ierapetra was Kamiros, like that of another city they had founded on Rhodes, but when their presence on Crete continued to foul up the weather, Zeus sent them elsewhere. The Doric name of the town was Ierapytna. It prospered in the Hellenistic period as the most powerful city in Eastern Crete, and although destroyed by the Romans, the last city in Crete to resist their invasion, it was rebuilt by them in even grander style. In the Byzantine period it was the seat of a bishop, but it was ruined by the Saracens and later by an earthquake in 1508. In the 13th century the Genoese or Venetians built Kastelli on the coast, a fort which is well preserved today. Nearby is the house where tradition claims that Napoleon spent the night of 26 June 1798 before his campaign in Egypt. Beside it is an interesting mosque and minaret. There are also a few Roman remains to be seen to the west of the town, including a theatre. The archaeology museum of Ierapetra contains a lovely sarcophagus found in the village of Eskopi to the north and finds from the Roman town. While in summer it can be very hot, Ierapetra is exceedingly pleasant in the winter. There is a youth hostel and some hotels, but the best beaches are towards Makriyialos. On 3 October every year a big festival celebrates the 1821 revolution.

Along the coast west of Ierapetra is **Myrtos,** where in 1968 the British School of Archaeology excavated an early Minoan town which had been a weaving centre, dating from 2500 to 2100 BC. Some of the finds are in the Myrtos school house, while the more important ones are in the Ag. Nikolaos museum. In nearby **Pyrgos** a villa has been found with large rooms and a stairway. One popular way of going to Myrtos, other than on the new road, is to walk through the river bed from Males, which has a frescoed Byzantine church, Panayia Messochoritissa (1431). There is another church, Ag. Georgios, further south in a ruined village.

Along the coast east of Ierapetra to **Makriyialos** there are small beaches and pensions and a camping site, and at Makriyialos itself there are many tavernas. To the north, the village **Etia** was one of the major towns in the Byzantine and Venetian periods, noted for its lovely setting. The region was ruled by the De Mezzo family, who built a palace fortress in the 15th century, considered one of the greatest Venetian constructions in Crete. It was three storeys high, with vaulted ceilings and sculptured decorations. The Turks were besieged in the palace, however, and a later fire and earthquake finished the destruction, although today it has been partially restored. Of the many outlying buildings, the wall and gate and fountain house bear inscriptions.

The **monastery Ag. Sofia** is close by, towards the village of Handras. During the Turkish occupation it served as a fortress and secret school, and was often besieged and destroyed. **Praisos,** the ancient city north of Handras, has three acropolises. Inhabitation dated from late

Minoan to Hellenistic times, and the walls and houses remain. The capital of the Eteocretans — the "true Cretans" or descendants of the Minoans, Praisos was destroyed by the city of Ierapetra in 155 BC. East of Praisos is **Zakro** with a restaurant called The Maestro's, where the Maestro serenades diners with his violin. Erotokritoa is the Maestro's competitor. A huge gorge from Zakro leads to the palace of **Kato Zakro,** called "the Gorge of Death" from the Minoan tombs found in it. One can also go by the road on top of the ravine.

The town of Zakro was excavated by the English archaeologist Hogarth in 1901, but the palace itself was found in 1961 by N. Platon, and because this side of Crete is sinking, part of it now lies in the water. Built in the Late Minoan period, the palace was destroyed by a sudden collapse, followed by fire. Of its remains are a central court, a west wing with inscriptions, magazines, a lustral basin, archives, and a once-decorated banquet hall. After the great destruction the surrounding town of narrow cobblestoned streets was rebuilt, but the palace lay untouched. The evidence of such a large settlement in Zakro, which could hardly have supported it, demonstrates how extensively the Minoans traded by sea. There are rooms to let in Kato Zakro and a pebble beach. In Zakro itself a Minoan villa has been uncovered with wall paintings and wine presses, and on a summit is a round, Hellenistic beacon tower.

The road north of Zakro leads to **Petsofas,** where a peak sanctuary was dedicated to the fertility goddess, and where many votive offerings have been found. Further north is **Palaikastro,** the last bus stop for **Vai,** a beach with palm trees said to have been brought by the Saracens on which a taverna operates in the summer. There is a late Minoan settlement with streets and houses by the sea, at a place called Roussolakos. Another site is Kastri on a hill by the shore, where remains dating from Geometric to Hellenistic times have been uncovered. A Classical temple to Diktean Zeus existed there, and a hymn to Zeus from the 4th century was found engraved on a stone. Palaikastro has a fine beach lined with restaurants and tavernas.

North on Cape Sideros lies ancient **Itanos,** which can be reached by the road from Palaikastro or Toplou. Also known as Erimoupolis, this was inhabited from early Minoan times, although the ruins existing today are Geometric to Hellenistic. Ptolemy used it as a naval station, and the city thrived on the trade of dyes and glass. Early Christian ruins are below, but this settlement, as well as the small 15th century village, was deserted because of the Saracen and pirate raids.

The famous **monastery of Toplou** lies south-west of Itanos. Its real name is Panayia Akroteriani, but the name toplou (meaning cannon in Turkish from the huge cannon once possessed by the monastery) is more popular. Believed to have been founded by the Kornaros family, Toplou was built in the late 15th century and was repaired after earthquake destruction in 1612. It is three storeys high and a veritable fortress with a tall Italianate bell tower dated 1558. Above the monastery gate is a hole, Fonias, through which the besieged monks used to pour hot oil onto their attackers. It has a long history as a place of refuge and resistance. At the beginning of the War of Independence in 1821, the Turks captured it and hung the bodies of twelve monks on the gate. At the end of the war, however, the Turks found themselves in turn attacked by Cretans. They surrendered the monastery when the Cretans offered to spare the lives of other Turkish prisoners and to give them transport. Cretan occupation ended when the Great Powers decided the island should remain Turkish. There is a very beautiful icon in the monastery painted by Ioannis Kornaros in 1770, one of the masterpieces of Cretan art. There are other icons, manuscripts and a Hellenistic inscription describing the arbitration of Magnesia in a argument between Itanos and Ierapytna. One of the aisles is believed to have been part of a chapel to Ag. Isidoros, built when Nikephoros Phokas liberated Crete, which also gave its name to Cape Sideros.

West of Toplou is the pretty town of **Sitia** (Sithia in the softer Cretan pronounciation; La Sitia in Venetian times, thus forming the name of the nomos Lassithi). The site was once occupied by ancient Eteia, which produced Myson, one of the Seven Sages of Greece. Sitia later produced Vincenzo Kornaros, author of the *Erotokritos,* the 17th century Cretan national epic of a love formed, lost, and found again between Erotokritos and Aretousa, daughter of the King of Athens. Once surrounded by Byzantine, Genoese, and Venetian walls, besides a Venetian fortress, little now remains of these defences, due to earthquake and the bombardment of Barbarossa. Today Sitia exports raisins and is known for its wine. In the middle of August, a 3-day wine festival is held there. There is a lovely youth hostel run by a slightly mad Englishman, and there are many tavernas and restaurants along the shady waterfront. **Buses** leave from Sitia for most of the villages in the nomos, and the **Karpathos-Rhodes ship** stops on the way from Ag. Nikolaos. There are also sea connections with Santorini and Piraeus.

South of Sitia is **Piskokephelo,** another peak sanctury, near which a farm house has been excavated. On 24 June a large festival is held in the village. **Zou** to the south has a Minoan villa, and a cave in **Maronia** contained Early Minoan finds. **Lithine** even further south is a charming village, with the remains of a once important Venetian tower. In **Chamezi** west of Sitia an oval, prehistoric house or sanctuary was discovered. Two bee hive tombs in **Mesa Mouliana** date from the end of the Bronze Age; and in **Exo Mouliana,** famous for its wine, is a frescoed church, Ag. Georgios (1426). **Myrsini** is a Venetian village with important Minoan tombs in the vicinity; and **Kavousi** had a small Sub-Minoan settlement and a peak sanctuary, although little remains of them.

Area Codes in Crete

Kissamos, Vathi, Topolia, Kaludiana, Platanos: 0822
Kandanos, Voutes, Paliochora, Rodovanion: 0823

Kolymvario, Ag. Marina, Voukoliai: 0824
Chania, Maleme, Galatas, Meskla, Lakkoi, Alikianos, Perivolia, Souda, Pazinos, Kounoupidiana: 0821
Vamos, Neo Choro, Kalyvai, Ag. Roumeli, Anopolis, Chora Sfakio, Patsianos, Vrysi, Georgioupolis: 0825
Rethymnon, Episkopi, Roustika, Armeni, Pigi: 0831
Spili, Myrtios, Ag. Galini, Melaves: 0832
Amario, Apodoulou: 0833
Perama, Mylopotamou, Panormos, Margariti, Koumerio, Anogia, Garagon: 0834
Ag. Varvara, Gergeri, Zaros: 0894
Myres, Vori, Tymbaki, Pompia, Ag. Deka: 0892
Herakleon, Rodia, Marados, Tylissos, Gazion, Ag. Myron: 081
Krouson, Arkane, Venerato, Prof. Elias, Hani Kokini, Pyrgos: 0893
Arkalohori, Thrapsano, Kastelli, Partira, Garipa: 0891
Ano Viannos, Emparos, Hondros, Arvi, Kefalo Vrisio: 0895
Ierapetra, Hiprokambos, Males, Pahia Ammos, Kavousi, Kato Chorio: 0842
Ag. Nikolaos, Neapolis, Skisma, Elounda, Krista: 0841
Tzermiadon, Ag. Georgios: 0844
Limin Kersonisou, Malia, Mohos, Gouves: 0897
Sitia, Skopi, Toplou, Stavrochorio, Handras, Zakro, Palaikastro: 0843

Cheap Accommodation in Crete
Ag. Nikolaos Youth Hostel, 3 Stratigou Koraka, tel. (0841) 28121
Chania Youth Hostel, 33 Drakonianou (Ag. Ioannes bus) tel. (0821) 53565
Herakleon Youth Hostel, 24 Handakos St., tel. (081) 286281
Ierapetra Youth Hostel, 32 Stratigou Samuel, tel. (0842) 22463
Malia Youth Hostel (open only 15/4-30/9), tel. (0897) 31355
Rethymnon YWCA, Timiou Stavrou, tel. (0831) 29330
Sitia Youth Hostel, 24 Agelaki St., tel. (0843) 22693
Camping sites exist near Chania, Mournies (nomos Chania), on the coast east of Rethymnon, 5 miles east of Ierapetra, and at Limin Kersonisou (nomos Herakleon). Many others are in the planning.

Hotels in Crete
The best hotel in Chania is the relatively modern, air conditioned Kydon (A) which is not far from the harbour. More modest and less expensive, Aptera Beach (C) is located about three miles from town. It is one of the slew of hotels that dot the sandy north coast of Crete, providing easy access to fine beaches while complicating transport to villages and sites. This has given rise to a prosperous tourist bus system that is not only convenient, but twice as expensive as local bus lines. More elaborate hotels served mainly by tourist buses are Knossosbeach and Candia

Beach (both A) outside Herakleon. In downtown Herakleon the Astir (A) is the most centrally located, boasting a fine restaurant on the roof. Two others, Atlantis (A) and Astoria (A), also in town, have air conditioning and swimming pools. However, in choosing a hotel in Herakleon, one of the largest cities in Greece, it is necessary to weigh the convenience against the noise. The Greeks are night people, and even though most of the discotheques and nightclubs are outside the city walls, the biggest complaint of guests is the racket outside.

In the somber medieval Rethymnon, where noise is rarely a problem, the Xenia (B) by the sea is very pleasant, although the town beach isn't as impeccably clean as those by the El Greco (A) and Rithymna (A), both about four miles from town. Mallia, outside one of the major Minoan sites, is little more than beach and accommodation, Ikaros Village (A) being one of the more imaginative (or less, depending on how one looks at it) as it is built like a typical Cretan village.

Ag. Nikolaos, as the tourist capital of Crete, has the grandest hotels on the island, beginning with the architecturally original Hermes (A) on the favourite sea-side promenade of cafés, tavernas, hotels, and nightclubs. Just beyond town is the beautifully situated Minos Beach Bungalows (L), popular with film makers, and the Mirabello (L-A) complex with a fabulous discotheque. The ultimate in hotels, however, is Elounda Beach (L), a few miles north of Ag. Nikolaos in the little fishing village Elounda. Not only does it offer every luxury, but it is considered one of the finest and loveliest hotels in Europe. Of course tours to almost any point on Crete can be initiated from these hotels themselves.

in Ag. Galini (Rethymnon): area code 0832
B: Galini (Furnished apartments)
C: Acropolis, Bizaniou St., tel. 91234/91264
C: Astoria, Bizaniou St., tel. 91253
C: Candia, 15 Arkadiou St., tel. 91203
C: Cristof, 2 Bizaniou St., tel. 91229
C: Dedalos, Arkadiou St., tel. 91214
C: Miramare, 12 Bizaniou St., tel. 91221
C: Selena
C: Soulia, tel. 91272
D: Angelo, 7 Bizaniou St., tel. 91257
D: Ikaros, tel. 91270
D: Livii, 25 J. Daskaloyanni, tel. 91216
D: Mathios, tel. 91205
D: Minos, tel. 91218/91292
E: Aktaeon, 5 Kountouriotou, tel. 91208
E: Kydon, 2 El. Venizelou, tel. 91228
E: Pantheon, Kountouriotou, tel. 91293
in Ag. Nikolaos (Lassithi): area code 0841
L: Minos Beach (bungalows), Akti Elia Sotirchou, Ammoudi, tel. 22345 or in Athens 3619785; teleg. Minosbeach.
L: Mirabello (bungalows), tel. 28400/28806; teleg. Mirabello

A: Mirabello, tel. 28400/28806; teleg. Mirabello
A: Hermes, Ammoudi, Akti Koundourou, tel. 28253; teleg. Hermeshotel
B: Ariadne Beach Bungalows, Gargadoros, tel. 22741; teleg. Ariadni
Aghios Nicolaos
B: Coral, Akti Koumoudourou, tel. 28363/28159; teleg. Hotelcoral
B: Ikaros (pension), Ammoudi St., Tel. 22623
B: Polydoros (pension), Ammoudi St., tel. 22623
C: Acratos, 19 28th Octovriou St., tel. 22721; teleg. Acratotel
C: Alcestis (Alkistis), 30 S. Koudourou, tel. 28170/22454; teleg. Alkistis
C: Argyro (pension), 1 Solonos, tel. 28707
C: Athina (pension), 34a Pringhipos Armostou Georgiou
C: Creta, 22 Sarolidi, tel. 22518/28893; teleg. Hotelcreta
C: Cronos, 4 N. Plastira, tel. 28761/22217
C: Delta, Tselepi, Kitroplatia, tel. 28991; teleg. Hoteldelta
C: Du Lac, 17 28th Octovriou, tel. 22711
C: Pergola (pension), Mykos
C: Rhea, 10 Marathonos & Milatou, tel. 28321/26109; teleg. Maris
D: Lato, 12 Iossif Koundourou, Limin, tel. 22319; teleg. Hotel Lato
E: Aegeon, 2 28th Octovriou, tel. 22773
in Amoudara (Herakleon); area code 081
A: Creta Beach, tel. 286301/216896
in Anogia (Rethymnon); area code 0834
E: Imarmeni, tel. 31242
E: Psiloritis, tel. 31231
in Arkadi (Rethymnon): area code 0834
B: Arkadi (ex Xenia), tel. 71227
in Arkanes (Herakleon): area code 081
B: Dias, tel. 75810
in Chania (Chania): area code 0821
A: Kydon, Platia S. Venizelou, tel. 26190; teleg. Kydonchania
B: Doma, 124 El. Venizelou, tel. 21772
B: Lissos, 68 Vas. Konstantinou, tel. 24671/24672; teleg. Lissotel Chania
B: Xenia, tel. 24562
B: Porto Veneziano (Eneticos Limin), Akti Enosseos, tel. 29311
B: Samaria, Kydonias & Zimvrakakidon, tel. 51551
C: Aptera Beach (bungalows), Paralia Ag. Apostolon, Aptera, tel.
22636/23973; teleg. Apterahotel Chania
C: Canea, 16 Platia 1866, tel. 24673; teleg. Caneahotel Chania
C: Diktynna, 1 Betollo, tel. 21101; teleg. Dictynnahotel
C: Elyros, 5 Mylonoyanni, tel. 22462
C: Hellinis, 68 Tzanakaki
C: Kriti, N. Phoca & Kyprou, tel. 21881
C: Kypros, 17 Tzanakaki, tel. 218815
C: Lucia, Akti Kountourioti, tel. 21821
C: Plaza, 1 Tombazi, tel. 22540
D: Avra, 30 Petrof, Nea Chora, tel. 23654
D: Hermes, 23 Yannari, tel. 22317

D: Nea Ionia, 3 Verovitch Passa, tel. 22706
E: Averof, 11 Platia 1866, tel. 23090
E: Piraeus, 14 Zabeliou, tel. 22754
E: Viennos, 27 Skalidi, tel. 22470
in Chora Sfakion (Chania): area code 0825
B: Xenia (pension), tel. 91202
in Elounda (Lassithi): area code 0841
L: Elounda Beach (hotel & bungalows), tel. 28461; teleg. Elotel
C: Aristea, Shisma, tel. 4301
in Episkopi (Rethymnon): area code 0831
D: Minos, tel. 61208/61249
in Gournes (Herakleon): area code 081
B: America, 42 25th Martiou, tel. 76231
in Gouves (Herakleon): area code 0897
A: Candia Beach, tel. 41241; teleg. Canbeach Hericliou
in Herakleon (Herakleon): area code 081
A: Astir, 25th Avgoustou, tel. 282222/285025/283265; teleg. Astirotel
A: Astoria, 5 Platia Eleftherias, tel. 286462/285025; teleg. Astoriotel
A: Atlantis, Meramvellou & Hygias, tel. 288241, teleg. Atlantisheraklion
A: Knossos Beach (hotel & bungalows), Hani Kokkini, tel. 288450/76204/282059; teleg. Knossosbeach
A: Xenia, Archiepiskopou Makariou, tel. 28400; teleg. Hotelxenia
B: Cosmopolit, 44 Evans, tel. 283313/284055; teleg. Cosmopolite
B: Esperia, 20 Idomeneos & Meramvellou, tel. 288211; teleg. Esperotel
B: Kastro, 20 Theotokopoulou, tel. 285020/284185; teleg. Kastrotel
B: Mediterranean, 1 Smyrnis, Platia Daskaloyanni, tel. 289331; teleg. Mediterranean
B: Xenon Georgiades (pension), 17 Kandanoleon, tel. 284808
C: Akti, 13th km. Ethnikis Odou, Hani Kokkini, tel. 761260
C: Daedalos, 15 Daedalou, tel. 224391
C: Domenico, 14 Almyrou, tel. 288231; teleg. Domenicoheracleion
C: El Greco, 4 1821 St., tel. 281071; teleg. Elgreco
C: Galini, 15 Aegeou Poros, tel. 288223
C: Gortis (pension), 4 Akrotiriou, tel. 280613
C: Heracleion, 128 Kalokairinou & Delimarcou, tel. 281881
C: Ilion (pension), 1 Priansou, Leoforos 62 Martyron, tel. 283867
C: Ivi (pension), 37 Rafkou, tel. 289039
C: Knossos, 43 25th Avgoustou, tel. 283247
C: Mirabello, 18 Theotokopoulou
C: Mykonos, 22 Minotavrou, tel. 287395
C: Olympic, Platia Kornarou, tel. 288861; teleg. Olympicotel
C: Park, 5 Coroneou, tel. 283934/284404; teleg. Parkhotel
C: Pasiphae, 34 Possidonos Poros, tel. 283135
C: Phaedra, 11 Satha Kamaraki, tel. 223950
C: Poseidon, 46 Possidonos Poros, tel. 285859/222545
C: Prince (Pringips), 44 Konitsis Poros, tel. 287107

C: Selena, 7 Androgeo, tel. 287660
D: Vines (Klimataries) (pension), 13 Koritsas Poros, tel. 285751
D: Arcadi, 235 Leoforos Kalokarinou, tel. 282077
D: Florida, 6 25th Avgoustou, tel. 283246
D: Minos, 24 Arch. Makariou, tel. 282256/282107
D: Palladion, 16 Chandakos, tel. 282563
D: Phaestos, 8 Tsakiri, tel. 283027
D: Venetia, 189 Leoforos Kalokairinou, tel. 283239
E: Ariadne, 26 Petlebouri, tel. 285675
E: Chania, 19 Kydonias, tel. 282832/284282
E: Criticon, 26 Evans, tel. 220211
E: Idaeon Andron, 1 Perdikari, tel. 283624
E: Ionia, 5 Evans, tel. 281795
E: Moderno, 202 Leoforos Kalokairinou, tel. 283006
in **Ierapetra** (Lassithi): area code 0842
C: Creta, Platia El. Venizelou, tel. 22316/22550
C: Lygia, Parodos Kyrba, tel. 28881/28882
C: Myrtos, Myrto
D: Alkyon, 16 M. Kothri Paralia, tel. 22211; teleg. Alkyon
D: Arcadi, 4 Dom. Theotokopoulou, tel. 28665
D: Ierapytna, Platia Ag. Ioannou Kale, tel. 28530
E: Livykon, 37 Navarcho Koundouriotou, tel. 22370/22371
E: Venizelos, 17 Koraka, tel. 28675
in **Kamilarion** (Herakleon): area code 0892
E: Oasis, tel. 22709
in **Karteros** (Herakleon): area code 081
B: Amnissos (bungalows), tel. 281332
B: Motel Xenia, tel. 281841
in **Kissamos** (Kastelli) (Chania): area code 0822
C: Castle (Kastron), Platia Castelliou, tel. 22140
D: Possidon, tel. 22424
E: Morpheus, tel. 22086/22475
in **Kolimbario** (Chania): area code 0824
D: Rose Marie, tel. 21220/21294
in **Limin Kersonissou** (Herakleon): area code 0897
A: Belvedere, tel. 22251/220105; teleg. Belotel
A: Creta Maris (hotel & bungalows), tel. 22115; teleg. Cremotel Greece
B: Nora, tel. 22271; teleg. Norotel
C: Avra, Kastri, tel. 22203
C: Eva, tel. 21090
C: Glaros
C: Helena, tel. 22226
in **Linoperamata** (Herakleon): area code 081
A: Zeus Beach, tel. 223761; teleg. Akti Zeus
in **Maleme** (Chania): area code 0821
B: Maleme Beach (hotel & bungalows), tel. 91221; teleg. Malotel
Chania

in Malia (Herakleon): area code 0897
A: Ikaros Village, tel. 31267; teleg. Ikaros Village
A: Kernos Beach (bungalows), tel. 31421; teleg. Kernoshotel
A: Sirens Beach, tel. 31321; teleg. Sirensmalia
B: Grammatikaki (pension), tel. 31366/31390
B: Malia Beach, tel. 31210/313013
D: Golden Bee (Chryssi Mellissa), tel. 31243
in Myres (Herakleon): area code 0892
D: Olympic, tel. 22777/22477
in Neapolis (Lassithi): area code 0841
D: Neapolis, 1 Evangelistrias, tel. 32268
in Omalos (Chania): area code 0821
B: Xenia (Pavillon), tel. 93237
in Paliokastro (Lassithi): area code 0843
E: Itanos, 22508/22227
in Paliochora (Chania): area code 0823
D: Livykon, tel. 41250
in Panormos (Rethymnon): area code 0834
B: Lavris, tel. 51226
D: Romantika
in Phaistos (Herakleon): area code 0892
D: Xenia (Pavillon), tel. 22836
in Plakias (Rethymnon): area code 0832
C: Alianthos, Kinotiki Odos Myrthiou-Plaka, tel. 31227
C: Livykon, tel. 31216
in Psykro (Lassithi): area code 0844
D: Zeus, tel. 31284
E: Dictaeon Andron
E: Heleni
in Rethymnon: area code 0831
A: El Greco (hotel & bungalows), Kampos Pigis, tel. 71281; teleg. Elgreco Rethymnon
A: Rithymna (hotel & bungalows), Adele, tel. 29492
B: Idaeon, 9 Nikolaou Plastira, tel. 28667/22346 (Reserv.), teleg. Ideon Rethymnon
B: Xenia, 30 N. Psarou, tel. 29111; teleg. Xenihotel
C: Brascos, Ch. Daskalaki & Th. Moatsou, tel. 28867
C: Minos, Perivolia, tel. 28439/29233
C: Park, 7 Igoumenou Gavriil, tel. 29958
C: Valari, 84 Kountouriotou, tel. 22236/29368
D: Acropole, Platia Heroon, tel. 29774
D: Minoa, 60 Arcadiou, tel. 22508
E: Achillion, 151 Arcadiou, tel. 22581
E: Diethnes, 20 Platia Tessaron Martyron, tel. 22547
E: Paradissos, 35 Igoumenou Gavriil, tel. 22419
in Sitia (Lassithi): area code 0843
C: Alice, 34 Papanastassiou, tel. 28450/28441, in Athens 3619684

C: Crystal, 17 Kapetan Sifi, tel. 22284/28484
C: Itanos, tel. 22146/22900; teleg. Itanos
C: Sitia, 28 Kapetan Sifi, tel. 28155/22316
D: Archontiko, 161 Kondylaki, tel. 28172
D: Flisvos, 4 C. Karamanli, tel. 22422
D: Minos, 31 Therissou, tel. 28331
D; Mysson, 82 Myssonos, tel. 22304
D: Praessos, 9 G. Mavrikaki, tel. 22325
D: Stars (Astra), 37 M. Kalyvaki
in Souda (Chania): area code 0821
D: Knossos, Platia Pringipos Georgiou, tel. 89282
D: Parthenon, Platia Pringipos Georgiou, tel. 89245
in Stalis (Herakleon): area code 0897
A: Anthoussa Beach, tel. 31380
B: Blue Sea (bungalows), tel. 31371; teleg. Achro Heraklion
in Tzermiadon (Lassithi): area code 0844
E: Dictaeon Andron
in Zakros (Lassithi): area code 0843
C: Zakros, 1 Eleftherias, tel. 28479

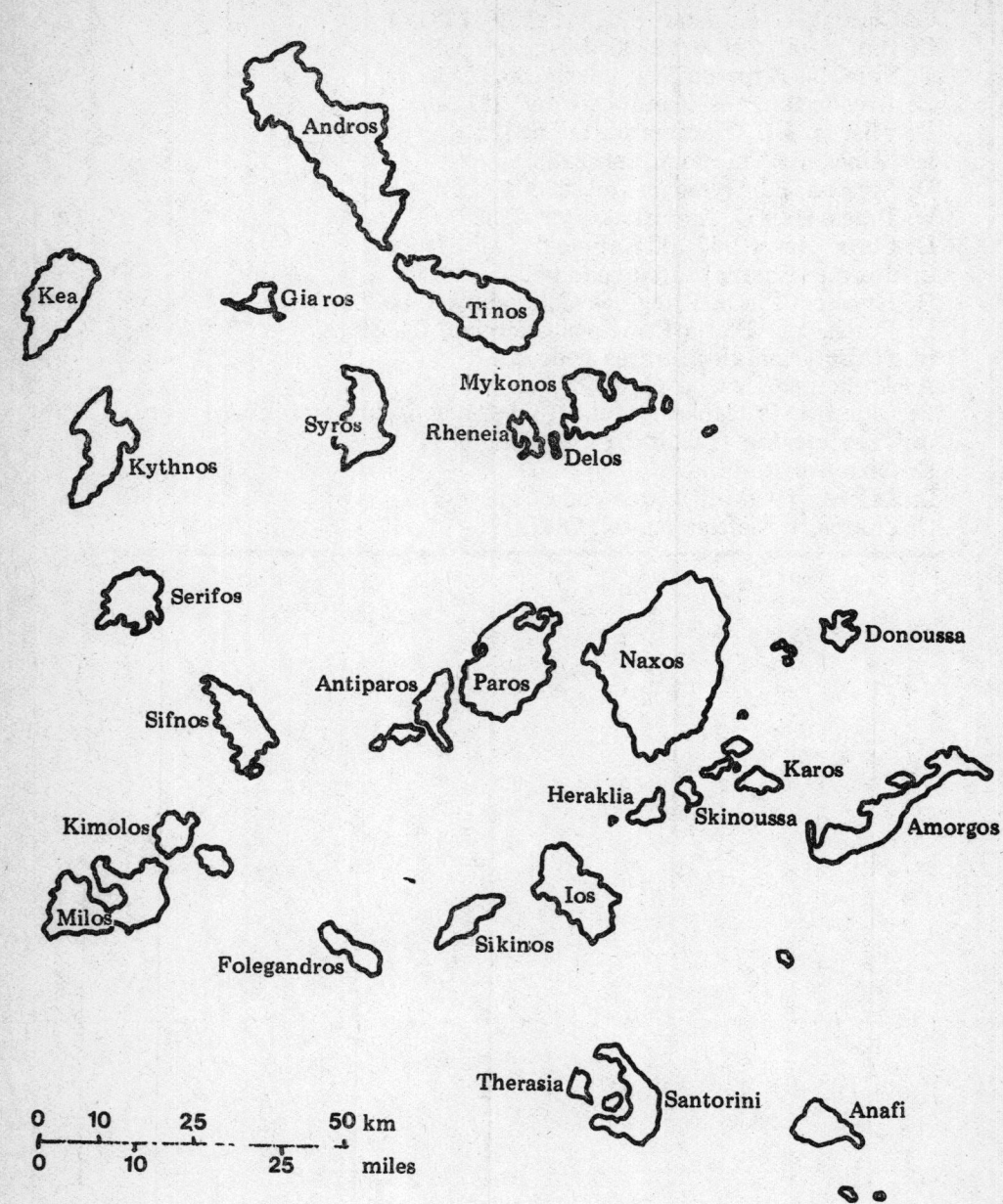

Andros

Kea

Giaros

Tinos

Mykonos

Syros

Rheneia

Delos

Kythnos

Serifos

Sifnos

Antiparos

Paros

Naxos

Donoussa

Kimolos

Heraklia

Karos

Skinoussa

Amorgos

Milos

Ios

Folegandros

Sikinos

Therasia

Santorini

Anafi

0   10   25   50 km
0   10   25   miles

The Cyclades

Part 7
The Cyclades

When imagining a Greek island, many people picture one of the Cyclades, with archetypal rocky terrain, asymmetrical white houses and narrow dwarf-like streets, with a church squeezed in at every corner. As they are relatively close together, one can visit a variety of the islands without losing much of the holiday in transit; in the summer there are daily communications between them. Yet within the Cyclades (the 'circling' islands around Delos, the tiny centre of ancient Greek spiritual life), one can find, besides such constant favourites as Mykonos, Santorini, and Paros, some of the most untouched islands in Greece such as Anafi and Kimolos.

Archaeological evidence suggests that the Cyclades have been inhabited since at least 6000 BC, the first settlers traditionally coming from Karia in Asia Minor and speaking a non-Greek language. Later the Karians were supplanted by the Phoenicians, who in the beginning of the Bronze Age developed a culture known as Early Cycladic, which lasted from 3000 to 2000 BC, or until the advent of the Cretan thalassocracy. The most familiar product of the Early Cycladic civilization are the sculptured figurines of the fertility goddess, so beautiful in their utter simplicity.

Mythology mentions Minos of Crete conquering the Aegean islands in order to rid himself of his overly just brother Rhadamanthus, whom he sent to administer the new Cretan colonies. This period of Minoan influence on the islands occurred during the Middle Cycladic period; the Late Cycladic period coincides with the fall of Crete and the rise of the

119

Myceneans. When the Myceneans in turn fell to their Dorian conquerors, a dark age fell on the islands which lasted for hundreds of years. Many islands, however, were under the Ionian influence, and spoke the Ionian dialect.

Towards the end of the 8th century BC, a new culture, the Archaic, flourished in Ionia and on the islands. The rise of the Persians, however, caused the Ionians to flee westwards to Attica, and the islands were left at the mercy of the Persians, whom some of them actively supported at Marathon and Salamis. The Athenians punished those who had sided with their enemy and obliged the islands to enter into the new maritime league they had formed at Delos in 478 BC. This replaced an older Ionian council, or Amphictyony. But what began as a council of allies gradually turned into a tribute to the Athenians, as their fleet was the only one capable of protecting the islands from the Persian menace. As the islands were proud of their independence, they naturally resented Athenian encroachment in their affairs, compelling the Athenians to put down many a rebellion and to extort the yearly contribution of money and ships through physical force.

During the Peloponnesian War the islands generally sided with the city on top at any given time, although many jumped at the chance to support Sparta against the Athenian oppressors. But when Athens recovered from the war in 378 BC, she formed a second Delian league, again subjugating the Cyclades. Most of these turned to Phillip of Macedon as his star rose into ascendancy and were later to become the subject of many battles between the generals of Alexander the Great.

In the beginning of the 2nd century BC the Romans captured the islands, bringing a certain amount of peace with their conquest. Some of the islands were later given to Rhodes, who proved a less kind ruler. The fall of Rome, however, spelt centuries of hardship for the islands. Although they were officially part of the Byzantine Empire, Constantinople could not protect the islands from the numerous marauders prowling the high seas and the islanders were left to fend for themselves, building villages in the most inaccessible places possible.

When Constantinople fell in 1207, the Frankish conquerors allotted the Aegean to the Venetians, and the islands became a free for all between young noblemen and the pirates (sometimes one and the same). The Cyclades became the special territory of Marco Sanudo, nephew of the leader of the Fourth Crusade, Doge Enrico Dandolo. Marco Sanudo as Duke of Naxos ruled that island and Paros by himself and gave the smaller islands to his barons, who still owed allegiance to Naxos. The Crispo dynasty followed the Sanudos in 1383, but as pirates and the growing Ottoman Empire caused increasing difficulties Venice herself stepped in to bring about a certain amount of control at the end of the 15th century. A few decades later, however, the islands were systematically decimated by the pirate admiral Khair-ed-din-Barbarossa, and by the mid-16th century they were under Turkish domination.

The Venetians had managed to convert many of the Greeks on the Cyclades to the Catholic faith, in particular on Syros, and during the Ottoman occupation both Orthodox and Catholic monasteries thrived. Nominally the islands continued to be ruled by the Duke of Naxos, but he was now a mere puppet of the Sultan. Turkish rule was only economically harsh on most of the islands, which were spared the cruelties inflicted on Crete. Following Catherine the Great's luckless adventure in the Aegean under the Orlavs in the 18th century, the Greek War of Independence broke out. Cycladic participation consisted mainly of naval support and harbouring refugees, since under French protection (for the Catholic population) many islands retained a neutral stance in the conflict. However, in the early years of the Greek nation the Cyclades were added to its territory. Syros led the ports of Greece at the time, but lost the position to Piraeus with the advent of the steamship. Today that island's capital, Ermoupoulis, is still the largest town and administrative centre of the Cyclades.

Most of the Cyclades have suffered a drastic drop in population in this century due to the lack of fertile soil and fresh water. The islanders who have remained make a living from fishing and tourism for the most part. The Cyclades have an excellent dry, comfortable climate, air conditioned naturally by the north Meltemi wind. On some islands there may be water shortages in the summer, which may cause the water to be turned off half the time. Little signs beg tourists to limit themselves to one shower a day and should be heeded.

Amorgos

Connections: In the summer there are daily boats from Naxos; in the winter the mail caique goes two or three times a week. There are also less frequent summer connections with Ios and Santorini and once a week with Rhodes, Kos, Kalymnos, Astypalaia, Folegandros and Piraeus.

History: Both Amorgos and its neighbouring islet Karos have produced artifacts from the pre-Mycenean period, certain tombs on Amorgos dating back to 3300 BC. In 1885 the German archaeologist Dummler found 11 ancient cemeteries, with many fine ceramics now to be seen in Oxford and Copenhagen. Much work in marble has also been found, along with signs of trade with Milos and Egypt. There were three ancient, independent cities on Amorgos in Cycladic times, each minting its own coins and worshipping Dionysus and Athena. Kastri (modern Arkesini) was settled by Naxians, Minoa by Samians, and Aegiali by Milians.

In the 5th century BC Amorgos joined the Delian Alliance; later the Alexandrian gods, Serapis and Isis, were worshipped widely, for Ptolemy of Egypt was the Hellenistic ruler of the island. In the Roman period exiles were sent to Amorgos, and this downhill trend continued when the island was ravaged by Goths, Vandals, and Slavs during the Byzantine period. One bright moment in this dark history was during the War of the

Iconoclasts, when a miraculous icon sailed to Amorgos, set adrift, according to tradition, by an icon-loving lady from Constantinople. As the icon showed a preference for staying by the cliffs on Amorgos' south coast, Emperor Alexis Comnenus founded the Chozoviotissa monastery there in 1088 to house it. In 1209 the Duke of Naxos, Marco Sanudo, seized the island with an army of Naxians, and Gizi later built the town castle, for pirates were a plague up until the 19th century. The 17th century saw an increase of wealth on the island despite Turkish occupation (1537-1823). Part of this new wealth came from the women who made extraordinary embroideries throughout the 17th to 19th centuries, some of which are on display at the Victoria and Albert Museum in London. So many cloths were exported that a hero of the revolution, General Makriyiannis, threatened to declare war on Amorgos should the island send any more abroad: but Amorgos heeded not. However, rather than battling with Makriyiannis, the island simply ran out of embroideries, and no one now remembers how to make them. The highlight of the island's later history occurred when Brigitte Bardot paid it a visit in 1973.

Amorgos today is divided in half, north and south, by the lack of road between the two sides. **Aegiali,** the village in the north, is a modest tourist resort reached by caique from the port Katapola. From Katapola the island's only road goes to the capital Amorgos, and to Arkesini. Enough fruit and oil is produced on the island to supply the needs of the 2000 inhabitants but little more. The women still do some embroidery. **Panayiéria** on Amorgos are unique in that they are run like pot-luck dinners: everyone brings a dish and eats for free. Those who shun the little hotels at Aegiali can find rooms in the southern part of the island even in the summer with little difficulty, as the island's tourist industry is of modest proportions.

Above the port **Katapola,** which has a **yacht supply station,** are the ruins of the ancient city of **Minoa,** on Mt. Profitis Elias. Walls of the city and the acropolis are preserved, along with a few remains of a temple of Apollo. The inhabitants believe the name Minoa comes from Minos, the King of the Mountain, or Minos, the King of Crete, although the great city states of Amorgos were a product of the Ionian culture; the island is closer to Asia Minor than the other Cyclades. It takes about an hour to hike up to Minoa, more commonly known today as Moundalia. Also near Katapola is **Rakidi** with the church Ag. Georgios on the site of an oracle used in antiquity.

The other ancient city in the south part of Amorgos is **Arkesini,** at the present village of **Kastri.** More extensive tombs, walls, and houses remain here than at the other two ancient sites. The town of **Amorgos,** also known as Chora, is a typical white Cycladic town, which sits more than 300 metres (1000 ft.) above sea level. In the middle of town, on a rocky mount, is the castle built by Geremia Gizi in 1290. The locals call it Apano Kastro, and steps lead up to it; it is well preserved and affords a panoramic view of the island. An ancient tower, almost completely intact, can be seen at Ag. Trias, quite a walk away.

A road has been built to the **monastery Chozoviotissa,** and cars now replace the mule as the most popular form of transport to this huge, white fortress monastery at the foot of an orange cliff 600 metres (200 ft.) high.

One huge wall encloses 100 rooms, two churches, and at the present time of writing four monks. The miraculous icon of the Madonna from Constantinople is still inside, along with 98 hand-written manuscripts in its library. For many years a mysterious spear, thrown by unknown, impossible hands, was stuck in the rock of the cliff over the monastery, and although it finally fell down, worn away by time, there are still many stories about it. In 1976 a less mysterious rock fell on the monastery and went through three floors, but repairs have been carried out by the government.

Although most people go to the northern side of the island by caique, there is a path through the rocky rugged region, guarded on either side by the occasional tower, and others can be seen in the Rekti ravine. **Aegiali** (also Egiali or Ghiale) has only a few remains of its ancient walls, but one can see the **Tholaria,** or Greek vaulted tombs dating from Roman times. In Aegiali are concentrated the island's hotels, restaurants, and one very nice sandy beach. Some of the windmills still turn in the mighty Aegean winds. Smaller beaches on Amorgos can be located at Ag. Panteleimon, Ag. Paraskevi, Ag. Anna, Kato Mera, and at Kolofanou.

Hotels: In Aegiali, Mike, rated C, is open July-September. Ideal for those seeking escape from worldly strife, it is simple but clean. The guaranteed freedom from crowds may be worth more than the luxury Mike lacks. There are also rooms in houses, both in Aegiali and the other villages.

Panayiéria: 21 November, at the Monastery Chozoviotissa; 26 July, Ag. Paraskevi at Arkesini.

Specialities: Fava beans and embroidered scarves.

Of the many **islets** which lie between Naxos and Amorgos, ships from Piraeus go twice a week to Heraklia and Donoussa. **Heraklia** has a large cave and an ancient Greek fort with a tower; **Donoussa** has signs of a prehistoric settlement. **Karos** produced signs of very early inhabitation, besides the medieval ruins situated in the north. Uninhabited **Skinoussa** was also inhabited in the Middle Ages, and there are fresh water springs and a type of mastic tree still growing on the islet. These places are hardly prepared for tourists, although ideal for lovers of the remote. Visitors should bring their own beds if not board along, as the islets are poor and the local shop may not sell very much.

Anafi
Connections: Twice a week from Piraeus, once a week from Santorini (inquire at the Domigos agency).

History: According to mythology, Anafi rose at the command of Apollo to shelter Jason and the Argonauts, besieged by a tempest, and has ever since kept its 28 sq. km. (11 sq. mile) head out of the water. In the 15th century BC, however, a great deal of volcanic rock, 5 metres (16 ft.) thick in some places, was added to Anafi from the explosion of Santorini, brought by wind and tidal wave. Both Apollo and Artemis were worshipped on the island from early times, and the ruins of their temple remain on the site of the ancient town. The twelfth Duke of Naxos, Giacamo Crispi, gave Anafi to his brother who built a castle, which did very little when the terror of the Aegean, Barbarossa, turned up, enslaving the entire population. For a long time Anafi remained deserted, people trickling back only when it was safer.

Anafi today is one of the most primitive islands in Greece; it has only one telephone, one real village, no roads, no hotels, no restaurants but three cafés, and one place to swim. Very few of the few people who live there can speak English. The visitor may find lodging in a private house, but dinner is more difficult and likely to be limited to bread and macaroni and perhaps a little fish. Fresh water is scarce, as is any fresh fruit or vegetables. Very little contact with the outside world has left many old customs intact, and some have suggested that the island's songs and *panayiéria* retain traits from the ancient cult of Apollo.

The temple of Apollo and Artemis is east of the present village of **Anafi,** surrounded by a pile of rock and wall which was once a town; down towards **Katalymatakia** are ruins of ancient houses. The castle built by Gulglielmo Crispi is further north, and half-ruined.

Panayiéria: 15 August at the Monastery Panayia Kalamiotissa, with special folk lore dances. Other festivities late in autumn.

Andros
Connections: Daily ferryboat from Rafina, connected by same line to Tinos and Syros.

History: The name Andros is thought to have derived from the Phoenician Arados, or perhaps from Andrea, the general sent by Rhadamanthus of Crete to govern the island. In 1000 BC Ionians colonized Andros, leading to its early cultural bloom in the Archaic period. Dionysos was the most popular god worshipped at the pantheon on Palaiopolis, the leading city at the time, and a certain temple of his had the remarkable talent of turning water into wine during the Dionysia.

After the Athenian victory at Salamis, Themostokles came to Andros in search of the Athenian tribute. As the Andrians refused to give it, he attacked the island, although unsuccessfully. Although the islanders later assisted the Greeks at Plataea, Athenians held a grudge against Andros, and in 448 BC Perikles divided the island between Athenian colonists, who taxed the inhabitants heavily. In response the Andrians supported

Athens' enemies whenever they could: when the Peloponnesian War broke out, they withdrew from the Delian alliance and sided with Sparta, supporting that city throughout the war, in spite of siege by Alcibiades and Konon. Spartan oppression, however, proved just as awful as Athenian oppression, and things were no better during the succession of Hellenistic rulers, although a magnificent statue of Hermes, the Conductor of the Dead, dating from the 1st or 2nd century BC and found at Palaiopolis, suggests that at least art survived the constant change of kings.

For putting up resistance to their conquest, the Romans banished the entire population of Andros to Boetia. When a later ruler permitted their return, the inhabitants found their homes pillaged and faced many a rough year. Byzantium proved a blessing compared with the past, despite Saracen raiding. In the Venetian free for all, another nephew of Doge Enrico Dandolo, Marino Dandolo, took Andros, and allied himself with his cousin Marco Sanudo, the Duke of Naxos. Most of the surviving fortifications were constructed during Dandolo's reign.

In 1566 the Turks took the island. Apart from collecting taxes, they left the island more or less to its own devices, and many Albanians from nearby Karystos, Evia settled on Andros. In 1821 Andros' famous son, the philosopher Theophilos Kairis, declared the revolution at the cathedral of Andros. The island contributed money and weapons to the struggle. In 1943 the Germans bombed the island for two days when the Italians stationed there refused to surrender.

One of the largest and most populated of the Cyclades **Andros** today is an island famed for sailors and ship owners; the latter have built large mansions in the capital. Vegetation and rock share the land equally, and there is much fresh water, especially mineral water which is commercially exploited. Only at Vatsi, with its villas, hotels, and sandy beach, are there many tourists; despite its size, Andros is one of the lesser known islands in the group.

At the very tip of the elongated capital **Andros,** or Chora, is the fortress **Kato Kastro,** built by Marino Dandolo, and partially destroyed in the 1943 bombardment. Below is a place called **Kamara,** where the locals dive into the deep blue sea. There is a good view of the town from here, surrounded by sandy beaches and occasionally blasted by winds. A street running through the middle of town, Dimitrio Pascale, was once a ravine, according to the locals, spanned by the drawbridge of a large castle. The port **Emborios,** no longer used for large boats (the ferryboat calls at Gavrion) is now a popular beach; a small church, **Ag. Thalassini** guards one end of the harbour on her throne of rock. The town's cathedral, **Ag. Georgios,** is built on the ruins of a 17th century church.

The following legend is told about a third church, **Theoskepasti,** built in 1555. When the wood for the church's roof arrived in Andros from Piraeus, the priest found that he couldn't afford the price demanded for it by the captain of the ship. Angrily, the captain set sail again only to run into a fierce, boiling tempest. The sailors prayed to the Virgin, promising to bring the wood back to Andros should she save their lives. Instantly the sea grew calm again, and Theoskepasti, or Roof of God, was completed without further difficulty. It was dedicated to the Virgin Mary, who also has a miracle-working icon inside the church.

The main street of Chora is closed to traffic. A little shop on it sells delicious cheese and custard pies. There is also a small **museum** that no one ever has a key to. Public offices have been located in some of the beautiful old mansions. **Post office, banks,** and **OTE** are towards the centre of town; and the **bus station** lies a hop and a skip away.

Restaurants: O Stathmos (by the bus station), O Frangouris, Panayiotis Nonas (Taverna), Exochikon (by the beach), Dimitrios Konstantinos, Georgios Athanasiou.

Discotheque: Dimitri Koutellis.

Panayiéria: Theoskepasti, 15 days before Easter; 19 June, Analapsis.

Specialities: bira, a special soft drink; froutalia omelette, made with cheese, sausage and potatoes.

From Chora frequent buses leave for the **island's villages.** Many go to Gavrion when a ship is coming in (always check the timetable at the bus station). At nearby **Stenies** is a lovely beach, Yialya. **Apikia** bottles the mineral water Sariza and owns the 16th century monastery Ag. Nikolaos to the north. **Menites,** a mountain village is gifted with waters and might have been the location of Dionysos's miraculous temple, at the church Panayias tis Koumulous. On 23 August this church sponsors a **panayiéri,** and the village has two restaurants. By Menites is the deserted medieval **Messaria,** with a church of the Taxiarchos built in 1158 by the Emperor Manuel Comnenos. Messaria was the home of a legendary nun named Rose. She lived during the 18th century, curing people and making an icon of Ag. Nikolaos from her hair, which she gave to the church of that saint, built in 1732. By Messaria and Menites is **Aladino,** where a cave named Chaos can be visited. The precise location is called Lathinou, and the cave has various chambers with stalactites (bring a light).

South of Chaos cave is the most important monastery of the island, **Panahranto,** founded shortly after Nikephoros Phokas' liberation of Crete in 961. By donkey it is a two-hour ride to the monastery, walled like a fortress in the mountains. Inside the church are many relics of the saints.

Above Korthion Bay is the **castle of the Old Woman,** so named for a certain lady who abhorred the Venetians. She tricked them into letting her inside the fort, and later opened the door to the Turks who committed great slaughter. Very upset by this, the old woman leapt from the castle and landed on a rock now known as "Tis Grias to Pidema" or Old Lady's Leap.

Palaiokastro, another fortification built by Dandola, is a bit north of Korthion, and in ruins. South is the beautifully situated church of **Zoodochos Pigi** (Spring of Life), built in 1640, which once belonged to the Monastery of Filetron. A crumbling tower protected the monks from sea raids. In the village of **Korthion** there is a small beach and a **panayiéri** on 15 August, the Assumption of the Virgin. The fishing in the bay has a reputation for being excellent, but if they aren't biting one can always eat at Evagellos Kalogridos' Restaurant.

Palaiopolis on the west coast was the ancient city of Andros, in-habited until around 1000 AD when the people moved to Messaria. An earthquake in the 4th century AD destroyed part of it, and pirates finish-ed the job. Walls and part of the acropolis are preserved, along with the ruins of buildings and temples, although the site has yet to be thoroughly explored. **Vatsi,** to the north, is Andros' most popular tourist resort, and Konstantinos Damiaros and Stamatis Thomas are two good restaurants among many to be found there. On the hill is a discotheque, Marabout.

A road from Vatsi leads to the **convent Zoodochos Pigi,** built in the 14th century and containing icons from that century onwards. The nuns of the convent run a weaving factory. **Arni,** further inland, is the little paradise of the island, with its greenery, trees, and water. **Gavrion** up the coast, by the beach Psili Ammos, is the port of Andros and not all that charming in itself. There are two good restaurants, Panayiotis Yian-nakaronis and Yiannoulis Valmas. From Gavrion it is a healthy walk to **Ag. Petros;** on the way the landscape squirms with stone walls that look like caterpillars with humps. Ag. Petros has a lovely tower of interlocking stones, dating from the time of the Pelasgians (the ancient seafarers) and perhaps used as a signalling station in antiquity.

Amolonos to the north is an isolated mountain village, known for its beauty. Another tower is located on the far north-west coast, a region of violent seas (the Cavo Doro canal) when the north wind blows.

Hotels in Andros: area code 0282
In Andros (Chora):
B: Paradissos, tel. 22187/9; 8012722 in Athens; teleg. Mantsotel.
B: Xenia, tel. 22270.
C: Aegli, tel. 22303.
In Apikia:
C: Helena B.
C: Pighi.
In Vatsi:
B: Lykion (pension), tel. 4214.
C: Chryssiakti, tel. 4236/7.
D: Avra, tel. 4216.
D: Krinos, tel. 4232.
In Gavrion:
B: Aphrodite, tel. 71209/71233; 3629863 in Athens.
E: Aktaeon, tel. 71246.

E: Athinaikon, 3 Ep. Embirikou, tel. 71234.
In Korthion
C: Korthion, tel. 6218.
Tourist Police: regular police station in Chora. Tel. 22300.

Antiparos
Connections: At least two boats a day from Paroika, Paros; caique from Pounda, Paros when one opens the church door.

Antiparos ('before' Paros) was the site of the ancient Oliaros, and once connected to its larger neighbour Paros by a causeway. In the time of Alexander the Great, a large, deep cave full of stalactites was discovered on Antiparos, which has been attracting tourists for 2000 years. Unprotected, the island was uninhabited in Byzantine times. The Venetians, under Leonardo Lorentani, built a tower there and what is left of it can still be seen in the town's harbour.

Antiparos is still inexpensive, and has become a popular place to build villas. Many tourists who find Paros too touristy end up on a quiet Antiparian **beach** (there are good beaches at Kastro, at Sifnaikos Yialos in the north, and Ag. Georgios in the south). Fish is plentiful, even in the restaurants, and there are many rooms to rent besides the three hotels. Of the islands off the coast, **Strogilonisi** and **Despotiko** are known for their rabbit hunting. On the islet **Saliagos,** a Neolithic fishing village from the 5th millennium has been excavated by John Evans and Colin Renfrew.

The **cave** is still the major attraction on the islet, despite the centuries of tourists taking free souvenirs. In the summer, a special caique leave Paroika for the cave at 9 am every morning. Entrance is 10 dr. and the caique is 50 dr. for the round trip. It is generally closed in the afternoons. From the boat landing stage one must ascend, half an hour by foot and less by donkey, and then descend into the 70-metre (230-ft.) deep chamber. The cave is about twice as deep, but the rest is closed. Steps have been built to prevent visitors from killing themselves with ropes. Inside, the cave is fantastic and spooky. To make up for the many stalactites that have been broken off, famous visitors of the past have smoked and carved their names on the walls, including Lord Byron and King Otto, the first King of Greece (1840). One stalactite attests to a mass held in the cave by the French Ambassador to Constantinople, Count Noandel, in 1673 which was attended by 500 people. The church by the entrance of the cave, **Ag. Ioannis,** was built in 1774. To see the cave in the winter, it is necessary to go to the village for the key.

In Antiparos there are two 17th century churches, the cathedral **Ag. Nikolaos** and **Evangelismos.**

Panayiéria: 23 April, Ag. Georgios; 21 May, Ag. Konstantinos at Kambos; and 8 May, Ag. Ioannis Theologos by the cave.

Hotels in Antiparos: area code 0284
C: Chryssi Akti, tel. 61286.
D: Anargyros, tel. 61206.
D: Madalena, tel. 61227.
   Tourist police: in Paros, summer only. Tel. 21673.

Delos
Connections: Caique from Mykonos daily at 9 am, returning at 12.30;
44 dr. round trip. To see the 1.35 sq. mile island, which is one big
archaeological site costs 50 dr. (7.50 with student card). The museum is
25 dr. (2.5 for students).

   Mythology: The ancient name of Delos was Ortygia, derived from
one of Zeus' love affairs, this time with a maiden named Asteria. Asteria
fled the lusty king of the gods in the form of a quail, and Zeus turned
himself into an eagle the better to pursue her. The pursuit proved so hot
that Asteria turned into a rock and fell into the sea. This rock was known
as Ortygia, or Adelos, the invisible one, as it floated all over Greece just
below the surface of the sea. A while later Zeus fell in love with Asteria's
sister Leto, whom he approached in the form of a swan to avoid the difficulties he had with her sister. But Zeus' wife, Hera, soon discovered the
affair and in a fit of jealousy begged Mother Earth not to allow Leto to
give birth anywhere under the sun. All over the world wandered poor,
suffering Leto, unable to find a rock to stand on, as all feared the wrath
of Hera. Finally in pity Zeus turned to his brother Poseidon and asked
him to help his miserable mistress. Poseidon thereupon ordered Órtygia
to halt, and anchored the islet with four columns of solid diamond. Thus
Adelos the Invisible, not under the sun but under the sea, became Delos,
the Visible. Delos, however, was reluctant to have Leto, fearing her son
would give her a resounding kick back into the sea. But Leto promised
the islet that no such thing would happen; indeed her son would make
Delos the richest sanctuary in Greece. The island conceded, and Leto
gave birth first to Artemis, goddess of the hunt and virginity, and then
nine days later to Apollo, the god of truth and light.

   History: In the 3rd millennium BC Delos was settled by the Karians,
and by 1000 BC the Ionians had made it their religious capital, introducing the cult of Apollo whom they believed to be the father of the
founder of their race, Ion. This cult is first mentioned in a Homeric
hymn of the 7th century BC. Games and pilgrimages took place, and
Delos was probably the centre of the Amphictyonic League of the
Ionians (a maritime confederation). In 550 BC Polycrates, the Tyrant of
Samos, conquered the Cyclades but respected Delos, giving the island
the islet Rheneia, and symbolically binding it to Delos with a chain.
   With the rise of Athens, notably under Pisistratos, Delos' greatest
glory and greatest difficulties begin. What was once entirely sacred

started to take on a political significance, and the Athenians invented stories to connect themselves to Delos — did not Erechtheus, the King of Athens, lead the first delegation to Delos? After slaying the Minotaur on Crete did not Theseus stop at Delos and dance around the altar of Apollo? In 543 BC the Athenians even managed to find an oracle at Delphi ordering the purification of the island, which meant removing the old tombs, a manoeuvre designed to alienate the Delians from their past and thus decreasing the island's importance in comparison to Athens'.

In 490 BC the population of Delos fled to Tinos before the Persians under Darius, who, according to Herodotus, respected the sacred site and sacrificed 300 talents worth of incense to Apollo. The Delians, further-more, were told they could return home in safety. The Persians lost the war, and after the Battle of Salamis the Athenians, to prevent further in-vasions, organized a new Amphictyonic league, or Delian Alliance, for its centre was to be at Delos. Only the Athenian fleet could guarantee protection to the island allies, who were required to contribute a yearly sum and ships to support the navy. Athenian archons administered the funds.

The Delian alliance was effective, despite the resentment among the islanders who disliked being lorded over by the Athenians, for the con-tributions were more like tributes. In 454 BC Perikles, in order better to "protect" or rather spend the league's treasury, placed it on Athens' akropolis; some of the money went to repair damage incurred during the previous Persian invasion, and some to beautify Athens generally. To make matters worse, a terrible plague hit Athens, and as it was deter-mined to have been caused by the wrath of Apollo, a second purification of Delos was called for. This time not only did the Athenians remove all the old tombs, but they forbade both births and death on Delos, forcing the pregnant and the dying to go to Rheneia. Thus the alienation of the Delians was complete. When the people turned to Sparta for aid during the Peloponnesian War, the Spartans remained unmoved: since the in-habitants couldn't be born or die on the island, it wasn't really their homeland, and why should they help a group of foreigners? In 422 BC Athens punished Delos for going to Sparta by exiling the entire popula-tion (for being "unpure") to Asia Minor, where all the leaders were slain by cunning. Athenians moved in to take the Delians' place, but Athens herself was punished by the gods for her greed and suffered many draw-backs in the Peloponnesian War. After a year, hoping to regain divine favour, Athens allowed the Delians to return home. From 403-394 Delos had a breath of independence due to Athens' defeat by the Spartans, and 50 years later the islanders applied to the Amphictyonic league to oust the Athenians from the shrine altogether. The head of the league at the time, Philip II of Macedon, refused the request, wishing to stay on good terms with the city that hated him most.

In the confusion following the death of Philip's son, Alexander the Great, Delos became free and prosperous, supported by the pious Macedonian kings. Many new buildings and shrines were constructed and by 250 BC Delos was a cosmopolitan, commercial port, flourishing through the business of merchants from all over the Mediterranean. When the Romans defeated the Macedonians in 166 BC they returned the island to Athens, who exiled the Delians to Achaia. But by 146 BC and the fall of Corinth, Delos was the centre of all east-west trade, and declared a free port by the Romans in order to undermine business at Rhodes. People from all over the world settled on the island and set up their own cults in complete tolerance. Roman trade guilds, each with its own lares, centred on the Italian Agora. New quays and piers were constructed to deal with the heavy flow of vessels. Markets thrived.

In the battle of the Romans with Mithridates of Pontus in 88 BC, Delos was robbed of many of her treasures. 20,000 people were killed, and the women and children carried off as slaves. This was the beginning of the end of Delos. General Sulla regained the ruined island, but 19 years later Delos was again destroyed by pirates allied to Mithridates, and the population was again dragged off to the slave markets. General Triarius retook the island and fortified it with walls, and Hadrian attempted to revive the waning cult of Apollo with new festivities but failed. Delos hit such a decline that when Athens tried to sell the wretched place, no one offered to buy it. In 363 AD the Emperor Julian the Apostate tried to renew paganism on Delos, but the oracles solemnly warned: "Delos shall become Adelos", and he gave up the idea. Later Theodossios the Great banned all heathen ceremonies. A small Christian community survived on Delos until the 6th century, when it was given over to the rule of pirates. House builders on Tinos and Mykonos used Delos for a marble quarry, and it became a pasture land.

After the independence of Greece, Delos and Rheneia were placed in the municipality of Mykonos. Major archaeological excavations were begun in 1872 by the French School of Archaeology at Athens under Dr. Lebeque, and work is still being continued. The island's only permanent population today are the guardians of the ruins, appointed by the Greek government, and a million or so lizards who play on the broken marble.

A trip to Delos begins as one struggles out of the caique and pays the entrance fee. After this the rest is easy. All the major sites are labelled, and at a normal walking pace everything of interest to the average dilettante can be seen in four hours. Basically Delos is laid out as follows.

To one's left from the boat landing stage is the **Agora of the Competalists.** Compita were Roman citizens or freed slaves who worshipped the Lares Competales, or crossroad gods. These established the Roman trade guilds, along with the others under the protection of Hermes, Apollo, or Zeus. Many of the remains in the Agora are votive offerings to these gods; there are also ruins of the shops. A road, once lined with statues, leads to the sanctuary of Apollo. To the left of the road is the long **Philip's Stoa,** built by Philip V of Macedon in 210 BC. Only the foundations remain of this once tall and splendid building of the Doric order. General Sulla once placed a votary statue inside it for his victory over Mithridates. The kings of Pergamon built the **Southern Stoa** in the 3rd century BC, and one can also see the remains of the **Delians' Agora,** the local market place in the area.

The **Sanctuary of Apollo** is announced by the **Propylaea,** a gateway built in the 2nd century BC of white marble. Little remains of the sanctuary itself, once crowded with temples, votive offerings, and statues. Next door to it is the **House of the Naxians,** built in the 6th century BC. Once a huge kouros, or statue of Apollo as a young man stood there, of which the pedestal remains. According to Plutarch the statue was destroyed by a huge bronze palm tree placed near it by the Athenians, which fell down in the wind and brought the Naxian Apollo down with it.

Next one comes upon the **three temples of Apollo.** The first and largest was begun by the Delians in 476 BC. The second was an Athenian construction of Pentelic marble, built during the Second Purification and the third, of porous stone, was made by the 6th century Athenian tyrant Pisistratos. Dimitrios the Besieger contributed the **Bull's Shrine** which held a sacred trireme in honour of the sacred delegation ship of Athens (the ship whose departure put off executions in Athens, namely that of Socrates, until its return). Other buildings in the area had an official purpose — the **Prytaneion of the Rectors** and the **Councillor's house.** Towards the museum is the **sanctuary of Dionysos** of the 4th century BC, flanked by its marble phalli. **The Stoa of Antigonos** was built by a Macedonian king of that name in the 3rd century BC. Outside the stoa is the **Tomb of the Hyperborean Virgins,** who came to help Leto give birth to Apollo and Artemis, thus making the tomb sacred and irremovable during the purifications.

On the other side of the Stoa stood the **Abaton,** the holy of holies, where only the priests could enter. The **Minoan fountain** nearby is from the 6th century BC. Through the **Italian Agora** one comes to the **Temple of Leto** (6th century) and the **Dodecathon,** dedicated to the twelve gods of Olympos in the 3rd century BC. Beyond, where the **Sacred Lake** has dried up, is the famous **Terrace of the lions,** exvotos made by the Naxians in the 7th century BC. The lake, sacred for having witnessed the birth of Apollo, was surrounded by a small wall which still exists. When Delos' torrent Inopos stopped flowing, the water evaporated. Along the shore are two **Palaestras** (buildings for exercises and lessons) along with the foundation of the **Archighession,** or temple to the first mythic settler on Delos, worshipped only on that island. Besides the **Gymnasium** and **Stadium,** there are the remains of a few houses and a **synogogue** built by the Phoenician Jews in the 2nd century BC.

A dirt path leads from the tourist pavilion and museum to Mt. Kynthos (110 metres/360ft.). Along the way one meets the **Sanctuary of the Syrian Gods** of 100 BC with a small religious theatre within. The first of **three Serapeions** follows, dedicated to the Egyptian god Serapis. All three shrines were built in the 2nd century BC. Between the first and second Serapeions is the **shrine to the Samothracian Great Gods,** the Cabri or underworld deities. Next is the third Serapeion, perhaps the main sanctuary, with temples to both Serapis and Isis, half a statue remaining. In the region are houses with mosaics, and a **temple to Hera** from 500 BC. **The Sacred Cave** is on the way to the top of Mt. Kynthos, where Apollo ran an oracle. Later it was dedicated to Herakles. On the mountain itself is the **Shrine of Good Luck,** built by Arsinoe Philadelphos, wife of her brother, the King of Egypt. On the summit of Kynthos signs of a settlement dating back to 3000 BC have been discovered.

The **Theatre Quarter** consists of the private houses surrounding the **Theatre of Delos** from the 2nd century BC, which seated 5,500; beside it is a lovely 8-arched **reservoir.** The houses of the quarter date from the Hellenistic and Roman ages and many have mosaics, some beautifully preserved, such as in the **House of the Dolphins** and the **House of the Masks.** All houses have a cistern beneath the floor, spaces for oil lamps and sewage systems. Some are built in the Peristyle "style of Rhodes" with a high-ceilinged guest room. Columns bordered the central courts, open to the sun. Other special houses include the **House of the Trident** (now closed, but perhaps to be reopened), and the **House of Dionysos,** both with mosaics, and the **House of Cleopatra and Dioscourides,** where the statues stand a headless guard over the once great town.

The **Museum of Delos,** which has recently been reopened, contains many interesting finds from Delos and the cemetries at Rheneia. The tourist pavilion next door sells expensive refreshments. Campers are allowed to pitch tents behind the museum, and are advised to bring their own provisions.

Hotel: B: Xenia, tel. (0289) 498. 4 rooms and 7 beds.

Surrounding Delos are the islets **Ag. Georgios,** named for the monastery there, **Karavonissi, Rheneia, Mikro** and **Megalo Rematiaris;** the latter was consecrated to Hecate, the Queen of the Night.

Folegandros

Connections: Twice a week with Piraeus; Capt. Petros' boat from Ios when the sea is calm; once a week with Rhodes, Kos, Kalymnos, Astypalaia and Amorgos.

The name Folegandros comes from the Phoenician "Phlegundum" meaning "the rocky island", a name which fits it well. The ancient city of the island is located on a high plateau above the modern capital, Chora, which itself dates back to the Middle Ages, set high above the sea away from would-be pirates. In the 13th century Marco Sanudo built a fortress by the ancient town; the houses themselves, two storeys high, formed a wall around Chora.

Folegandros is a small dry island of 650 inhabitants, one of the smallest in Greece with a permanent population. It has become a popular place for escapists. **Chora,** the capital, is a pretty village almost 300 metres (1000ft.) above sea level. From there one can see the **ancient city** within the wall, besides the ruins of **Marco Sanudo's fortress,** high above two bays. The **post office** and **OTE** are located at Chora, and there are two **restaurants:** Popadopoulos and Kritikos barbeque. North of Chora is a large cave, **Chrisispilio,** the Golden Cave, with stalactites and stalagmites, although access is rather difficult — ask in the village for someone to guide you.

The port of the islet, **Karovostasis,** is an hour's walk from Chora, but the special bus greatly shortens the trip on Folegandros' one road. Good restaurants can also be found here, and there is a beach, **Livadi,** nearby. To go to the other beach, **Ag. Georgios,** take a path from Chora. By the lovely church **Panayia** one can find another Venetian castle, balancing on a cliff above the sea.

As there is only one little hotel on the island and a few rooms, most visitors who stay over night sleep outside. Captain Petros of Ios makes round trips designed for a one-day excursion. The island's specialities include the little known Folegandrian biscuit and cheese.

Panayiéria: 15 August, the Assumption of the Virgin; and Easter, when an icon is paraded and trips are made in boats around the island.

Hotel: Danassis E

Ios
Connections: Daily in the summer with Santorini, Paros, Mykonos, Piraeus; less frequently with Sikinos, Folegandros, Tinos, Herakleon, Anafi, Milos; with Sifnos and Serifos once a week.

Traditionally the mother of Homer came from Ios, and it is to this island that the great poet returned at the end of his life. **Homer's tomb** is at Plakotos on the mountain, although an earthquake has left only the rock which constructed it. Plakotos itself, an ancient town that once had a temple to Apollo, slid down the cliff and one can look down and see the ruined houses, although a tower, Psarapyrgos, remains.

Present-day Ios and Gialos are built on the sites of ancient towns, and at Ios some of the ancient walls are preserved. Aegina on Ag. Theodotis Bay is another ancient town; above it is Paliokastro, a fortress built in the Middle Ages. Legend recounts that on one occasion attacking pirates managed to bore a hole in the gate, big enough to allow one man in at a time — only to be scalded to death in burning oil by the besieged men and women. All the pirates perished, and the anniversary of the victory over the marauders is celebrated every year with great pomp. The Venetian Lord of Ios, Marco I Crispi, built another fortress in 1400 by the present town of Ios, although little remains of it.

Another local story shows how close the inhabitants of the smaller islands were to the big political events of Greek history: King Otto, the first King of Greece, paid a visit to Ios, and greeted the villagers in the café, buying them all a drink. To top that off, he promised that he would pay to have the village cleaned up for them. The grateful Niotes, scarcely knowing what a king was, toasted him saying: "To the health of the King, Ios' new garbageman!"

In the earthquake of 1951, all the water was sucked out of Ios Bay and rushed back, flooding the town and causing much damage. If tourists hadn't popularized Ios, the chances are that the island would be deserted today.

The **tourists** who visit Ios are for the most part a rare breed of Europeans under 30 who haven't realized that the 1960s have turned into the 1980s. Flower children still bring their guitars and sing in the street and wear clothes from Berkeley, California. The locals shake their heads and wish they had more money. Water, or the lack of it, is a major problem on Ios in the summer; for innumerable years a massive reservoir served the needs of the populace, until some smarties decided to improve it and only succeeded in breaking it. One waterless toilet in Gialos is used by all.

Gialos is the port of the island and has a yacht supply station. As only one or two ships come directly to the pier, a loud speaker constantly announces in Greek and English when it is time to board the caiques to be taken to the ships. There is a beach in the bay, but it is very subject to wind. The **Marino discotheque** is by the shore, and at the port are the **restaurants** Tasos, Kostopoulos, Frangakis, Lambaras and Kristovoulos. From Gialos a road goes up to Ios village: there are also steps which take 15 minutes to climb. On the way is the **Ios Club**, which plays classical music from 7pm-9pm (programme posted). Popular music dominates the rest of the night.

Ios town is a fine Cyclades town in the best tradition, although many of the houses now contain tourist shops. Of the 18 original windmills behind the town, 12 remain, along with three olive oil "factories". The **bus stop** for Gialos and Milopotamos is on the edge of town, by the **OTE** and **post office.** In the same area are the **police** and **doctor,** and the swing where Niotes once courted their ladies fair. Ghosts are rumoured to dance in the square when no one is looking. From the bus stop one can also visit the cemetery where people are buried not in the ground but in boxes covered with a slab of marble. Two very old churches stand half-ruined on the hill above the town, where supposedly a tunnel connects Ios to Plakotos, used as a hiding place during pirate times.

Restaurants: Mastrodonakis, Elias Kyriakis, Boulouvasis, Stratis, Plakiotis, Kostopoulos and Katsavis.

Discotheques: Petris Club, Kukuvaiya, Romeo, Windmill (live folk), Fanari I and Fanari II.

A bus leaves Ios every half-hour for the beach **Milopotamos,** which also has tavernas and a camping place, Souli. The church, Milo-

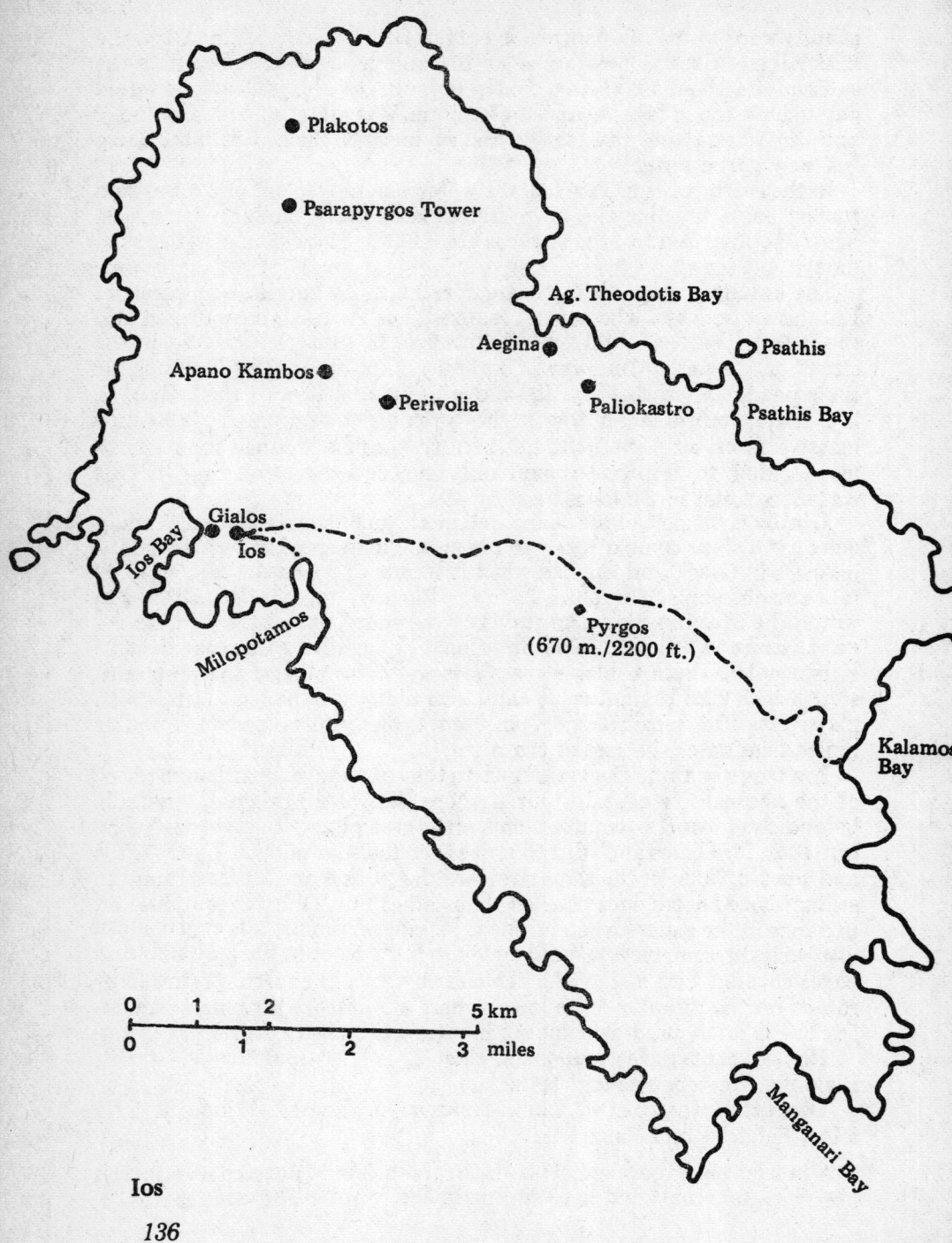

Plakotos

Psarapyrgos Tower

Ag. Theodotis Bay

Aegina

Psathis

Apano Kambos

Perivolia

Paliokastro

Psathis Bay

Gialos

Ios

Ios Bay

Milopotamos

Pyrgos
(670 m./2200 ft.)

Kalamos
Bay

0   1   2   5 km

0   1   2   3   miles

Manganari Bay

Ios

potamo, Panayia at Messenia, has a *panayiéri* on 23 August. South of Milopotamos is **Manganari Bay,** a German tourist resort with a lovely beach. Caiques leave Gialos daily to Manganari. **Psathis Bay** to the north is three hours by foot from Ios town and has become very frequented by wealthy Athenians. A certain church of the Virgin fell into the sea there; at another church, **Ag. Ioannes Kalamos,** a huge *panayiéri* takes place on 29 August. Greeks and tourists board little caiques to attend, as it costs nothing to eat there.

Just north of Psathi is **Ag. Theodotis Bay** of the famous Paliokastro. At the nearby monastery, Ag. Theodotis, one can even see the door the pirates broke through on the way to their doom. On 8 September a big celebration there commemorates the event with food and dance. **Perivolia,** a small settlement in the middle of the island, has water and trees; a church in the valley, **Ag. Barbara,** has a *panayiéri* on 26 July. **Apano Kambos,** once inhabited by a hundred families but today reduced to three or four, is another pretty place. Nearby at a place called Hellinika are huge monoliths of mysterious origin.

Speciality: Megithra cheese, a hard white cheese similar to parmesan, mixed with perfumes and kept in a goat's skin.

Hotels in Ios: area code 0286

Nissos Ios (D) is the hotel for poor Bohemians. One has to crawl only a few yards to the loveliest beach on the island, Milopotamos, a few yards to a good taverna, and a few yards to the frequent buses to Chora for more sophisticated entertainment. The hotel itself is merely adequate, but no Bohemian worth his salt spends his day in a hotel.

In Ios Town
B: Chryssi Akti (pension), tel. 91255
C: Amadoros, tel. 91201/91253; 3450282 in Athens
D: Aktaeon, tel. 91207
E: Avra
In Gialos
C: Sea Breeze (Thalassis Avra), tel. 91285/91440
In Kambos
E: Helena, tel. 91276
In Milopotamos
D: Nissos Ios, tel. 91306
In Manganari
Manganmari (bungalows), tel: 91258.

Tourist police: regular police at Ios town, or Akteio ticket office, Gialos, for any tourist information.

Kea (Tsia)

Connections: Daily ferryboat from Rafina; once a week with Lavrion, Kythnos and Piraeus.

History: At a site called Kephala signs of a Neolithic fishing settlement have been discovered, dating the inhabitation of Kea back to 3000 BC. A recently discovered Minoan colony, a mile away by the village of Vourkari, suggests that these early peoples were later subjugated. The colony is called Ag. Irene, after the church on the small peninsula of the settlement, and was discovered by John L. Caskey of the University of Cincinnati. Minos himself supposedly visited Kea, had an affair with a woman named Dexithea and thus created the Kean race. He also left behind many Minoans to colonize the island. They settled at Ag. Irene in about 1650 BC, building a palace at the site of the present-day church, besides roads, gates, an underground cistern, and strong walls on the landward side of the little peninsula to protect the colonists from the locals. No defence was necessary on the shore as the Minoans ruled the seas. Many of the ruins of Ag. Irene can only be seen in the water, however, as the Mediterranean has risen over 2 metres (6 ft.) since the Minoans lived and built there. At Troulos, overlooking three bays, a tower once stood which could signal any danger from sea to the inhabitants.

When the Minoan civilization on Crete fell in the 15th century BC, Ag. Irene had connections with the Myceneans on the mainland. Later Kea was dominated by the four ancient towns: Ioulis, located near the present capital of the island; Karthea, Poiessa, and Koressia. The poets Simonides and Bacchylides were sons of Kea, along with the physician Erasistratos. In Venetian times, namely 1210, Domenico Michell built a fortress by the capital of Kea out of the temple of Apollo at Ioulis, and for that reason the Greek government had much of the fort destroyed. The castle protected the Venetian aristocracy, who built mansions inside, many of which are still there with coats-of-arms inscribed on the walls. Even during the Turkish occupation Catholic descendants of the Venetians continued to live on in their grandfathers' homes.

Kea today is becoming increasingly popular as a summer time resort with both Greeks and foreigners, who have built numerous villas and houses on the island. Although rugged and rocky, there are two green valleys, where vineyards produce the red wine Mavriti with its aromatic bouquet. Valanides in the centre of the island is also very green, and there are some lovely beaches, besides a growing number of hotels to accommodate tourists.

Chora, the capital of Kea, is located inland, high above the sea as are so many Cycladic towns, recalling the uncertain days of piracy. A bus makes the trip from the port Korissia. In Chora a small **museum** should be ready by now, housing finds from Ag. Irene and the four ancient cities. The present town itself dates from the Middle Ages. It is situated in an amphitheatre on a hill, and divided into four quarters: Kastro, on the top, Messatha, Ag. Spiridon, and Panochori. At Kastro was the ancient acropolis of **Ioulis,** where the Venetian commander built his castle. Some of the walls of Ioulis are preserved along with signs of the **temple**

of Apollo and a cistern. The old **Venetian mansions** can also be found up at Kaştro. **Pyscopi** and **Ag. Anna** are two churches at Chora dating back to Byzantine times: in **Ag. Philothe** are bones of the saint. At **Panayias Kastrianni** (The Virgin of the Castle) is an icon which worked many a miracle during the Turkish Occupation of Kea (its *panayiéri*is on 15 August). Another church is dedicated to Kea's patron saint **Ag. Charalambos,** who protected the island from the plague, and on 10 February the entire island celebrates this feat; even Keans who have moved to Athens at Phalero have a *panayiéri* on that day.

The **bank, OTE** and **post office** are all located at Chora. If one isn't charmed enough by the lovely white village, the **Leon Petrinos** (a lion sculptured in the rock), and the inhabitants, a drink of the **Tourokomeno** waters guarantees that no visitor will ever leave Kea.

Restaurants: Lepouras taverna, Dimostenis, Tsiotiko Steki (souvlaki and often music) and O Tiriandas, which also has music.

Specialities: Apricot jam, almonds, honey, Vromosis greens and Tloumisio cheese, besides the red Mavriti wine.

The port of Kea, **Korissia,** also called Limin Ag. Nikolaos, has a beach, Yialiskari. The hotel Itzia mas has a restaurant and a discotheque called Medusa. A road leads along the bay to Ag. Irene at **Vourkari,** a village with a nice beach, a taverna Oreo Voukaki and restaurant Tassos Psilas. As well as the **Minoan colony,** the walls of ancient **Koressia** can also be seen. Further down the road is **Otzias,** another beach and village. Stephas is a restaurant there, and on 7 September a *panayiéri* takes place for Ag. Soustas.

South of Otzias are the ruins of **Karthaea,** one of the largest ancient towns of Kea. Inside the walls are the seats from the theatre, an asklepeieon, a monument, and temples of Demeter and Athena. A huge statue of Apollo from Karthaea is now in Copenhagen. The fourth ancient city, **Poiessa,** also spelled Poieessa or even Pisses, is south of Korissia near the **monastery Ag. Marina** *(panayiéri* 17 July). A few fortifications remain at the ancient city, but at the monastery a huge tower has been preserved and restored, dating from the Classical period, which is considered one of the most beautiful ancient towers of Greece. Other similar towers are also in the immediate region. At Poiessa the beach is of golden sand. Another beach is at **Koundoros,** by the Kea Beach Hotel.

Hotels in Kea: area code 0288
In Chora
B: Ioulis (pension), tel. 21577
In Korissia
B: Itzia mas (motel), tel. 31305:3633083 in Athens; teleg. Logothnik Athens
C: Carthea, tel. 31222/31204
In Koundouros
B: Kea Beach (hotel & bungalows), tel. 21411/21544; 9220152 in Athens;

teleg Tasvlahos
In Poiessa
D: Akroyali, tel: 21411.

Tourist police: at Chora in summer only, tel. 31300

Kimolos
Connections: Twice a week with Piraeus, Serifos, Sifnos; caique twice a day from Apollonia, Milos (30 dr.).

The name of the island is thought to be derived from its first inhabitant. But Kimolia means chalk in Greek, and whether the name comes from the producer (chalk was once a main export of Kimolos) or the other way around, no one is quite sure. A long time ago Kimolos was connected to nearby Milos, and an ancient town was built where the sea now flows. However, the cemetery of this settlement remains on Kimolos at a site called Elliniko, dating back to 2500 BC.

Today the only chalk on Kimolos is in the school house at **Chora,** a 15 minute walk up from the port. On the way one passes the largest building on the island, a philanthropic gift to the old people of Kimolos, where they live for free. In the basement are a few items known as the **museum** of Kimolos, which one can see if the key-holding person happens to be around.

In the small village are a few cafés and a 17th century church, **Evangelistra.** Nearby at **Paliokastro** are the ruins of a Venetian castle, Arzandeira, and inside is **Christos,** the oldest church on the island.

Psathi, the very quiet port of Kimolos, relays passengers to ships in caiques. The little village nearby, **Oupa,** derives its name from a certain kind of fish the people once scooped out of the sea by the basket full. **Prassa,** 4 miles away, is a radioactive source although it hasn't been developed. There is a kafenion there. To see the **Elliniko** cemetery one goes by horse and must take the archaeologists along, as the dig is still in process. The small islet in the bay, **Poliegos,** has a lot of goats.

There are about 50 beds to accommodate visitors on this small, dry island, and there are **beaches at Aliki, Bounatsa, Mavro Spilia,** and **Klima** that some people camp on. For seekers of peace and quiet, Kimolos has a lot to offer, if they are prepared to rough it a little.

Panayiéria: 27 August, Ag. Fanouris; 27 July, Ag. Panteleimonos; 21 November, Panayias; 20 July, Profitis Elias; 4 August, Ag. Theothoso.

Kythnos
Connections: Three times a week with Piraeus, Serifos, Sifnos, Milos, Syros and Santorini.

History: Kythnos was once uninhabited because of a large quantity of wild animals and snakes; Ofioso, the ancient name for the island, means snake. After the Minoans left the island, the Driopes came, and their King Kythnos gave his name to his kingdom in the 6th century BC centered at a town still known today as Dryopis. During the Hellenistic period Kythnos was dominated by Rhodes. Two great painters came from the island, Timatheus (416-376 BC), who was known in antiquity for a certain portrayal of Iphegenia, and Kydian. In 198 BC all of Kythnos was pillaged, except for Vyrokastro by Merihas which proved impregnable. Marco Sanudo later took the island, and for 200 years it was under the rule of the Cozzadini family who still live in Bologna today. In order to maintain their authority the Cozzadini paid taxes to both the Venetians and the Turks. The French pirate Bonné built the Kastro tou Kephalou in the north in the 18th century, presiding by force rather than tribute until he was removed.

Kythnos today: As the snake population has been controlled and as there are not many rooms on the island, most visitors to Kythnos sleep under the stars. On festive occasions the islanders still like to don their traditional costumes, especially during carnival. Fishing and farming are the major occupations and many inhabitants weave baskets.

The capital, called **Chora** or Kythnos, is 6 miles from the port. Although the **post office** etc. are there, it isn't all that interesting. It has more fresh water, though, than anywhere on the islands, and has a restaurant, Georgios Bittakes. Tourists for the most part prefer to stay in Merihas, Loutra, or Dryopis. **Loutra** has the thermal baths of the Cyclades, fed by two springs and used since ancient times, reputed to cure rheumatism and arthritis. **Pirate Bonné's fort** is nearby, as is the beach **Ag. Irene.** Four buses daily leave Chora for Loutra, which has a discotheque, Kythnos, and two restaurants, Estathio and Vassalos.

At **Merihas,** the port, there are rooms to rent besides the hotel. O Yialos, Geo. Gardarakis and Ant. Goanides are three restaurants there.

On 2 November, a *panayiéri* is held for Ag. Akindinos. On the edge of town there are a few ruins of a fort. At **Dryopis** walls remain of the ancient city, along with the more recently built fortress Vryokastro. A cave by the village was used as a refuge during pirate raids. Every Sunday local music and dancing top off a day of rest.

Kolona is one of the nicest beaches of the island, where hot water flows and various statues have been discovered. At **Katakefala** one can see the Oriastro Kastro, a ruined castle with houses and churches from the Middle Ages. **Kanala,** another fine beach, is by a monastery of the Panayia, celebrating 15 August and 8 September. Other beaches on Kythnos include **Fikiado, Lefkas,** and **Episcopi.**

Specialities: Baskets and kounoura paximathi, a very hard bread that has to be soaked in water before it can be chewed.

Hotels in Kythnos: area code 0281.
in Kythnos town:
C: Xenia-Anagenissis, tel. 31217

in Merihas

C: Possidonion, tel. 31244

Tourist police: Loutra, summer only. Tel. 31220.

Milos

Connections: Once a week in summer with Ios and Santorini; daily with Piraeus, Sifnos, and Serifos; less frequently with Kimolos and Kythnos.

History: Milos has the oldest Neolithic settlement of the Cyclades, at Phylakope, which might have been settled by Phoenicians or Cypriots, attracted by the obsidian (a black volcanic rock) in which Milos abounded. Obsidian tools from Milos have been found in the earliest Minoan, and even Pre-Minoan settlements on Crete, dating before 3000 BC. Under the Cretans and later the Myceneans the island became rich from the obsidian which was traded all over the Mediterranean. As the inhabitants of Milos in later years were Dorian, they sided with the Dorian Spartans in the Peloponnesian War. When the Athenians made war in the east, the Milians again refused to fight with them. These factors led up to that most moving tragedy in Thucycides when the Athenians castigated the Milians by slaying the entire male population and enslaving the rest. After the fall of Athens, however, the island prospered until the inhabitants asked the Romans to come to protect them from the pirates. General Pompey put an end to the pirates, but the Romans moved in for good at Klema, the Dorian town the Athenians had previously destroyed, and asserted their authority. Christianity came to Milos in the 1st century and the faithful built a great series of catacombs. Marco and his brother Angelo Sanudo captured Milos and the island was later placed under the Crispi dynasty. In 1580 Turkish rule began even though Milos was infested with pirates. One of them, John Kapsis declared himself King of Milos, a claim which Venice recognized for three years, until the Turks tricked Kapsis into coming to Istanbul where they slew him.

In 1820 George Kentrotis or Betonis, a farmer, found a cave while planting his corn. Inside was a lovely statue, now known as the Venus of Milo. George's friends in the village told him that it should be taken away from Milos, out of reach of the Turks, and so the Venus was sold to the French Council at Istanbul (during which time she lost her arms). It was then brought to France and given to Louis XVIII, who put it in the Louvre.

In 1835 Cretan rebels from Sfakia fled to Milos and founded the village Adamas, the present port. During the Crimean War the French navy docked at the great harbour of Milos and left many monuments, as they did during World War I.

Milos today is one of the richer Cyclades and doesn't need tourism to maintain a healthy economy. A volcanic island, its wealth is in the rocks, as is its beauty: the whole island is a geological playground of colour and formations worthy of a Dr. Seuss. The natural harbour of Milos is vast and safe, considered one of the best in the Mediterranean.

Plaka the present-day capital of Milos, has two museums. The **Archaeology Museum** is near the bus stop, marked by a line of broken statues, and contains some of the finds on Milos dating back to Neolithic times; in a back room is a plaster cast of the Venus Milos lost, a consolation prize from the French. Many signs direct one to the **Folklore and Laographic Museum,** which is worthy of a visit especially if you can find someone to tell you the stories behind the exhibits, which include almost everything from a kitchen to a grape press. Plaka, a modern village, lacks the Cycladic charm, and although there are a few rooms to rent, most tourists stay at the port Adamas, while campers pitch tents at the second port Pollonia.

A short walk from Plaka brings you to **Klema** (ask for Tripiti if you go by bus), the town the Athenians destroyed and the Roman capital of the island. Here you can see the **Catacombs:** open 9 am - 1 pm and 4 pm - 6 pm. Entrance 25 dr.; 2.5 dr. with student card. Dating from the first century after Christ, this is one of the best preserved Early Christian monuments in the world. The church area and long corridors lined with arched tombs remain, each with a little light before it that you can move about in order to examine an area more closely. When first discovered, the Catacombs were still full of bones, but the air turned them dust. Some tombs held five or six bodies; others are buried in the floor. On some of the tombs inscriptions in red still remain (all writing in black is later graffiti). Strangely enough, the modern cemetery of Milos near Plaka is constructed like a row of catacombs above ground.

A path from the catacombs leads to the place where the Venus of Milos was discovered (there is a marker by the fig tree) and past the tall walls to the well preserved **Roman Theatre,** where spectators looked out over the sea. Part of the stage remains, but the fact that there are still three tiers of seats left unexcavated is claimed to be a manifestation of the Milians' lack of interest in tourism. However, a theatre company from Athens performs in the theatre in August. There are also the remains of a **temple** on the path back to the main road.

In **Mandrakia** to the east you can drink the **waters of Tsillorneri** which "clear the system". It is a small fishing village with a beach nearby. **Kastro,** above Plaka, affords a good view of the island. **Platina** to the west has a beach and is near the rock **Arkoudes,** or 'bear', which is visible when entering the harbour by ship. **Adamas,** founded by the Cretans, also has icons from Crete in the church **Ag. Charalmbos.** One picture, dating from 1576, portrays a boat attacked by a mad fish. The captain prayed to Mary, who resolved the struggle by snipping off the fish's nose. Another church, **Ag. Triada,** is the second oldest in Milos and also has some lovely Cretan icons. Besides being the main port of the island, Adamas has most of the tourist **accommodation** and

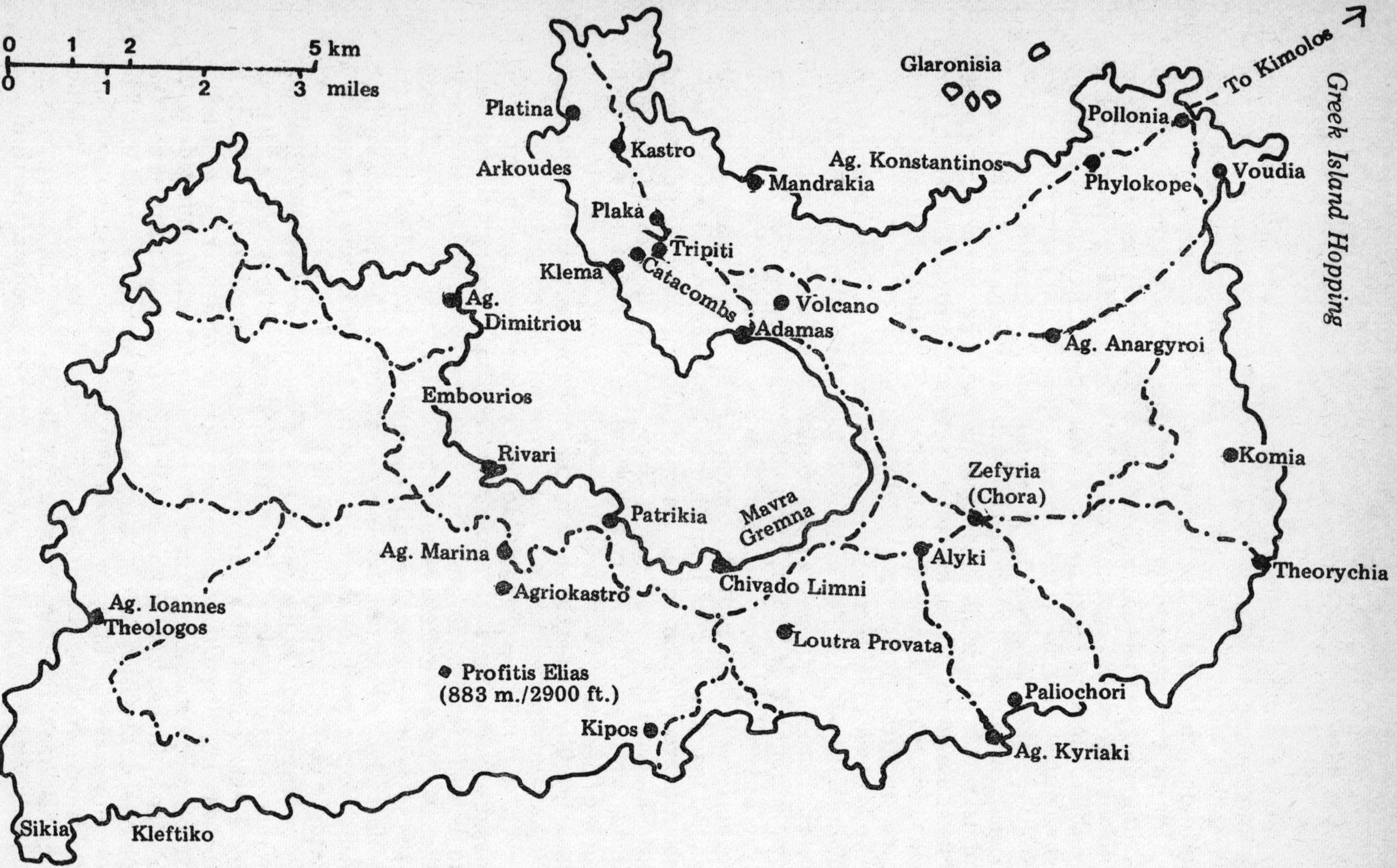

To Kimolos

Voudia

Theorychia

Komia

Pollonia

Phylokope

Ag. Anargyroi

Paliochori

Ag. Kyriaki

Glaronisia

Zefyria
(Chora)

Alyki

Ag. Konstantinos

Volcano

Loutra Provata

Mandrakia

Adamas

Mavra
Gremna

Chivado Limni

Kastro

Tripiti

Catacombs

Patrikia

Plaka

Klema

Agriokastro

Kipos

Platina

Arkoudes

Ag.
Dimitriou

Embourios

Rivari

Ag. Marina

Profitis Elias
(883 m./2900 ft.)

Ag. Ioannes
Theologos

Silkia

Kleftiko

5 km
miles

3

2

2

1

1

0

restaurants, among them Venus Village at the hotel, Akroyanni, Adamas, Antonio Panoria, and Geo. Lilies. Zorbas and Yangos are two discotheques and there is also a beach. Above the village, the **volcano** still smokes.

Buses leave both Adamas and Plaka for **Pollonia,** from whence the caique leaves for little Kimolos. In Pollonia there are many trees, tavernas, fresh fish and places to camp. The site **Phylakope** is very near, with its three successive levels of cities, from the Early Cycladic (3500 BC) to the Late Cycladic periods. Houses, roads, a palace, and walls remain of this great centre of Cycladic civilization, some of which has been engulfed in the rising Mediterranean. Part of the cemetery Elliniko remains on Kimilos across the channel.

At **Komia** to the south are the ruins of Byzantine churches, and nearby at **Demenayaki** are some of Milos' obsidian mines. **Zefyria** further inland is also known as Chora, for it was the capital of Milos in the Middle Ages, up till the 18th century. Panayia Portani was the main church of the village. A story recounts that a priest of this church was guilty of fornication. When accused by the villagers he denied it, but the villagers refused to believe him. With that the priest angrily cursed the people, which is why everyone left Chora. Zefyria today is a very quiet village of old crumbling houses surrounded by olive trees. Alyki on the bay is a good beach near the **Mavra Grema,** the black cliffs, strange formations in the rock.

At **Loutra Provata** you can see remains of Roman mosaics, and then take a sauna. The waters there are known for curing rheumatism; indeed from Hippocrates onward, the waters of Milos have been praised for their healing properties. **Kipos,** towards the south coast, has two churches. One, the Panayia tou Kipou is the oldest in Milos, dating back to the 5th century. The old monastery Chalaka is at **Ag. Marina,** along with a well. From here one can climb to the top of **Profitis Elias,** from where all of Milos and other islands are visible. Beaches can be found both at **Patrikia** and **Embourios,** a small fishing village with rooms to rent. **Ag. Dimitriou,** another beach further north is often windy.

Ag. Ioannes Theologos, in the south-west corner of Milos, has the biggest panayiéri on the island, on 7 May. Ag. Ioannes is also known here as the Iron Saint, for during one panayiéri the party goers were attacked by pirates. The people begged the saint to save them, and he complied by turning the door of the church to iron (one can still see a scrap of a dress caught in the door as the last woman entered). The pirates could not break in, and when one of them tried to kill someone left outside, Ag. Ioannes made his arm fall off!

South of Ag. Ioannes are the fantastic rock formations at **Kleftiko,** only attainable by caique. The largest of the four **Glaronisia** (seagull islands) on the north of Milos is shaped like a pipe organ. Throughout Milos one can find rocks and hills of scarlet, green, and yellow, and there are many caves. **Antimilos** to the north-west is inhabited only by goats.

Panayiéria: 17 July, Ag. Marina; 19 July, Profitis Elias on the mountain; 20 June and 31 October, Ag. Anargyroi (Byzantine church); 7 May and 25 September, Ag. Ioannes, Theologos and Chalaka; 14 August at Chora; 28 August, Ag. Ioannes Prodromou; 5 August, Sotiris at Paraskopou; 26 July, Ag. Panteleimonos at Chora; and 25 July, Ag. Paraskevı at Pollonia.

Specialities: pottery.

Hotels in Milos: area code 0287
in Adamas
B: Adamas (pension), 2 Griara, tel. 41844
C: Chronis (bungalows), tel. 41625 / 41829
C: Corali, tel. 41633 / 41800 /
D: Delfini, Lagada, tel. 41741
D: Semiramis, tel. 41617; 4179751 in Piraeus

Tourist Police: see regular police in Adamas.

Mykonos

Connections: Twice a day with Piraeus, Tinos, Naxos, and Paros; once a week with Samos and Ikaria; twice a week with Leros, Kalymnos, Rhodes, Kos; two or three times a week with Syros, Ios, Santorini, Thessaloniki, and Herakleon; boats also from Rafina and Andros. By air from Athens at least once a day.

History: In mythology Mykonos is the rock tomb of the last giant slain by the hero Herakles; it also has the grave of Ajax of Oileus, one of the Achaean heroes of the Trojan War. (This Ajax is called little Ajax to differentiate between another hero of the same name, who committed suicide when the arms of the dead Achilleus were not given to him but to Odysseus.) After the capture of Troy, little Ajax raped Priam's daughter Kassandra who sought protection in a sanctuary of Athena. Athena avenged this blasphemy by wrecking Ajax's ship as he was returning home, off the coast of Mykonos. Poseidon saved him in the storm but rather than being grateful, Ajax declared that he would have been perfectly able to have saved himself without the god's assistance. Poseidon's trident finished Ajax then and there, and his Mycenean tomb can still be seen at Linos.

The Ionians, who settled on the island, built three cities, one on the isthmus south of Chora, the second at Dimastos, dating back to 2000 BC, and the third at Panormos by Paliokastro. During the war between the Romans and Mithridates of Pontos, all of these ancient cities were destroyed. Chora was re-built during the Byzantine period, and the Venetians surrounded it with a wall that no longer exists; however, at Paliokastro a fort built by the Guizzi rulers still remains.

In recent years Mykonos, the most notorious and most popular of all the Cyclades, has toned down a bit. The jet set and the gay world are less obvious, people dress decently in the street and only swim nude at

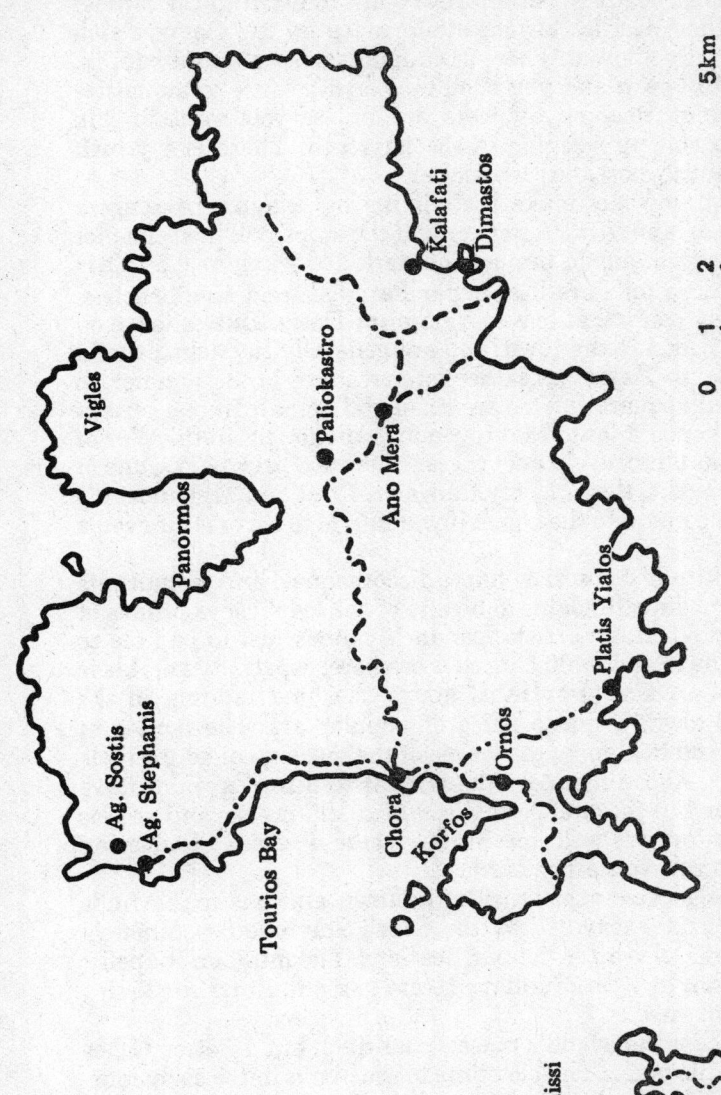

The Cyclades

Tragonissi

5km
3 miles

Kalafati
Dimastos

Vigles

Paliokastro

Ano Mera

Panormos

Platis Yialos

Ag. Sostis
Ag. Stephanis

Ornos

Chora
Korfos

Tourlos Bay

Frassonissia

Delos

Kounelonissi

Megalo
Rematiaris

Rheneia

Mykonos

the official naturalist beaches. All **campers** are referred to the official camping site by the Paradise beach; others sleep on the Chora beach although it's not really allowed. There are numerous **hotels and rooms,** both in and outside town: and you should always be sure to memorize carefully where your sleeping quarters are unless you want to join the lost souls who end up sleeping in the haystack. There is a **youth hostel** in town, but it closes in September.

A group of caique owners make their living by relaying passengers from the steamers to land. After 9 pm at night the ships pull in at the pier down the road, a very dramatic business on dark and windy nights. **Caiques** also leave Chora for Paradise, Super Paradise, and Hell beaches, along with the daily boats that leave at 9 am for Delos. **Buses** leave on the hour from just outside the town, and are generally so packed that a fly couldn't squeeze in. **Taxis** are rather rare creatures in the summer, to be found in the main square (prices are fixed and listed). Here a bust of the heroine of Mykonos, Manto Mavroyenous, who fought in the War of Independence, looks out bravely above a sea of orange back packs, one of the safest places to leave them. Many things are "lost" on Mykonos: it's silly to take a good camera to the beach if you intend to leave it for even a five-minute swim.

Despite the multitude of tourist shops, discotheques, and restaurants at **Chora,** the town can still claim to be one of the loveliest examples of Cycladic architecture. Many artists live on Mykonos just to be able to paint it. Many of the island's 400 churches are here; especially notable is the famous **Panayia Paraportiani,** above the boat landing in the Kastro quarter of town, a masterpiece of popular art. The houses at **Alefkandra,** tall and beaten by the waves of the sea, are called the little Venice of Mykonos. Above them are the famous **windmills** which have all stopped working but for one, Nikola's, which still creaks and groans over its wheat. Visitors are welcome inside, where a rather Chaucerian miller will offer to sell you a postcard.

The **museum** is located just outside the town and has many finds from the islet Rheneia, excavated by the Greek Stavropoulos. Rheneia was the cemetery of Delos after the purifications. The museum is open 9 am to 1 pm and 6 pm to 8 pm; Sundays 10 am to 2 pm. Entrance 25 dr.; 2.5 dr. with student card.

Petros the pelican, the island's mascot, has died, but a Petros II has been found to take his place. The best time to see him is in the early morning. If you miss seeing the bird you can at least see his house, which is properly labelled. The fishermen of Mykonos still wear their baggy fishermen's clothes and are very friendly, as are all the inhabitants in the off season.

Prices in Mykonos, however, are some of the highest in Greece. Cheap food can be found by the square, either souvlaki or the various pies sold at the two bakeries.

Restaurants: Good and less expensive are Adoninis, Georges, Makis, Alefkandra, Mykos and Marko Polo. Very good but not cheap are

Edem, Manto, Philipi, El Greco, and Katherine.

Discotheques: Remetso (the best), Nine Muses (second best), Windmill, Pavlos Bar, AX-BX, Bamboulas, Mykonos, Marquise, Thalami (Greek music), Minotauvros, Bills Bar, Copacobana, Venekara, Ankyra, Bar Pirous, Steps, Seven Sins, Bar Sunday, Bar Kastro, Venetia, Montparnasse, Number One.

Specialities: Koupanisti cheese, lousa (big rabbit sausages made in October), and xinogalo, the extra special yoghurt. There are also many woven items.

The only other real settlement on the island is at **Ano Mera,** where the **Tourliani monastery** with its 15th century carved steeple is the main attraction. Inside the monastery church is a carved wooden iconostasis and Bishop's throne. North of Ano Mera is **Panormos Bay,** where one can see the ancient city and Venetian fortress. South at **Dimastos** was the oldest town of Mykonos. The island **Tragonissi** has many caves and seals, but the dragon has departed. At **Linos** the tower and walls date back to the 6th century BC, and at a place called **Portes** is the tomb of Ajax, the trouble causer. **Paradise Camping** is a 20-minute walk from the road. Besides the nude beaches there, other **beaches** include Ag. Stephanis, Platis Yialos, Petinos, Theokaris, Salvator, and Ornos. Almost all of these beaches including Paradise have tavernas or cafés.

Hotels in Mykonos: area code 0289

The Leto (A), with a fine view over the harbour, is where the celebrities check in. It is the best hotel near Chora, and the best place to stay if one wishes to sample the somewhat decadent delights of the island (reserve well in advance, however). Other hotels by the golden beaches of Mykonos afford a better night's sleep, but as usual transportation to the action in town is a problem. The Alkistis Bungalows (B), however, on Ag. Stephanis beach are not too far, offering good food in their restaurant and some greenery and flowers to recommend themselves on this popular but barren island.

A: Leto, tel. 22207; teleg. Letohotel

B: Aphroditi (bungalows), Kalafati Beach, tel. 71367/71388; 8674878 in Athens; teleg. Aphrhotel

B: Alkistis (bungalows), Ag. Stephanis Beach, tel. 22332/3; 3639475 in Athens; teleg. Alkistel

B: Kouneni, Tria Pigadia (in Chora), tel. 22301

B: Rhenia (bungalows), tel. 22300/22777

B: Theoxenia, tel. 22230

C: Artemis, Ag. Stephanis Beach, tel. 22345

C: Bellou, Megali Ammos, tel. 22589; teleg. Hotel Belu

C: Mangas, Vryssi, tel. 22577

C: Manto, 1 Evangelistrias, tel. 22330

C: Marios, Limni, tel. 22704

C: Mykonos Beach (bungalows), Megali Ammos, tel. 22572/3

C: Paralos Beach, Ornos Beach, tel. 22500/22600/22800; teleg. Paralos
C: Petinos, Platis Yialos, tel. 22127
D: Apollon, Paralia, tel. 22223
D: Maria, Platis, Yialos Beach, tel. 22343

Tourist Police: at Chora, by the boat landing stage. Tel. 22482.

Naxos

Connections: Tourist boat every day to Mykonos and almost every day from Piraeus; in summer, caique every day to Amorgos; frequent connections with Paros, Ios, Santorini, Syros, and Tinos in the summer; twice a week with Rhodes, Kos, Kalymnos.

History: The first inhabitants of Naxos, the largest island of the Cyclades, were probably Thracian, later supplanted by the Karians, whose early leader gave his name to the island. Besides the present town of Naxos, inhabited from 3000 BC, are the sea-eroded remains of a Cycladic town at Grotta, and at Kastraki there is a Cycladic akropolis by the Mycenaean fort. In mythology, Theseus and the Cretan princess Ariadne stopped off at Naxos on their way to Athens, after the destruction of the Minotaur. Then, for some unknown reason, Theseus deserted the girl who had assisted him so greatly and left for Athens with the other Athenians. This myth supposedly demonstrates the rise of a late Cycladic culture after the fall of Crete, which itself eventually gave way to the Ionian and Athenian. As for poor Ariadne, she later married the god of wine, Dionysos, who happened to be on Naxos at the time, teaching the Naxians how to make wine.

The greatest enemies of powerful ancient Naxos were the Miletians from Asia Minor. Many battles were fought between the two rivals at the fort called Delion, of which a few vestiges remain by Naxos town. It was here that the Naxian heroine Polykrite fled when her island was besieged by these enemies, only to find the gate of the fortress already closed. One of the Miletian leaders found her there and fell so much in love with her that he agreed to help her people, informing her of all the movements of his armies. Thus the Naxians were able to make a sudden and vicious attack on the Miletians. However, in the confusion of the battle, Polykrite's lover, turned traitor for her sake, also perished, and the girl died in sorrow the next day, despite being acclaimed a great heroine.

Naxos was one of the first islands to work in marble, later producing in the Archaic period the lions of Delos and huge koures statues. Two of these were left in the quarries because they were flawed. In 523 BC the tyrant Lugdami decided to make the buildings of Naxos the highest and most glorious of all Greece. The only remaining sign of Lugdami's determination is the huge lintel from the gate of the temple of Apollo, located next to the town on the islet Palatia. An ancient mole connects Palatia to the mainland, attesting to the former glory of Naxos when the island was the leader of the Ionic Amphictyonic League. As with most of the islands, Naxos declined in importance in the Classical age. In Hellenistic times it was governed by Ptolemy of Egypt who fortified Apano Kastro and Chimaru. The Byzantines continued to build defences on this rich and strategic island: and at their Castle T'apaliru, Marco Sanudo besieged them for two months in 1207.

With the taking of T'apaliru, Marco Sanudo became the Duke of Naxos and held sway over all the Venetians who had seized the Aegean islands in the free for all after the sack of Constantinople. Under the Venetians a small part of the population were converted to the Catholic church, and a cathedral was built along with the Palace of the Dukes, of which only one tower and a few walls remain on the top of Naxos town. The Duke's other residence was at Apano Kastro, used in defence against both outsiders and rebellious islanders. Even after the Turkish conquest in 1564 the Dukes of Naxos remained in nominal control of Naxos and the Cyclades, although always answerable to the Sultan.

A latter-day Naxian, Petros Protopapadakis, planned the Corinth canal and gave many public works to the island. He was the Minister of Economics in 1922 during the misadventure in Asia Minor, and was executed with other members of that sad government by the following regime. His statue now stands by the port.

Economically Naxos is the most important of the Cyclades. It is also one of the most beautiful. A great deal of farming takes place in its rich valleys, the cultivation of lemon trees being particularly important — the liqueur Kitro is made from the leaves. Wheat, potatoes, and dairy products are also to be found in great quantity. Signs of Ancient, Byzantine, and Venetian history abound throughout the island, and the capital town, also called Naxos, has fine examples of both Cycladic and Venetian architecture.

Naxos today: The first thing one sees when entering the port of Naxos is the lonely lintel from the **temple of Apollo,** begun in 522 BC but never finished, perhaps because it was too large. The ruins on the islet are open until sunset and require some clambering to examine. A small sandy beach curves down on one side of the **ancient mole,** although most people prefer to swim at **Ag. Georgios beach** on the other side of town. Here the large hotels, tavernas, discos, and an impromptu bamboo camping site are also located. In the upper part of town, below the Venetian tower, is a **youth hostel** and the **Naxos Archaeology Museum,** housed in the former French commercial school: Open 9am-1pm and 4pm-6pm; 10am-2pm Sunday; closed Tuesday. Entrance 25dr., 2.5dr. with student card; free Thursday and Sunday. There are a great many Cycladic sculptures inside, pottery, a mosaic of Europa, and a very funny figurine of a pig about to be sick in a sack.

In the upper town one can also see many **Venetian mansions** still bearing their owner's coats of arms, and imagine how great the **Palace of the Dukes** once was, with its seven towers. Nearby is the 13th century Catholic cathedral built by Marco Sanudo, called **Ypapandi** or

Candlemas, and the Orthodox Cathedral, or **Mitropolis of Zoodochos Pigi,** built in the 18th century out of an old temple and older churches. The iconostasis was painted by Dimitrios Valvis of the Cretan school. Other interesting churches in the town are the **Church of Pantanassa,** once the church of a Byzantine monastery, dating back to the 11th century and containing an 8th century icon of the Virgin. By **Grotta,** where the remains of a Cycladic town are in the sea, is the church **Ag. Georgios,** built in 1200, with an excellent carved wooden iconostasis. On an islet by Ag. Georgios beach is **Panayia Myrtidiotissa.**

In the town itself is the **House of the Kallivrousi,** where the Naxian saint, Ag. Nikodimos, was born in 1749 and where he lived for many years, writing books on theology. His panayiéri on 14 July is one of the largest in Naxos. Also in the town is the **old market,** with snake-like streets so narrow one must walk in single file. The wooden floors of the houses extend directly overhead, forming many tunnels and narrow passageways.

In Naxos harbour there is a **yacht supply station,** offering general provisioning.

Restaurants: Meltemi, Kavouri, Neraida, Trata, Paradissos; with music Platanos, Kasanakia, and Asteria.

Discotheques: Medusa, Rock, Naxos Club, Flisvos.

Specialities: Kitrou liqueur, Tsinotiri (only for the strong hearted).

As an alternative to taking a bus (from the harbour) or a taxi, there are three places in Naxos where one can rent a scooter to see the rest of the island. The south road from Naxos leads to the village **Galanado,** with the Bolognia Castle built by the Venetians and the ruins of Hellenistic walls. In **Glinado** further south is the monastery Ag. Saranta (17th century), containing post-Byzantine icons. **Tripodes,** officially known as Vivlos, once the capital of the district of Vivlian wine, has an ancient fort Paliopyrgos, supposedly constructed by the Thracians in a contest over a woman. Ag. Matheos nearby is built on an early Christian basilica. **Kastraki,** situated in a region of fine beaches (the one named Kastraki has four tavernas) has a Mycenaean fortress with the remains of a Cycladic acropolis. **T'apaliru,** a Byzantine castle to the east, is high on a rock and defied Marco Sanudo and his mercenaries for two months before the Venetian took the island.

Sagri to the north is actually three small villages, with many old buildings dating from the Byzantine period, including the fortified monastery Timios Stavros, dating from the 16th century. Ag. Ioannes Gyroulas was built on a temple of Demeter, and three other churches, **Ag. Nikolaos** (11th century), **Kaloritsa** (14th century) and **Panayia Arkulou** (13th century) have frescoes.

Halki in the heart of the island is situated by the fertile Tragea valley, where both the Byzantines and the Venetians made a point of building towers: **Francopoulo,** right in the centre of the village, and the Byzantine **Apano Kastro** located on a high rock, contain many ruined

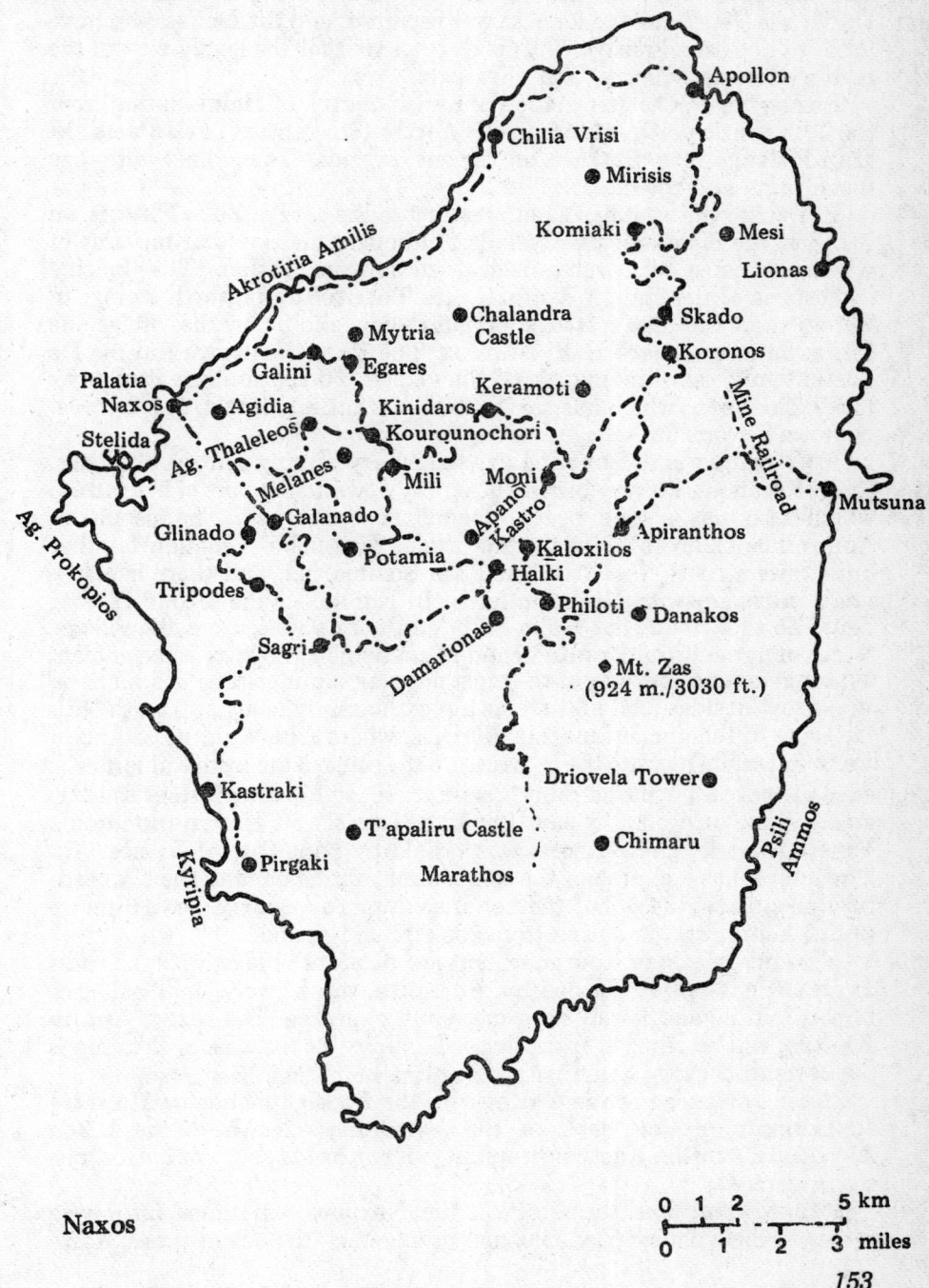

Apollon

Chilia Vrisi

Mirisis

Komiaki   Mesi

Lionas

Akrotiria Amilis

Chalandra Castle

Skado

Mytria   Koronos

Galini   Egares

Keramoti

Palatia
Naxos   Agidia   Kinidaros
Stelida   Kourounochori

Ag. Thaleleos

Mine Railroad

Melanes   Mili   Moni

Galanado   Apano Kastro   Mutsuna

Glinado   Potamia   Apiranthos

Kaloxilos
Halki

Tripodes   Philoti   Danakos

Sagri   Damarionas

Mt. Zas
(924 m./3030 ft.)

Ag. Prokopios

Driovela Tower

Kastraki

T'apaliru Castle   Chimaru

Kyripia   Pirgaki   Marathos

Psili Ammos

Naxos

0 1 2   5 km
0 1   2   3 miles

churches and houses. Apano Kastro was built on a Cylopean foundation, and Mycenaean tombs have been discovered in the immediate area. Under the Venetians the fortress was repaired, and the Dukes may have used it as a second residence. It is worth a visit for the lovely view of the region's forests, villages, and olive trees.

Panayias Protothronis is the parish church of Halki, dating from the 12th century. **Ag. Georgios Diasrtis** (9th century) and **Panayia Damiotissa** have frescoes of various periods. The village also has restaurants and rooms.

Philoti to the west has a path leading to the cave of **Zeus Philoti,** on Mt. Zas, the highest of the Cyclades, although it is closed at the time of writing because of archaeological discoveries inside. The marble iconostasis of the church **Koimisis tis Theotokou** is worth seeing. In Philoti there are also restaurants and rooms, and below the village one can swim at the beach **Psili Ammos.** The **Venetian tower** of the De Lastic family is in the middle of the village. To the south is Ptolemy's tower **Chimaru,** which has survived almost entirely intact. It is a three-hour walk from the village.

Apiranthos and **Koronos** are the emery mining centres of Naxos. From Koronos a railway brings the emery down to the port of **Mutsuna,** which also has a fine beach, rooms, and tavernas. The people of Apiranthos claim to be of Cretan origin. Two noble Venetian families built towers there, the Crispi and the Sommaripa, and there is also a small **museum** with Neolithic finds. In Koronos is the second cave of Zeus, **Zeus Korona,** or Kako Spilio, an hour's walk from the village. North of agricultural **Komiaki** and **Mesi** (which also have some ancient remains) is **Apollon,** one of the most popular summer-time destinations on Naxos. Besides food and rooms along the sandy beach, up on the hill are some of the ancient marble quarries, where a huge statue of Apollo lies unfinished. Opposite the quarries are the ruins of the medieval fort called **Kalogeros** for the summit it is built on. By **Mytria** further south is an old stone bridge and a cave known as Genisis. At **Kourounochori** a Venetian castle, Della Rocca, was visited by King Otto of Greece. **Ag. Thaleleos** has a church of the same name, dating back to the 13th century. **Melanes,** the site of another ancient marble quarry, has a 6-metre (20ft.) kouros statue dating from the Archaic period.

Kinidaros east of Kourounochori is a pleasant village, with the ruins of an ancient settlement nearby. **Potamia,** three lovely small villages, upper, middle and lower, have many old churches. The castle, **Apano Kastro,** can be reached from Upper Potamia. To the west of Potamia is the seventh-century church **Ag. Mamas** which has been restored.

Closer to Naxos town is **Galini** with the fortified monastry **Moni tis Ipsiloteras,** dating back to the Byzantines. North is the beach **Akrotiria Amilis.** Another beach, **Ag. Prokopios** south of Naxos, has six tavernas.

Panayiéria: like the Cretans, the Naxians sometimes improvise verses at their panayiéria, a custom dating back to ancient times. Some of the many celebrations are: 20 May, Ag. Thaleleos; 17 July, at Koronos; 15 August, Panayia at Philoti; 1 July, Ag. Anargyroi at Sagri; 23 August, at Tripodes; 14 July, Ag. Nikodimos at Naxos; 29 August, Ag. Ioannes at Apollon and Apiranthos; 23 April, Ag. Georgios at Kinidaros.

Hotels in Naxos: area code 0285
B: Ariadne (pension), 1 Ariadnis, tel. 22452.
C: Acroyali, Ag. Georgios, tel. 22922
C: Aegeon, Pigadakia, tel. 22852
C: Anessi, Ag. Georgios, tel. 22758
C: Apollon, 61 Neofytou, tel. 22468
C: Barbouni, tel. 22535/22474
C: Coronis, Paraliaki Leoforos, tel. 22626/22297. Teleg. Coronotel
C: Hermes, 7 Protopapadaki, tel. 22220. Teleg. Hermesho
C: Nissaki, Ag. Georgios, tel. 22876
C: Panorama, Amphitritis, Kastro, tel. 22330.
C: Renetta
C: Zeus, Ag. Georgios, tel. 22912
D: Anixis, 330 Amphitritis, tel. 22782
D: Dionyssos, 110 Persefonis, tel. 22331
D: Oceanis, 11 Damirali, tel. 22826/22436
D: Panormos, Ag. Georgios, tel. 22510
D: Pantheon, tel. 22436
D: Proto, Paralia, tel. 22394

Tourist police: regular police in town.

Paros
Connections: per week, in summer — 12 with Naxos, 19 with Piraeus, 4 with Herakleon, Crete, 11 with Ios, 7 with Syros, 3 with Leros, Kos, Kalymnos and Rhodes, 9 with Santorini, 4 with Mykonos, 2 with Amorgos and Anafi, 1 with Heraklia and Dounnoussa; frequent daily connections with Antiparos.

History: With the trade of the famous Parian marble, the island of Paros prospered very early in history. An Early Cycladic town thrived, and was connected with Knossos and the Mycenaeans in the Late Cycladic period (1100 BC). In the 8th century BC Ionians settled the island and brought it a second prosperity. The poet Archilochos and the sculptor Ariston were famous sons of ancient Paros. During the Persian wars the Parians supported the Persians at both Marathon and Salamis. When Athens' General Miltiades came to punish them after Marathon, they withstood his month-long siege, leaving Miltiades to go home with a broken leg and die of gangrene. During the destructive Peloponnesian wars Paros remained neutral until forced to join the second Delian League in 378 BC. The great sculptor Skopas came from Paros in the Hellenistic period, and the island did well until Roman times, trading its marble which was used in the Temple of Solomon, the Venus of Milo, many of the structures on Delos and later Napoleon's tomb. When the Romans took over Paros, they also took over the marble business. After various other invaders the island was then left practically uninhabited. In 1207 Marco Sanudo ruled Paros from Naxos. The pirate Barbarossa, that red-bearded terror, took the island in 1536, and from then the Turks ruled via the Duke of Naxos. At this time the interior village of Lefkas became the capital of Paros, due to the innumerable pirate raids. The Catholics set up Capuchin schools and missions but had little success in coverting the locals. In 1770 the Russians began to fortify Paros against the Turks, but they left long before the work was finished. Paros joined the War of Independence, and the heroine Manto Mavroyenous, whose parents were from Paros and Mykonos, came to Paros after the revolution and died there. She had led guerilla attacks against the Turks throughout Greece.

Paros today: Although Paros is one of the more frequented isles of the Cyclades, it still retains a quiet rural charm. Although it is not blessed with a great deal of fresh water, the inhabitants still manage to farm, producing sweet red wine and barley. One of the most beautiful churches in Greece is at the capital, Paroikia. Besides this town, Dryos, Marpissa, and Naousa are popular and well supplied with tourist facilities.

Three of the most important things in **Paroikia** are located directly opposite the landing pier; the **tourist police** in the windmill, the **bus stop** for villages on the rest of the island, and the 'Nudity is Forbidden' sign. A small beach 15 metres (50ft.) away is a handy place to sleep if one's ship arrives at 4 in the morning; a quieter place can be found in the pine forest by the church Ekatontapyliani. There are innumerable rooms and donkeys for rent. The architecture of the town is pure Cycladic, and, what is more, one can explore it without climbing hundreds of stairs. The main street winds through the centre of town, lined by shops, both tourist and non-tourist. Near the heart of the town a narrow **13th century wall** is amalgamated into neighbouring houses, built out of the temples of Apollo and Demeter. Some objects in the museums are from this strange conglomerate.

The most important attraction of Paroikia is the church of a hundred doors, the **Ekatontapyliani,** founded by Justinian in the 6th century, and built by Ignatius, an apprentice of the master architect of Ag. Sophia in Constantinople, the most beautiful church within the Orthodox religion. A story runs that Ignatius made the Ekatontapyliani so lovely that when his master came to visit it, he was consumed by jealousy and pushed Ignatius off the roof of the church — but not before Ignatius had seized his foot and dragged him down, too. Around the church is a building with cells, built to protect the villagers during the days of piracy. The church bells hang in a tree. As an earthquake damaged much of the original building, the present church was reconstructed in the 10th century out of Classical and older Byzantine materials. Pagan tombs and a well are beneath the church flooor.

On the carved wooden iconostasis is an icon of the Virgin, worshipped for its healing virtues; the church also contains the mortal remains of the Parian Saint Ag. Theoktisti, and a painting illustrates her story. Captured by pirates, she managed to flee into the trees of Paros. For 30 years she lived a sacred life alone in the wilderness. A hunter finally found her, and when he brought her the communion bread she asked for, she died. For a good omen he cut off her hand (now on exhibit in a box) and made to sail away, but he was unable to depart until he had returned it to the saint's body. Beneath a liftable wooden cover is Theoktisti's foot print: the Greeks take off their shoes and fit their feet into her's for good luck. Behind the iconostasis are frescoes and a carved marble Holy Table. The Baptistry next to the church has a sunken font.

Near the church is the **museum:** open 9am-1pm and 4pm-6pm; closed Tuesday. It contains the Hellenistic Parian Chronicle with the history of Greece carved in the marble, finds from the temple of Apollo and a mosaic of Herakles. The small church of **Ag. Nikolaos** is also nearby, built at the same time as the Ekatontapyliani. Just outside Paroikia, by a spring, are the Classical ruins of an **Asklepeieon** (temple to the god of healing). Nearby was a temple to Pythian Apollo, which no longer remains, although by **Livadia Camping** (the official site) are a few signs of a temple of **Delian Apollo. The Cave of the Neraidas,** or nymphs, can be seen by the Xenia Hotel.

Also in Paroikia is the **Aegean School of Fine Arts,** founded by Brett Taylor in 1966 and accredited with many American Universities. In June and July there are even chamber music concerts. A good alternative to the small and not so clean town beach, is **Argo beach,** by the Argo taverna, and near Livadia Camping.

Restaurants: Oasis, Livadia, Katerina, Nissiotissa, Alligaria, Efkalyptos, Limnataria, Kalamnys, Fanari, Pandorsos.

Tavernas: Rodies and Retos.

Bazookia: Elitas and Cecilia.

Discotheques: Paros, Psarades, and Lemon Tree.

Specialities: Parian wine, souma liqueur.

In Paroikia one can rent a bicycle, car, or donkey or take a bus to see the rest of the island. South-west of the town is **Betaloudes,** also called Psychopiani, by the ruins of a 17th century **Venetian tower.** It is full of butterflies and flowers. A convent nearby, **Christos sto Dasos,** has the tomb of Ag. Arsenios, a school teacher, abbot, and prophet canonized in 1867. Men are not allowed inside. At **Pounta** there is a small boat which makes the short trip across the straits to Antiparos: the signal to call it over is to open the church door. **Alyki** has new houses and good fish tavernas, and an airport will soon be operating nearby. A dirt road leads from **Agkairia** to Dryos or to the **Monastery Ag. Theodoron** where the nuns are expert weavers. Above **Glifa beach** is a small church in a cave, Ag. Ioannes Spiliotis.

Platis Ammos

Langeri

Santa Maria

Ag. Ioannis
Prodromos

Filizi

Ambelas

Glifades

Tsou Kalia

Prasonisi

Krispi

Drionisi

Kolimbithres

Naousa

Marmara

Chrysi Akti

Fikia

Treis Ekklises

Longovardes Monastery

Marathi

Kostos

Younia

Lefkas

Prodromos

Marpissa

Ag. Theodoron Monastery

Lagadas

Spilion

Molos

Kalampaki

Aspro Chorio

Kalami

Thapsana

Ag. Theodoron Monastery

Piso Livadi

Dryos

Delion

Argo

Asklepeion

Mt. Profitis Elias

Betaloudes

Kamari

Agkairia

Akrotiri

Tripiti

Glifa

Krios

Paroika

Saliagos

Strogilonisi

Pounta

Kanali

Vathia Psaria

Alyki

Voutakos

Pandro

Kavouras

Antiparos

Panayia

Dipla

Sifnaikos

Yialos

Kambos

Antiparos

Cave

Ag. Georgios

Despotiko

Paros

0 1 2
0 1 2 3 miles
0 5 km

There are many beaches in the **Dryos** region, which has made it a popular place to build hotels. **Piso Livadi** to the north-east was the port of Marathi and is well stocked with beaches, restaurants and hotels. This region has the best fishing in Paros. At **Marpissa,** above the windmills, are the ruins of a 15th century **Venetian fortress** and the **Ag. Antonios monastery** (16th century), made from classical ruins and containing lovely paintings and marbles.

In the town of Dryos itself is the 17th century **Cathedral of the Metamorphosis. Marmara,** a bit to the north as its name implies, is full of marble — in the streets and the churches. A favourite beach, Molos, is below the village. **Prodromos** is an old farming village. **Lefkas,** one of the loveliest villages of Paros and its medieval capital, is located high above the sea. Much farming is done there, and the inhabitants make textiles and ceramics.

Beside Lefkas is **Marathi,** the site of the ancient marble mines. Lychnites or candlelit marble, the finest marble in the world, was produced here. Be sure to bring a flashlight to explore the mines, which are no longer in use for economical reasons. The lovely 16th century fortified monastery, **Ag. Minas,** is less than half an hour's walk away.

North-east of Paroikia is the temple of **Delion Apollo,** of which the marble foundation and altar remain. Along with temples on Delos and Naxos this temple forms part of a perfect equilateral triangle. The **Treis Ekklises** are the ruins of three 17th century churches, built from the ruins of a 7th century church which was in turn built from a 4th century BC Heroon of Archilochos. The **monastery Longovardes** is the largest on Paros and was established in 1683 by Christophros Palaiologos. There are many old icons and paintings and an icon painting school, but women are not allowed inside. **Naousa** is the second port of Paros and the most popular destination for most visitors because of the many beaches nearby, in particular **Santa Maria** and **Langeri.** The restaurants and tavernas usually have good fresh fish. On 23 August a big festival takes place there in celebration of a victory over the Turks. **Ambelas** on the east coast is a small quiet village with a hotel and few tourists.

Panayiéria: 15 August, Ekatontapyliani at Paroikia; 23 April, Ag. Georgios at Agkairia; 21 May, Ag. Konstantinos at Paroikia; 40 days after Orthodox Easter, Analypsis at Piso Livadi; 24 June, Ag. Ionnes Baptist at Prodromos; 2 days in late June, Ag. Pnevmatas at Lefkas and 1 July at the monastery; 23 August, at Naousa; 9 November, Ag. Theoktisti at Paroikia.

Hotels in Paros: area code 0284
in Dryos
C: Ivi (Hebe), tel. 41249 ext. 20
D: Dryos, tel. 41249 ext. 4
in Ambelas
C: Ambelas, tel. 51324

in Marpissa
B: Marpissa (pension), Piso Livadi, tel. 41288
C: Leto, tel. 41283; 3628864 in Athens
C: Logaras, tel. 6591829 in Athens
C: Piso Livadi
C: Vicky, Piso Livadi, tel. 41277
in Naousa
B: Naousa (pension), tel. 51207
C: Ambelas, tel. 51324
C: Galini
C: Hippocambus (bungalows), tel. 51223/4; 3249993 in Athens; teleg. Hippocambotel
C: Piperi
D: Drossia, tel. 51213
in Paroikia
B: Xenia, tel. 21394; 3605611 in Athens
C: Alkion, tel. 21506
C: Argonaftis, tel. 21656
C: Ermis, tel. 21217
C: Galini, tel. 21280
C: Georgy, tel. 21667
C: Paros, tel. 21319
C: Stella, tel. 21502
C: Tzortzis, tel. 21667
D: Kontes, tel. 21246
D: Kypraiou, tel. 21383
D: Oasis, tel. 21227
E: Pandrossos, tel. 21229
E: Cairo, tel. 21325

Tourist Police: In windmill, Paroikia, summer only. Tel. 21673.

Santorini
Connections: Frequent connections with Herakleon, Crete, Naxos, Ios, Mykonos, Paros and Piraeus; once a week with Ag. Nikolaos and Sitia (Crete), Kassos, Karpathos, Diafani, Halki, and Rhodes; once a week with Anafi. Daily flights from Athens.

History: The history of Santorini, or Fira, is tied up with its geology. In the long distant past the island was created from volcanic debris. It was circular in shape, with a volcano called Strogyle in the centre. Since prehistoric times, regular volcanic eruptions created a rich, volcanic soil, which attracted inhabitants very early. First came the Karians, who were chased out by the Cretans. Their colony at Akrotiri dates back to the height of the Minoan civilization. Then, in approximately 1450 BC the volcano erupted again, destroying not only Akrotiri, but causing irreparable damage to the mighty Minoan civilization in Crete.

This relatively recent theory, now accepted by most of the learned, found its major exponent in the Greek archaeologist Spirydon Marinatos. In 1939 he decided that the destruction of Amnisos, the port of Knossos on Crete, could only have been caused by a massive natural disaster, such as a tidal wave from the north. What, he wondered, could have caused such a catastrophic force? There were the following clues: south-east of Santorini oceanographers discovered volcanic ash from Strogyle on the sea bed, covering an area of 900 x 300 sq. km. (350 x 115 sq. miles); on nearby Anafi and Eastern Crete itself is a layer of volcanic tephra 20 cm. (8 ins.) thick. This, thin as it was, would suffice to destroy existing plant growth and cause a famine. A Classical clue came from the Athenian reformer and writer Solon, who in 600 BC wrote of his journey to Egypt, where the scribes told him of the disappearance of Kreftia (Crete?) 9000 years ago, which Solon might have mistaken for a more correct 900. The Egyptians, who had steadily traded with Crete and Santorini, described a lost land of Atlantis, which had red, white and black volcanic rock (like Santorini today); they spoke of the ancient city vanishing in 24 hours under a tremendous wave. In his *Critias* Plato describes Atlantis as being composed of one round island and one long island, connected by one culture and rule (Santorini and Crete, under Minos?). He describes Atlantis as a sweet land of art, flowers, and fruit (which are portrayed on the frescoes discovered at Akrotiri). In the 19th century French archaeologists discovered Minoan pots at Akrotiri, and it was there that Marinatos began to dig in 1967, bringing to light a wonderful ancient Minoan city.

Whether or not Santorini was the glorified Atlantis of the ancients, the theory of the ruin of Minoan life by its volcanic explosion and subsequent tidal waves and earthquakes has recent support in a similar explosion in 1883. This is when the volcano Krakatoa exploded creating a caldera (a crater left by an explosion) of 8.3 sq. km. (3¼ sq. miles). This vacancy caused a tidal wave more than 200 metres (660 ft.) high, spreading great damage over 150 km. (100 miles). The caldera caused by Strogyle, i.e. the present bay of Santorini, is 22 sq. km. (8½ sq. miles). After the volcano had sunk into it, it was filled by a rushing sea, which caused a truly enormous wave. As no bodies have been found at Akrotiri it is supposed that earthquakes and other omens warned the inhabitants in time for them to flee. The present islets of Therasia and Aspronisi mark the edges of the caldera.

In the 8th century BC the Dorians settled at Santorini, building their capital at Mesa Vouna on Mt. Profitis Elias, which was inhabited until the early decades after Christ. Ptolemy of Egypt had close contacts with Mesa Vouna, and he built a temple dedicated to Dionysos and to his family there, along with military barracks. The founder of the Doric colony was named Thira, from whence derives the island's second name. The Thirians also established the city of Cyrene in Libya.

Like the Ptolemies, the Byzantines also considered the island to be of strategic importance and fortified it, but most of these fortifications have since been destroyed in earthquakes. Skaros near Imerovigli became the Frankish capital when Marco Sanudo captured the island, eventually taken over by the Crispi family. At this time the island was called after its patron saint Saint Irene, which has been elided into Santorini. In 1534 the pirate admiral Barbarossa stopped by and gave the island to the Turks. Later, in 1956, a great earthquake shook the island and levelled most of the houses. The inhabitants say that the present town in no way equals the past, although if you look between the earthquake-proof structures you can gain some idea of what the pre-1956 town looked like.

Santorini today: Whatever its architectural deficiencies, the present **capital town of Santorini** is the most splendidly situated of all the island towns of Greece, on the edge of a 275-metre (900 ft.) striped cliff plunging into the sea below. It looks directly over the volcano and bay, an often spectacular sight at sundown. To reach the town from the cruise ships and yachts (ferry boats now call at Athinios) it is still necessary to climb the huge stairway cut into the rock, or to rent a donkey to make the trip up. The rest of the island, with its hilly swirling vineyards and long black beaches, has an unusual beauty which attracts not only artists but tourists from all over the world.

Fira, as the capital is known, has been given over to tourism. Coffee shops and bars (generally rather expensive) hang on the edge of the cliff, affording customers a most lovely view while they sip their drinks. The **museum** is in the north part of the town: open 9 am to 1 pm and 4 pm to 6 pm; 10 am to 2 pm Sunday. Closed Tuesday. Entrance 25 dr., 2.5 dr. with student card; free Thursdays and Sunday. It houses finds from Akrotiri and ancient Thira, and pottery from Minoan to Hellenistic times. The famous frescoes, however, are in the National Archaeology Museum of Athens. Beside the museum little signs direct one to a **handicraft workshop** where the women weave large carpets on looms. There are many sophisticated bars but very few unsophisticated ones; the typical Greek kafeníon does not exist. In some places, however, one can sample local wines by the glass.

The **Youth Hostel** is a few blocks from the bus station square, by the Olympic Airways Office. The **Post Office, OTE** and **bank** are close by in the opposite direction. It is best to arrive early at this bank, if you want to avoid crowds in the summer. The bus station square also has the cheapest food (souvlaki, etc) in town. The numerous tourist shops sell typical handicrafts and custom made jewellery. Also on the square is the **Damingos Tourist Office** which handles most of the excurions made on the island, including those to the volcano.

Restaurants: Atlantis (in the hotel), Bobby's, Aris, Drakotos, Leschi.

Discotheques: Neptune, Volcan, and Yellow Donkey.

Specialities: Wine, white and rosé in particular under the labels of Atlantis, Santina, Kaldera, Nikteri, Volcan and Vissanto.

Three or four buses a day go to the **Akrotiri** site in the south of the

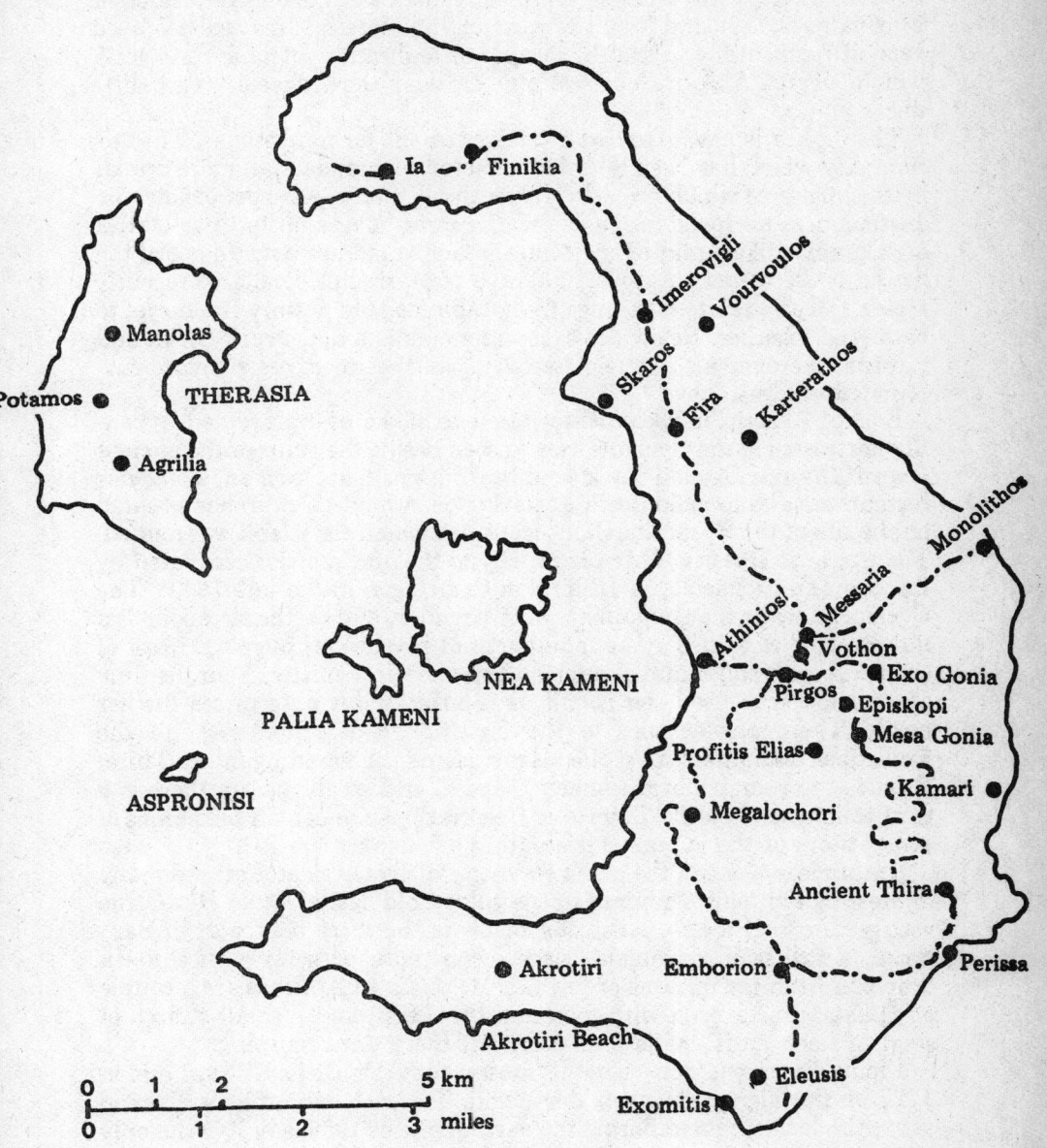

THERASIA

Manolas

Potamos

Agrilia

PALIA KAMENI

NEA KAMENI

ASPRONISI

Ia   Finikia

Imerovigli   Vourvoulos

Skaros   Karterathos

Fira

Monolithos

Athinios   Messaria

Vothon

Pirgos   Exo Gonia

Episkopi

Profitis Elias   Mesa Gonia

Kamari

Megalochori

Ancient Thira

Emborion   Perissa

Akrotiri

Akrotiri Beach

Eleusis

Exomitis

0	1	2		5 km
0	1	2	3	miles

Santorini (Thira)

island (schedule posted): open 9 am to 1 pm and 4 pm to 6 pm; entrance 25 dr., 5 dr. with student card. The dig was begun by Professor Marinatos in 1967 and is still very much in progress. Excavation proved very difficult owing to the thick layer of tephra, or volcanic glass rock, which covered Akrotiri: one can see how deep the archaeologists had to dig.

The tephra is now quarried to make cement for tombstones. The ancient city which has been revealed is incredible, made even more unreal by the huge roof which protects it from the elements. A carpet of volcanic dust silences all footsteps as one walks amid houses up to three stories high, many still containing their huge pithoi, or storage pots. In one of the houses is the rather controversial grave of Marinatos, who died recently after a fall on the site. The huge filing cabinets hold pottery shreds yet to be pieced together. Below the excavation site is a black rock beach and taverna; there are also some coffee shops and rooms in the vineyard surrounded villages above.

East of Akrotiri is **Exomitis** where one of the best preserved Byzantine fortresses of the Cyclades can be seen beside the ruins of the ancient town of **Eleusis**. A good black sand beach is north at **Perissa,** which has restaurants and bazooki music at weekends. A modern church is situated on the site of the Byzantine Saint Irene, for whom the island was named. The **ancient Dorian Thira** is nearby to the north, a site excavated by the German archaeologist Hiller von Gortringen in the late 1800s. The Cyclopean walls that remain are very peculiar, and on the akropolis is a monstrous eight-sided stone monument of mysterious purpose. Most of the houses which remain at ancient Thira are Hellenistic, from the time of Ptolemy who used the island as a base for his enterprises further north. There are temples to the Egyptian gods, Dionysos and the Ptolemies, and others to Apollo Karneius and the founding father Thira. Besides the remains of a cemetery, agora, and small theatre there is a gymnasium, and on the Terrace of Celebrations are carved the names of competitors of the gymnopedies dating back from 800 BC.

Emborion is one of the oldest surviving villages of Santorini, and many interesting old houses remain in the ruined old castle. Other Byzantine vestiges are at **Pirgos**. **Athinios** below is the ferry-boat port of Santorini, a rather inconvenient place when more passengers disembark than can fit in the one bus or few taxis to town. At Athinios are a couple of cafés and a taverna with food and breakfast, and a small stretch of sand to sleep on if one is forced to wait there until morning.

From Pirgos one can visit the **monastery Profitis Elias**, built in 1712 on the highest point of the island. This not only affords a grand view; the locals, remembering the earthquake of 1956, say it is the only place on Santorini which will remain above sea level when the rest of the island sinks into the sea to join its other half. Profitis Elias has a museum of valuable church objects, diamond gospels, the mitre of Gregory V, a crusader's cross, and local folklore. At the foot of Profitis Elias, by the village of Mesa Gonia is **Panayia Episcopi** or Kimisis Theotokou, built in the 11th century. The Venetians converted the church to the Catholic faith when they conquered Santorini, but under the Turks the Orthodox recovered their own. Inside are Byzantine icons, and on 15 August the biggest *panayiéri* on the island takes place there.

Kamari by the sea is on the site of an ancient town, of which a few vestiges may still be seen. It has a good beach, fine fish restaurants, and a discotheque. **Monolithos** is the closest beach to Fira, further north, and many people camp there. **Skaros,** on the way to Ia or Oia was the medieval capital of Santorini, but has been greatly damaged by earthquakes. Ag. Stephanos there is the oldest church on the island, and there are also the crumbling ruins of a Catholic convent of Santa Katerina, built after a young girl's vision in 1596. The nuns lived a life of hardship until they changed residence in 1818 for Fira, and now the desolate convent is about to tumble down. In **Imerovigli** is another convent still inhabited, dedicated to Ag. Nikolaos and built in 1674. **Ia** is the second port of Santorini, where most ferryboats stop. If one arrives during the night, it may be best to disembark at Ia, where there are rooms to rent and places to eat, rather than at the rather desolate Athinios. Frequent buses connect Ia to Fira.

Boats leave daily from Fira to **Therasia,** once part of Strongyle and separated from it by the explosion. Ruins of a **Middle Cycladic settlement** have been discovered in the south part of the islet, predating the colony at Akrotiri. Other ruins are in the north, of the **ancient town of Therasia.** Most of the population make a living from the sea, so there are very few men on the islet in the summer. It is rumoured that male visitors are very welcome at this time. At the largest of the three villages, **Manolas,** it is possible to find a room and food. Other boats leave for the volcano, where you can climb into the crater: however, be warned that half the visitors find it rather unimpressive, no matter how romantic it sounds.

Panayiéria: 19 and 20 July, at Profitis Elias; 1 September, at Fira; 20 October, Ag. Artemiou in Fira; 26 October, Ag. Dimitriou in Karterado; 15 August, at Mesa Gonia.

Hotels in Santorini: area code 0286.

The most comfortable hotel in Fira is the Atlantis (B). The view from its windows is one of the most spectacular in the world, looking down at the volcano and its islet offspring serene in the sapphire sea. The sunsets are particularly enchanting. The Yellow Donkey discotheque, the best on Santorini, is located at the hotel.

in Fira

B: Atlantis, tel. 22232
C: Kavalari, tel. 22455
C: Panorama, tel. 22481/22479/22271
D: Tataki, tel. 22389/22391
E: Lucas, tel. 22481

Elsewhere
 C: Artemidoros, Messaria, tel. 22502/22245
 C: Christina (Christi), Perissa, tel. 22562
 C: Kamari, Kamari, tel. 31243/31216
 D: Archaea Elefsina, Emborion, tel. 22643

Tourist Police: Regular police by Olympic Airways or the Damingos
Agency on the square is also very helpful.

Serifos
Connections: Daily with Piraeus, Kythnos, Milos and Sifnos; Ios and
Santorini twice a week.

History: Serifos, the "bare island" once had great iron and copper
deposits, considered some of the best in Greece and mined from an early
period. However, due to more economically mined sources discovered in
Africa, the mines are now deserted and the population has gone
elsewhere. Historically the fate of the island follows that of the other
Cyclades; Chora high above the sea was once fortified with a Byzantine-
Venetian castle and walls, and here and there on the island are vestiges
left by other conquerors.

What Serifos may lack in historical interest is more than compensated
for by its **mythology,** for it was the destination of Princess Danae, who
was set adrift in a box with her infant son Perseus. This cruel deed was
done by her own father, the King, for it had been prophesied that a son
of Danae would slay him. In order to foil the oracle the King had locked
his daughter in a tower, but even there her beauty did not fail to attract
the amorous attentions of Zeus, who came to Danae in a shower of golden
rain and fathered Perseus.

Enraged but unable to put his daughter or grandson to death, the King
decided to leave the issue to fate and set them adrift in the box. Zeus
guided them to the shores of Serifos, where a fisherman discovered them
and brought them to Polydectes, the King of the Island. Struck by her
beauty, Polydectes wanted to wed Danae but she refused him, and as
Perseus grew older he supported his mother's position. Although
Polydectes pretended then to lose interest in the woman, he desired her
more than ever and plotted to remove Perseus by asking a favour of him.
Perseus, glad that the King had stopped chasing his mother, could not
refuse. Then Polydectes explained what he wanted: nothing less than the
head of the gorgon Medusa, the only mortal of the three horrible sisters
whose hair was of living snakes, whose eyes bulged and whose teeth were
fangs. They were so ugly that a mere glance at one of them turned a
human to stone.

Despite Danae's horror at this treachery of Polydectes, Perseus
accepted the task and went about accomplishing it, assisted by the goddess
Athena whose mirrorlike shield, winged shoes, and cloak of invisibility
proved a great help in the success of the venture. With Medusa's awful

head in his pouch Perseus returned to Serifos (saving Andromeda from a sea monster on the way), to find his mother hiding in the hut of the fisherman who had saved them so long ago, for Polydectes had tried to force her to marry him. Angrily Perseus went up to the palace, where he found a very surprised Polydectes at a great banquet. Perseus told him that he had succeeded in his quest and held up the prize as proof, instantly turning everyone in the room into stone.

The kind fisherman was declared King of Serifos by Perseus, who with his mother went home to the mainland. Still fearing the old prophesy, Danae's father fled before them. But fate caught up with the old King when he later met Perseus in another town. They did not recognize one another and Perseus accidently killed his grandfather.

Serifos today: Although called "the Bare", Serifos has a lot of water, so much, in fact, that in 1977 part of the road to Chora was washed out in a flood. Fishing and farming the two fertile valleys are the main occupations of the Serifiotes. A small number of tourists are attracted by the lovely beaches on the island, although there are few tourist facilities.

Serifos, or **Chora,** the capital, is a 20 minute walk from the port. There is also an hourly bus service. It is a pretty town, still retaining some medieval characteristics. Some of the houses are made from pieces of the old fortress and others date back centuries. One can see the old windmills, beside a certain rare carnation which is only grown on Serifos. The **bank, post office,** and **OTE** are all located here, along with the **restaurants** Stavros Kamoudies, Elene Livaniou and Kostas Vounaries; the latter often has music.

Livadi, the port and beach, is more popular with tourists and there are many rooms to rent. A sweet shop makes delicious hot Loukomades, or doughnuts in honey, which attracts most of the locals and tourists like Pooh bears at night. **Restaurants** in the village include George Mochas, Stamatis Xypnitos and Vassileos Kapernaros, and in the summer a discotheque, Psathi, entertains visitors at night. At **Mesa Akrotiri,** a 2-hour walk from Livadi, are two caves, one the Cave of the Cyclops Polythemus with stalactites, and Koutala, where signs of an ancient people were found.

Megalo Livadi, the second port of Serifos, is connected by road and bus to Chora. It was once the huge loading port for the ores mined on the island, but the village declined with the mines. However, tourists still go there for its beach. One can also see the White Castle (O Aspro Kastro) said to date back to the 6th century AD. By the church Ag. Karalambos is a round tower.

Sikamia with its beach and one store is a good place to get away from it all, for there are also trees and fresh water. Galini, another beach with the restaurant Micheal Kyritsis, is half an hour by foot from Sikamia, and from here one can visit the **Monastery Taxiarchos,** built in 1500. Inside is a lovely old table, 18th century frescoes, and Byzantine manuscripts in the library. The oldest church on Serifos is at **Panayia** village, built in the 10th century. **Kallistos**, not far from Galini, is another green place with two restaurants.

Other **beaches** on Serifos are Karavi, Lia, Vouss, Ag. Soustas, Psili Ammos (one of the best), Platys Yialos, Koutalas, Halara and Ganima. Most of these are remote and attainable only by foot.

Panayiéria: Fava beans are the big speciality at these celebrations: 15 August, Panayia at Panayia; 27 July, Ag. Panteleimonos at Livadi; 7 September, Ag. Sosoudos at Livadi; 6 August, Sotiros at Kalobelli; 15-17 August, Panayia near the Monastery (a different village each day).

Hotels in Serifos: area code 0281
in Livadi
B: Perseus (Persefs) (pension)
C: Maistrali, tel. 51381 / 51298 / 51220

Tourist police: regular police at Chora.

Sifnos
Connections: Daily with Piraeus, Serifos, Milos; five weekly with Paros; two weekly with Ios and Santorini; frequently with Kythnos.

History: The Phoenicians, one of the first people to settle Sifnos, named the island Meropia (mentioned in Pliny) and began to mine for gold. They were followed by the Cretans, who founded Minoa near Apollonia, and were in return replaced by the Ionians who lived near Ag. Andreas and elsewhere. Meropia, meanwhile, had become famous for its wealth of gold. In later times the island sent an annual egg of solid gold to Apollo at Delphi, supposedly a tenth of each year's total production. The Treasury of Sifnos at Delphi was one of the richest there, and decorated with beautiful statues.

Then one year the Sifniotes decided they needed the gold more than Apollo and sent the god a gilded rock. Apollo accepted this fraud, but soon discovered he had been duped and cursed the island. This gave Polycrates, the Tyrant of Samos, a good excuse to extract a huge fine from Sifnos, and it also caused the mines to sink and dry up. Thus the island became empty, or 'Sifnos', which is what the name means. Nowadays most of the ancient mines are underwater, at Ag. Mina, Kapsalos, and Ag. Suzon.

After these inconveniences the island went into decline and the inhabitants moved to Kastro, where a Roman cemetery has been discovered. In 1307 the Da Koronia family ruled the island in place of Venice. In 1456 Kozadinos, the Lord of Kythnos, married into the family and the Kozadini ruled Sifnos until the Turks took the island in 1617.

Sifnos today is one of the wetter and greener Cyclades, and it has the best cuisine of Greece. A Sifniote chef is fought for in the kitchens of Athens, Tselemendes being the most famous. The soil is very fertile, and produces the best olive oil of the Cyclades, along with a decent wine.

Platys Yialos with its long sandy beach has plans to become a large resort area.

Apollonia is the present capital of the island, a delightful 20-minute bus ride from the port. It is spread out on the hills and forms a circle of white from the distance. A **folk art museum** is at the bus stop square, open 7 am - 10 am, and contains furniture, textiles and other examples of local art. Two churches in the town, Stavro and Ouranofora, are built from the stone of ancient temples. There are many dovecots in the region with triangular designs which are repeated in the architecture of some of the houses. The island's **banks, telephone,** etc. are to be found in Apollonia. Local music is often played on Sundays.

Restaurants: Hotel Sifnos, Kypros, Kali Karthia, Sophias, and Koutsionouri.

Discotheques: Kilistria, and Aloni Night Club, which often plays Greek music.

Kamares is the port of the island. A sign advises the arriving visitor to "Look at the prises before live the island." There are various pottery workshops in the town, and a beach where people swim and camp. The waterfront is shady, with cafés, restaurants, a taverna and the Boulis discotheque. The island's one **bus route** begins here, going on to Apollonia, Artemon, Chrissopigi and Platys Yialos.

Artemon with its windmills is the second largest village of Sifnos, with rooms for rent and restaurants. It was named for the goddess of the chase, who once had a temple where the present Konies church is. Another church, Ag. Georgi tou Afendi, was built in 1630 and in the Panayia Gounia there are some interesting frescoes. Large white mansions dominate the town. **Kastro,** south-east of Artemon, was the Classical and medieval capital of the island. It is a charming village, situated on a hill by the sea, surrounded by Byzantine-style walls made from the backs of the houses. On some of the old houses one can still discern Venetian coats-of-arms. Ruins of the Classical akropolis and walls remain, and there are many interesting churches, among them the two of the Panayia, Eleoussa (1653) and Koimmissi (1593), and Ag. Aekaterini (1665). All of these churches have noteworthy floors.

The monastery of **Chrissopigi,** by the seaside village **Apokofto** was built in 1650 on a holy rock. Long ago two women fled to the monastery from a band of approaching pirates. Desperately they prayed to Mary for help and she answered their pleas by splitting the cape right in the pirates' path, creating a gap 18 metres (60 ft.) wide, which today is spanned by a bridge. The icon of the Virgin in the church was discovered in the sea by fishermen attracted by the light it radiated. To see the church ask the bus driver to let you off at Chrissopigi and walk down the mule path. There is also a paved road. The village Apokofto has a beach and cafés.

Platys Yialos is a sandy beach with a good restaurant and camping place. From there the small **boat** leaves five times a week for Paros. Another beach, **Vathi,** is connected to the port Kamares by **caique** every morning. It also has rooms to rent and restaurants. The monastery, there, **Taxiarchos,** dates from the 16th century. Another monastery on Sifnos is located by the village Exambello, called **Vrissi,** built in 1612 and containing many old manuscripts and objects of religious art.

Panayiéria: 1 September, Ag. Simeon near Kameres; 20 July, Profitis Elias near Kamares; 29 August, Ag. Ioannes in Vathi; 25 March and 21 November, Panayia tou Vounou.

Specialities: Rivithia tou Fournou (oven baked chick peas every Sunday), Manouri cheese, dipped in wine.

Hotels in Sifnos: area code 0284.

Platys Gialos (B) is one of those relatively recent attempts at creating a resort, which indeed this fine beach is quickly becoming. An excellent taverna with a bigger menu than most takes care of nutritional needs. It is very easy to be lazy there, and the evenings, as yet, are quiet and star filled.

in Apollonia
B: Apollonia (pension), tel. 31490
C: Sifnos, tel. 31624.
C: Sofia.
in Artemon
C: Artemon, 3 Ag. Konstantinou, tel. 31303.
in Platys Yialos
B: Platys Gialos, tel. 31224

Tourist Police: regular police in Apollonia.

Syros
Connections: everyday with Piraeus; twice a week with Ikaria and Samos, and frequent connections with Paros, Tinos, Mykonos, Ios, Naxos, Santorini; daily boat from Rafina via Andros and Tinos.

History: In Homer Syros is called Syriin, first settled by the Phoenicians at Dellagracia and Finikas. Poseidon was worshipped on the island, and in connection with his cult one of the first observatories in the world, a heliotrope, was built there. It was constructed by the philosopher Ferekides, who also designed sundials and was a teacher of Pythagoros. In Roman times the population emigrated to Ermoupolis, at that time known as 'the Happy,' with its two tall hills, Ano Syros and Vrontatho. In the 13th century the Venetians founded a city on the first hill and converted many of the locals to Catholicism. The Turks took the island in 1566 but permitted the Catholic and Orthodox free worship. Under French protection, Syros remained neutral during the War of Independence. In 1822 war refugees from Chios, Psara, and Smyrna founded a second city on the other hill, Vrontatho. The port of Ermoupolis then was much larger than it is today and ships were built and repaired in the vast shipyards. This harbour, together with the island's central location, and its escape from any war damages enabled Syros to become the premier port of all Greece.

Both commercial and artistic advancement took place, and for 50 years the island was the undisputed leader of trade and culture. Huge Neoclassical mansions were built by the wealthy captains and merchants, who also constructed the Theatre Apollon, a miniature copy of La Scala in which an Italian opera season ran until 1914. This period also saw the construction of immense public buildings, such as the town hall, and the world's first monument to an unknown warrior, sculpted by Vitalis and located in Ermoupolis. In 1870, however, the advent of the steamship and the growth of Piraeus spelt doom to the glory of Syros.

Syros today is better known for its Turkish Delight, or *loukoumia*, than for its ships. The sweet is considered the best in Greece, and ships from the eastern islands often call at Syros, not so much for embarkations but to allow the passengers to purchase their *loukoumia*. The vendors rush on in a frenzy, attacked by equally mad buyers who want to get their yearly supply before the boat leaves.

Ermoupolis, the city of Hermes, the god of commerce, is still the largest town of the Cyclades and their administrative capital, but it is now quiet and almost haunted, with closed mansions and few tourists. A modern shipyard was recently built in the harbour in an attempt to restore a little of Syros' former fame. Built at a 20° angle, the city is headed by two hills which one can climb by road or endless steps. Everywhere are signs of Syros' past prosperity: the large churches are rich and splendid, especially **Ag. Nikolaos** (patron saint of seamen), the grandest of all, with its lovely painting of the Last Supper. Some of the mansions still have their ornate interiors and painted ceilings — the lobby of the Elmot Hotel is a typical example. The **Town Hall** faces a large shady square. Inside are full length portraits of King George I and Queen Olga painted by Prossalendis. **The Archaeology Museum** is up the steps next door to the town hall: open 10 am-1 pm and 4 pm-6 pm; 10.30 am-2.30 pm Sunday; closed Tuesday; entrance 25 dr, 2.5 dr. with student card, free Thursday and Sunday. It contains proto-Cycladic and Roman finds from Syros and other islands. In front of the town hall is a statue of the revolution's hero — admiral Miaoulis and a bandstand with seven muses. On Sunday afternoon the local philharmonic society gives a concert there, and at around 7 pm every evening in the region of Ag. Nikolaos you can hear them practising with a great blast of sound. The little La Scala, the **Apollon Theatre** is worth a visit.

On top of **Vrontathi Hill** is the church Anastasis with a few old icons and a superb view of the surrounding area, including Tinos and Mykonos. More interesting, though, is the other hill, **Ano Syros,** where the medieval Venetian town still exists, dominated by **St. George,** the large Catholic cathedral on top. A large **Capuchin convent of St. Jean** was founded there in 1535 by the French King Louis XIII, and it is very

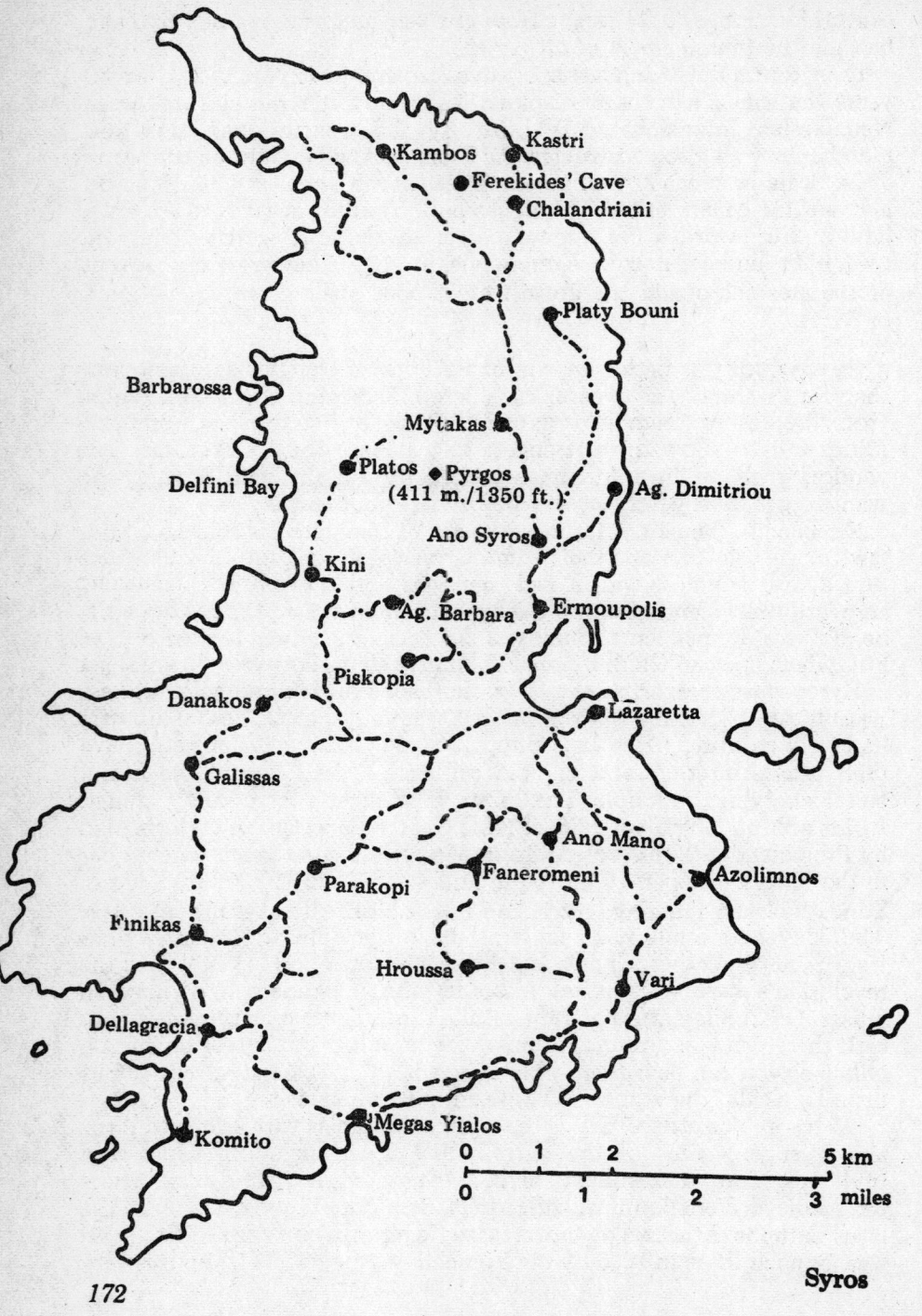

Kastri

Kambos

Ferekides' Cave

Chalandriani

Platy Bouni

Barbarossa

Mytakas

Platos ◆ Pyrgos
(411 m./1350 ft.)

Delfini Bay

Ag. Dimitriou

Ano Syros

Kini

Ag. Barbara

Ermoupolis

Piskopia

Danakos

Lazaretta

Galissas

Ano Mano

Parakopi

Faneromeni

Azolimnos

Finikas

Hroussa

Vari

Dellagracia

Megas Yialos

Komito

| 0 | 1 | 2 | | 5 km |
| 0 | | 1 | 2 | 3 miles |

Syros

beautiful. Another church, **St. Nicolaos,** was founded in the 15th century as a house for the poor. Many of the families who live in Ano Syros have been Catholic from the time of the Crusaders and some still live in the picturesque old mansions. Every year the **Apano Syria** takes place there in May or October (outside the high tourist season) celebrating the glorious history of Syros. There is a **yacht supply station** in the port.

Restaurants: Stavropoulos, Biraki, Hermes in the hotel.

Bazookia: Moulin Rouge (Markos Vanvakaris, one of the early popularizers of bazooki music in Greece, was a son of Syros).

Specialities: Loukoumia, nougat, halva, Vryosyr cheese and mineral water from the Syrigas mountain.

A 45-minute walk from Ermoupolis brings one to the pretty seaside church of **Ag. Dimitriou,** founded after the discovery of an icon there. Another excursion close to the city is a 15-minute walk to the **temple of Isis** at Dili, built in 200 BC. At **Lazaretta** across the harbour there was once a temple of Poseidon dating from the 5th century BC, although all that remains are a few objects in the museum. The ancients in Homer's time believed that the people of Syros never died of natural causes, but were struck down by the divine arrows of Apollo and Artemis. However, as these two deities have no temple on Syros, they probably had to come from Delos to accomplish this. A **cemetery** from Roman times is at Pefkakia, also near Ermoupolis.

Other ancient sites are in the north of the island. At **Grammaton Bay** a blessing to protect ships from sinking is carved in the rock, dating back to Hellenistic times. **Kastri,** a bit north of Chalandriani, was settled in the Bronze Age, and walls, the foundations of houses, and a cemetery remain. Signs suggest it was later inhabited for a brief period around 8000 BC. The **cave** where the philosopher Ferekides supposedly lived in the summer is a bit north of Kastri; his winter cave is at Alythini.

Kini and **Galissas** are two fishing villages with beaches that have grown popular in recent years; at Kini there is even a discotheque. The Phoenicians settled in **Finikas** (Phoenix), and Kyklades is a good restaurant there. **Vari** has become a major resort, while **Dellagracia** (Poseidonia), **Megas Yialos,** and **Azolimnos** have fewer tourists. **Piskopio** in the middle of the island has the oldest Byzantine church on Syros, Profitis Elias, situated in the piney hills. **Ag. Barbara,** a pleasant Orthodox monastery, has an orphanage for girls and produces items of popular art. **Hroussa,** an inland, pine shaded village has become a popular place to build villas.

Panayiéria: 6 December, Ag. Nikolaos in Ermoupolis; the last Sunday in May, the finding of the icon at Ag. Dimitriou; 26 October, also at Ag. Dimitriou; 24 September, an Orthodox and Catholic celebration at Faneromeni.

Hotels in Syros: area code 0281

In Ermoupolis the modern Hermes (B), a few feet from the ferry landing, is definitely the most comfortable hotel on the island, but the turn of the century Elmot up the hill is more fun. It is not even an official hotel, but rather a neo-classical mansion with rooms for rent run by a very efficient family with an advanced system for taking showers. The doors and windows are tall and narrow, and the heroes of the Revolution painted on the ceiling beam down on the guest like their Olympian fore-fathers.

in Finikas:
C: Olympia, tel. 42212
in Ermoupolis
B: Hermes, Platia Kanari, tel. 28011 / 23011/2 / 28510
C: Europe, 74 Stam. Prioiou, tel. 28771/2
C: Nissaki, 2 E. Papadam, tel. 28200/1
D: Cycladikon, Platia Miaouli, tel. 22280
E: Akteon, tel. 22675
E: Hellas
in Dellagracia
B: Delagrazia (pension), Agathopae, tel. 42225
C: Poseidonion, tel. 42300
in Vari
C: Achladi, tel. 22704
C: Alexandra, Megas Yalos, tel. 42540
C: Domenica, tel. 22704
C: Kamelo, tel. 22704
C: Romantica, tel. 22704
D: Emily, Achladi Beach, tel. 22704

Tourist police: regular police in Ermoupolis, or the Tourist and Shipping Agency of Panayiotis Boudouris.

Tinos
Connections: Ferryboat daily from Athens and Rafina via Andros; daily connection with Mykonos, Syros; twice a week with Leros, Patmos, Kalymnos, Rhodes, Kos, Ikaria and Samos; more frequently with Paros and Naxos.

History: Inhabited by the Ionians in Archaic times, Tinos was occupied by the Persians in 490 BC, but set free after the Battle of Marathon. In the 4th century a sanctury of the sea god Poseidon was founded on the island (after he cleared it of snakes) and it became a sacred place, where pilgrims would come to be cured by the god and to participate in the Poseidonia, December festivals. There were two ancient cities on the island, both named Tinos, one where the present town is and the other at Xombourgo. When the war between the Romans and Mithridates of Pontos broke out in 88 BC, the latter destroyed Tinos. In the 13th century the Venetians built a fortress at Xombourgo, out of the ancient akropolis and city there, and called it Santa Elena. It was one of the strongest fortresses of the Cyclades, and stood impregnable to eleven assaults by the Turks. Even the terrible Barbarossa was defeated by Santa Elena and its Venetian and Greek defenders. The frustrated Turks often pillaged and destroyed the rest of Tinos, venting their anger at Santa Elena's defiance.

In 1715, long after the rest of Greece had submitted to Ottoman rule, the Turkish admiral finally arrived in Tinos with a massive fleet and army. After sustaining a terrible attack, the Venetians decided that this time Santa Elena would not hold out, and, to the surprise of the Greeks, surrendered. The Turks allowed the Venetians to leave in safety, but in Venice the officers were put on trial for treason. It was decided that they had been bribed to surrender, and all were executed. Meanwhile the Turks blew up a good deal of Santa Elena in case the Venetians should change their minds and come back. Tinos was thus the last territorial gain of the Ottoman Empire.

In 1822, during the Greek War of Independence, a nun of the convent Kehrovouni, Sister Pelagia (now a saint), had a vision of the Virgin directing her to a certain rock. Here she discovered a miraculous icon of Mary and the Archangel at the Annunciation. The icon was found to have incredible healing powers for the faithful, and a church was soon built for it in Tinos town, called Panayia Evangelistra or Christopiliopsia. This has become the most important place of pilgrimage in Greece, called the Lourdes of the Aegean, and thus making Tinos the most visited island in all of Greece. On 15 August 1940, during the huge annual celebration at the church, an Italian submarine entered the harbour of Tinos and sank the Greek cruise boat *Elli* — one of the major incidents directly before the war with Mussolini. In the recent reign of the junta the entire island was declared a holy place (part of this government's so-called "moral cleansing") and the women of Tinos were required to behave at all times as if they were in church, by wearing skirts, etc. This rule, however, was abolished along with the junta.

Tinos today: Although most of the Greek visitors to Tinos stay in the town with its millions of shops selling candles, holy pictures, incense, bottles, and other pilgrimage paraphernalia, there is no reason why other visitors must. The rest of Tinos is charming, dotted with 1848 white dovecots and many masterpieces of folk art. The villages are so pretty that in one of them, Pyrgos, an art school was founded. Most of the island's famous sons, in fact, were artists, including Guizzes, Halepas, Soxos and Litra.

The biggest attraction of the capital **Tinos,** of course, is the church **Panayia Evangelistra** with the wonderful icon. It is open to visitors 8.30 am - 8.30 pm every day, as are the numerous museums inside the church complex (so complex that little signposts direct visitors to the various sites within). The church itself is rather small and crowded with ex votos of the faithful in gold and silver, creating a rather magical effect above the hundreds of lighted candles. Certain men spend the whole day removing these from the stands so that new arrivals will in turn have somewhere to put their own candles. Some of these candles are so huge one wonders how the pilgrims carried them up the hill. The icon itself, which people queue to kiss, can hardly be seen under the gold and diamonds and pearls. Around the church four houses have been built for those waiting to be healed by the icon, but there is not enough room and many people camp out patiently in the church yard.

A **picture gallery** (gifts from grateful worshippers from all over the world) is right across from the actual church, and includes works by the Ionian school, a Rubens or two, works by Greek artists, china figurines and a few ghastly mirrors. Another museum contains the works of the Tiniote sculptor **Antonios Soxos;** above it is the **Sculpture Museum** housing works by a variety of Greek sculptors such as Ioannis Boulgaros and Vitalis. The **Byzantine Museum** has many old icons; and another museum contains items used in the church service. Beneath the church one can visit the **crypt** where Ag. Pelagia found the icon. The water there is supposed to have curative properties. A **mausoleum** of the men who died on the *Elli* is by the crypt. On 15 August and 25 March pilgrims from all over Greece throng the church to pay their respects to the icon (2 out of 3 are women), forming a line all the way down to the harbour. Around these times, one should never come to Tinos expecting to find anything which remotely resembles a hotel room.

One of the streets, Evangelistra, which leads up to the church is a solid line of shops; the other, more spacious street is where one can find the **Archaeology Museum:** 9 am - 1 pm and 4 pm - 6 pm; 10.30 am - 2 pm Sunday; closed Tuesday. Entrance 24 dr., 2.5 dr. with student card; free Thursday and Sunday. This contains finds from the Sanctuary of Poseidon and Amphitrite, including a sun dial and a sea monster in various pieces. There are also huge archaic storage vases with fine decorations. In **Nikolaos Pokamisas' art gallery** on Evangelistra street are some lovely paintings of Tiniote villages, and there are other galleries in town. One unofficial gallery is at a little restaurant called **Koutouki,** owned by a Greek American Sotiris Fisas, who is almost as much of an institution as the icon. Les objets d'art range from fat mermaids to My Friend Mike, along with photographs of ships Mr. Fisas was sunk on during the war. There is also a large collection of photos and drawings of Mr. Fisas himself given by his staunch patrons.

Although blessed with numerous eating and drinking establishments, Tinos town never has enough chairs for visitors in the summer, just as the ships from Tinos to Athens often lack seats, although surplus passengers are let on all the same. Two landing areas operate, often simultaneously, and it is always best to ask the ticket agent which pier to queue up at in the tourist pens. There is a **yacht supply station** in the port.

There is a **weaving school** in the town which can be visited. Last but not least, mention must be made of the town itself, which has retained much of its typical white Cycladic architecture. Some of the houses repeat the embroidery-like ornamentation of the dovecots, while

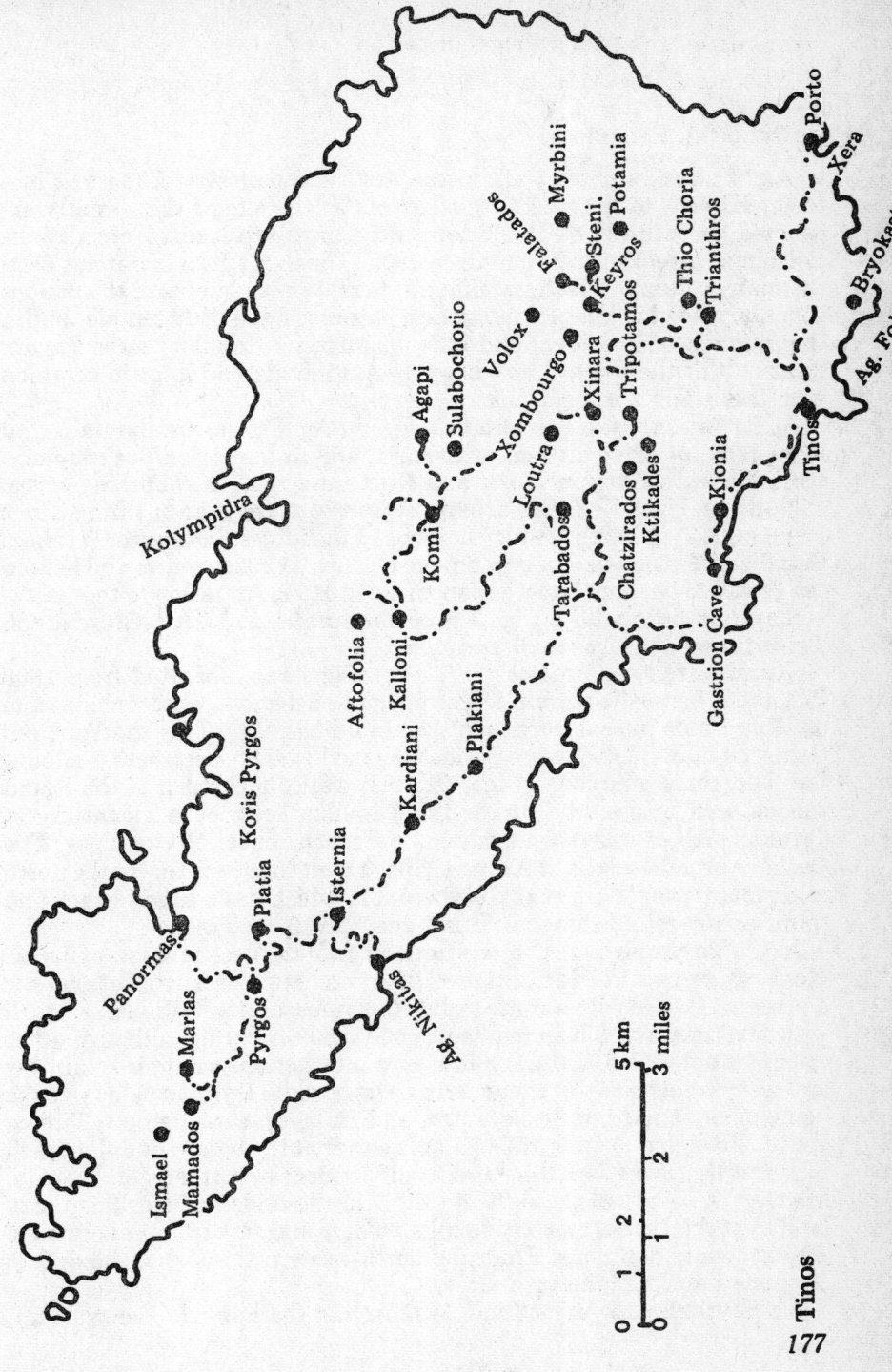

Kolympidra

Porto
Xera
Bryokastro
Ag. Fokas

Myrbini
Steni
Potamia
Keyros
Falatados
Thio Choria
Trianthros

Volox
Sulabochorio
Agapi
Xombourgo
Xinara
Tripotamos
Tinos
Loutra
Chatzirados
Komi
Ktikades
Kionia
Tarabados
Gastrion Cave

Aftofolia
Kalloni
Kardiani
Plakiani

Koris Pyrgos
Platia
Isternia
Ag. Niklas

Panormas
Pyrgos
Marlas
Mamados
Ismael

5 km
3 miles

2
2
1
1
0
0

Tinos

others date back to the Venetian period.

Restaurants: Afdonia, Aigli, Falara, Plaka, Kymata and many more.

Bazooki: Panorama.

Ag. Fokas, a short walk to the east, is the closest beach to Tinos town; **Kionia** to the west is further but is the site of the recently excavated **Sanctuary of Poseidon and Amphitrite,** discovered by the Belgian archaeologist Demoulin in 1902. The name Kionia derives from the many columns which were found there. What remains of the famous sanctuary are the temple, treasuries, entrances, the little temple, baths, the fountain of Poseidon, and inns for pilgrims. In many ways the ancient cult of the sea god and his wife Amphitrite had a lot in common with the island's present cult of Mary.

At **Bryokastro,** a few minutes beyond Ag. Fokas, are the walls and other remains of an ancient settlement, and in the region one may also see a Hellenistic tower. **Xera** and **Porto** are remote swimming coves.

North of Tinos is the **Kehrovouni Convent** (regular bus from Tinos pier), built in the 12th century and one of the largest in Greece. It is here that Sister Pelagia had her dream of such great consequence, and her old cell is still to be seen. She was canonized in 1972. **Arnados** to the west is a charming little village with a good restaurant, and **Thio Choria** and **Trianthros** are also small and quiet.

Xombourgo, 520 metres (1700 ft.) high, was inhabited from 1000 BC, and a few walls remain of this ancient settlement. Later inhabitants used the ruins to construct their own buildings, especially the Venetian Gizi, who built Santa Elena. Besides the medieval houses, there is a fountain and three churches in the Venetian walls, and much of the island can be seen below. At **Loutra** the Catholics founded a monastery of Jesuits (17th century), and there is a French school of Ursulines. The Catholic archdiocese is at **Xinara** village a bit to the south. On the north coast many people camp at **Kolympidra,** which has a sandy beach and small eating establishments. Buses run here from Tinos.

In the **Tarabados** region one finds some of the best dovecots of Tinos. **Koris Pyrgos** and **Plakiani** are old towers. Further north, **Isternia** is a pleasant village with a road leading to Ormos, or **Ag. Nikitas,** a beach with tavernas, etc. This area has a good deal of marble, although other considerations were also taken into account when the sculpture, painting and weaving schools were founded at pretty white **Pyrgos.** This was the home or birthplace of Soxos, Litra, and Halepas, three famous Tiniote artists. Food and lodging are available either at the village or at its beach **Panormas** below. In the town itself student works are on display. **Marlas,** a small village to the north, is in the midsts of marble quarry land. A special green marble is exploited here and sent from Panormas to Tinos town and Athens. From the north-western tip of the island, it is only one nautical mile to Andros.

Panayiéria: 15 August and 25 March at the Panayia Evangelistra, the two largest in Greece; 15 June, Ag. Triada at Kardiani; 26 October, Ag. Dimitriou in Tinos town; 21 December, Issodia of Mary at Tripotamos; 20 October, Ag. Artemiou at Falatados; 29 August, Ag. Ioannes at Komi (Catholic); 19 January, Megalomatas at Ktikades.

Hotels in Tinos: area code 0283

Tinos Beach (A), between the church of the sacred icon and the ruins of the sanctuary of Poseidon at Kioni, has the more recent attractions of a swimming pool and tennis courts. It is quiet and restful, away from the swarms of pilgrims.

in Tinos town:

A: Tinos Beach (hotel and bungalows), tel. 22626/8; 716730 in Athens; teleg. Tinos Beach Tinos

B: Favie Souzane (pension), 21 Antoniou Sochou, tel. 22693/22593; 7773266 in Athens

B: Theoxenia, tel. 22274

B: Tinion, 1 C. Alavanou, tel. 22261; teleg. Tinion Tinos

C: Argo, Angali, tel. 22588; teleg. Hotelargo Tinos

C: Asteria, Leo. Stavrou-Kionion, Kallithea, tel. 22132/22070

C: Avra, Paralia, tel. 22242

C: Delfinia, Paralia, tel. 22289/3622311 in Athens

C: Flisvos, Paralia, tel. 22243/22032

C: Galini, tel. 22260

C: Leto, Paralia, tel. 22791/2

C: Meltemi, 3 D. Philippoti, Leof. Megalocharis, tel. 22881/4; 5245862 in Athens; teleg. Meltemi Tinos

C: Oasis, 1 Evangelistra, tel. 22455

C: Oceanis, 3 Akti G. Drossou, tel. 22452

C: Poseidonion, 4 Paralia, tel. 22245/22566

D: Aegli, 7 El. Venizelou, tel. 22240

D: Eleana, tel. 22561

Tourist Police: Tinos town, summer only. Tel. 22255.

Patmos

Lipsi

Leros

Kalymnos

TURKEY

Bodrum

Kos

TURKEY

Marmaris

Astypalaia

Nissyros

Symi

Tilos

Halki

Rhodes

Saria

Karpathos

0	10	25		50 km
0		10	25	miles

Kassos

The Dodecanese

Part 8
The Dodecanese

The Dodecanese ("the Twelve", although there are actually thirteen
main islands) is a grouping derived from the 750 AD Byzantine subdivi-
sion of the empire into themes. As most of these islands are off the coast
of Asia Minor, the exchange of ideas between east and west which inevitably came their way caused them to flourish early. Various ancient
peoples now known as "the Aegeans" were the original inhabitants of the
islands, who were later subjugated by the sea-faring Minoans. When
Crete fell in the 15th century BC, the Achaeans held sway over the
Dodecanese, and many islands sent ships to aid the Greek cause at Troy.
In the 12th-11th centuries BC the Dorians invaded the Dodecanese
(although on some islands Ionians eventually replaced them), heralding
the Dark Age of Greece which lasted for three centuries.

By the archaic period cities on the islands, particularly on Rhodes and
Kos, flourished and established colonies abroad. The Persians invaded
the islands which did not support them in their ventures against Greece,
although when they were defeated the Dodecanese joined the Athenian
league. Their great distance from Athens, however, allowed them a
greater independence and prosperity than that known by the Cyclades,
and they produced many great artists and intellectuals, the most famous
being Hippocrates, the Father of Medicine.

After the death of Alexander the Great, Ptolemy of Egypt controlled
most of the Dodecanese. One of the greatest sieges in antiquity took place
when one of Ptolemy's rival generals, Antigonos, sent his son Dimitrios to
take Rhodes from Ptolemy: the island was the victor. In 164 BC powerful

Rhodes made an alliance with Rome, enabling her to exert a great imperialistic influence of her own over many of the Greek islands.

St. Paul visited some of the Dodecanese and began their early conversion to the Christian faith. St. John the Theologian was exiled from Asia Minor to Patmos, where he converted the inhabitants, besides writing the *Apocalypse.* The islands were later incorporated into the Byzantine Empire. At the end of the 11th century the Crusaders began to pass through the Greek Islands, and especially through the Dodecanese, marking the beginning of the end of Byzantium. Although their ostensible purpose was to rid the Holy Land of infidels, they were not adverse to plunder and to carving out their own little principalities in the captured lands. One of the greatest ironies in history occurred in 1204 when they sacked Constantinople itself, a Christian capital as great as Rome.

Jerusalem fell to the Ottoman Empire in 1291, and the Knights of the Order of St. John, who came from many countries in Europe and ran a hospital for pilgrims in Jerusalem, retreated to Cyprus. 18 years later they set up their headquarters on Rhodes, buying it and the rest of the Dodecanese from Admiral Vinioli, the head Genoese pirate there at the time. In 1309 they built a hospital and fortified Rhodes and the other islands against the numerous would-be invaders and adventurers of the day. The Knights themselves played pirates quite often in swift vessels made on Simi. As could be expected, the Sultan of the Ottoman Empire did not view these ventures in a favourable light, especially since the Knights let Christian pirates through their territory unmolested, but stopped ships carrying Moslem pilgrims.

In 1522 Sultan Suleiman the Magnificent attacked Rhodes (the third major Moslem offence on the Knights) and all the islanders of the Dodecanese who were able rallied to the defence. Only the information of a traitor caused the defeat of the Knights after a long siege. Suleiman permitted them and their followers to depart in safety with their possessions to Malta. Turkish occupation lasted until 1912, when the Italians took "temporary possession" of the Dodecanese, although their massive building, road construction and reafforestation programmes proclaimed that they scarcely considered the occupation temporary. While Turkish rule had been depressing and sometimes brutal, Fascist Italian rule in its attempts to outlaw the Greek religion and language was just as awful. After the Second World War, the islands were united with Greece, the last territory gained by the government, which quickly went about exploiting their rich tourist potential.

Two of the Dodecaneses, Rhodes and Kos, have succeeded in becoming two of the major holiday centres of Greece, particularly with Germans and Scandinavians. The climate, beaches, and natural beauty of these islands make them popular year round. Another island very frequented in the summer is Patmos, with its magnificent monastery of St. John. The other Dodecanese are less well known but none the less charming. A certain village on Karpathos maintains the dress and customs of 300 years ago; tiny Kastellorizo, tucked under the bulge of Turkey, is haunted with war-ruined mansions; Kalymnos is the sponge capital of Greece; the volcano on Nissyros still smokes; rocky Kassos has a glorious but tragic history; lovely neo-Classical mansions decorate Simi; Astypalaea, Halki, and Tilos are small and serene; and Leros, the island of Artemis, often serenades the visitor with the strains of the santouri, or hammer dulcimer.

Besides the Athens-based ships to the islands, one can fly to Rhodes, Kos or Karpathos from Athens, and to Rhodes directly from abroad. Two small ships, the noble *Panormitis* and the *Miaoulis,* connect most of the Dodecanese with one another, and most popular connections can be made daily in the summer on the tourist caiques, although one pays about double the price of the ferry for their services.

Astypalaia

Connections: Once a week with Piraeus and Amorgos; twice weekly with Kos, Rhodes and Kalymnos; once a week with Folegandros.

History: The name Astypalaia means "old city" in Greek, but mythology claims that the name is derived from a sister of Europa, the mother of King Minos. It is thought by some that inhabitants from this island settled the ancient capital of Kos, which was also called Astypalaia. The Venetian Quirini family occupied the island from the 13th century until 1522, styling themselves the Counts of Astynea, and building a castle in Choria. During the Italian occupation of the Dodecanese another fortification called Kastellano was built in the east of the island, south of Vathi.

The westernmost island of the Dodecanese, Astypalaia has much of the character of a Cyclade, particularly in the architecture of the houses. Although it is also rocky like a Cyclade, there is a rich valley, Livadia, half an hour's hike from the port, where the island's agriculture is centred. The coastline offers many sheltered bays renowned for their fishing.

The capital of the island, **Astypalaia,** is situated around the harbour below the Venetian castle. A port capable of taking large ships should be finished very soon, facilitating disembarkations. In the pretty white town, or rather village, are the island's restaurants, hotels and rooms and houses for rent.

Choria, above the town was the Venetian capital; on the gate of the **fortress** one can still see the Quirini coat-of-arms. Within its walls are the ruins of the houses on tiny streets, and two churches, **St. George** and **La Madonna of the Castle.** The fortress is being slowly restored.

Livadia, with the island's beach, is a bit to the west. A little bit further to the south is Astypalaia's unofficial nude beach. The island's highest point, 610 metres (2000 ft.) is just behind Livadia. From Astypalaia town one can hike to the monastery, **Ag. Libies,** or go by bus or taxi to the more remote villages of **Analypsis** and **Vathi,** which is by the Italian **Kastellana.**

Panayiéria: 21 May, Ag. Konstantinos; 15 August, Panayia.

Hotels in Astypalaia: area code 0242
In Astypalaia
D: Astynea, 21 Mich. Karageorgi, tel. 61209; tel. Astyotel
D: Paradissos, 24 Mich. Karageorgi, tel. 61224

Tourist Police: Regular police at Astypalaia.

Halki

Connections: Twice a week with Rhodes, and with Ag. Nikolaos and Sitia (Crete), Karpathos, Kassos and Piraeus.

The name Halki (also spelled Chalki, Khalkia, etc.) comes from the word for copper in Greek, which was mined on the island long ago. An ancient city once existed where Chorio is today, and the Knights of St. John built a castle there on the old acropolis.

Small rocky Halki is a fishermen's island, an occupation held by about 75 per cent of the population which isn't already away at sea. Very few tourists visit the island, despite its proximity to Rhodes, nor are the islanders very sure of what to do with tourists when they do come. In the port, called **Halki,** there are three kafenions and a small inn. The little town is dominated by enormous bell towers; one church in fact, **Ag. Nikolaos,** has the distinction of having the tallest bell tower of the Dodecanese. Halki's beach, **Pontamos,** is an hour's walk from town, or one can hike north towards **Pefkia** where there are a few ancient ruins.

Choria, the old capital of the island, is connected to the port by the island's one road. The interior of the **castle** on a nearby rock is very damaged, although a few frescoes remain in a church inside. The climb up to the castle is worthwhile for the view. The old windmill, which ground the wheat to bake bread in the island's one oven, no longer turns. Most of Halki's food comes from Rhodes, although it is far easier to find fresh fish here than on its more popular neighbour.

Panayiéria: 29 August, Ag. Yeno (the biggest); 15 August, Panayia.

Kalymnos

Connections: Twice a week with Piraeus and Leros; three times a week with Kos and Patmos; four times a week with Rhodes; once a week with Mykonos, Samos, Astypalaia, Karpathos, Simi, Nissyros, Lipsi and Tilos; caique every day to Pserimos.

History: Neolithic remains have been found at Vothini, along with a cave shrine to Zeus, dating inhabitation of Kalymnos back into prehistoric times. After the destruction of Crete, Dorians from Argos settled the island, naming their capital after their mother city. Homer mentions ships from Kalymnos at Troy, and archaeologists have uncovered Homeric tombs on the island which yielded the Skomi treasure now in the British Museum. An ally of Persia, the Queen of Halikarnassos, conquered the island at the beginning of the 5th century BC, but after Persia's defeat Kalymnos joined the Athenian league.

In the 11th century AD the Turks launched a sudden attack on the island and killed almost everyone. The few survivors fled to fortified positions at Kastelli and Kastro, the latter of which grew to be the capital of the island in a position virtually impregnable. The Genoese Vinioli family occupied Kalymnos, but later sold it to the Knights of St. John, who strengthened the fortress of Kastro. In 1522 they abandoned it to succour Rhodes and the Turks quickly took their place. Despite a revolt in 1821, the island followed the fate of the rest of the Dodecanese and only became Greek in 1945.

Kalymnos today: Kalymnos as even the most fleeting visitor will note is very much preoccupied with sponges. It is the only island in Greece that still has an active fleet of sponge divers. In the past the sponge fleet left home for seven months of the year to work off the coast of North Africa. Today it makes only one four-month trip a year, diving (due to political considerations) in Greek and Italian waters. The fleet leaves a week after Easter, this being designated Sponge Week on Kalymnos. This is the occasion for a big celebration of food, free drinks, local costumes and dances. In the Sponge Dance, the local school master pantomimes the part of the sponge fishermen while his pupils play the sponges. The last night of Sponge Week is tenderly known as To Hypnos tis Agapis, or the Sleep of the Lovers. It ends with the pealing of church bells, calling the divers to their boats for another dangerous four months at sea.

Sponge fishing is defintely an art. In ancient times the divers strapped heavy stones to their chests to take them down to the sea bed, speared the sponges with tridents, and were then raised to the surface by a lifeline when they gave the signal. Today the divers wear oxygen tanks and attack the sponges with axes, going down to a depth of 90 metres (300 ft.). When fresh from the sea the sponges are smelly and black, and have to be stomped on and soaked until they are clean. Later some are treated to achieve the familiar yellow colour. In Pothia a school for sponge divers runs three-month courses, and there is also a private school, Gonatos, which supplies all necessary equipment for anyone interested in learning the art. Almost all the famous sponge divers in Tampa, Florida are sons of Kalymnos.

Pothia, the port, is also the capital of this island, the second most populated of the Dodecanese. It is a large, sprawled out town, not really very pretty, although not for any lack of effort. All over the town are **statues by Michail Kokkinos** and his daughter Irene. Octopi dangle on lines and poles along the waterfront, and sponges of all shapes and sizes decorate the shops. At night the sea sparkles with the many lights of the night fishermen; during the day a lazy pastel charm falls on the town. A sandy beach with 3 dr. showers is by the local yachting club which can

0   2   5 km
0   1   2   3 miles

Emporios

Skala

Kalabros

TELENDOS

Arginonta

Kastelli

Telendos   Massouri

Myrties

Profitis Elias
(701 m./2300 ft.)

Monastery
Kyra Psilas

Platis Yialos

Linaria

Lasos   Vathis

Panormos

Chorio

Argos

Ag. Nickolaos

Kalymnos
(Pothia)

Thermapiges

To Leros

Kephalos
Cave Vothini

To Kos

Nera

To Piraeus

Kalymnos
186

provide supplies, winter berthing etc. **Thermapigies** nearby is a radioactive spring known for curing rheumatism, arthritis, digestive and kidney troubles. Its large white buildings house facilities for visitors. Above the town is a huge cement cross which lights up at night. The main reason for this, according to locals, is to attract curious tourists in passing boats, who will stop at Kalymnos to ask what it is doing there.

At Myli is a castle built by the Genoese Vinioli, which still bears his coat of arms. It is called either **Pera Kastro** or Chryssocheria (Golden Hand), for the church to the Virgin later built inside it, on the site of an ancient temple of the Twins. A treasure was once supposedly found there, and the area has since been thoroughly combed on the offchance of there being any more. Another site in this region, a bit above Pothia, is the church **Christ of Jerusalem**, constructed by the Byzantine Emperor Arkadios in thanks for his shelter at Kalymnos during a terrible tempest. On the site a famous temple of Apollo Kalymnian once stood. Another church by Christ of Jerusalem is a basilica of **Ag. Anastasis** founded by Ag. Elene. Both these churches are now in ruins. By the hospital is the **Cave of the Nymphs,** known more recently as the Cave of the Seven Virgins, for seven maidens who hid themselves there from the Turks and were never seen again. A few traces of ancient worship have been found inside.

Restaurants: Stelios Svinos, Kadouni (music) and Linoatsis Ioannis.

Discotheques: Korina, Jack.

Specialities: Dolmades (stuffed grapeleaves) and tangerines. Sponges and shells.

From Pothia one may go by caique to **Nera** islet, south of Kalymnos, where there is a monastery and coffee house; another caique trip takes two hours to the **Kephalos Cave** of Zeus, also called Daskaleion Cave, which is full of stalactites and stalagmites. **Vothini** village is just south of Pothia; at the convent of Ag. Katerina the nuns produce rugs and handicrafts. Traces of a Neolithic settlement were found there. 2 km. (1¼ miles) above Pothia is **Chorio,** the old capital of Kalymnos, which grew out of the medieval settlement in the **Kastro.** This castle rises above the village, looking as if it would be more at home in a Hollywood set of Transylvania than on a sunny isle of Greece. The town of Kastro, which was inhabited from the 11th to 17th centuries, is preserved as well as the actual fort and surrounding walls. On a dark day, wandering through Kastro can be quite an eerie experience. Chorio itself is a pretty white village announced by three imposing windmills as one climbs from Pothia. It has a good restaurant, Asteria.

A road branching off at Chorio brings one to **Argos,** named by the Dorian settlers who came from Argos on the mainland of Greece. Although there are some ruins there, scholars do not think that the Doric city was at precisely the same location as the present village. North of Chorio the road passes Kalymnos' best beaches: **Massouri,** considered the finest of all, with three restaurants, Pizania, Ellina, and Kiriakos Kokkinides. **Myrties** (with the Stala restaurant) is another fine beach to the south, and it is from here that the caique makes its 15-minute trip to **Telendos** islet.

In the 6th century AD Telendos broke off from Kalymnos in an earthquake. Facing the strait is a monastery of Ag. **Konstantinou** and a fort, **Kastro,** both dating back to the Middle Ages. Another monastery, **Ag. Vassilos** is in better condition than the dilapidated Ag. Konstantinou. One may also see the ruins of **Roman houses** on the islet and there are two small beaches. Fishermen live there for the most part, and are privileged with magnificent sunsets. On the mountain of Telendos one can see the form of the sleeping or **marble princess.** A similar marble prince faces her on the Kalymnos side of the strait.

Other good beaches in the area are **Platis Yidlos** and **Linaria,** the latter with food at Geo. Vaporis. North of these beaches is **Kastelli,** where the survivors of the terrible Turkish massacre fled. Kastelli overlooks the sea in a wild region of rocky cave mouths full of fangs. The church **Panayia** is below. **Arginonta** gives its name to the entire northern peninsula, which is perfect for rugged, isolated hikes in the hills. Non-hikers must take taxis as public transport does not reach so far. **Emporios,** the northernmost village, is within walking distance of some exceptional countryside, and **cyclopean walls** and a tower are very close by.

Vathi, the second most populated village on the island, is east of Pothia, at the end of a wiggling mountain road, from where one has a lovely view of the village's superb situation at the mouth of a Norwegian-like fjord. The growing of tangerines and lemons is the main business of Vathi ('the deep') and houses and white-walled roads fill in the gaps between the orchards. There are many tavernas. North of Vathi one can walk to the fortress-monastery of Kyra Pailas, the Tall Lady.

Panayiéria: 15 August, Panayia; 14 September, Stavros on Nera islet; 27 July, Ag. Panteleimonos at Brosta; a week after Easter, the Iprogros (sponge week), and when the divers return, although each boat is likely to come in at a different time and celebrations are not as general as at the Iprogros.

Hotels in Kalymnos: area code 0243
in Pothia
C: Olympic, tel. 28801/3/ teleg. Jolympitis Kalymnos
C: Thermae, tel. 29425
D: Alma, 8 Patr. Maximou, tel. 28969; teleg. Alma
D: Crystal, Platia 25th Martiou, tel. 28893
D: Panormos, Mariaska, tel. 47228
E: Vazanellis, 22 Patriarchou Maximou
in Panormos
C: Drossos, tel. 47301/28918; teleg. Drososhotel
C: Plaza, tel. 28907/47281

D: Katina, tel. 47262/28906
in Myrties
C: Delfini, Messologiou, tel. 28914/28919/29233; teleg. Delfini Kalymnos
D: Marilena (bungalows), tel. 47289
D: Myrties, tel. 28912

Tourist Police: Regular police at Pothia.

Karpathos
Connections: In the summer, two daily flights from Rhodes; by ship twice a week with Rhodes, Halki, Kassos, Sitia, Ag. Nikolaos (Crete) and Santorini.

History: One of the many ancient names of Karpathos was Porfiris, or "Red", for a red dye once manufactured on the island and used for the clothes of kings. Other ancient names described the number of cities on Karpathos, from Tripolis to Tetrapolis, Hetapolis and Oktopolis. The present name is thought to derive from the days of the pirates, when the Vrontis gulf hid pirate ships which would rush out to attack and plunder any passing vessel. Disgruntled captains dubbed the island Arpaktos, or "robbery island," and the name was eventually corrupted to Karpathos.

Four ancient cities are known to have existed on the island. One, Nissyros, is on the islet of Saria to the north and is believed to have been founded by people from the island of Nissyros. Iron and silver were mined during these ancient days at Assimovorni. A certain kind of delicious fish, the scarus, is caught in the sea by Karpathos, and Luculus, the Emperor of Rome, would send special ships to Karpathos to catch these fish for his dinner. These signs of prosperity had long ended when the pirates made Karpathos their centre and one of its villages, Arkessia, a slave market. Things were so rough that the Turks, it seems, didn't really want Karpathos. They only sent a cadi, or judge, to the island a few times a year, and he never stayed longer than necessary, having to rely on the Greeks to protect him from the pirates. Today the Vrontis gulf and bay at Arkessia are said to be full of sunken pirate treasure.

Karpathos today: Karpathos is a rugged but beautiful island off the beaten track. One can often hear its own special music, played at a furious pace on the goat skin bagpipe tsabouna and the three-stringed lyre (the Cretan lyre has four strings). Karpathian dances are fast and difficult to pick up. They can be seen in purist form at the village Olympos which is 300 or more years behind the rest of the island, originally because of its inaccessibility. A road is being built there, however, which will probably modernize this original village or turn it into a tourist attraction, or both.

Pigathia, the capital of Karpathos, was once called Poseidonion and claimed to be the sea god's home town. A few remains of the ancient town are just outside the present capital, at a site called **Posi,** and on the rocky hill above Pigathia Mycenaean tombs and even older remains have been uncovered. Two white churches now dominate the area above the town. The largest building in Pigathia is the Italian-constructed **town hall** by the post office; just past it the road leads to the long sandy beach on **Vrontis Bay,** and there is a good restaurant in the Proferis hotel above. On the road by the beach the ruins of the 5th-7th century **church** were recently discovered by accident, and a few columns are still standing. Across the bay from the beach one can distinguish the little **monastery of Ag. Nikolaos,** now deserted; a cave there, **Kamara,** has sweet water. Another good beach very close to Pigathia is **Amorpi,** with a good barbecue restaurant by the sea. Buses leave Pigathia for most of the villages.

  Restaurants: Proferis, George's (by the bank and cheaper). There is often music and dancing in the town's tavernas.
Discotheque: El Greco.
Specialities: Quince jelly.

  In the far south of the island is the airport, with a beach nearby. This was the site of the ancient kingdom of **Thaetho,** although little now remains. More can be seen of ancient **Arkessia** to the north. The surrounding cliffs are riddled with caves that have offered shelter to shepherds for centuries. By the sea are the ruins of an early Byzantine church, **Ag. Sophia.** If you brush aside the dirt and plants you will see brightly coloured mosaics. The coast below is jagged and wild, but there is a small beach. **Finiki,** a small harbour with a good inexpensive restaurant, is a stopping point for the sponge divers of Kalymnos. Although the sea on this western side of Karpathos, facing Crete, is usually calm, it can be very rough between Karpathos and Rhodes.

  Off the coast at **Lefkos** is an islet, **Sokastro,** with a medieval castle. **Othos,** inland, has more greenery than the other villages of the island, and one can enjoy the shade while eating lunch at one of the three restaurants there. Neighbouring **Volada** is the start of the mountain walk path to Spoa and Olympos (3 hours). There is a medieval fortress on a hill by the village. **Aperi** in the mountains above Pigathia has been built up largely with funds sent home from America; almost everyone in the village speaks English with a Chicago accent. Some of the old men emigrated at the turn of the century and are full of early American tales. A local hero, Nikolaidos, contributed the money for many of the village's large buildings. A story is told of him, recounting how when he was young and orphaned, an evil woman pushed him off the highest point of the village; he was miraculously saved by the Virgin, who kept him warm during the night until someone found him the next morning. In later life he went to America and became a prominent lawyer. One of the high spots of a visit to Aperi is the Eleftheria Café, with a fresh water spring inside and a small private museum in the back room that must be seen to be believed. **Ahata** below is a beach with mountain water that

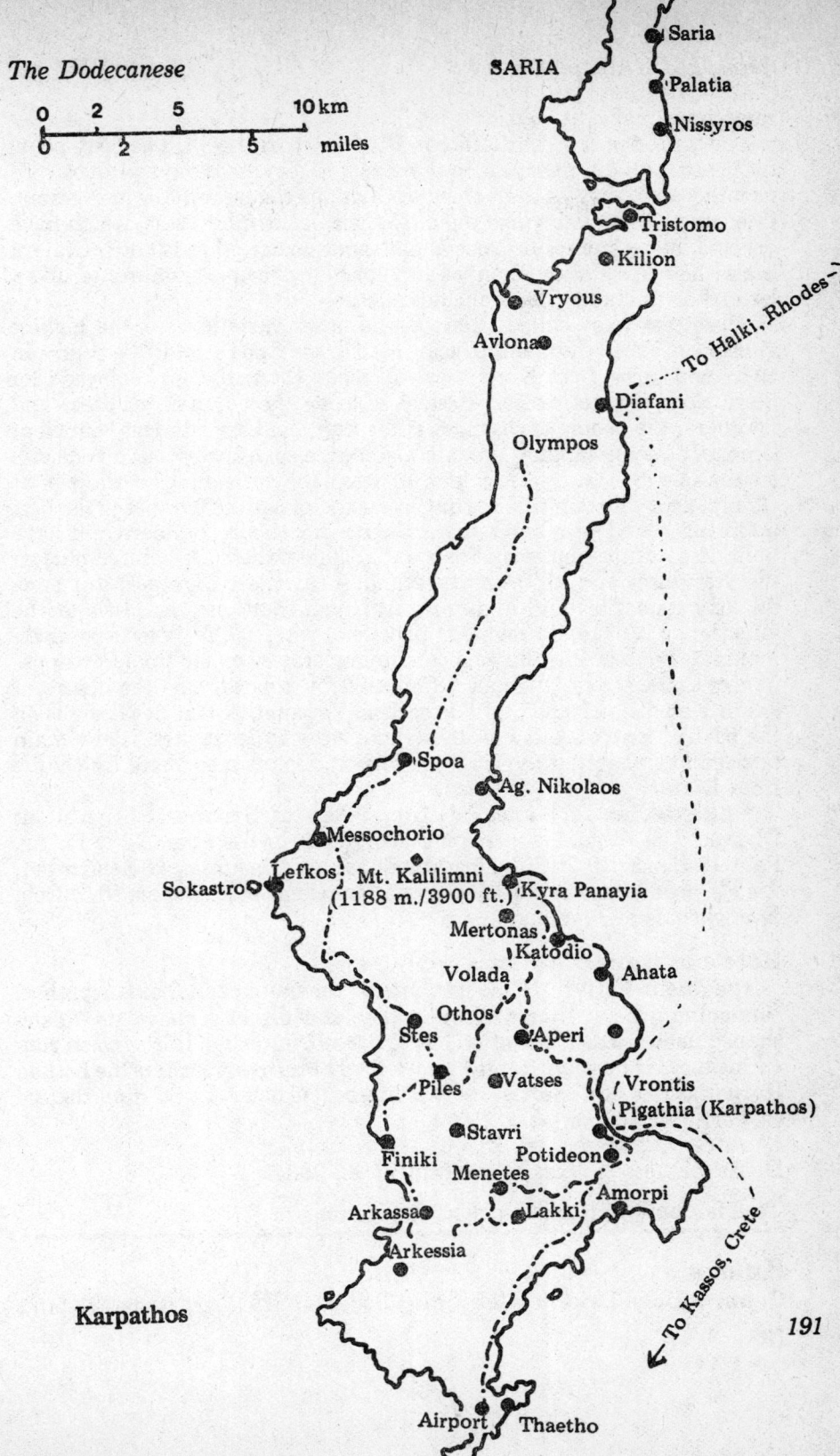

The Dodecanese

0   2   5   10 km
0   2   5   miles

SARIA

● Saria
● Palatia
● Nissyros

◉ Tristomo
◉ Kilion
● Vryous
Avlona ●

● Diafani

Olympos

To Halki, Rhodes →

● Spoa
● Ag. Nikolaos

● Messochorio
Lefkos ●
Sokastro ◐
Mt. Kalilimni
(1188 m./3900 ft.)
● Kyra Panayia

● Mertonas
● Katodio
Volada
● Ahata

Othos
Stes ●
● Aperi
Piles ●
● Vatses
Vrontis
Pigathia (Karpathos)

● Stavri
Potideon
Menetes
Finiki ●
● Amorpi
Arkassa ●
● Lakki

Arkessia ●

Karpathos

To Kassos, Crete →

191

Airport ● Thaetho

sometimes makes it cold.

The second port of Karpathos is **Diafani** in the north. The ferry boats to Pigathia almost always stop there as well. On other days caiques connect the two ports, for the women of Olympos come shopping in Pigathia. One can always distinguish them by their beautiful dresses, which have become folk costumes for special occasions on the other islands. Diafani is a 1½ hour walk from Olympos and has many rooms, restaurants, and a lot of fish, including the delicious scarus.

Olympos (also called Olimvos and other variations) is the highest village on Karpathos. A surfaced road from Spoa should be ready in 1979, and buses from Karpathos will make the trip, once renowned for its difficulty, much easier. Besides wearing the old style of dress and jewellery, the people of Olympos still speak in a Doric dialect of ancient Greek. If they wish, they can talk together in such a way that no one else on the island has the least idea of what they're saying. Weddings at Olympos may last up to three days, and the music of Olympos is the best in Karpathos. The inhabitants are renowned house builders and have built many of the houses on the island. Some of these are painted blue on the first storey and white on the second. A cave near Olympos, **Vorgunda,** has stalactites and a church. Although there are no hotels at the village, one can stay in rooms at private houses: ask for Vassileos Pharmakides. Back in Pigathia one can buy records of music from Olympos.

Vrykous above Olympos (connected by a path) was the centre of another ancient kingdom of Karpathos. Yet another was at Nissyros on the islet of **Saria.** A few walls remain near **Palatia,** the islet's main settlement, inhabited by a few shepherds. One can go there by caique from Diafani.

Panayiéria: 14 September, Ag. Pileas at Stavro: 15 August, at Olympos; 29 August, Ag. Ioannes Vorgunda in the cave: 27 July, Ag. Panteliemonos; 19-20 July, Profitis Elias on the mountain; 8 September, Tis Playa at Messochorio; 23 August, Panayia near Mertonas; 25 March, Evanglismos at Pigathia.

Hotels in Karpathos: Area code 0245

The serene Porfyris (C) is just outside the quiet capital of Karpathos, overlooking the sheltered Vrontis bay and directly above its sickle-shaped beach, which one often has to oneself. Although it is pension run, eating there is no sacrifice: the Greek food in the restaurant is the best on Karpathos, as one can tell by the number of natives who dine there.
C: Porfyris (pension), tel. 25294
D: Anessis, 2 Metaa, tel. 25256
D: Karpathos, 25 Vas. Konstantinou, tel. 25347

Tourist police: Regular police at Pigathia.

Kassos
Connections: Twice a week with Rhodes, Halki, Karpathos, Diafani,

Sitia, Ag. Nikolaos (Crete), Santorini; once a week with Piraeus.

History: Homer mentions Kassos in the *Iliad,* for the island sent ships to Troy to aid the Achaeans. An ancient city was built where the present village of Poli is today, and at Hellenokamara cave there are Pelasgian walls (Mycenean). During the Turkish Occupation, Kassos retained a good deal of its autonomy, especially with regard to its ships, which it quickly put at the disposal of the Greek cause when the War of Independence was declared, in 1821. For the first three years of the war the Greeks generally came out ahead in the struggle, but the Sultan, angered by these set-backs, prepared powerful counter-attacks through Ibrahim Pasha, son of the Ottoman Empire's governor of Egypt. In July 1824 Ibrahim left Egypt with a massive fleet to crush the Greek rebellion. His first stop was Kassos, which he decimated, slaying the men and taking the women and children as slaves. The few who managed to escape went to an islet off the north-western coast of Crete, Grambousa, where they were forced to turn to piracy for survival, flying the Greek flag proudly in Turkish waters. But Kapodistria and the Great Powers put a stop to their activities, and their refuge Grambousa returned to Turkish rule.

Kassos today: The southernmost Dodecanese and one of the most remote, Kassos has a rocky coast lined with sea caves, with a few small beaches wedged in between. The port is small, and if the sea is a bit rough the ships won't go near it. Caiques then relay passengers to and fro, a process which takes about an hour. Of its many surrounding islets, Armathia has a small village and beach, which can be reached by caique.

Fry is the little capital and port of the island, where the islanders' main occupation, fishing, is much in evidence. Every year on 7 July a ceremony is held there in memory of the massacre of 1824, and many people from Karpathos also attend, coming on the special boats which run that day. Although there are no hotels on the island, there is a small inn and a taverna at the village.

There are hardly any trees on Kassos because, it is claimed,Ibrahim Pasha burnt them all down, but a lot of lighthouses stick out above the rocky terrain. A road connects the major villages of the island with Fry. The ancient fort of the island is at **Poli,** on the acropolis, and one can visit the lovely cave **Hellenokamera,** also known as Sellai, with its large stalactites. It is surrounded by **Pelasgian walls** and was used as a refuge during hard times.

Panayiéria: 14 August, at Ag. Marina; 23 April, Ag. Georgios; 7 July, at Fry.

Tourist police: Regular police at Fry.

Kastellorizo (Megisti)
Connections: Boat twice a week from Rhodes.

History: According to tradition, Kastellorizo's first settler was King Meges of Echinada, who gave his name to the island. He must have come early indeed, as signs prove that Kastollorizo was inhabited from Neolithic times. Mycenean graves have also been discovered, and Homer mentions the island's ships at Troy. When the Dorians came, they began to fortify their new home, building two forts on the island, the Kastro by the present town and one above on the mountain, called Palaeo-kastro — the acropolis of the ancient capital. Apollo and the Diskouri, the patron gods of sailors were worshipped, and the island had a great fleet of ships based in its large sheltered harbour, which traded with ancient Lykia in Asia Minor, bringing its wood to ports in Africa and the Middle East. From 350-300 BC the island was ruled by Rhodes, and in Roman times the pirates of Cassius used it as their hideout. The island was converted to Christianity from the time of St. Paul, who preached on the coast of Asia Minor at Myra.

During the Byzantine period Kastellorizo's fortifications were repaired, and this work was continued by the Knights of St. John in the 13th century. They gave the island its present name, for the red rock of the castle which they used as a prison for knights who misbehaved on Rhodes. The Sultan of Egypt captured the island in 1440, but ten years later the King of Naples, Alfonso I of Aragon, took it back. Although Kastellorizo belonged to the Ottoman empire by 1523, the Venetians later occupied it twice during their struggles against the Turks, in 1570 and in 1659. In the War of Independence the islanders, the first in the Dodecanese to join the cause, seized their two fortresses from the Turks, but were forced by the Great Powers to give them back in 1833. In 1913 Kastellorizo revolted again only to be subjugated by the French. During the First World War the island was bombarded from the Turkish coast. In 1927 an earthquake caused extensive damages but the Italians, then in charge, did nothing to repair the island as it had failed to co-operate with their programme of dehellenization. Another revolt took place in 1933, but was crushed by soldiers from Rhodes. By now the island was in sharp decline — in 1941 only 1500 inhabitants remained of an initial 15,000, living mostly from the sea and the lands they owned on the coast of Asia Minor.

This, however, does not end the tale of misfortunes suffered by this tiny but brave island. During the Second World War the Allies, fearing a conflict, sent everyone to the Middle East. Although this was done for their safety, the islanders were not allowed to take most of their more precious belongings with them, and the occupying troops pillaged the houses. To hide their crime, they burnt the town, destroying more than 1500 homes. As if this were not enough, the ship carrying the refugees home after the war sank, and many people were killed. Those who survived came home to discover that they had lost literally everything, and that there was nothing to do but emigrate.

Kastellorizo today: The furthest east of all Greek territories,

Kastellorizo has a difficult time holding on to its remaining 250 people. Having lost their lands in Asia Minor, the islanders' only occupation is fishing, and the few boats that go out supply only enough for the island's meagre population. The soil of the island, essentially a big rock, is uncultivatable, and the people feel isolated and threatened by the proximity of Turkey, little more than a nautical mile away. Everyone wants to leave, and the only reason they don't is to keep the island Greek. Should there be less than 200 people of Greek blood on Kastellorizo, the island will revert to Turkey as it is in Turkish waters. Thus the Greek government pays the Kastellorizonites not to move (although most have apartments in Athens), and has built them a desalination plant, made special efforts to bring them Greek radio and television, and creates jobs for them, such as repairing the Kastro.

There is only one town on the island, also called **Kastellorizo,** full of ruined houses and mansions, some burnt, others crumbling from earthquakes or bombardments. One can see how wealthy some of the inhabitants once were from the remaining interiors, today the property of chickens, cats, and turkeys. Small tavernas line the waterfront, so close that it is relatively easy to dispose of an unpopular dinner companion in the sea. A hotel occupies one lip of the harbour, and on the other is the **fort** (kastro), last repaired by the eighth Grand Master of the Knights of St. John, Juan Fernando Heredia, whose red coat of arms is another possible explanation for the name of the island. A ladder takes one to the top, which affords a fine view of the surrounding seascape and of Antipholos, the Turkish village which is geographically so close but in all other senses totally remote from Kastellorizo. No boats link the two, nor is it an official port of entry. Recently an inscription in Doric Greek was discovered at the fort, proving the existence of an ancient castle at the same site. A tomb nearby yielded a golden crown, and in the **mosque** is a small **museum** (open 5 pm - 7.30 pm) containing photographs of the days of past prosperity, a few frescoes, folk costumes and items found in the harbour.

From the fort one can take the high road to the school with its black and white pebble mosaics. There is also a **weaving school** where two girls will spend two months making just one large rug. A long staircase leads to the mountain above the town, where there are four white churches and the fortress Palaeokastro, dating back to ancient times with Doric inscriptions from the 3rd century BC.

There are no beaches on the island, but the sea is clean, and there are a multitude of tiny islets to swim out to. An excursion which should not be missed is to the **Blue Cave,** or Parastas, a half-hour caique ride from the town. It is best to go in the morning when some light filters in, for the entrance is very low. One must duck to enter. The blue effects of the water inside have led to comparisons with the Blue Cave of Capri. There are many stalactites and a seal who lives inside; if you bring a light there's a chance you may see him.

Panayiéria: 20 July, Profits Elias; 21 May, Ag. Konstantinos; 24

April, Ag. Georgios.
Tourist Police: Regular police in town.

Kos

Connections: Daily flights from Athens. Connections by sea — daily with Rhodes; less frequently with Patmos, Nissyros, Leros, and Pserimos; six times a week with Piraeus, Kalymnos; four times a week with Patmos and Leros; three times a week with Nissyros, Samos, and Mykonos; twice a week with Ikaria, Astypalaia, Simi, Tilos, Naxos, Paros, Limnos, Lesbos, Chios; once a week with Arki, Lipsi, Thessaloniki, Kavala, Amorgos, Folegandros, and Agathonisi; Turkish boat to Bodrun, Turkey; daily tourist boat excursions to Kalymnos.

History: Two of the island's early names were Meropis, for its mythical king, and Nymphaeon, for its numerous nymphs. The modern name, however, has more obscure origins. Astypalaia was the ancient capital, although in 366 BC the inhabitants founded the new city of Kos, on the same site as the present-day capital. Poised between the west and east (the ancient city of Halicarnasse, present-day Bodrun in Turkey, is very near), Kos flourished with the trade of precious goods — and ideas. Halicarnasse was the birthplace of the father of history, Herodotus, and in the 5th century Kos gave birth to the father of medicine, Hippocrates. His school on the island was rated the best in Greece, where he taught pupils a theory of medicine based on waters, observations, and special diets. Doctors today still take the Hippocratic Oath when entering practice. When Hippocrates died, an Asklepeion was founded on the island (a temple to the god of healing), which along with Epidavros and Triki was one of the most sacred in Greece. Up to Roman times, people from all over the world came to be cured at its hospital.

Verdant Kos also produced the school of Bucolic poetry, with Theokritus from Sicily as its major exponent. The Hellenistic ruler, Ptolemy II Philadelphos, was also born here.

Kos's wealth and position excited the envy of others, and from the 6th century it was invaded by Persians, Romans, and Saracens. The gods themselves, it seems, were jealous, and earthquakes in AD 142, 469, 554, and 1933 levelled most of the island's buildings. In 1315 the Knights of St. John took control of Kos, and built fortifications beginning in 1391, using material from the ancient city. Later Grand Masters who continued the work had no qualms about using the works of art from the Asklepeion to furnish the stone for their walls. In 1457 and 1477 the Turks besieged the Knights without success, but they gained the fortress after the fall of Rhodes.

Kos today: Dolphin-shaped Kos with its natural beauties, climate, beaches, and antiquities is Rhodes's major Dodecanese rival in the tourist industry. It is so successful that there are never enough rooms for its summertime visitors, even with the new hotels that have been erected recently. Yet despite the throngs, the island has managed to retain a charm that Rhodes has lost, and still pleases even the tourist-hating tourists. Part of this charm comes from the locals themselves, who are still not hardened by the dollar or the package tour. In Kos one does not find the petty greed of a duty-free port as in Rhodes, and the food is also much better, costing about half the price.

Kos capital lies in the region of the dolphin's eye. A wealth of greenery, flowers, and trees makes up for what it lacks in architectural beauties, for most of the houses were constructed on anti-seismic principles following the 1933 earthquake. The disaster had one good side effect, however, for it opened up new archaeological explorations. Some of the recent finds may be seen in the **museum** on the main square (open 9 am - 1 pm and 4 pm - 6 pm; closed Sunday. Entrance 25 dr., 2.5 dr. with student card. Free Thursdays). The prize exhibit is the statue of Hippocrates from the 4th century BC, and there are some fine Hellenistic sculptures from the Casa Romana and the Asklepeion.

Dominated by the 18th century **Defterdar Mosque**, the square before the museum has the best sweet shops on the island, offering a superb baklava. To the left of the mosque the street leads to the **Ancient Agora**, once walled in by the Knights; nearby are the ruins of a **temple of Aphrodite**. Continuing down the same street one arrives at the huge **plane tree,** under which Hippocrates supposedly taught. It is 14 metres (46 ft.) in diameter and supported on all sides by posts and Classical pillars. Although tree experts say that the tree is not quite old enough to fit its legend, it might very well be the oldest tree in Europe. On 1 September it is customary to give it a pat to ensure one's long life. By the tree is the Loggia Mosque and remains of the **ancient harbour quarter** excavated in 1934. A stone bridge leads to the **castle of the Knight of St. John** (open 9 am - 1 pm and 4 pm - 6 pm; entrance 5 dr., 2.5 dr. with student card), finished in 1514 by Grand Master Fabrizio del Carretto. It is well preserved, the walls containing many coats of arms and bas-reliefs, some dating from Classical times, such as the famous lion. Besides splendid areas of multicoloured weeds, the Kastro also contains many sculptures, inscriptions, columns and so on which are occasionally dug up in town and brought here for safe keeping, forming lines of defunct marble.

Back at the museum square, if you head off in the opposite direction along the harbour towards the Olympic Airways office, you will eventually see the **Casa Romana.** Surrounded by extensive ruins of **Roman baths,** the Casa Romana is described on a plaque as "A reconstructed house of Kos," dating from the Hellenistic or Roman periods, and excavated in 1933 by Laurenzi. (It has the same opening hours and entrance fees as the Kastro). Both it and the baths beside it fell in the earthquake of 554 AD, and the reconstruction affords a good idea of the spacious elegance of the wealthy before the birth of Christ. To the left is the **House of Europa** with mosaics, the **Xystrion,** and the **ancient gymnasium.** The **ancient Odeum** is across the street, containing

Hellenistic seats; once in a while dramas are still performed there. Â small **Temple of Dionysos or Herakles** is a skip away off Vas. Pavlou Street.

Kos harbour is an official port of entry for yachts, and it has a supply station. Beside it is one of the hardest worked tourist offices in Greece, distinguished by the rucksacks parked in front of it. The post office is behind it. There are two sandy beaches by the town for swimmers and for those who didn't reserve a room in advance. Many good tavernas and restaurants line the waterfront. A twenty-minute walk will take you to the start of the night places, with song and dance until late in the evening.

Restaurants: Turko Manolis (fish), Throsia, Limnos, Mavro Matis, Prestone, Prassini Akti and many more.

Bazookia: Aquarius, Olympia, Tria Adelphia, Rhoda, and Kambourio (very good).

Discotheques: Miropidis, Apollon.

Specialities: honey pastries, wine (Golden Retsina, Glafkos, Theokritos Vinko.)

Many places in Kos rent bicycles, the ideal transport to the **Asklepeion** a few kilometres inland. Discovered by the German Herzog in 1902, following the description in Strabo, it has been somewhat restored by the Italians (open 9 am - 1 pm and 4 pm - 6 pm; entrance 25 dr., 2.5 dr. with student card; free Thursday and Sunday). This was one of the most sacred shrines to the healing god Asklepios, worshipped by the Asklepiada, a secret order of priests who found that baths in a beautiful setting did much to remedy the ills of body and soul. Snakes were the symbol of the cult, as they were believed to search out healing herbs. Built after the death of Hippocrates in the 4th century BC, the Asklepeion is essentially Hellenistic with some Asiatic influences on the different levels. The lowest level is occupied by a large series of Roman baths; on the second level are the remains of a chapel built by Gaios Startinios Xenophon, a Roman doctor, what may have been a hospital, and a fountain, where water has been flowing for more than 2000 years; on the third level is the altar of Asklepios, and Ionic temples of Apollo and Asklepios (a few of the columns have been reconstructed by the Italians); on the fourth level was a Doric temple of Asklepios from the second century BC, the grandest and most sacred of all. The view from this top level is superb. On the way back to the capital, the village **Platani** has some good tavernas and cafés.

A modern establishment with healing waters is located at **Ag. Fokas** on the south coast of the island. Its thermal waters are known as an aid for arthritis and rheumatism. A beach stretches between the villages **Tolari** and **Kardemena** further down the coast. At Kardemena once stood the ancient and most important Carian town on the island, Halasarniton. It is a lively place in the summer (with rooms and restaurants) and besides farming and fishing, the locals produce pottery.

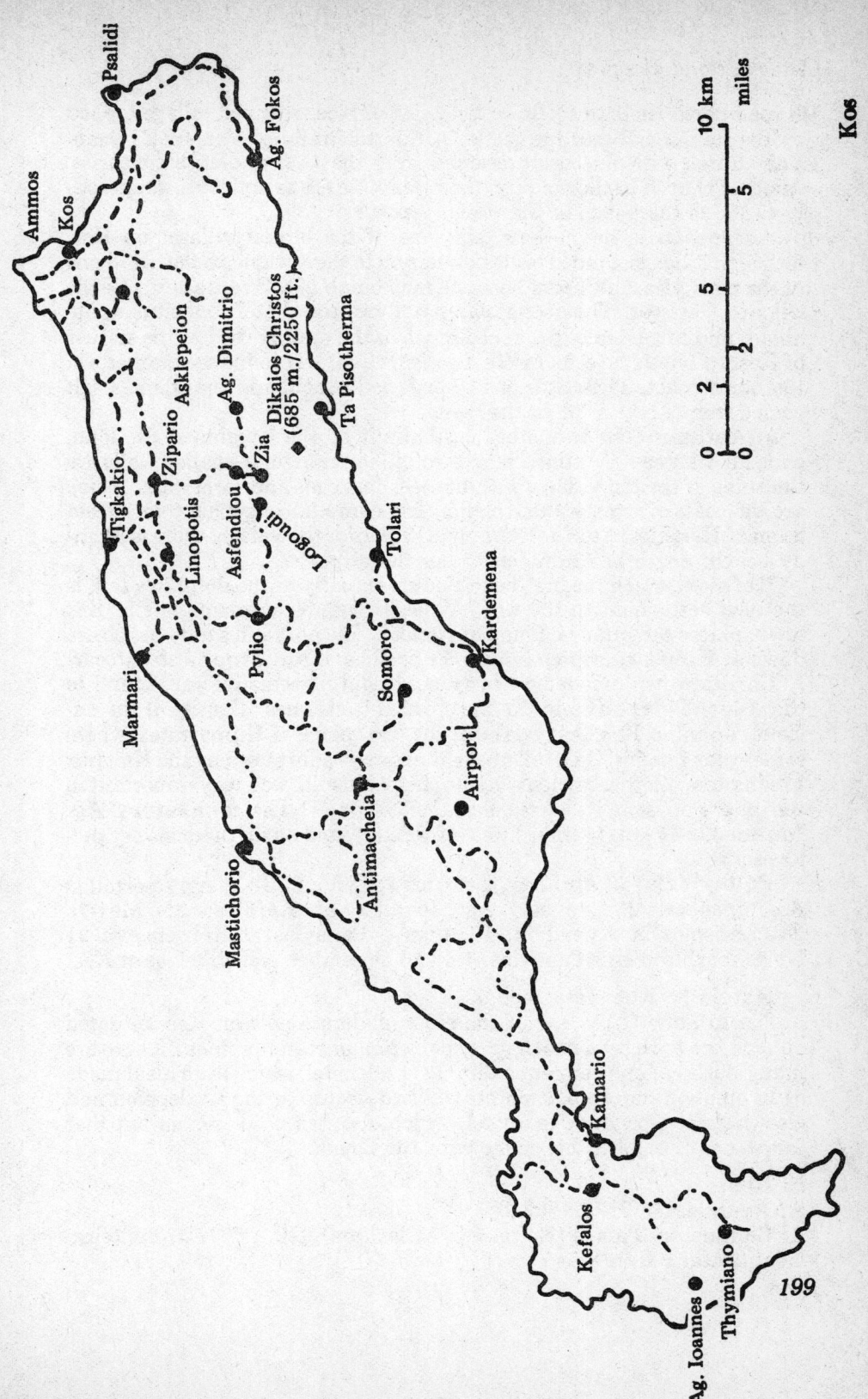

Kos

Psalidi
Ag. Fokos
Ammos
Kos
Ag. Dimitrio
Ziparo Asklepeion
Ta Pisotherma
Tigkakio
Zia
Dikaios Christos
(685 m./2250 ft.)
Linopotis
Asfendiou
Logoudi
Pylio
Tolari
Somoro
Marmari
Kardemena
Antimacheia
Airport
Mastichorio
Kamario
Kefalos
Thymiano
Ag. Ioannes

10 km
5
5
2
2
0
0
miles

199

A road north leads to **Pylio** in the heart of Kos, a ruined village topped by the ruin of a Byzantine castle. Within the walls one can see a Byzantine church with frescoes preserved from the 14th and 15th centuries. Another church in the vicinity, the Byzantine **Charmyleion,** supposedly contains the bones of the twelve Apostles.

Asfendiou is to the east, still one of the largest villages on Kos, although it has lost much of its population to the lowlands below, and one of the most pleasant. From here one may climb **Mt. Oromedon,** or even **Dikaios Christos**. This is the region of Pyxioton that Theokritus wrote about, and Mt. Dikaios produced much of the marble used in the statues of Kos. At Niotis taverna in **Zia** a wine festival is held in the summer. On the north coast, **Tigkakio** has a very good beach, and the island's salt comes from Alyki a bit to the west.

At **Antimacheia** is another castle built by the Knights of St. John, called le Chateau d'Antimacheia. Around its triangular-shaped walls are the ruins of the old village, with houses, churches and reservoirs. Inside are the coats of arms of the Knights. The name Antimacheia comes from a son of Herakles. At **Mastichorio,** the port of the village, there is a sandy beach. South of Antimacheia lies the airport.

Kefalos, which means "head" but is actually in the dolphin's tail, is the next settlement to the west. When there are no rooms left in Kos town, places can often be found at Kefalos. The port and sandy beach are down at **Kamario,** which is near the basilica of **Ag. Stephanis,** an early Christian monument now in ruins. Neolithic remains were found in the **Aspri Petri cave** by Kefalos, which is also near the site of the ancient capital of Kos, **Astypalaia,** the birthplace of Hippocrates, where some ruins remain. On a hill above the town is a fort used by the Knights. Isthmioton, another ancient city on the peninsula, was very important in the past and sent its own delegation to Delos. The **monastery Ag. Ioannes** is 6½ km. (4 miles) west of Kefalos, and a trip there is very picturesque.

Panayiéria: 23 April, Ag. Georgios at Pylio; 29 July, Ag. Apostoli at Antimacheia; 29 August, Ag. Ioannes at Kefalos; 25 March, Evangalismos at Asfendiou; 15 August, Panayias at Kardemena; 21 November, Isodia tis Panayias at Zia; 6 December, Ag. Nikolaos at Kos.

Hotels in Kos: area code 0242

The Atlantis (A) is one of the most modern hotels on Kos. Situated outside the town by a beach, transportation poses no problem. There are many buses, or one can rent a bicycle at the hotel, which is an ideal mode of locomotion on the not too hilly island. Tours to the Asklepeion and elsewhere can begin at the hotel, which also has a fair restaurant that serves continental dishes along with the Greek.

in Kos:
A: Atlantis, tel. 28731/292182
A: Continental Palace (Epirotikon Melathron), tel. 22737/28239; teleg. Continental Palace Kos

B: Alexandra, 1 25th Martiou, tel. 28301; teleg. Alexotel
B: Constanta (Pension), Artemissias, tel. 28244
B. Dimitra Beach (Bungalows), Ag. Fokas, tel.28581/2;teleg. Dimitrotel
B: Fotini (Pension), 3 Veriopoulou, tel. 28784.
B: Irene (Pension), Lambi, tel. 28186.
B: Kos, 31 Vas Georgios, tel. 22480/1
B: Theoxenia, 4 Vas Georgios, tel. 22310/2
C: Acropole, 4 Panagi Tsaldari, tel. 22244/22448
C: Christina, 3 Harmylou, tel. 22466; 9702173 in Athens
C: Ekaterini (Catherine), 8 P. Tsaldari, tel. 28285
C: Elli, 10 Themistoklwous, tel. 28401/2
C: Elisabeth, 9 El. Venizelou, tel. 22543
C: Ibiscus (Iviskos), 2 Akti Miaouli, tel. 22214
C: Koulias, 11 Riga Ferreou, tel. 28261/3
C: Milva, Platia Konitsis & Meropidos, tel. 28250/1; teleg. Milvahotel
C: Oscar, 59 El. Venizelou, tel. 28090/1
C: Veroniki, 2 P. Tsaldari, tel. 28122/3
C: Zephyros, 34 Vas. Georgios, tel. 22245/22288
D: Dodecanessus, 2 Alex. Ipsilantou, tel. 28460
D: Hara, 6 Halkonos, tel. 22500; teleg. Hotelhara
D: Helena, tel. 22740
E: Asklepeion, Grigoriou E, Marmaroto, tel. 28616
E: Kalymnos
in Kardemena:
D: Paralia, 21 25th Martiou, tel. 51205
in Kefalos:
D: Sidney

Tourist Police: National Tourist Office by harbour, tel. 28572.

Off the north coast of Kos is the islet **Pserimos**. It is connected daily by caiques from Kalymnos, and day excursions from Kos run on Mondays, Wednesdays, and Friday, costing about 350 dr. It has a lovely sandy beach, fresh fish, and few houses (less than 100 people live there). The old town is mostly abandoned. In the summer two cafés and tavernas have food; the people who stay overnight on Pserimos sleep out on the beach. On 15 August there is a panayiéri to the Virgin.

Leros
Connections: Four times a week with Piraeus; six times a week with Kalymnos, Kos, and Rhodes; three to six times a week with Patmos; once a week with Arki, Lipsi, Agathonisi, Kavala, Thessaloniki; three times a week with Samos; twice a week with Ikaria, Chios, Lesbos, and Limnos; once a week with Mykonos and Tinos.

History: When the hero Meleagros died, his sisters mourned him so passionately that Artemis turned them into guinea fowls and put them in

her temple at Leros, the wooded island dedicated to her. This worship of
the goddess of the chase and the guinea fowl might be traced back to the
Ionians, who took Leros from the original invaders, the Dorians. The Ionian city Ephesus, with the huge temple of Artemis, one of the Seven Ancient Wonders of the world, is relatively close on the Asia Minor coast.
Like the other Dodecanese, Leros sent ships to Troy, and was conquered
later by Darius, the Persian King of Kings, although the island was
liberated when his ships floundered in Salamis. Leros sided with Sparta
in the Peloponnesian War, despite its Ionian ancestry. Under the Byzantines, it was part of the theme of Samos, but in 1316 it was sold to
the Knights of St. John and governed by the Duke of Naxos as part of
the monastic state of Patmos. The Italians built a naval base in one of
the many sheltered harbours, which was bombed badly in the war.
During the later Cyprus dispute the Greek government dismantled the
base, to show that it had no warlike intentions against Turkey. When
the junta took power in 1967, communist dissidents were exiled on
Leros and kept under the strictest surveillance.

Leros today: With one of the most serrated coastlines of all the
islands, Leros is often forgotten in the tourist guides, perhaps because it
defies easy description. Neither big nor small, green but also rocky, with
some tourists but not too many, good swimming but few stretches of
sand, pretty but typical architecture, quiet but not too quiet — what can
one say to make the island distinct from all others, except that it has a
large mental hospital? Sociologically it was one of the last places in
Greece to hold on to the ancient traditions of matrilineal inheritance, all
property going to the eldest daughter who carried on the family line. Today, though, the daughters of Leros receive only a house and dowry when
they marry, like other Greek women.

Ag. Marina in the interior is the capital of the island, topped by the
Kastro, a Byzantine fortress renovated by both the Knights of St. John
and the Venetians. An easy footpath leads to the top, which commands a
splendid view of "four seas": the bays Panteli, Alindas, Gournas, and
Lakkiou. Two old churches have been repaired by the Greek
Archaeology Service, **Moni Megalochiro** and **Kyras Kastrou.** The
latter has the following legend: during the Turkish occupation a
miraculous icon of the Virgin with a candle set sail from Constantinople
and landed at Leros. The inhabitants, led by the bishops, met it and
carried it in great procession to the cathedral. The next day, however,
the icon was nowhere to be found, but before dismay had spread too far
the Turkish captain of the Kastro found it with its candle in the powder
stores, a strange incident considering that the door was firmly bolted and
locked. The icon was returned to the cathedral, but the next night the
very same thing occurred. And the next night, and the next. Finally the
Turkish captain grew weary of the affair and gave the powder storeroom
to the Christians, who turned it into the church Kyras Kastro. Here the
wilful icon has decided to remain ever since. During the Second World

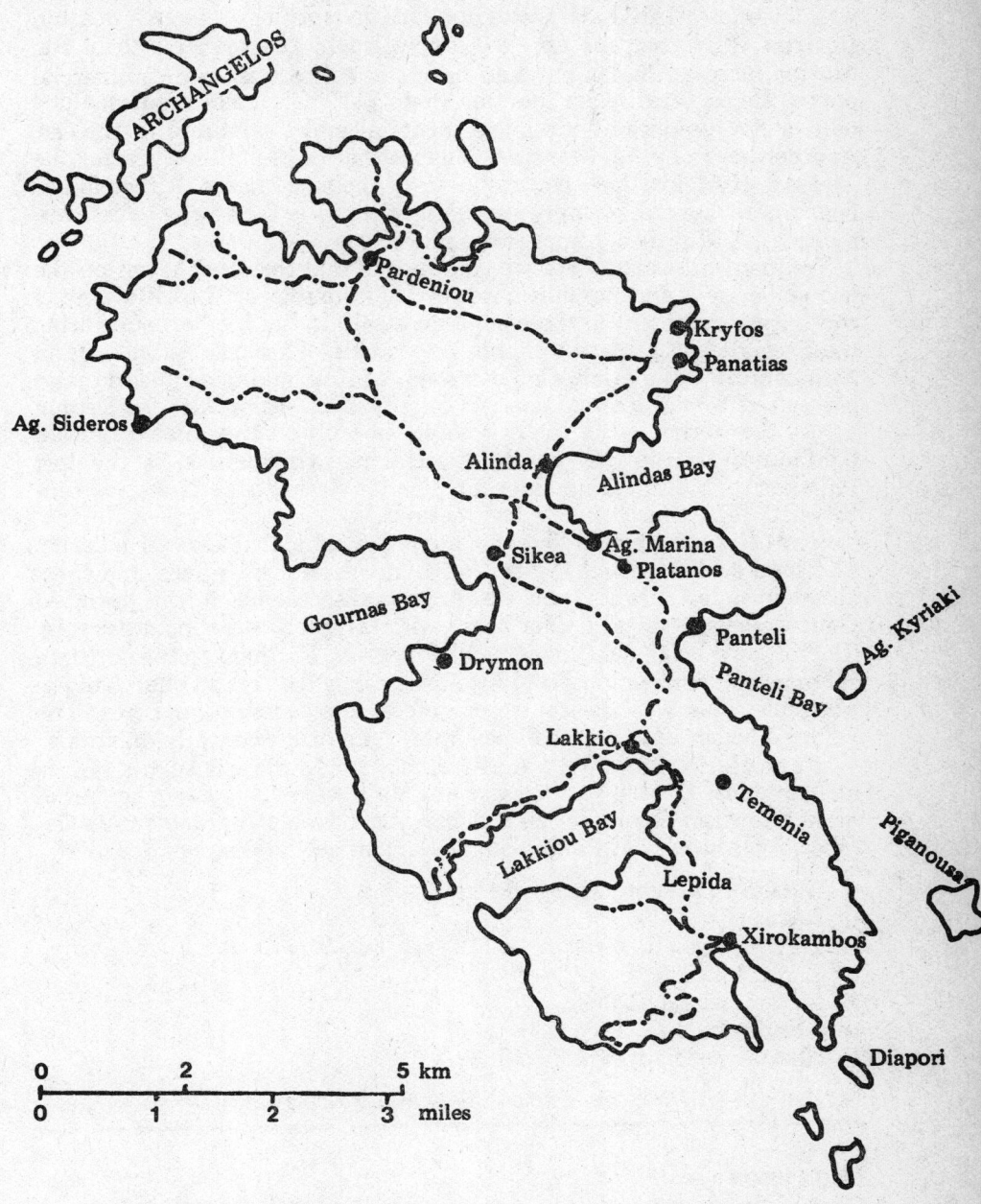

ARCHANGELOS

Pardeniou

Kryfos

Panatias

Ag. Sideros

Alinda

Alindas Bay

Ag. Marina

Sikea

Platanos

Gournas Bay

Panteli

Ag. Kyriaki

Drymon

Panteli Bay

Lakkio

Temenia

Piganousa

Lakkiou Bay

Lepida

Xirokambos

Diapori

0		2		5 km
0	1		2	3 miles

Leros

War the Germans and the Italians used Kastro as an observatory.

In Ag. Marina there is also a small **museum** housing local finds, which is most likely to be found open in the morning. A church nearby, **Sotiros Christos,** has an exceedingly bright red roof. North of Ag. Marina, across Alindas bay and beach, is **Alinda,** the old commercial port of Leros. Nearby are the ruins of an Early Christian basilica, along with a few vestiges of the ancient capital and a windmill in the sea. Another beach by Ag. Marina is Vromolithos in Panteli bay, facing the islet Ag. Kyriaki which has a church of the same name. Although the beach is rocky, trees supply shade and the sea is very clean. There are tavernas, and a restaurant, Savopoulos.

Frequent buses run between Ag. Marina and the other towns on the island. There is an especially good service from the port **Lakkio.** On the shore is a monument to those sunk on a ship in Lakkio harbour during the Second World War. A church Ag. Ioannes Theologos is built on an 11th century foundation. One can swim at Koulouki beach nearby and eat at the Efstathiades, Leros, or Possidonion restaurants. At Lepida across the harbour, the Moni Panayia is built on the ruins of an old lighthouse, and further south, overlooking Xirokambos, is the fort Paliokastro, built near an older fortification dating back to the 3rd century BC. The church inside has mosaics.

Panteli by the bay of the same name is a fishing village with a beach. The medieval aqueduct Pigathi tou Genovezou is near here, and there are rooms, restaurants, and the Anemis discotheque in the town. At Gournas bay, besides another beach with tavernas, is the monastery Ag. Sideros, on a small islet connected to the coast. Partheni on the northern shore had an ancient temple to Artemis, nearby the present church of Ag. Matrona. This was the centre of guinea fowl worship on Leros. The village's beach has tavernas known for their fish, especially mavrakis.

Panayiéria: 16-17 July, Ag. Marina at Ag. Marina; 6 August, Sotiros at Plantanos; 15 August, Panayias at Plantanos; 20 August, in honour of foreign tourists at Alinda; 20 October, Ag. Kyras at Pardeniou; 28 October, Ag. Matrona at Pardeniou; 26 September, Ag. Ioannes at Lakkio.

Hotels in Leros: area code 0247
in Lakkio
B: Zenon Angelou (pension), tel. 22514/22149
C: Leros, tel. 22940
C: Miramare, tel. 22053
in Alinda
B: Alinda (pension), tel. 23266

Tourist Police: Regular police at Ag. Marina.

Nissyros
Connections: three times or more a week with Kos, Kalymnos and Rhodes; tourist boat three times a week from Kos; twice a week with

Tilos, Symi, Astypalaia, Amorgos, and Piraeus; once a week with Ios, Folegandros.

History: Once Kos and Nissyros were one island, but when the latter's volcano exploded they were separated. In early days the inhabitants founded a city on Saria islet north of Karpathos, but they returned home when the pirates became too much of a problem. The rest of the fortunes of this tiny island follow those of the other Dodecanese, and it was fortified by the Knights of St. John.

Nissyros today: Nissyros manages to be a few degrees cooler than the other Dodecanese, and despite a lack of water, its rich volcanic soil keeps it green. Water melons, figs, and lemons are the major crops. On the islet **Yiali** between Kos and Nissyros are vast porous rock quarries with the houses of the workers; a similar quarry exists on Nissyros. If you visit the island at the right time, you will see chalked on the doors of the houses "Kalesmenoi", which means "you're invited to a wedding".

Mandraki is the village capital of the island, a charming place of old houses with white painted snakes in the streets. The **Kastro,** built in 1315, is to be seen above the town, and below it is the **Panayia Spiliani,** once a cave, and now a church (1825), filled with silver and gold and carved wood. From the roof there is a grand view of the sunset. In the main square of Mandraki a monument refers to the ancient Spartan maxim concerning the shield: "Come back with it or on it." Ten minutes from Mandraki is the island's sandy beach **Miramare,** and at **Loutra** are thermal baths. There are no hotels, but one can find rooms to rent.

Restaurants: Stavros, Franzis and Paradissi, which can be very lively at night.

One excursion not to be missed on Nissyros is to the **volcano** (Iphestios). A minibus leaves when the tourist boat from Kos arrives, and the road takes one almost all the way across the little, round, but scenic island. It passes **Loutra, Poloi** (another seaside village), and **Emborios** above on the mountain with its fort and 600 BC walls. **Nikia** is across the volcano on the other side. One can actually walk down the dusty path into the crater, which smells of sulphur and is still smoking in places. Although there are no trees in the area, it is very colourful, the volcano white and yellow, the mountains red and brown and the sky its eternal azure.

Panayiéria: 29 June, at Poloi, Ag. Apostoli; 27 July, Ag. Panteliemonos at Mikia; 15 August, Panayias, at Mandraki.

Tourist Police: Regular police at Mandraki.

Patmos
Connections: daily tourist boat in summer from Pythagorio, Samos; four times a week with Kalymnos, Leros, Kos, and Rhodes; three times a week with Piraeus; twice a week with Lipsos and Ikaria, Samos, Tinos, Syros, Nissyros, Symi, Agathonisi, Chios, Lesbos, and Limnos; once a

week with Naxos, Kavala, and Thessaloniki.

History: Patmos was inhabited from the 14th century BC, with the capital at present-day Skala and the acropolis and fortifications on Mt. Kastello. It was subjugated to Asia Minor and not very important. In 95 AD a certain John of Epheses was exiled to Patmos, there he converted the inhabitants and wrote the *Book of the Apocalypse,* or *Revelations.* Patmos was abandoned from the 7th to 11th centuries, however, and was only inhabited again when the Blessed Christodulos, a saintly hermit, founded the monastery of St. John the Theologian there, on the site of an ancient temple of Artemis and an old basilica. The money for the building came from the Byzantine Emperor Alexis Comnenus. When Alexis's fortunes were down, Christodulos had predicted his ascent to the throne, whereupon Alexis promised that should his words come true, he would grant him any wish in his power. When events in 1088 did indeed fall as the hermit had foretold, Alexis kept his promise. The entire island of Patmos was given to the monastery, which managed to retain absolute control of it for centuries against a thousand afflictions ranging from poverty to pirate raids. Under the Duke of Naxos, Patmos was left a relatively independent monastic state. In the 13th century the village Chora was founded in the shadow of the monastery, so that when in danger the population could take refuge behind its powerful walls. Patmos flourished particularly during the 16th to 19th centuries, and its school of theology and liberal arts, founded in 1713, cast a healthy glow over the long dark domination of the Turks. The monastery's control of the inhabitants lessened as the latter grew rich from trade at sea. By 1720 the monks and laymen divided the land between them, and Patmos began to establish colonies abroad. With the advent of the steamship the island declined like other island shipping centres.

Patmos today: Composed of volcanic masses, Patmos has many bays but little vegetation. Fresh water is supplied by the desalination plant at Skala, one of the largest in the world. There are many beaches, although transport to them isn't always easy. Although the island has known a great surge of tourism in recent years, it is a quiet group of tourists who come, and at night Patmos, for the most part, sleeps.

Chora on the hill is the capital of Patmos, containing some of the old mansions built when the island thrived on sea trade. A whole day can be spent visiting the old churches of the town: **Ag. Dimitrios** is the oldest, built shortly after the monastery. There are two convents, **Agia tou Agion** (open 3 pm - 5 pm) and **Zoodochos Pigi** (1607), and the **Evangelismos,** which runs the National Orphanage for Girls. All have interesting icons. Chora's most visited religious institution, of course, is the **Monastery of Ag. Ioannes Theologos,** one of the richest in Orthodoxy, both in wealth and art work. Inside its huge fortifications (restored after heavy damage in the earthquake of 1956) are the remains of its founder, the Blessed Christodulos, along with an icon of St. John given to the monastery by Alexis. Beautiful frescoes cover almost all

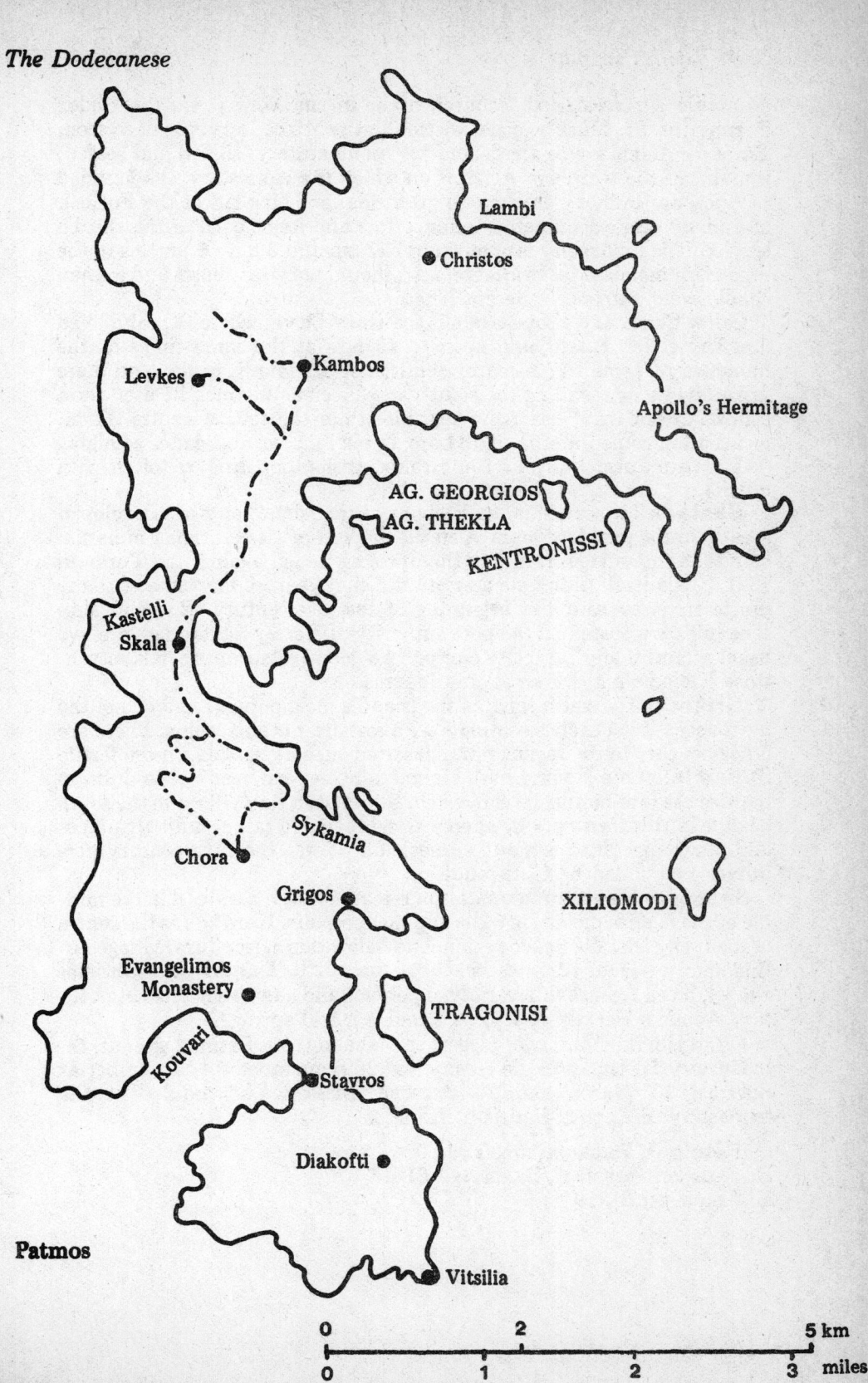

The Dodecanese

Lambi

● Christos

Levkes ●   ● Kambos

Apollo's Hermitage

AG. GEORGIOS
AG. THEKLA

KENTRONISSI

Kastelli
Skala ●

Sykamia

Chora ●

Grigos ●

XILIOMODI

Evangelimos
Monastery ●

TRAGONISI

Kouvari

● Stavros

Diakofti ●

Patmos

● Vitsilia

| 0 | | 2 | | 5 km |

| 0 | 1 | 2 | 3 miles |

paintable surfaces in the church area. In the library are the Codex Porphyrius, St. Mark's gospel written in the 5th century; the deed from Emperor Alexis giving the island to the monastery, signed and sealed; remains of the temple of Artemis on which the monastery was founded (supposedly built by Orestes, in gratitude for being rid of the Furies), and many other documents, manuscripts and items used in the church service. The monastery is open 8 am - 12 am and 3 pm - 6 pm. As in the case of all monasteries in Greece, men should not wear shorts and women should wear skirts of a decent length.

Below Chora and above Skala is the **Holy Cave,** where St. John lived and wrote the *Apocalypse,* open to visitors at the same times as the monastery. A small 17th century church of St. John is inside, and there are a few items recalling the saint's stay, such as the rock he used for a pillow. Chora itself has more nightlife than the tourist centre Skala; locals often come into the small bars, to play music, and dance at night.

Restaurants: Vangelis Ganbirakis, Ipsilantis Christos (often with music).

Skala below serves as the harbour of the island, and has developed greatly in the past few years. A statue of Protergatis Xanthos Emmanial stands in the village, recalling the uprising he led against the Turks in 1821. Skala itself didn't even exist until that year, so fearsome were the pirate raids even at the beginning of the last century. Bus and ship schedules are posted on the port authority office. By Skala there are two beaches and many places to camp. Two good restaurants are Konstantinos Kleiodis and Mavroyannis Ioannis.

Grigos in the south rates as the island's most popular and one of the most accessible beaches complete with restaurants and rooms. There are other beaches in the region, often deserted such as Sapsila. In the fertile Sykamia an old Roman bath claims to have been used by St. John to baptize the inhabitants he converted. **Stavros,** a tiny village to the south has the **Kalikatsou rock,** where carved rooms in rather unlikely places and other signs lead some to suggest that it was the 11th century hermitage mentioned by Christodulos.

Signs of very ancient inhabitation remain on **Mt. Kastelli** in the middle of the island, including walls and an acropolis. **Kambos** is the centre of the rocky island's fertile region, and below this agricultural village is a fine sandy beach. Another beach to the north, **Lambi** near Christos chapel, has a remarkable variety of pebbles and a taverna. The 19th century Apollo's Hermitage is by a small mineral spring.

Panayiéria: The two biggest panayaéria on Patmos are at the monastery for St. John, on 8 May and 26 September; 14 September at Stavros; 16 March and 20 October, Blessed Christodulos at the monastery; 6 August, Sotiris at Kambos.

Hotels in Patmos: area code 0247.
B: Patmion (pension), Skala, tel. 31313
B: Xenia, tel 31219

C: Astoria, Skala, tel. 31205
C: Chris, Skala, tel. 31001/31403
D: Diethnes, Skala, tel. 31357
D: Rex, Skala, tel. 31242
D: Rodon, Skala, tel. 31371
D: Vamvakos, Grigos
E: Neon, Skala, tel. 31218

Tourist Police: Regular police at Skala.

Of the three major islets in the administrative district of Patmos, **Lipsi** is the largest; quiet, carless, and almost untouched by tourism, it has two fine beaches, both close to the village. The 750 people who live on Lipsi fish and herd cattle, and good wine is to be had. One legend claims that is the isle of Calypso: there is certainly a similarity in the names of the enchantress and the islet. The ruined castle on the hill may be reached by mule. Caiques in the summer make the two-hour trip from Ag. Marina, Leros, and twice a week ships on the Dodecanese route call there between Patmos and Leros.

More remote is **Agathonissi,** connected only once a week with the outside world, like the even smaller **Arki.** (The ship's route is: Rhodes, Kos, Kalymnos, Leros, Agathonissi, Arki, Lipsi, Patmos and Samos.) These are poor islets, inhabited only by a few fishing families. On Agathonissi are two villages, Megalo Chorio and Mikro Chorio, and a few ancient remains have been found there.

Rhodes (Rodos)
Connections: By air — weekly night flights direct from London, Germany, the Netherlands, Italy, Finland, Norway, Lebanon, Denmark, Belgium, Austria, New York and Boston; three flights a day from Athens, and in the summer from Karpathos and Herakleon, Crete; one flight a week from Cyprus. By ship — May to Nov. ferry boats from Brindisi, Ancona, less frequently from Venice, Genoa, and Naples, Italy; from Limassol (Cyprus), Haifa (Israel) and Marseilles. Ferry boat daily from Piraeus; tourist boat to Marmaries (Turkey), Simi and Panormitis. Island connections — four times a week with Leros, Patmos; three times a week with Nissyros, Tilos, Karpathos, Kassos, Santorini, Halki; two times a week with Sitia, Ag. Nikolaos (Crete), Kastellorizo, Ikaria, Samos, Chios, Lesbos, Limnos, Mykonos; once a week with Thessaloniki, Kavala, Milos; daily ferry boat to Kos and Kalymnos.

History: Inhabited from the Stone Age, Rhodes was later invaded by the Minoans who built shrines to the moon at Philerimos, Lindos, and Kamiros. The Achaeans took the island in the 15th century BC, and Homer mentions that the Rhodians sent nine ships to Troy. In antiquity three ancient Dorian cities ruled the island, Lindos, Ialysos, and Kamiros, and the position of Rhodes on the trade route between the Middle East and the West led to an early importance both in trade and naval power. Around 1000 BC the three cities formed the famous Hexapolis with Kos and two cities of Asia Minos, Knide and Halicarnasse, a confederacy which was united politically, religiously, and economically. For four centuries they knew great prosperity and colonized from Naples to the Costa Brava in Spain.

Rhodes sided with the Persians in both their major campaigns against Greece, but upon their defeat joined the Athenian league. In 480 BC, in order to prevent rivalries among themselves and to increase their wealth and strength, the three ancient cities united and founded one central city, Rhodes, on the northern tip of the island. Hippodamos of Miletus, the geometrician and city planner, designed the new town with straight streets, as he had with Piraeus. It was considered one of the most beautiful cities of ancient times, and surrounded by walls encompassing a much greater area than that delineated by the existing medieval walls. Famous schools of Philosophy, Philology, and Oratory were founded, and the port had facilities far in advance of its time. Although Lindos, Kamiros and Ialysos still existed, they lost all their importance and most of their populations to the mighty new city.

During the Peloponnesian War, Rhodes sided with whichever power was in the ascendancy at any given time, and later supported Alexander the Great. He in turn lent his support to Rhodes in order to increase the island's commercial importance in contrast to that of Athens. The Rhodians surpassed that city, taking in most of the Mediterranean trade and building up a great navy that ruled the waves. Rhodian colonies were founded all over the known world. Under Alexander and after his death a thriving trade began with Egypt, and although the island was independent, it allied itself with Ptolemy in the Hellenistic struggles between the generals of Alexander. The other great powers at the time left the Rhodian fleet with the task of controlling piracy and creating trade and navigation laws; these were later adopted by the Romans and indeed by commercial traders today.

Then another general of Alexander, Antigonas, in his campaign to unit the old empire, ordered the Rhodians to fight with him against his rivals, mainly Ptolemy of Egypt. Loath to lose their lucrative Egyptian trade, the Rhodians refused, and so Antigonas sent his son Dimitrios Poliorketes (The Besieger) into the attack with the army of Syria and the Phoenician fleet. The ensuing year-long siege by one of the greatest generals of all time against the greatest city of the day has gone down in history, not only as a contest of great strength and endurance, but for the battle of wits between the two sides. Over and over again Dimitrios would invent some new ingenious siege machine, such as the 10-storey high Helepolis siege tower, only to have it ingeniously foiled by the defenders (who dug a hidden, shallow ditch in the path of the great Helepolis, thus tumbling it to the ground). After a year both sides grew weary of the affair and made a truce, Rhodes agreeing to assist Dimitrios' father Antigonas except in battles against Ptolemy. They also sent important hostages with Dimitrios to guarantee their promises.

So Dimitrios departed, leaving the Rhodians all of his vast siege machinery. This they either sold or melted down, either way in order to construct a great statue of their patron god Helius, the sun, by now associated with Phoebus Apollo. The famous sculptor Chares of Lindos was put in charge of the project. The Colossus of Rhodes, as it was later called, took him twelve years to cast and was almost 30 metres (100ft.) tall. The Rhodians placed it somewhere in the harbour, although the exact location is not known. Considered one of the Seven Ancient Wonders of the World, it lasted only from 290 to 225 BC, when an earthquake brought it crashing to the ground. There it lay for almost ten centuries, until 653 AD when the Saracens who had captured Rhodes, sold it as scrap metal to a merchant from Edessa. According to legend, 900 camels transported it to the ships.

In 164 BC, when they had repaired their city and walls from the siege of Dimitrios (the city at that time was even larger than it is today), the Rhodians made a treaty with Rome. Alexandria was then the only rival of Rhodes in wealth, and tiny Delos its only rival in Mediterranean trade. A famous school of rhetoric on Rhodes attracted Romans such as Cicero, Cassius, Julius Caesar and Mark Anthony. However, entanglement in Roman politics and the oscillations of power within the Roman Empire often brought evils to Rhodes along with privileges. When Rhodes supported the successors of Julius Caesar, Cassius cruelly sacked the island and sent many of its treasures to Rome. This began the decline of Rhodes, who lost control of the many islands she administered, along with much of the trade she once had. This trade had fallen off almost completely by the time of the end of the empire and Pax Romanica. In the first century St. Paul preached on the island and converted many of the inhabitants to Christianity.

Byzantium brought many invaders and adventurers to Rhodes, including the Arabs, the Genoese, the Venetians, and the Crusaders. In 1191 King Richard the Lion-heart and Phillip Augustus of France came to Rhodes in search of mercenaries. After the fall of Jerusalem in 1291, the Knights Hospitallers of St. John took refuge on Cyprus, but by 1306 they had become interested in the wealthier and better positioned Rhodes. They asked the Emperor Andronic Palaeologus to cede them the island in return for their loyalty, but the rulers of Byzantium knew better than to trust the Franks after they had sacked Constantinople in 1204. The Knights, under Grand Master Foulques de Villaret, then took the matter into their own hands. Although they purchased the Dodecanese from the ruling Genoese pirates, it was a prize they had to fight for, spending three years besieging the inhabitants.

By 1309, with the help of the Pope, the Knights had Rhodes and began to build their hospital and inns, eight in all, one for each of the "tongues", or different nationalities which comprised the Order (England, France, Germany, Italy, Castile, Aragon, Auvergne and Provence). Each tongue had a master, and they in turn elected the Grand

Master of the Knights, who lived in a special palace. There were about 600 men in the Order, originally devoted to the care of pilgrims who came to the Holy Land. As occasion dictated they became more and more warlike, and although they built a hospital on Rhodes, defence and raiding were their two primary concerns. They were also extraordinarily wealthy, especially after the other great Order of the Middle Ages, the Knights Templars, was dissolved in 1312. The popes gave much of their wealth and property to the Knights of St. John.

The Knights erected a new wall around the town, replacing the outdated Byzantine fortifications. Italian engineers, the best of their time, designed the new works throughout the 14th, 15th and 16th centuries, some of the most splendid of the day. The knights were besieged without success by the Sultan of Egypt in 1444, and by Mohammed II the Conqueror in 1480; but in 1522 Sultan Suleiman the Magnificent conquered the island. The siege lasted for six months, and Suleiman was on the point of giving up when a traitor told him that the Knights could not hold out. So he redoubled his efforts and the Knights were forced to surrender. They were permitted to leave in safety for Malta, with their Christian retainers and possessions, and thus became the Knights of Malta. In 1831 they ended up in Rome.

Turkish rule brought 400 years of darkness to Rhodes. When the inhabitants revolted during the War of Independence, the Turks reacted by slaughtering a quarter of the population. The Italian rulers in 1912 brought material prosperity but spiritual tyranny. They claimed that the island was their inheritance from the Knights of St. John, although of course only an eighth of the knights had been Italian. Mussolini even had the Palace of the Grand Masters reconstructed (it and many other of the medieval buildings of the old town were destroyed in the Great Gun Powder Explosion of 1856, when lightning struck an old Turkish powder magazine). During the Second World War Rhodes remained in the hands of a German garrison until May 1945. Before then a large part of the Jewish population on the island, almost 2000, had been slain in Nazi prison camps. Rhodes with the rest of the Dodecanese officially joined Greece in 1945, whereupon the government declared it a free port, boosting its already great tourist potential.

Mythology: Long ago, when Father Zeus handed out lands to all the gods and goddesses, he forgot to leave a portion for Helius, the god of the sun. Dismayed, Zeus asked Helius what he could do to make up for his omission. The sun god replied that he knew of an island just emerging off the coast of Asia Minor, which would suit him just fine. Zeus gave it to him willingly and Helius named this new home of his "Rhodes" after his nymph wife, the daughter of Poseidon and a Telchine. The nine Telchines, with their flippers and dog heads, were the first inhabitants of the island, and are accredited with founding the three ancient cities of Kamiros, Ialysos, and Lindos. The three grandsons of Rhodes and Helius with these names are other possible founders, as is Tlepolemos, who led the nine ships of Rhodes to Troy.

Kamiros even had a fourth mythological founder, Althaemenes, son of the Cretan king Catreus, himself the son of Minos. An oracle predicted that Catreus would be slain by one of his offspring. To prevent the prediction from coming true, Althaemenes went to Rhodes, where he founded Kamiros and built an altar of Zeus, surrounding it with magic metal bulls that would bellow were the island invaded.

Oracles, however, are not made for nothing, and in later life we find Catreus going to Rhodes to visit his son, whom he had missed dearly for so many years. He arrived at night, and what with the darkness and the bellowing of the mistaken metal bulls, Althaemenes could neither see nor hear, and was thus unable to identify his father and the Cretans. Naturally thinking that they were invaders, he slew them. When he realized his error in the morning he begged Mother Earth to swallow him up, which she did.

Rhodes today: Called more beautiful than the sun in antiquity, Rhodes has a new nickname today: "The island of Eternal Summer". Indeed it has more annual hours of sunshine than most places in Greece, attracting cold northern Europeans year-round, in the same way that Florida attracts cold north Americans. The island is endowed with tourist facilities of every kind, including a casino and golf course, and many shops make it easy for the visitor to take advantage of Rhodes' duty-free port. Despite all this cosmopolitanism, quiet villages remain on the island where one may enjoy the sunshine and not knock elbows with a tourist every minute.

Rhodes capital is divided into the Old Town within the walls and the New Town outside them. Those looking for cheap accommodation and food will have better luck in the old town. There are three harbours: **Mandraki** for yachts, small passenger ships and tourist boats; **Emborio,** or the commercial harbour, and **Acandia,** used by the large cruise and ferry boats. The **Yacht Supply Station** offers yachtsmen berthing, over-wintering, repairs, and general provisioning. The **Yacht Club** is located to the north of Mandraki harbour. Rhodes is an official port of entry and exit.

The **Old Town** is surrounded by the **Great Wall,** constructed on Byzantine foundations mainly under four Grand Masters: d'Aubusson, d'Amboise, del Carretto, and Villers de l'Isle Adam. Averaging 12 metres (40 ft.) thick, it is curved in order to deflect missiles better, and the landward sides were surrounded by a large moat, 30 metres (100 ft.) wide. Each tongue of the Knights was assigned a certain area of the wall to defend (Catalan and Aragon together). Bastions and towers strengthened the defence of the wall, and many gates connected the old town with the village outside, the most magnificent of these being the **Gate of Emery d'Amboise** located by the Palace of the Grand Masters and built in 1512. The Turks later blocked up the two harbour gates; they also made a law that all Greeks had to be outside the inner walls by sundown or forfeit their heads. On Mondays and Saturdays there is a tour of the **perimeter of the medieval wall,** starting at 4 pm at the Palace of the Grand Master.

Inside the inner wall, or **Collachium,** which the Knights could defend if the outer wall were taken, are the different Inns and the **Palace of the Grand Masters,** also called Castello, for indeed it is more of a castle than a palace. It is open from 1 April to 16 October, 7.30 am - 7.30 pm; 10 am - 6 pm Sunday; closed Tuesdays. The actual construction of the palace, on the site of a sanctuary of Helios, was completed in the 14th century, and it survived intact under the Turks (who used it as a prison) until the Great Gunpowder Explosion of 1856 left it in ruins. Mussolini ordered its reconstruction as it stands today, and the Italians filled it with lovely mosaics and Hellenistic sculptures brought from Kos. A **Sound and Light Show** takes place here in the evening, from 1 April to 31 October, performed in English among other languages. Performances begin at 7.30 pm and finish at 10.15 pm. Tickets may be purchased at the gate and cost 50 dr., 25 dr. for students and 10 dr. for children.

The medieval **Ippoton Street** (the Street of the Knights) leads down from the palace. The remaining Inns of the different tongues are in this area, including the French Inn, the Italian Inn, and the House of Villaragout on the street itself. The Inn of Provence and one of the Spanish Inns are on an alley by the French Inn. At the end of the street, if you turn toward Argyrokastro Square you will find the fine Auvergne Inn, today a cultural centre, and a 14th century building constructed by Grand Master Roger de Pins and perhaps the original hospital of the Knights. The English Inn is nearby, built in 1483, but hard hit by an earthquake in 1851. Rebuilt by the British, it was bombed and rennovated again in 1947. This was a praiseworthy effort, especially since the English left the Order of St. John when the Pope excommunicated Henry VIII. The British Counsul of Rhodes (Polidou Street, tel: (0241) 27306 and open 8.30 am - 1.30 pm) has the key to it.

The later Hospital of the Knights on Platia Symis now houses the **Rhodes Museum** (open 7.30 am - 7.30 pm; 10 am - 6 pm Sunday; closed Tuesday. Entrance 25 dr., 2.5 dr. with student card. Free Sunday and Thursday). It contains a collection of statues, stelai, and inscriptions, the prize of the collection being the Aphrodite of Rhodes, or the Marine Venus, found when a hotel was being constructed. An excellent book on the island by Lawrence Durrell takes its title from the statue: *Reflections on a Marine Venus.*

Also in Platia Symis are the ruins of a **temple of Aphrodite,** dating from the 3rd century BC and discovered by the Italians in 1922. Another temple of the same epoch was dedicated to **Dionysos** and can be found near a corner in the wall behind the Ionian and Popular Bank. On Mondays, Wednesdays, and Fridays, from 9 am - 1 pm, one may also visit the **Museum of Decorative Arts.** The **fountain** on Argyrokastro Square is a reconstruction, found in the Byzantine fort at Arnitha. Stores in the region sell objects made from onyx stone, to be seen in increasing frequency as one approaches the major shopping street of the old town, **Sokratous,** dominated by the slender minaret of the lovely **Mosque of Suleiman,** across from the clock tower. It is the only Turkish mosque in Greece which still holds services, and is generally closed; those who find it open must remove their shoes before entering. Suleiman the Magnificent had it built in 1523 after he conquered Rhodes.

The mosque marks the start of an area known as the **Turkish Quarter,** a fascinating zigzag of narrow streets. Turkish balconies of latticed wood project overhead beside crumbling stone arches and houses built directly over the street. On the square off Archelaos Street are the **Turkish baths,** built in 1765. Although heavily bombed, they have been restored to full working order by the city, and one may take a Turkish bath for about 75 dr. The **Turkish library** is near the Mosque of Suleiman, containing some rare Persian and Arabian manuscripts. Another mosque, **Ibrahim Pasha** is off Sophokles Street. It was built in 1531, and the minaret was restored by the Italians.

Kastellania Palace, on Hippocrates Square, was built by d'Amboise in 1507 and served as a tribunal. It is near the **Evriaki,** or Jewish quarter of town. The Platia Evrion Martyron (the Square of Hebrew Martyrs) recalls the Jewish inhabitants of Rhodes sent off to die in the concentration camps. At the end of Sokratous Street still stand the ruins of the **Virgin of Victory,** built by the Knights in thanksgiving for their defeat of the Turks in 1480.

The **New Town** has an **Aquarium** at its northern tip, the only one in Greece and the Balkans. Along the quay from the yacht club to Mandraki the buildings are lit up at night, somehow complementing the Babylonian air of the city after dark. The most important of the large public buildings is the **Governor's palace,** and beside it the **Mosque of Mourad Reis** who was the head pirate of the Egyptian Sultan, killed at Rhodes in 1522, and buried in the Turkish cemetery by the mosque. The modern church **Evangelismos** is a replica of a Byzantine Church of St. John destroyed in 1925. Behind the colonnade of sweet shops by the long Eleftherias Square is the **market place** and **bus stop** to outer Rhodes (a few buses also leave from nearby Alexandrou Papagou Street). In the market one can find cheap food and fast service. At the corner of A. Papagou and Archiepiskopou Makariou Streets is the large office of the **National Tourist Organization of Greece,** with its push-button light-up map for the lost tourist. The office is open 8 am - 2 pm and 5 pm - 8 pm.

By **Mandraki** itself are a few derelict windmills, and the **fortress of Ag. Nikolaos,** built in 1464 on the site of a church of the same name, with funds provided by the Duke of Burgundy. At the mouth of the harbour, where the Colossus might have stood, are **statues of the Rhodian deer,** which have become the symbol of the island. Along the waterfront of the city are many beaches, including one at Emborios, the commercial harbour and others by Akti Miaoulis and to the east of the cape.

Many places in town rent bicycles and scooters and cars, but any reasonably active visitor can even walk to **Mt. Smith,** named after Admiral Sydney Smith who kept watch on Napoleon's Egyptian escapades from here. On the way there (north Epirous Street) are the ruins of an **Asklepeion,** or temple to the god of healing, and the **Cave of the Nymphs.** Mt. Smith was the ancient acropolis of the Rhodians. On the top, the Italians have partly reconstructed a **temple of Pythian Apollo** (later associated with the sun god Helius). It belongs to the Doric order and dates from the 2nd century BC. A few columns also remain of temples of Zeus and Athena, and one can distinguish the outline of a 3rd century BC **stadium.** The **ancient theatre** has been reconstructed, and hosts classical dramas in July (see the Tourist Office for programme details).

Other Rhodian efforts to amuse visitors include the **Casino at the Grand Hotel on Akti Miaoulis,** where the guests may win or lose their fortunes at roulette and baccarat nightly from 7 pm to 4 am. **Folk dances** by the Nelly Dimoglou company are performed in the Old City Theatre from June until October. Tickets are 120 dr., 60 dr. for students, and the shows begin at 9.15 pm (there is no show on Saturdays). For information call (0241) 20157 or 27524. At **Rodini Park,** where the Rhetoric School of Aeschines was built in 330 BC after his political defeat by Demosthenes, the **Wine Festival** runs from the beginning of July to the beginning of September. It is open from 7 pm to 1 am in the morning, and buses bring revellers to and from Mandraki harbour. Entrance is 50 dr., or 40 dr. for individuals in groups of more than 20. Besides Rhodian wines and other Greek varieties, there is music, dance, and food, although one must pay for the latter.

Restaurants: Rose Marie on Akti Miaoulis; Deloukis, Norden, No. 13 on Kos Street; Kontiki, Astoria by Mandraki; Oscar on Plams Street; Piccolo on Kastellorizo; Loukoulos on Amerikis; Scandia on Vas. Marias; Jason, corner of Griva; Posseidon on Pythagora; Nouri on Komninon Street; Maison Fleuri on Vas. Friderikis; Arapaki on The. Soufili; Neorion on 21 April Street; Vlachos on Themistokoleous. Cheaper restaurants can be found in the Old Town; generally speaking, the more out of the way, the cheaper the restaurant, and sometimes the better if one likes Greek-tasting food.

Night Clubs: Cosmopolitan at Koumptpiroptou Square; Sultana on Riga Fereou; Zorbas on Vas. Marias; Isabella on Akti Miaoulis; Copacabana on Australias; Kastro on Arionos; Rhodian Cellar on Riga Fereou; Golden Chevalier on Griva Street; Rodini at Rodini Park; Pergola on Alex. Diakou; Chevalies on Platonos; Rhodes Palace on Leof. Triaton; Golden Beach on Akti Triaton; No. 1 at Ixia Triaton; Spilia at Ixia Triaton; Dionyssos on Sokratous; and Elli at Platia Kountouriotou.

Discotheques: Aquarius on Voriou Ipirou; Kilimatzaro and Vikings on Akti Mialoulis; Milord on S. Venizelou; Mittato on Papalouka; VIP's on Sokratous; 2001 on Vas. Marias; Fat Albert on Plutarchou Plessa; Step by Step on Papalouka; and Can Can on Ammohostou.

Specialities: Rice pudding (rizagalo), bougasta (custard pastry), and wine, especially Chevalier de Rhodes (red), Grande Maitre and Lindos Blanc Sec. Ceramics are the main local product; duty free items such as furs, jewellery, and spirits are in great abundance.

Buses and taxis serve the rest of the island with great efficiency, and tourist agencies run many guided tours to places of interest. South-west of the town, **Therme Kallitheas** has thermal waters for bile, liver, and intestinal troubles. There is a beach and a restaurant in an artificial cave. **Faliraki,** a popular resort area by a beach, has many restaurants, Geo. Iandreou and Geo. Ianakles being two of the better ones. One can play golf at **Afantou,** one of the three golf courses in Greece. It has 18 holes and there are also tennis courts. There are fine beaches in the bay below, and at **Ladiko** Anthony Quinn has his very own stretch of sand. At **Kolymbia** village down the coast many large farms are supplied with water from the tiny village **Epta Pigi,** the Seven Springs.

Archangelos, continuing down the main highway, rates as the largest village on Rhodes. From there one may visit the two churches Archangelos Gabriel and Archangelos Micheal (the village church), considered two of the prettiest on the island. The people of Archangelos have a reputation for great musical talents, and they also make a good variety of peasant boot. The fort on the hill dates from the Knights of St. John.

One of the strongest forts of the Knights is below Malona at **Feraclos.** It was occupied originally by pirates, whom the Knights chased out, repairing the walls and using it as a prison. Even after the rest of the island was conquered the Castle of Feraclos held out against the Turks, only falling after a long, determined siege. There is also a cave there and a lovely enclosed beach.

Beautifully situated **Lindos** is the second most important town of Rhodes, both historically and touristically. Of the three ancient cities it was the largest and most important, inhabited from 2000 BC; the first temple on its magnificent acropolis dated back to 1510 BC. Of its many colonies, the city which has become Naples, Italy, is the most famous. Part of its early importance lies in its natural harbour, the only one on Rhodes, and in its early ruler Cleobulos, one of the Seven Sages of Greece, who lived during the 6th century BC: his maxim "Nothing to Excess" was engraved on the oracle at Delphi. He created a reservoir which supplies water to Lindos to this day.

One can take a donkey or walk up the narrow curving streets to the **acropolis,** lined with a solid display of blouses, tableclothes, and other items put out to sale by the good women of Lindos, who sit by their wares, needlepoint in hand, as if weaving the fates of the thousands of tourists who pass them every day. The acropolis is open 7.30 am - 7.30 pm, 10 am - 8 pm Sunday; 25 dr. entrance, 2.5 dr. with student card; free on Thursday and Sunday. It is reached by a tall stair built by the Knights of St. John. Note the trireme carved in the rock before climbing; a statue of Agesander, priest of Poseidon, once stood there, sculpted by Pythocretes, better known for his Victory of Samothrace.

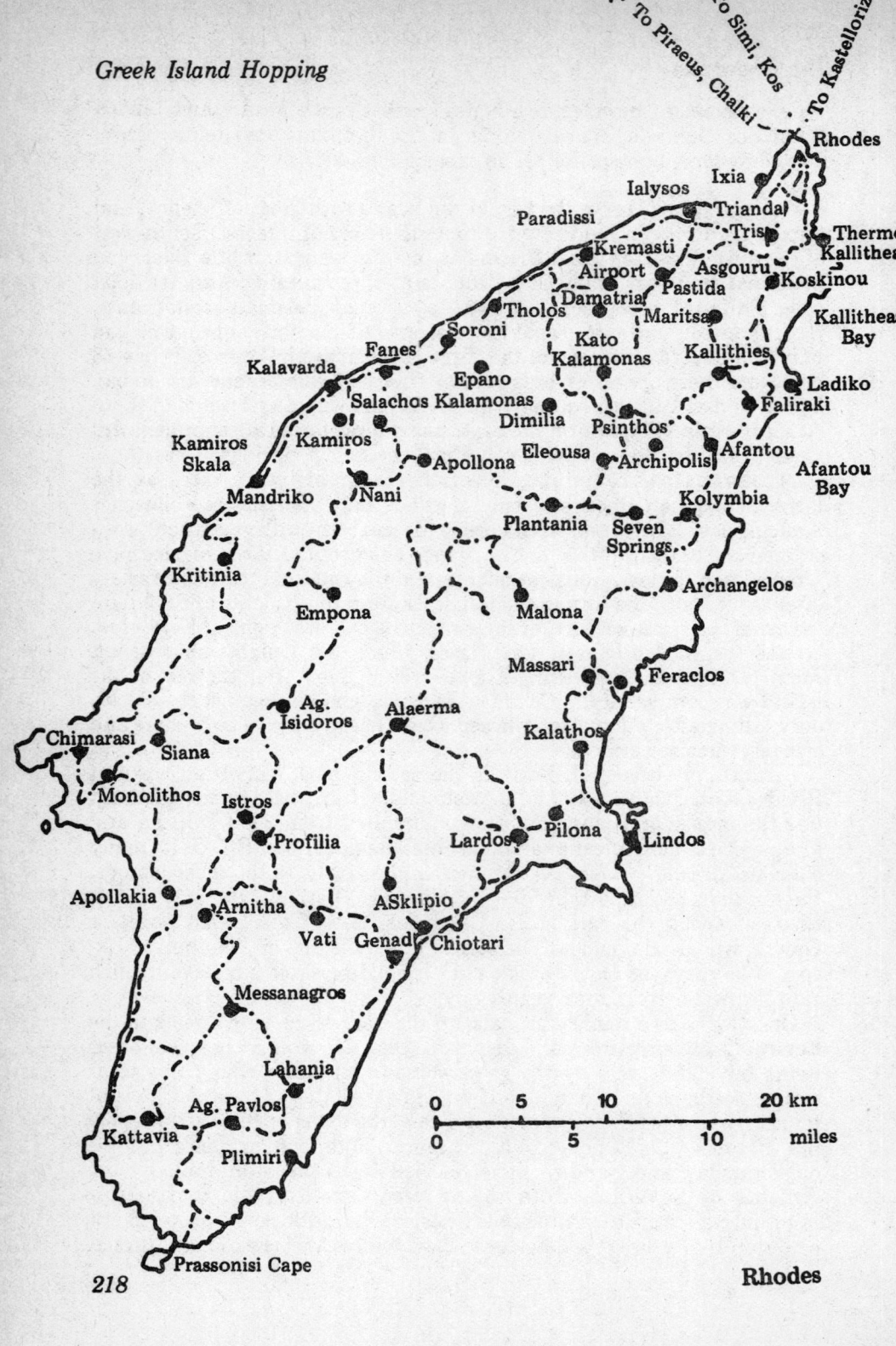

Greek Island Hopping

To Piraeus, Chalki
To Simi, Kos
To Kastellorizo

Rhodes
Ixia
Ialysos
Trianda
Tris
Paradissi
Therme
Kremasti
Kallitheas
Airport
Asgouru
Koskinou
Damatria
Pastida
Tholos
Maritsa
Kallitheas
Soroni
Bay
Kato
Fanes
Kalamonas
Kallithies
Kalavarda
Epano
Ladiko
Kalamonas
Salachos
Faliraki
Kamiros
Dimilia
Kamiros
Psinthos
Skala
Eleousa
Afantou
Apollona
Archipolis
Mandriko
Afantou
Nani
Bay
Kolymbia
Plantania
Kritinia
Seven
Springs
Empona
Archangelos
Malona
Massari
Feraclos
Ag.
Isidoros
Alaerma
Chimarasi
Kalathos
Siana
Monolithos
Istros
Lardos
Pilona
Lindos
Profilia
Apollakia
Arnitha
ASklipio
Vati
Genad
Chiotari
Messanagros
Lahania
Ag. Pavlos
Kattavia
Plimiri

0   5   10   20 km
0   5   10   miles

Prassonisi Cape

Rhodes

On top of the stair one passes through two medieval vaulted rooms. To the right is a 13th century **Church of St. John** in poor repair, and straight ahead is the raised Dorian arcade of Lindias Athenas, the patron goddess of the city. The **Propylaea** and the temple itself, of which only seven columns are standing, were built in the 4th century BC and reconstructed by the Italians. The pride of the temple was the golden inscription it once contained of Pindar's Seventh Ode.

The view from the acropolis encompasses a wide area, most striking towards the small, deep blue harbour where St. Paul landed in 58 AD. The small chapel dedicated to him has a huge panayiéri on 28 June. In the larger bay the once great Lindian navy of 500 ships berthed. The buildings, invariably white, of the town below date from the 17th century. The older ones have tall roofs and lovely wood work, besides collections of the famous Lindian ware, painted plates occasionally dating back to Byzantium. The inhabitants learned the art from the East and produced some true masterpieces in the folk tradition, a few of which can be seen at the **Papakonstandis** mansion, now the Lindos museum. Lindos also had a reputation for embroideries dating back to the time of Alexander the Great. A sperveri, the fine bridal dress that all Lindian girls once wore, can be seen at **Kashines house.** In the **Panayia church** in the centre of town are many excellent Byzantine works of art. The Church itself was founded in 1779. There is a beach, Palestra, many restaurants, and a huge plane tree in the square which makes waiting for the bus a comfortable business. At a distance, by the harbour, is the **tomb of Cleobulos,** now converted to the church Ag. Milianos.

Lardos west of Lindos is a pretty little village. The beach below it has sand dunes: indeed the whole south-east coast of Rhodes is a series of sandy beaches, many of them deserted, while the west coast, beaten by a rough sea, is rugged and wild. At the southernmost tip, **Prassonisi Cape,** the landscape takes on an other wordly aspect in its desolation. Skiadi Monastery is the only place in the region to spend the night. **Apollakia** on the west coast, a charming village, produces the best water melons on Rhodes. Further up the coast, **Monolithos** is the most important village of the region, surrounded as its name implies by huge monoliths. On a rocky cliff 200 metres (650 ft.) high is a castle built by the Grand Master d'Aubusson.

Inside is a frescoed church, Ag. Pantelimonos. A footpath winds its way up to the top, and the energetic climber will be rewarded magnificently, for the view of the sun setting over Halki island from the castle of Monolithos is divine. Below, the small bay of Fourni has caves with signs of ancient occupation, and not far is the monastery Ag. Anastasia.

One of the most traditional villages left on Rhodes is **Empona** in the mountains, where the dances of the women are exceptional. Old people wear their traditional dress every day. **Mt. Atavros,** with the ruins of a temple of Zeus Attrivirus, is a two-hour climb from Empona. At almost 1200 metres (4000 ft.) it is the highest mountain of the island. On a clear day one can see Crete from the peak; perhaps poor Althaemenes used to come up when pining, like all Cretans, for his mother island. Althaemenes supposedly founded the village below Empona, **Kritinia,** which he named in honour of Crete. **Kamiros Skala** below, which also claims Althaemenes, has frequent caiques to Halki.

Kamiros itself, one of the ancient cities of Rhodes, lay forgotten until 1859, when excavators began to bring to light a remarkable number of ancient buildings. The **cemetery,** in particular, rendered many beautiful items and in archaeological terms was one of the richest ever discovered in Greece. An excellent water and drainage system, supplied by a large reservoir, served the many houses which have been excavated. An agora and a temple of Apollo **Kamiros** have also been discovered.

On a high hill over the village of **Salachos** are the ruins of another medieval fort; the village below is praised for its shade and fresh water, some of which comes from the Spring of the Nymphs. **Mt. Profitis Elias** (790 metres/2600 ft.) above Salachos has two hotels on the top, besides the monastery of the Prophet Elija. The most popular site in this region of Rhodes is the **Valley of the Butterflies,** or Betaloudes, by **Kato Kalamonas.** Buses go there in the summer, and entrance is 3 dr. Intersected by a tiny stream, the valley is long and shady, full of fairy-tale trees and wooden bridges. From June till September a sooty orange species of butterfly (Callimorpha Quadripuctaria) flocks here, attracted by the sweet resin of the trees, which is used to make frankincense. The butterflies rise in a flutter when people jingle car keys or clap their hands. A bit up the road is a monastery, **Panayia Kalopetra,** claimed to have been built by the hero who began the Greek revolution in 1821, Alexander Ypsilantis. Below Kalamonas is the very popular beach Paradissi.

Kremasti, a village of few tourists, is best known for its wonder-working icon, Panayias Kremasti, for which one of the biggest panayiéria of the Dodecanese takes place between 15 and 23 August, climaxing on the 23rd. Villagers bring out their native costumes and are said to dance a mean sousta. On **Mt. Philerimos** nearby stood the acropolis of the ancient city of **Ialysos,** called Orychoime (open 1 pm-6pm, 10.30am-2.30pm). Ialysos, the least important of the three ancient cities, is situated by Trianda village, but its acropolis presents the greatest interest. On the site of an older Phoenician temple are the remains of a **temple of Athena** from the 3rd century BC, and a 4th-century **Doric fountain,** discovered by the Italians. A basilica built in the first millennium has been restored with frescoes. The **cemetery** yielded finds from Mycenaean to Hellenistic times. At the Byzantine fortress at Olychoime, Our Lady of Philerimos, the Genoese fought John Cantacuzene in 1248; there are a few Byzantine churches nearby.

Nearby **Trianda,** a resort area, was settled by Minoans in 1600 BC, and might have been damaged in the explosions and subsequent tidal wave from Santorini. Some people at **Asgouru** practise the Moslem faith, and the mosque and minaret there were once part of a church of St. John. There are many oak trees in the area around Rodini Park.

Caiques leave Mandraki in the morning for the following beaches: **Lardos, Tsambika, Faliraki, Kallithea, Ladiko and Kolymbia.** Most are on the east coast.

Panayiéria: In August, dance festivals at Kallithies, Maritsa and Empona; 29-30 July, Ag. Soula at Soroni, an occasion for donkey races; 28 June at Lindos; 14 June, Profitis Ammos at Philerimos; 26 July, Ag. Pantelemeimon at Siana; 7 September, at Monastery Tsabikas, when barren women go to pray for fertility; 15-23 August at Kremasti; 26 August, Ag. Fanourious in the Old Town; 5 September, Ag. Tris by Rhodes; 13 September, Stavros at Apollona and Kallithies; 26 September, Ag. Ioannes Theologos at Artamiti; 18 October, Ag. Lukos at Afantou; 7 November at Archangelos; Carnival at Apokries.

Hotels in Rhodes: area code 0241

Rhodes, an attraction all year round, is the island of super hotels by any standards. The smallest C rated there is better than anything on many islands. In Rhodes town the Grand Hotel (L) by the beach contains the island's casino, a nightclub, tennis courts, and a huge swimming pool said to be the largest in the country. A little further down the road, on the long, hotel lined Ixia beach, Rhodes Palace (L) is the queen, although it does not give directly on to the beach itself like Miramare Beach. Another hotel in the vicinity is the Metropolitan Kapsis (A) reputedly the biggest in Greece, with a pool, tennis courts, and a sauna. Yet another, Rodos Bay (A) Hotel and Bungalows, has a private beach, besides a swimming pool. Its restaurant, on top of the hotel, not only sports a fine view but has good Greek and continental dishes. For any one wishing to escape the throngs of beach and town, the Elafos Elafina (A) ('The Buck and Doe') is a Swiss chalet-type lodge built on the slopes on Mt. Profitis Elias by a tiny village of the same name, lost in the shady pine forests.

In Rhodes town
L: Grand Hotel, Astir Palance, Akti Miaouli, tel. 26284; teleg. Grandrhodes
L: Miramare Beach (hotel and bungalows), Ixia, tel. 24251/27154; teleg. Miramarerhodes
L: Rhodes Palace (hotel and bungalows), Leof. Trianton, Ixia, tel. 25222; teleg. Rodos Palace
A: Apollonia (furnished apartments), Leof. Trianton, Ixia, tel. 25961.
A: Avra Beach (hotel and bungalows), Leof. Trianton, Ixia, tel. 25284/20150; teleg. Avra Beach.
A: Bel Air, Leof. Trianton, Ixia, tel. 2371; teleg. Belhotel
A: Belvedere, Akti Kanari, tel. 24471; teleg. Belvedere Rhodes
A: Blue Sky, Paltia Psaropoulas, tel. 24091; teleg. Bluesky Rhodes
A: Cairon Place, 28 Makariou, tel. 24328/27600
A: Chevaliers Place, 3 Griva, tel. 22781; teleg. Chevatel

A: Dionyssos, Ippoton, Faneromenis-Ixia, tel. 23021; teleg. Dioniotel
A: Eden Roc, Reni Koskinou, tel. 23851/23859; teleg. Edenroc
A: Ibiscus (Iviskos), 17 Nissyrou, tel. 24421/23326; teleg. Ibiscus Rhodes
A: Imperial, 23 Vas. Konstantinou, tel. 22431/24067; teleg. Imperial
A: Kamiros, 1 25th Martiou, tel 22591; teleg. Kamiroshotel
A: Mediterranean, 35-37 Ko, tel. 24661; teleg. Mediterranean
A: Metroplitan Capsis, Leof. Trianton, tel. 25015; teleg. Capsotel
A: Oceanis, Leof. Trianton, tel. 24881; teleg. Oceanishotel
A: Park, 12 Riga Ferreou, tel. 24611; teleg. Marvelrhodes
A: Regina, 20 Makariou, tel. 22171
A: Riviera, 2 Akti Miaouli, tel. 22581/24801; teleg. Hotelriviera
A: Rhodes Bay (hotel and bungalows), Ixia Trianta, tel. 23661; teleg. Rodosbay
A: Siravast, Platia Vas. Pavlou, tel. 23551; teleg. Siravast Rhodes
B: Acandia, 6 Vas. Marias, tel. 22251; teleg. Messotour
B: Aglaia, 35 Apol. Amerikis, tel. 22061; teleg. Aglahotel
B: Alexia, Orthonos-Amalias-Orfanidou, tel. 24061; teleg. Alexotel
B: Amphitryon, 10 Alex. Diacou, tel. 26880/3628080 in Athens
B: Angela, 7 28th Octovriou, tel. 24614/24014; teleg. Hotelangela
B: Athina, Georgiou Leonto & Amalias, tel. 22631; teleg. Athinhotel
B: Cactus, 14 Ko, tel. 26100/26088/24237
B: Constantinos, 65 Amerikis, tel. 22971/24758
B: Corali, 28 Vas. Konstantinos & Patmou, tel. 24911; teleg. Coralhotel
B: Delfini, 45 E. Makariou, tel. 24691; teleg. Retour
B: Despo, 40 Vas. Sophias, tel. 22571
B: Esperia, 5 Griva, tel. 23941
B: Europa, 94 28th Octovriou, tel. 22711/24810
B: Leto, Leof. Trianton, Ixia, tel. 23511; teleg. Litohotel
B: Manousos, 25 C. Leontos, tel. 22741; teleg. Manousotel
B: Olympic, 12 Platia Vas. Pavlou, tel. 24311; teleg. Olympic hotel
B: Phoenix (Palm), 2 Exarchou Panteleimonos, tel. 24531; 6435796 in Athens; teleg. Palmhotel
B: Plaza, 7 Ierou Lohou, tel. 22501; teleg. Plazahotelrhodes
B: Poseidon, 1 Akti Kritika, tel. 24541
B: Solemar, Ixia, tel. 22941; teleg. Solemar Rhodes
B: Spartalis, 2 N. Plastira, tel. 24371; teleg. Hotel Spartalis
B: Stella (Pension), 58 Dilberaki
B: Thermai, Makariou, tel. 24351; teleg. Thermotel
C: Achillion, 14 Platia Vas. Pavlou, tel. 24604
C: Adonis, 7 Vas. Konstantinou, tel. 27791
C: Aegli, 90 Kolokotroni, tel. 22789/24659; teleg. Hotel Aegli
C: Africa, 63 Alex. Diakou, tel. 24979/24645; teleg. Africhotel
C: Als, 10 Platia Vas. Pavlou, tel. 22481; teleg. Hotelals
C: Amaryllis, 44 Othonos & Amalias, tel. 24522
C: Ambassadeur, 53 Othonos & Amalias, tel. 24679
C: Anthoula (pension), 46 Alex. Diakou

C: Aphroditie (Venus), 50 Othonos & Amalias, tel. 24668
C: Arion, 17 Ethnarchou Makariou, tel. 23125/27441; teleg. Hotelarion
C: Astoria, 39 Vas. Sophias, tel. 24804
C: Atlantis, 29 I. Dragoumi, tel. 24821
C: Caracas, 19 Th. Sofouli, tel. 22371
C: Carina, 56 Grivas, tel. 22381
C: Colossos, 9 Haile Selassie, tel. 24331; teleg. Marvel
C: Diana, 18 Stratigou Griva, tel. 24677
C: Diethnes (International), 12 I. Kazouli, tel. 24595; teleg, Diethnes
C: Dora (pension), 37 Aristophanes, tel. 24523
C: Egeon (Eageon), 3 Erythrou Stavrou, tel. 22491
C: El Greco, 2 Georgiou Efstathiou, tel. 24071
C: Elite, 15 Exarchou Panteleimonos, tel. 22391/20981; teleg. Elithotel
C: Embona, 61 G. Griva, tel. 24139
C: Flora, 13 28th Octovriou, tel. 24538/26130
C: Florida, 5 Amarantou, tel. 22111/26843
C: Galaxy, 68 Vas. Annis-Marias, tel. 22401/29203
C: Gloria, 6 Ammochostou, tel. 24631
C: Helena, 78 Griva, tel. 24755; teleg. Hotelena
C: Hermes, 5 N. Plastira, tel. 27677
C: Irene, 9 25th Martiou, tel. 24761
C: Isabella, 12 Ammochostou, tel. 22651
C: Karpathos, 9 Vas. Sophias, tel. 22151
C: Laokoon, 31 E. Markariou, tel. 24579
C: Lydia, 17 25th Martiou, tel. 22871
C: Majestic, A. Zervou & I. Metaxa, tel. 22031
C: Mandraki, 39 D. Theodoraki
C: Marie, 7 Ko, tel. 22751
C: Mimosa, 4 G. Efstathiou, tel. 24026
C: Minos, 10 Alex. S. Diakou, tel. 24041/20291
C: Moschos, 5 Ethelonton Dodecanission, tel. 24764
C: New York, 36 Ionos Dragoumi, tel. 22841
C: Noufara, 35 Vas. Sophias, tel. 24545
C: Parthenon, Anthoulas Zervou, tel. 22351; teleg. Hotel Partheon
C: Pavlidid, 15 28th Octovriou, tel. 20281/21892
C: Perle (Magaritari), 15 Griva, tel. 22420
C: Petalouda (Butterfly), 49 Ammochostou, tel. 24207
C: Phaedra (Fedra), 7 Aracadiou, tel. 24207/22791
C: Royal (Vassillikon), 50 Vas. Sophias, tel. 24601
C: Saronis, 51 Othonos & Amalias, tel. 22811
C: Savoy, 9 E. Dodecanission, tel. 20721
C: Semiramis, 18 J. Metaxa, tel. 20741; teleg. Semiranmishotel
C: Soleil, 2 Democratias, tel. 24190/28564/24290; teleg. Soleilrhodes
C: Sylvia, 114 Kolokotroni, tel. 22551
C: Tilos, 46 E. Makariou, tel. 24591
C: Vassilia, 55 Othonos & Amalias, tel. 24051
C: Vellois, Leof. Trianton, tel. 24615/21045; teleg. Velloishotel

C: Victoria, 22 25th Martiou, tel. 24626
C: Villa Rodos, 36 G. Leontos, tel. 22631
D: Aleka, 37 Apol. Rodiou
D: Anastasia, 46 28th Octovriou, tel. 21815/28007
D: Atlas, 44 Orfandidou & 5 Kritis, tel. 24022
D: Australia, 29 Lohogou Fanouraki, tel. 24817
D: Belmar, 3 Nikolaou Sava, tel. 24920
D: Congo, 145 Dendrinou, tel. 24023
D: D'or, 81 Apoll. Rodiou & Orfanidou, tel. 22911; teleg. Hotel D'or Rhodes
D: Efrossyni, 31a Apoll. Rodiou
D: Iris, 46 Orfandiou & Kritis, tel. 26182/24035
D: Pantheon, 11 Tarpon Springs, tel. 24557
D: Rhodiakon, 20 Apollonos Amerikis, tel. 22051
D: Roma, tel. 24447
D: San Antonio (Ag. Antonios), 7 Ionos Dragoumi, tel. 24971
D: Villa Astereo, 19 Lochagou Fanouraki, tel. 23750
D: Xanthi, 18 Papalouka, tel. 24996
D: Zephyros, 133 Dendrinou, tel. 22826
D: Zeus, 72 Ag. Nikolaou, tel. 23129
E: Stassa, 2 Ag. Fanouriou
Out of town
A: Apollo Beach, Faliraki, tel. 85251/28781
A: Doretta Beach, Tholos, tel. 41441
A: Elafos-Elafina, Profitis Elias (alt. 710 metres, 2330 ft.), tel. 21221 teleg. Hotel Rodos
A: Electra Palace, Paralia Trianda, tel. 92521/92333
A: Elisabeth (furnished apartments), Paralia Ialissou, Ixia, Trianda, tel. 92491/22602
A: Faliraki Beach, Faliraki, tel. 85301, teleg. Hotelfalirakı Rhodes
A: Golden Beach (Bungalotel), Trianda, tel. 92411, teleg. Gold Beach
A: Sunwing, Kallithies, tel. 28600, teleg. Sunwing Rhodes
B: Esperides, Faliraki, tel. 85267/85206; teleg. P.O. Box 202
B: Xenia, Afantou, tel. 51121, teleg. Xenia Golf
C: Lido, Faliraki, tel. 85226; teleg. Hotel Lido Rhodes
E: Archangelos, 184 7th Martiou, Archangelos, tel. (0244) 21230

Tourist Police: Next to the National Tourist Office on Archiepiskopou Makariou & Papagos Streets. Tel: 27423. Telex: NTOG: 23255/23655

Symi

Connections: boat at 8.30 every morning from Rhodes to Symi and Panormitis; connected three times a week with Tilos, Nissyros and Astypalaia; twice a week with Kos.

History: One of the island's ancient names was Aegli, for the daughter

of Apollo who gave birth to the three Graces. "Symi" was a princess of
Ialysos on Rhodes, who either did something sufficiently evil to warrant
exile, or was stolen away by the hero Glaukos (who had built the Argo).
In either case she finished up on the rocky little island which took her
name. A less responsible myth has Prometheus creating the first men on
Symi, whereupon Zeus, in his displeasure, punished him by turning him
into a monkey, thus giving us the word Simian.

Pelasgian walls in Chorio attest to the prehistoric settlement of Symi,
the first inhabitants probably coming from Karia. In the *Iliad* Homer
tells how the island mustered three ships for the Achaeans at Troy,
led by King Nireus. After Achilles Nireus was the most beautiful of all
the Greeks, but that didn't prevent the Trojans from killing him. After
the Dorian invasion, Symi joined the Hexapolis (Knidos, Halikarnasos,
Kos, and the three cities of Rhodes), starting the island's domination by
Rhodes, which lasted throughout antiquity. The Romans fortified the
acropolis at Chorio, which became a Byzantine fort, later renovated by
the first Grand Master of the Knights of Rhodes, Foulques de Villaret.
From the Kastro the Knights could signal to Rhodes, and they favoured
the swift Symiote skiffs for their raiding activities.

During this time the island began to know a certain measure of
prosperity, primarily through ship building and trade. When Sulleiman
the Magnificent came to the Dodecanese in 1522, the Symiotes avoided a
battle by offering him beautiful sponges, which became their yearly
tribute to the Sultan in return for a relative degree of independence. Like
the Knights, the Turks made use of the swift Symiote ships, this time for
relaying messages. In order to keep Symi thriving, the Sultan declared it
a free port and gave the inhabitants the rights to dive freely for sponges
in Turkish waters.

Little, barren Symi thus became the third most important island of
the Dodecanese, a position it held from the 17th to the 19th century.
Rich mansions were constructed befitting the islanders' new prosperity.
Many of them also bought land in Asia Minor. Schools thrived. Even
after certain privileges were withdrawn because of its participation in the
1821 revolution, the island continued to flourish, as is demonstrated by
the huge Neoclassical mansions which dominate the town today. The
Italian Occupation and the steamship, however, spelt the end of Symi's
glory. The Italians closed up the lands of Asia Minor and thus the
island's lumber source for ship building, and the steamship killed the demand for wooden sailing vessels altogether. At the end of the Second
World War the treaty giving the Dodecanese to Greece was signed on
Symi on 8 May, 1945.

Symi today: Symi is a quiet place, as it has no cars; indeed, its streets
are mostly steps, and to visit places on the island one must rely on foot,
donkey, or caique. Although a boat-load of tourists arrives daily from
Rhodes, most leave the same day and at night the island offers a sweet
serenity to those who stay behind.

Symi's capital is divided into two quarters: **Yialos** in the harbour region and Chorio, the older settlement on the hill. In **Yialos** are centred most of the tourist facilities and one of the island's remaining trades, ship building. In honour of this trade a copy of the stone-carved trireme of the Lindos acropolis has been erected by the harbour. Near it is the restaurant and pension Les Katerinettes, where a plaque commemorates the signing of the 1945 treaty in the building. William the parrot also lives inside. Beyond the statue of the fishing boy and the Nireus hotel, is the small bay **Charani** where many ships wait to be finished or repaired. Here especially one can see the result of the bombing during the Second World War, which damaged so many of Symi's lovely old houses. A place called Nos is at the end of Charani, where the locals swim by the island's discotheque.

Most of the houses in Yialos date from the 19th century. Many that have been left empty for decades are now being repaired, especially by islanders who have moved elsewhere, but who like to come back in the summer. Older architecture may be seen at **Chorio,** connected to the port by a dirt road or the stairway from Platia tis Skala. Mansions, mostly Neoclassical, line the way up. By the derelict windmills is a **stone monument** erected by the Spartans for their victory over the Athenians off the coast of Symi, a battle mentioned by Thucycides. Houses in Chorio are more similar to Cycladic houses, small and asymmetrical, although the residents have often incorporated Neoclassical elements to ornament their doorways and windows. Many houses have very lovely interiors with carved woodwork, and the people are usually flattered to show the curious around their homes.

Among the most interesting buildings at Chorio are the **19th century pharmacy;** the fortress-mansion **Chatziagapitos,** and the churches with their pebble mosaics of evil mermaids sinking hapless ships. One whole section of town consists of old stone houses on narrow streets, half-ruined and deserted. The island's **museum** is also up at Chorio, containing objects dating from Hellenistic times to the present. At the **Kastro,** the Byzantine and medieval wall were built from ancient material, including the temple of Athena referred to in an ancient inscription. The coat of arms belongs to d'Aubusson, and the most interesting church of the village is by the walls, called **Megali Panayia,** with frescoes and post-Byzantine icons.

From Chorio it is a short walk to **Pedhi,** the only fertile area of Simi. On a small bay, it has a good beach and is the best place to camp out on the island.

Restaurants: Symi, Zephyrous, and Les Katerinettes.

Discotheques: Nos, also the Night Club in Yialos.

Specialities: Lobster.

The most visited site outside of Yialos and Chorio is the famous monastery of Symi's patron, who has also been adopted by Greek sailors, **Taxiarchis Michael Panormitis.** The ship from Rhodes calls here, or one may take a caique from Yialos, the trip averaging little more than an hour. The monastery dates from the 18th century (at least). The **iconostasis** in the church is a remarkable work of carved wood, and there are many 18th century frescoes and gold and silver ship votives. In the **sacristy** are more rich gifts from faithful sailors, and little bottles which drifted to shore with money for the monastery. Panormitis also has one of the best beaches on the island, and there are restaurants and cafes. **Seskli,** an islet near Panormitis, belongs to the monastery. Its ancient name was Teutlousa, and Thucydides writes that it was here that the defeated Athenians took refuge after their sea battle with the Spartans during the Peloponnesian War. A few Pelasgian walls remain, and there are also a few ruins on the nearby islet **Stroggilos.**

The other sites of Symi are also religious in nature. Of the 77 churches, the most interesting is **Michael Roukoumiotis,** an hour's walk from Yialos. Built in the 18th century, it is a rather strange combination of Gothic and folk architecture. Its *panayiéri* is held beneath the old umbrella-shaped cyprus tree. Ag. Emilianos is on an islet in the bay of the same name, connected to the shore by a causeway with a pebbly beach nearby. On the mountain **Kelaria** are Byzantine and even older remains. Ag. Noulias (18th century) is a half-hour walk from Chorio, and nearby Ag. Marina had a famous school before the revolution broke out.

Panayiéria: 2 May, Ag. Athanasios; 21 May, Ag. Konstantinos; 24 June, Ag. Ioannes; 27 July, Ag. Marina; 20 July, Profitis Elias; 6 August, Nymborio and Panormitis; 15 August, Panayias; 18 November, Taxiarchis, and Panormitis; 9 December, Ag. Anna on Profitis Ilias for marriage or fertility.

Hotel in Symi: area code 0241
B: Nireus (pension), 2 Platia Vas, Georgiou, tel. 71386

Tourist Police: Regular police at Yialos.

Tilos

Connections: Once a week with Piraeus; twice a week with Rhodes, Symi, Nissyros, Astypalaia, and Kos.

From the large prehistoric walls by Megalo Chora, it can be deducted that inhabitation on Tilos dates back to very ancient times. The Venetians fortified the ancient acropolis, the island then being called Piskopi, or 'Look out' for a Byzantine tower that once surveyed the region from the coast.

Very few visitors come to Tilos, and although it is situated between two mighty attractions, Kos and Rhodes, the little island lives in isolation. No one is ever sure when and what boat may arrive next; a sort of vague dreaminess surrounds all practical activity, and the visitor who forgets to wind his watch will lose all track of time. The women of Tilos still wear their traditional embroidered costumes, and the island's mechanical transport consists of a triatodia, or a three-wheeled contraption. One major shortcoming of Tilos, however, is a lack of fresh fruit and vegetables.

Megalo Chorio (to differentiate it from Mikro Chorio) is the village capital of the island. Besides the **Pelasgian walls,** other fortifications include the **Kastro** with its Classical gate (the Kastro itself is composed of ancient materials found on the old acropolis) and a few ruined **towers** said to have been built by the Genoese. All the island's public services are here. To the west of the village, **Plaka** beach is ideal for isolated camping, and further on is the monastery of Tilos, **Ag. Panteleimonos.** One may also take a boat there from the port **Livadia,** which consists of a few houses, a few rooms to rent, a not so good restaurant (all fish caught are sent straight to Rhodes) and a very long sandy beach with some shade. The only really fertile region of Tilos is by Megalo Chorio, where a little farming is done.

Panayiéri: 27 July, Ag. Panteleimonos; 28 June, Ag. Pavlos.

Tourist Police: Regular police at Megalo Chorio.

Part 9
The Ionian Islands

The seven Ionian islands were first grouped together during the age of Byzantium, when they formed the Theme of Kephallonia. Six of the seven are situated between Greece and Italy, a fact which has separated them for centuries from the mainstream of Greek politics, although from the beginning of their history to the present day the inhabitants have remained undeniably Hellenes. Not to be confused with the country of Asia Minor, the name Ionian is derived rather from Io of mythology, one of the victims of Zeus' love whom Hera, his wife, unjustly punished. About to be caught in the company of Io, Zeus changed the girl into a white cow, but Hera was not to be fooled. She asked Zeus to give her the cow as a present, and kept it under careful surveillance. With the help of Hermes, Io escaped, only to be followed by a terrible stinging gad fly which chased her all over the world. One of the first places through which she fled was the eastern part of the Adriatic sea, which has since been named Ionian in honour of the tormented girl.

Very little remains of the ancient past on the islands, although they were probably settled in the Stone Age by people from Illyria (present-day Albania) and then by the Eretrians. Homer was the first to mention them, and were he the last they would still be immortal as the homeland of immortal, crafty Odysseus. From the 8th century BC, mercantile Corinth colonized the islands and they held no small importance in trade and relations between Greece and the colonies to the west, particularly in Italy. One of them, Corfu, became so strong that when Corinth's policies went counter to her will, she challenged and defeated

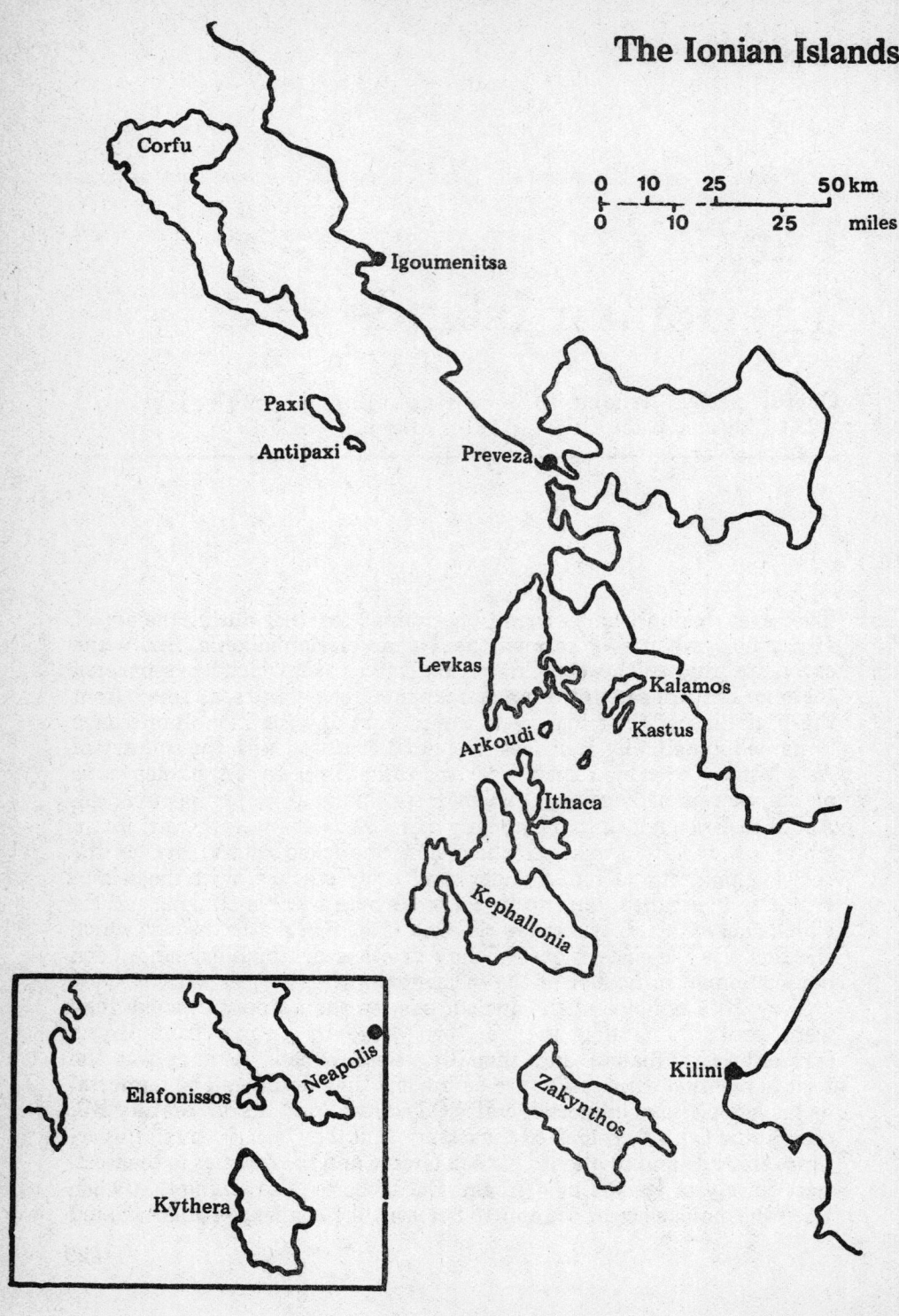

The Ionian Islands

0   10   25   50 km
0   10   25   miles

Corfu

Igoumenitsa

Paxi

Antipaxi

Preveza

Levkas

Kalamos

Arkoudi

Kastus

Ithaca

Kephallonia

Zakynthos

Kilini

Elafonissos

Neapolis

Kythera

at sea the mother city, allying herself with Athens. (Corinth was an ally of Sparta). This event triggered off the disasterous Peloponnesian War, as it forced the Lacedemonians either to submit to this expansion of the Athenian empire and control of western trade, or to attack. They chose the latter.

The Romans incorporated the Ionian islands in their province Achaia, a classification still current today in Greek administration. After the fall of the Roman Empire, Goths from Italy overran the islands, and it is because of their wholesale decimations that so few monuments of antiquity remain today. The Byzantine Empire realized the strategic importance of the islands as a bridge between east and west and fortified them. During the Second Crusade, however, the Normans took the islands by surprise and established garrisons on them, which they used as bases to plunder the rest of Greece. With a great deal of difficulty the Byzantines succeeded in forcing them out of Corfu at least, although the Normans were almost immediately replaced by the Venetians, who claimed the islands in the land grab after the Sack of Constantinople in 1204. The southern islands became part of the County Palatine of Kephallonia when the claims of the Sicilian Norman pirates, Vetrano and Count Orsini, were eliminated by the crucifixion of the former. Corfu, however, was occupied for 150 years by the Angevins, a rule so bitter that the inhabitants surrendered their island to the "protection" of Venice.

Venetian rule was hardly a bed of roses, even though Christian (the Orthodox and the Catholics never stopped considering each other heretics). The average Greek in fact preferred the Turks, who allowed the people a measure of self-government and demanded fewer taxes. Some of the Ionian islands actually did come under Turkish rule. The Ottomans were expelled in 1499, although they returned as the Venetian Republic weakened. Despite all their faults, the Venetians were at least more tolerant to artists than the Turks, as Moslems forbade all representations of the human figure, and in the 17th century the Ionian islands provided a refuge for painters, especially from Crete. The Ionian school of art was thus formed, noted for its fusion of Byzantine and Renaissance styles.

In 1796, after Napoleon had conquered the Venetian Republic, he considered the Ionian islands of the utmost importance to his schemes and took them with the Treaty of Campo Formio. In 1799 a combined Russo-Turkish fleet took the islands from him forming the independent Septinsular Republic under their protection (and safeguarding the islands against any danger of attack from the notorious Tyrant of of Epirus, Ali Pasha, who coveted them).

Although the Septinsular Republic did not last long (it was nullified by the Treaty of Tilsit in 1807 which returned the islands to. Napoleon), it was the first time in almost four centuries that any Greek was allowed independent rule, and it helped to inspire the later revolution in 1821; the British taking of the Ionian islands in 1815 was considered another sign of encouragement.

Although the British re-formed the Ionian State, they retained the right of military protection and appointed an English High Commissioner who took precedence over the Ionian parliament. Sir Thomas Maitland, the first High Commissioner, has gone down in history as probably the worst British representative ever to govern what was de facto a British colony. He deeply offended the Greeks by giving the city Parga, an important port on the mainland to the tyrant Ali Pasha, obeying an obscure clause in the 1815 treaty that no one expected him to comply with. All the Pargians in their turn immigrated to Corfu, rather than submitting to Ali Pasha. Other High Commissioners were little better (at least from the Greek point of view) and the Ionian State never stopped demanding, or conspiring for union with Greece. The British (since they now had Cyprus) agreed to cede the islands in 1864 — but only after blowing up all the fortresses on Corfu. During the Second World War Italy took the islands, but Mussolini's dream of creating another Ionian State under Italian protection shattered in 1943 when the Germans occupied the islands. Many of the Italian troops joined the Greeks in their resistance, and many were killed by their former allies in the Axis. In 1953 a terrible earthquake left the buildings on the islands in ruins.

The Ionian islands today, although lacking most of the elegant Venetian architecture which once embellished them, are still more endowed by Mother Nature than all the other Greek islands. Constant rain during the winter keeps them fresh, green and blooming throughout spring and summer. Easily attained from Greece or Italy, they have become very popular in recent years. To visit all of them, however, is quite a task, and is likely to be more of a crawl than a hop. From Zachynthos to Kythera (which probably shouldn't even be an an Ionian island, although tradition places it in the group) is a 24-hour boat-taxi-train-bus-taxi-boat trip. Islands are connected to the mainland rather than to each other for the most part, and thus visitors tend to concentrate on only one or two islands. And in fact each island is so lovely that it is no deprivation to spend even years on just one.

Corfu (Kerkyra)

Connections: Daily flights from Athens, and frequent flights from London, Rome, Lecce, Dusseldorf, Vienna, Paris, Munich and Frankfurt. Daily ferry from Brindisi, leaving at 10 pm (an 8 hour trip); other car ferries leave from Venice, Ancona and Bari. Bus three times a day from Athens (station 100 Kifissou St.); ferry boat six times a day from Igoumenitsa. Once a week a ship connects Corfu, Paxi and Kephallonia. There are daily trips to Paxi.

History: The ancient name of Corfu was Corcyra, after a mistress of the sea god Poseidon. She bore him a son on the island, called Phaeax, who became head of the Phaeacian race; their king's daughter Nausica found the travel-worn Odysseus washed up on the shore of Corcyra. In 734 BC the Corinthians colonized the island, settling the ancient city at Paliapolis. Modern Analypsis was the site of the citadel-acropolis.

Thriving on trade, Corcyra became the richest of the Ionian islands, but internally it was cursed with violent political rivalries between the democrats and the oligarchs. Although the Corcyrian fleet defeated the ships of mother Corinth when the island rebelled, strife among the inhabitants had weakened Corcyra so much that by the beginning of the 4th century BC it was captured by Syracuse, and then in turn by King Pyrrhus of Epirus and in 229 BC by the Illyrians. The Romans later flourished on Corcyra, Nero himself making a special visit to the island, but their civilization was put to an end by the Gothic invasion.

The islanders who survived eventually founded a new town where they would be better protected. This was on the two hills of the modern town ("Corypho" in Greek means two peaks, thus the name "Corfu"). In the 8th century, walls, castles and moats fortified the town, but they fell to the surprise attack of the Normans in 1081. The Normans, especially under Robert Guiscard and his son, proved a great menance to the Byzantine Empire, and in 1148 the Emperor Emmanuel Comenus sent a special force and fleet to dislodge them. When the siege of the Byzantines made no progress, Emmanuel came himself to lead the attack the following year. By causing subversion among the Normans themselves, he succeeded in winning back the island.

In 1204, when Venice came to make her claim on Corfu, the inhabitants resisted strongly, and although the Venetians succeeded in taking the island's forts, the islanders aligned themselves with the Despotat of Epirus, an Orthodox state. Fifty years later, however, the King of Naples, Charles I of Anjou, took Corfu and the rest of Achaia when his son wed the princess of Villehardouin. Angevin rule, which lasted 120 years, was intolerant and hateful, forcing the Corfiots to turn to Venice in 1386, to give their island to the "protection" of the Republic.

In 1537 a serious threat, not only to Corfu but to all of Europe, landed at Igoumenitsa in the form of Sultan Suleiman the Magnificent. Suleiman, the greatest of the Turkish rulers, was determined to take Corfu and from there base his attack on Italy and Western Europe. This was in spite of a peace treaty between Turkey and Venice, which did little more than to allow Suleiman to plan his attack in the utmost secrecy. When the Corfiots discovered, only a few days in advance, what was in store for them, the people tore down their houses to repair the fortress and in order to leave nothing behind for the Turks. The terrible pirate admiral Barbarossa was the first to land on the island and begin the siege of the city, during which he suffered massive losses without success. But he was not the only one: thousands of Corfiots had been pitilessly abandoned outside the fortress, caught between the Venetians and the Turks, and prey to the worst of Barbarossa's fits of rage at his setbacks. Those who were not slaughtered were taken to the slave markets of Constantinople when Suleiman, discouraged by his losses and bad weather, ordered the withdrawal of the seige.

Only 21 years later Venice, under pressure from the Corfiots, increased the fortifications of Corfu. The canal between the present town and the fortress was dug at this time. Many houses in town were left unprotected, however, and when the Turks reappeared in 1571 under Ouloudj Ali, these and the rest of the homes, trees, and vineyards on Corfu were destroyed. This time the Turks took no prisoners, contenting themselves with massacring the population. The devastation was underlined two years later by another pirate admiral, Sinan Pasha: of the entire Corfiot population, only a tenth survived on the island after the three Turkish rampages.

In 1576 Venice finally began to build the necessary walls for the safety of the Corfiots, together with the Fortezza Nuova, designed by the great expert Sammicheli, and a vast number of other fortifications that no longer exist but were considered superb in their day. The Turks came again in 1716, attacking the new fortifications for one terrible month, only to be dispersed by a tempest, and as legend claims, Ag. Spyridon, the patron saint of Corfu.

After the fall of Venice, the French occupied Corfu but quickly lost it again in a fierce battle against the Russo-Turkish fleet. When Napoloen finally got back what he considered his own, he himself designed the new fortifications of the town. They were so strong that the British, when allotted the Ionian Islands, did not care to attack them, even though the French commander Donzelot refused to give them up. The French Government finally had to send word to Donzelot to come home, and in 1814 Corfu came under British rule, according to the wish of Count John Capodistria. Capodistria, soon to be the first president of Greece, was a son of Corfu and at that time working for the Tzar of Russia.

But while Capodistria had asked for "military protection," the British, centred on Corfu, took upon themselves all the affairs of the Ionian state. One of the first things they did was to demolish part of the Venetian fortifications in order to build new, more powerful ones in their place, calling upon the Ionian government to pay more than a million gold sovereigns to cover the cost of these marvellous new structures. But in 1864, when Britain had decided to pull out, their condition for letting the Ionian islanders unite with Greece was the destruction of the fortresses of Corfu — those same fortresses the British themselves had just built, and the more historic Venetian buildings. A wave of protest from all corners of the Greek world failed to change the British mind, and in 1864 the fortifications were blown up, leaving the few ruined relics one can still see today. In 1923 Mussolini bombarded and occupied Corfu after the assassination on Greek territory of an Italian delegate to the Greek-Albanian border council. At the end of the year, however, the League of Nations forced him to withdraw.

Corfu today is considered one of the most beautiful islands in the world. Some of the visitors in the spring are fervent English gardeners who leave their home plots just to admire the island's wild flowers.

Unlike the other Ionian islands, Corfu was spared from the terrible earthquake of 1956, and today retains much of its elegant old Venetian architecture. Lovely beaches exist on most of the island's coasts, and a very healthy supply of hotels and restaurants accommodates the thousands of summer visitors. Winter in Corfu, with its grey skies and rain, attracts few foreigners, but it is the best time to go if you wish to make the acquaintance of the refined and charming Corfiots.

The capital of the island is also called Corfu or Kerkyra, subdivided into **Ag. Nikolaos** in the north and **Garitsa** in the south. Most places of interest, however, are close together in Ag. Nikolaos. Those arriving by ship, from Italy, enter Corfu through the back door at **Mandouki,** the international harbour. This is not one of the more attractive parts of town, although there are good cheap tavernas in the streets to the west of the customs buildings, and bazookias and discotheques further down the shore which are very active at night. The monastery Platyera nearby houses the tombs of Capodistria and Dzarellos. From Mandouki to the centre of town one walks up the hill by Avrami Street to **Platia Theotoki,** the centre of the business district. Buses from here leave for the immediate region of the city, while buses to the villages leave from Solomou Street by the Nuova Fortezza (Neon Frourion in Greek).

The new fortress, **Nuova Fortezza,** was built by the Venetians following the third decimation of the island. Its walls originally encompassed a much greater area in order to protect the town, but these were destroyed by the British. It stood the main brunt of the Turks' siege of 1716. Not far from it is the house of **Edward Lear,** the great English limerick writer. To the north, by the square where many locals take their evening volta and refreshments, is the domestic port and ticket offices. The **tourist police** live on Arseniou Street a few blocks to the east. Further along the quay is the **Sino Japanese Museum,** housed in the former residence of the Lord High Commissioner. It was built in 1823 in the Regency style by the British architect Sir George Whitmore, and used as the king's palace on Corfu from 1864. In 1924 it became a museum (open 8.30 am-10 am and 4 pm-6 pm; closed Saturday and Sunday afternoons. Entrance 25 dr., 2.5 dr. with student card), housing a collection brought from Japan by the diplomat Manos. It is the only collection of Oriental art in Greece (except for a few items in the Benaki Museum in Athens) containing more than 8000 pieces dating from Neolithic times. The Corfu municipal library is also housed in the building.

The museum faces the famous **Spianada,** one of the largest public squares in Europe, and one of the most beautiful with a wealth of trees, flowers and cafés. On the museum side of the Spianada is the only **cricket ground** in Greece, where little boys play football until their older white clad brothers kick them off the field. In the summer matches are held, pitting the British against the natives. Enthusiasts can apply to play at the Gymnasticos Syllogos, tel. 22377. The **Ionian rotunda** in the Spianada is dedicated to the infamous Sir Thomas Maitland and on Sundays the local philharmonic society gives performances there. Other memorials to British officials peer out here and there through the trees.

The old fortress, or **Paleon Frourion,** separated by the canal or contra fossa from the Spianada, can be visited from 5 pm to 7 pm. Scholars have identified the site with the Heraion acropolis mentioned by Thucydides. Of the huge, mighty walls, the work of centuries, which surrounded the fortress, only a few Byzantine and Venetian fortifications remain, along with a church to St. George. The **Corfu Sound and Light Show** is held at the old fortress from 15 May to the end of September. The Corfu Ballet performs Greek folk dancing from 8.30 pm to 9 pm, and the Sound and Light Show takes place from 9 pm to 9.45 in English on weekdays. Tickets for both performances are 70 dr., students 50 dr.; tickets for just the Sound and Light Show are 50 dr., students 25 dr. For further information see the National Tourist Office or telephone 30520 or 30360.

The church of the patron saint **Ag. Spyridon** is in the old town, not far from the Ionian and Popular Bank of Greece. The church is easy to find, as its bell tower protrudes above the town like the mast of a ship, with its flags and Christmas lights. Ag. Spyridon was the Bishop of Cyprus in the 4th century; when Constantinople fell, his bones were brought in a sack of straw to Corfu. The church was built in 1596 to house the precious relics, now contained in a silver Renaissance reliquary by the inconostasis and brought out with great pomp on the panayiéria of the saint. According to the Corfiots, the good saint has brought them safely through many trials, frightening both cholera (who struggled so hard at San Isidore Cape that it left claw marks in the rock) and the Turks away from his beloved worshippers. He even gave the Catholics a good scare when they considered placing an altar in his church; the night before its dedication, he blew up a powder magazine in the Old Fortress with a stroke of lighting, to show his displeasure. The Orthodox Palm Sunday, Easter Saturday, 11 August and the first Sunday in November are dedicated to huge celebrations for Ag. Spyridon.

A Catholic Church, **Ag. Frangiscos,** is further up N. Theotoki Street and another block down towards Fileninon Street is the **Orthodox Cathderal of Ag. Theodora Augusta and Ag. Vlassios,** housing the headless remains of Ag. Theodora. Back through the lovely maze of the **Old Town,** built between 1577 and 1630 and decorated daily with banner-like laundry hung out to dry, is the **town hall** on E. Voulgareos, built by the Venetians as a club in 1663. The **Catholic cathderal of Ag. Iakovos and Christoforos** is close by on Glifford Street. At the end of this street is the **British Consulate.** Up the hill the **OTE, post office** and the **National Tourist Office** are bunched together by a remnant of the Venetian wall. The tourist office has a list of people who rent rooms in town; for lodging outside of town see the **tourist police** on 4 Polychroniou Konstata.

The **Tennis Club of Kerkyra,** open to non members, is a few blocks south on Romanou Street (tel. 22021 or 29542). On the quay the

Nautical Club, tel. 28470, has compressed air for divers. The **Archaeology Museum** (open 9 am-1 pm and 4 pm-6 pm; 10 am-2 pm Sunday; closed Tuesdays. Entrance 25 dr., 2.5 dr. with student card, free Thursday and Sunday) contains items found on Corfu, most spectacularly a huge freize from the 5th century BC, found at the Temple of Artemis along Kastrades Bay. Other items are from the **Tomb of Menecrates,** discovered on the junction of Marassli and Kiprou Streets in the Garitsa quarter. Further south begins the suburb of **Anenmomylos,** where one can swim at the beach Mon Repos for a slight charge. Mon Repos palace above was built by Sir Frederic, the second High Commissioner of the Ionian State, for his Corfiot wife. The Greek royal family later adopted it as a summer villa and the Duke of Edinburgh is said to have been born there. The 11th-century church of Ag. Iassonos and Sosipater (two martyrs instructed by St. Paul) can also be visited at Anenmomylos. The martyrs' tombs and rare icons are inside.

It is a short stroll to **Analypsis,** just south of Mon Repos, where in mythology Jason and Medea spent their wedding night on the Golden Fleece they had just captured. A spring of clear, cold water by the sea is palatable, but be warned that all who drink of it never leave Corfu, bewitched by its magic spell. In the village the 11th century church **Ag. Kerkyra** was left in ruins by an earthquake. **Kanoni,** at the southern tip of the little peninsula, is named for the old canon once situated on the bluff, where two less threatening cafés now overlook the pretty bay, the harbour of ancient Corcyra. Two islets protected it: that of the picturesque convent **Panaya Vlancharina,** now connected to the shore by a causeway, and **Pontikonissi,** the Isle of the Mouse, with a 13th century chapel **Ag. Pnevmatos.** Pontikonissi was the Phaenician ship that brought Odysseus home to Ithaka, but which, on its way home, the angry Poseidon smote "with his open palm, and made the ship a rock, fast rooted in the bed of the deep sea," according to the *Odyssey.* **Bus no. 2** from Corfu town passes all the above suburbs of gardens and trees, its route ending at Kanoni.

Another islet to the north of Corfu is **Vidos,** extensively fortified prior to the British dismantling. Here the vastly outnumbered French troops fought a heroic battle in 1800 before surrendering to the Russo-Turkish fleet. On Vidos and **Lazaretto,** another islet, are buried many Yugoslavians killed in the Second World War.

An official **port of entry,** Corfu harbour offers yachts over-wintering, berthing and supplies.

Restaurants: Averof on N. Theotoki; Aegli on Liston Square; Pantheon on N. Theotoki; Hellas on Xenophon Stratigou; Yiaias on Glifford Street; Grysi and Krisomatlis on Ag. Panton; Pallas Athena and Neftikon on N. Theotoki.

Bazookia: Kiklamina; Kastro, and Corfu by Night.

Discotheques: Fantasia, Bola Bola; Zodiac, Galaxias, Kuruvaia, No. 1.

Specialities: Cumquat liqueur and sofrito (meat with sauce).

The island's two **youth hostels** are located outside of town, one at Ag. Ioannes, 10 km (6 miles) from Corfu, (tel. 28408), and Kontokali, 7 km (4 miles) from Corfu (tel. 91102). There are also six **official camping sites:**

Kontokali: Pyrgi Camping, tel. 93283, 100 persons capacity; and Kontokali Akti Diethnes, tel. 91202, 300 persons capacity.

Dassia: Kar-tol Camping, tel. 932230, 212 persons capacity.

Ipsos: Ipsos Camping, tel. 93243, 100 persons capacity; and Kerkyra Camping, tel. 93246, 147 persons capacity.

Korakiana: Dionyssos Camping, tel. 91417, 270 persons capacity.

If you want to camp further off the tourist track, Kassiopi and Paliokastritsa are good bets, although sites are not officially listed for either location.

The roads on the rest of Corfu are very good. The most popular way to see the island is on the back of a scooter (there are 14 places to rent scooters and bikes in Corfu town). Buses leave from the New Fortress, but as they are likely to be crowded one should arrive at the station early. To the immediate north begins a long series of beach, hotel and restaurant complexes, along with most of the camping sites, including **Kontokali, Gouvia, Dassia, Ipsos** and **Pirgi. Kouloura** further north is less than a mile from the rugged Albanian coast. The brothers Durrell have left their mark on this part of Corfu: Lawrence Durrell in his excellent book on the island, *Prospero's Cell* (Corfu is thought to be the setting of Shakespeare's *The Tempest)*, and Gerald Durrell's picture is in many of the local cafés. At Kouloura the 16th-century **Kouartanou Gennata** is part Venetian mansion and part fortified tower, and there are two other 17-century mansions, **Vassila** and **Prosalenti.**

Kassiopi lies at the northern end of the good paved road. This once important town was founded by Pyrrhus of Epirus in the Hellenistic Age, and it flourished in particular under the Romans who built great walls around it. A famous shrine of Zeus Cassius attracted the Emperor Nero in 67 AD, and Cicero also visited the town. Robert Giscard with his Normans took the Byzantine fortress and then conquered the rest of the island from here. Indeed as all pirates and adventurers from the north passed by Kassiopi to reach Corfu town, the history of the town is crowded with bloody battles, especially against the Venetians. When the latter finally took the fortress they destroyed it to avenge themselves on the locals. Without their defences the Kassiopians suffered unduly at the hands of the Turks and the town lost all of its former status. One can still see the ruined fortress above the village, now full of wild flowers and sheep. Although still a fishing village, Kassiopi has discovered the profits to be made from the tourist trade. Every night there is dancing in the tavernas.

In the interior of the island near Kassiopi is **Perithia,** an all but aban-

To Othonoi

To Erikoussa

To Mathraki

Sidari

Astrakeri

Peroulades

Avliotes

Karoussades

Roda

Ag. Spiridon

Loutses

Magoulades

Kassiopi

Arillas

Episkepsis

Perithia

Afionas

Kouloura

Choreopiskopi

Manatrades

Nissaki

Kora

Kiana

Pirgi

ngelokastro

Makrades

Lakones

Ipsos

Paliokastritsa

Liapades

Dassia

Gouvia

Dafnila

Giannades

Kontokali

Mandouki

Ermones

Alykae

Kerkyra (Corfu)

Pelekas

Mon Repos

Glyfada

Analypsis

Kanoni

Perama

Pontikonissi

Sinarades

Achilleion

Gastouri

Ag. Gordias

Benitses

Ano Pavliana

Mt. Ag. Deka
(549 m./1800 ft.)

Miramare

Ag. Mathias

Moraitika

Mt. Ag. Mathias
(427 m./1400 ft.)

Messoghi

Mt. Kava Louvouno (213 m./700 ft.)

Hlomos

Limni

Korission

Kouspades

Alikes Lefkimmis

Ionian Sea

Lefkimi

Corfu Sea

To Brindisi

To Igoumenitsa

To Paxos

Kavos

0   2   5   10 km

0   2   5   miles

Corfu

doned village on the slopes of Mt. Pantocrator, over 823 metres (2700 ft.) above sea level. To go there take the bus all the way to **Loutses,** then walk up the mountain with its ruins of Venetian forts and good general views of the whole area. **Ag. Panteleimonos,** another village in the interior, has the huge ruined tower mansion **Polylas,** complete with prisons used during the Venetian occupation. All along the north coast from **Roda** to **Sidari** are fine sandy beaches, considered the best on Corfu. From Sidari one can walk to the undeveloped beach at **Peroulades** for an isolated swim. At Karoussades just east of Sidari is a 16th century mansion, Theotoki-Kalokardiari.

North-west of Corfu are three islets, **Othonoi** (the largest), **Ekikoussa,** and **Mathraki,** the westernmost territory of Greece. One may visit these isles from either Corfu town or Kassiopi. Trips are neither regular nor very frequent, but run at least once a week from Corfu. On Othonos a well preserved medieval fort, **Kastri,** can be seen on a pine-covered hill. Olives and grapes are produced locally, and fresh fish is always available. Many places on the islets are still without electricity, and the population consists mainly of women as their husbands fish or work in America.

On the north-west coast of Corfu itself is the peninsula **Mourgi,** forming a large sandy bay by the village **Afionas.** An ancient fortified town once existed on the far end of the peninsula, and Afionas itself was walled in later years, to protect the inhabitants from pirates. In the same vicinity is another ruined town, **Paliokastro,** by the small village of Perlepsimades.

Paliokastritsa has become a major resort area in west Corfu. On a hill above the town the famous **Paliokastritsa monastery** was built in 1228 at the site of an old Venetian fortress. Inside a one-room museum contains some very old icons; from outside there is a pleasant view of the sapphire sea below. Along with Kassiopi, Paliokastritsa is considered to be a possible home of the princess Nausica, where the shipwrecked Odysseus found shelter.

Above **Paliokastritsa** (either an 8 km/5 mile walk uphill or a 200 dr. taxi trip) is the formidable **Angelokastro** mentioned in Henry Miller's book, *The Colossus of Maroussi.* It was built in the 13th century by the Despot of Epirus, either Michael Angelos I or more probably Michael Angelos II, and it makes a very imposing sight on the wild red rocks. The fortress played a very important role during the various raids on the island, sheltering the surrounding villagers (as well as the Venetian governor, who lived there). However the defending Corfiots were rarely content to stay behind the walls of Angelokastro, often attacking their attackers instead. They twice pinned hordes of Genoese pirates between themselves and the Corfiots from town, much to the dismay of the Genoese.

Further south along the coast both **Ermones** and **Glyfada** are growing resort areas. The island's golf course, Ropas Meadow, is at Pelekas. Besides 18 holes, it has a club house and swimming pool. At Pelekas the sunset is somehow more beautiful than elsewhere on the island, and the beach has become the unofficial retreat of nature children. In the village itself is the 13th century mansion **Pieri Mideon Barony,** half-ruined by a fire in the last century. **Ag. Gordias** further south has beaches and hotels. A Byzantine fortress at **Gardiki,** south of Ag. Cordias, was also constructed by the Despot of Epirus, Michael Angelos II, answering a great need during troubled times. Lagoudia, two islets off the south-west coast, are the home of a tribe of donkeys, some of whom were eaten by a boatload of Frenchmen who were wrecked there for three days.

Fine beaches, deserted for the most part, line the south-west coast to **Ag. Georgios. Lefkimi,** in the centre of a large fertile plain, is the second most important village of the island but not very interesting for the tourist; nearby **Kavos,** however, has an important **monastery Prokopios** and an excellent beach, as does **Asprocavos.** Heading north **Moraitkia, Miramare** and **Benitses** are tourist villages. Corfu's casino is in the **Achilleion** by Gastouri, a palace famous for its ostentatious ugliness. It was built by the Empress Elisabeth of Austria, and dedicated to that lady's passion for the hero of Homer's *Iliad.* Inside there are many bizarre paintings of Achilleus, and in the park a statue of the wounded Achilleus. When Elisabeth was assassinated, Wilhelm II bought the Achilleion, and in 1963 it became the small museum and casino it is today. **Perama,** across the bay from Kanoni, offers more luxury than any other place on this luxurious island, and many people rent villas there.

Panayiéria: 10 July, Ag. Proskopios at Kavos; 14 August, The Procession of Lights at Mandouki; first Friday after Easter, Paliokastritsa; 5-8 July, at Lefkimi; 15 August, Panayias at Kassiopi; 21 May, Union with Greece.

Hotels in Corfu

In Kerkyra, the most luxurious hotel is the Corfu Palace (L) with swimming pool, tennis, and access to the beach; however, the small Cavalieri Corfu (A), actually an old Venetian mansion converted to a hotel, is more interesting. Not only is it air conditioned, but it looks out over the splendid Esplanade, the old fortress, and the sea. The Castello (A) at Dassia north of town, is another case of renovation, this time from an idyllic country mansion, offering a frequent bus service to the nearby beach. In the other direction, at Eden-like Kanoni, both the new Corfu Hilton (L) and the Corfu Kanoni (A) are very distinguished and provide services to beach and town. They are within walking distance of the Achilleion museum and casino. Further afield, on the west coast of Corfu, Ermones Beach (A) is modernity in isolation.

In Corfu town: area code 0661
L: Corfu Palace, Leof. Democratias, tel. 39485; teleg. Corfupalace
A: Cavalieri, 4 Kapodistriou, tel. 39336/39283/39041; teleg. Cavaliericorfu
B: Astron, 15 Donzelotou, tel. 39505/39986

B: King Alkinos, 29 Dimarchou Panou, Zaphiropoulou, tel. 39300
B: Olympiakon, 4 Doukissis Marias, tel. 30532; teleg. Olympic
C: Arcadion, 44 Kapodistriou, tel. 37670; teleg. Arcadioncorfu
C: Atlantis, Xen. Stratigou, tel. 35560/35561/35562
C: Bretagne, 27 Stadiou, tel. 30724/35690; teleg. Hotelbretagne
C: Calypso, 4 Vraila, tel. 30723
C: Dalia, 9 Platia Ethnikou Stadiou, Garitsa, tel. 32341/26048
C: Hermes, 14 G. Markora, tel. 39321/39268
C: Ionion, 46 Xen. Stratigou, Neos Limin, tel. 39915/30628
C: Splendid, 39 Eugeniou Voulgareos, tel. 39863/90034
C: Suisse (Helvetia), 13 Kapodistriou, tel. 39815
D: Acropole, 3 C. Zavitsianou, tel. 39569
D: Anessis, 3 C. Zavitsianou, tel. 31695
D: Constantinopolis, 11 C. Zavitsianou, tel. 39826
D: Europa, Mandoukion, Neos Limin, tel. 39304
D: Mitropolis, 24 Leof. Konstantinou
D: Nea Yorki, 21 Ypapantis
D: Saroko, 10 J. Theotoki, tel. 36640/30170
E: Criti, 23 N. Theotoki, tel. 23691
E: Elpis, 4 N. Theotoki, tel. 30289
E: Epanissos, 156 N. Theotoki, tel. 30075
E: Kypros, 13 Ag. Pateron, tel. 30032
in Ag. Gordios: area code 0661
D: Diethnes (International), tel. 30407
in Ag. Ioannis Peristeron: area code 0661
L: Marbella Beach, tel. 39755/39853/8239779 in Athens; teleg. Marbella Beach Corfu
A: Marbella Beach (furnished apartments), tel. 39755/39853/8239779 in Athens; teleg. Marbella Beach Corfu
in Alykae: area code 0661
A: Kerkyra Golf, tel. 31785; teleg. Golfhotel
in Anemomylos: area code 0661
B: Arion, 5 Emm. Theotoki, tel. 39750/23904; teleg. Arionhotel
B: Marina, tel. 32783; teleg. Hotel Marina
in Ano Pavliana: area code 0661
D: Iliovassilema, Panamonas, tel. 95249
in Arillas (Magoulades): area code 0663
C: Arilla Beach, tel. 31401
C: Marina, tel. 31400
in Benitses: area code 0661
B: Potamaki, tel. 30889/92201
C: Benitses Inn, tel. 92258/92342
D: Avra, tel. 39269
D: Benitsa, tel. 92248/99269
in Dafnila: area code 0661
L: Eva Palace, tel. 91237/91286

in Dassia (Kato Korakiana): area code 0661
L: Castello, tel. 30184/93201
A: Chandris Corfu (hotel, bungalows and villas), tel. 33871; 4520715 in Piraeus; teleg. Chandrotel Corfu
A: Chandris Dassia, tel. 93351/4520715 in Piraeus; teleg. Chandrotel Corfu
C: Dassia, tel. 93224
D: Scheria, tel. 93233
in Gastouri: area code 0661
C: Achillon, tel. 30531/23629
in Glyfada: area code 0661
A: Grand Hotel Glyfada Beach, tel. 94201/22919/22574; teleg. Grandhotel Corfu
in Gouvia: area code 0661
A: Corcyra Beach (bungalows), tel. 30770/91308; teleg. Grekamer
C: Galaxias, tel. 91120
in Hermones: area code 0661
A: Ermones Beach (bungalows), tel. 94241; teleg. Harmones Greece
A: Ariti, 40 Nafsikas, tel. 33885/33163; teleg. Ariti Corfu
in Kanoni: area code 0661
L: Corfu Hilton (hotel and bungalows), tel. 36540
A: Corfu Kanoni, 20 Nafsikas, tel. 28996/37980; teleg. Kanoniotel
C: Royal (Vassilikon), 110 Figareto, tel. 37512
C: Salvos, 108 Figareto, tel. 30429/30889; teleg. Salotel
in Kontokali: are code 0661
A: Kontolaki Palace, tel. 23736; teleg. Kopa Kerkyra
in Kouspades:
C: Boukari
in Liapades: are code 0663
C: Chryssi Akti, tel. 41294
in Messoghi: are code 0661
C: Rossis, tel. 92352
C: Roulis, tel. 92353
In Moraitika: area code 0661
L: Miramare Beach (bungalow hotel), tel. 30183/30226; 3224855 in Athens; teleg. Miremare
A: Delfina (motel), tel. 30318/32808
B: Messonghi Beach, tel. 38684/3223415 in Athens
C: Sea Bird (Thalassopouli)
in Nissaki: area code 0663
A: Nissaki Beach, Crouzeri, tel. 91232/91233/91234/91235/91236; 717076 in Athens; teleg. Nissaki Beach Corfu
in Paliokastritsa: area code 0663
A: Akrotiri Beach, tel. 41275
B: Oceanis, tel. 41229
B: Paleokastritsa, tel. 41207/41217
B: Pavillon "Xenia", tel. 41208

C: Odysseus, tel. 41209/21280
D: Zephyros, tel. 41211/41220; teleg. Hotelzefyros
in Perama (Gastouri): area code 0661
B: Aeolos Beach (bungalows), 6 Mantzarou, tel. 331324; teleg.
Aeolotel Corfu
B: Akti (motel), tel. 39445/30574/36868
C: Aegli, tel. 39812
C: Argo, tel. 29468
C: Oassis, tel. 23190/33120; teleg. Hoteloassis Corfu
in Pyrgi: are code 0661
C: Emerald (Smaragdi). tel. 93209/93266
in Roda: area code 0663
B: Aeolos Beach (bungalows), 6 Mantzarou, tel. 33132; teleg. Aeolotel
Corfu
in Ipsos: area code 0661
B: Ipsos Beach, tel. 93232/93247
C: Mega, tel. 93208/93216
C: Ionian Sea, tel. 93241
D: Costas, tel. 93205

Tourist Police: In town, 35 Arseniou Street, tel. 28265. Outside of town at 4 Polychroniou Konstanta, tel. 320669.

Ithaca
Connections: Ship three times a week from Patras via Kephallonia; once a week from Kephallonia to Frikes and Vathi. Bus from Athens three times a week.

History: Inhabited from 2000 BC, Ithaca, home of the intrepid Odysseus, has become the eternal symbol of the journey's end. The island and the four cities of Kephallonia were probably the extent of Odysseus' Mycenean kingdom, but the inhabitants of Ithaca will have no part in the theory of the German archaeologist Dorpfeld that Nidri on Lefkas was the Ithaca of Homer. Of course they have a great deal of proof that Ithaca was indeed Ithaca: pottery decorated with the cock, the symbol of Odysseus, has been found on the island. Homer describes the palace of Odysseus as above "three seas" and a hillock in Stavros matches the description; furthermore it is the site of two ancient fortifications which might have been used for signals and beacons to the palace. There are candidates for the Fountains of Arethusa, where Odysseus found his faithful swineherd, and for the cave where he hid the treasure the Phaenicians gave him in Corfu. Not only do the Ithacians claim Odysseus, but some claim that the voyage of the Odyssey was a trip around the world, thus putting an Ithacian far ahead of Magellan. While this is rather improbable, others have suggested that he at least went through the straits of Gibraltar and perhaps even to Britain and Scandinavia.

Ithaca today: One of the rockier and drier of the Ionian Islands lacking long stretches of sand, Ithaca fails to attract much of the sun and fun crowd. Outside of July and August, the typical tourist at Ithaca has his Homer under his arm and his hiking shoes on his feet. Roads in Ithaca seem to be an afterthought of the highway department, but they are passable. A daily caique runs between the ports Frikes, Kioni and Vathi if one prefers to avoid them altogether. Most of the modern Ithacians take after their countryman Odysseus and spend their time at sea.

Vathi, rounding the end of a long sheltered bay, is the capital of the island, although little larger than a village itself. Its beautiful harbour attracts a good many yachts during the summer, and the locals claim it is the second most popular port in all of Greece. In town is the **mansion of the Drakolis family,** who brought the first steamship to Greece, which they named the *Ithaka*. **The Archaeology Museum** (open 9.30 am-12.30 am) is behind the Mentor Hotel, housing a collection of vases, offerings and other objects, many dating from Homeric times. From Vathi one can walk to the **Marmarospilia,** where Odysseus is said to have hidden his Phaenican treasure until he regained his throne and wife after killing the wretched suitors. Visitors should wear sturdy shoes and bring a flashlight. The way is signposted. Below the cave is the Harbour of Phorcys, the Old Man of the Sea. The people say that a secret road leads from the sea to the cave, as someone who left a rooster in the cave found it two days later by the shore.

Restaurants: Ithiaki, Nea Ithaki, Lido, Cherry Beach; self service at the Mentor Hotel.

Specialities: Roveni (a sweet made of honey, sugar and rice), cherapa chicken.

South of Vathi is **Parapigdio,** better known as the **Fountain of Arethusa,** the mother who wept so much when her son Coryx was killed that she turned into a spring of tears. Odysseus, disguised as a beggar, found his loyal swineherd here, and today it is a popular destination for picknickers. The water of the spring is very good to drink, and it has a reputation for increasing hunger. **Parachorio** is another village south of Vathi where a small wine festival takes place in the summer. The two restaurants there are famed for their chicken, and one can take the path around Mt. Stefano to the medieval ruins of the **Taxiarchos monastery.**

"Odysseus' Castle" is west of Vathi, also known as the fort of Pisaetos. Although a more likely candidate for Odysseus' palace is in the north part of the island, Pisaetos was the citadel of the ancient town Alkaklomena. Cyclopean walls and a tower-like structure remain. There is a beach in the bay below the castle, and the road continues its precarious way on a neck of land only 550 metres (600 yards) wide. From the height of the **Kadaro Monastery** one can see to the Gulf of Patras. **Kioni,** on a small protected bay is a fishing village with a few rooms to rent, a place to swim and dancing every Saturday night. Up the road is another similar village, **Frikes.** Many of the larger ships stop here and there is

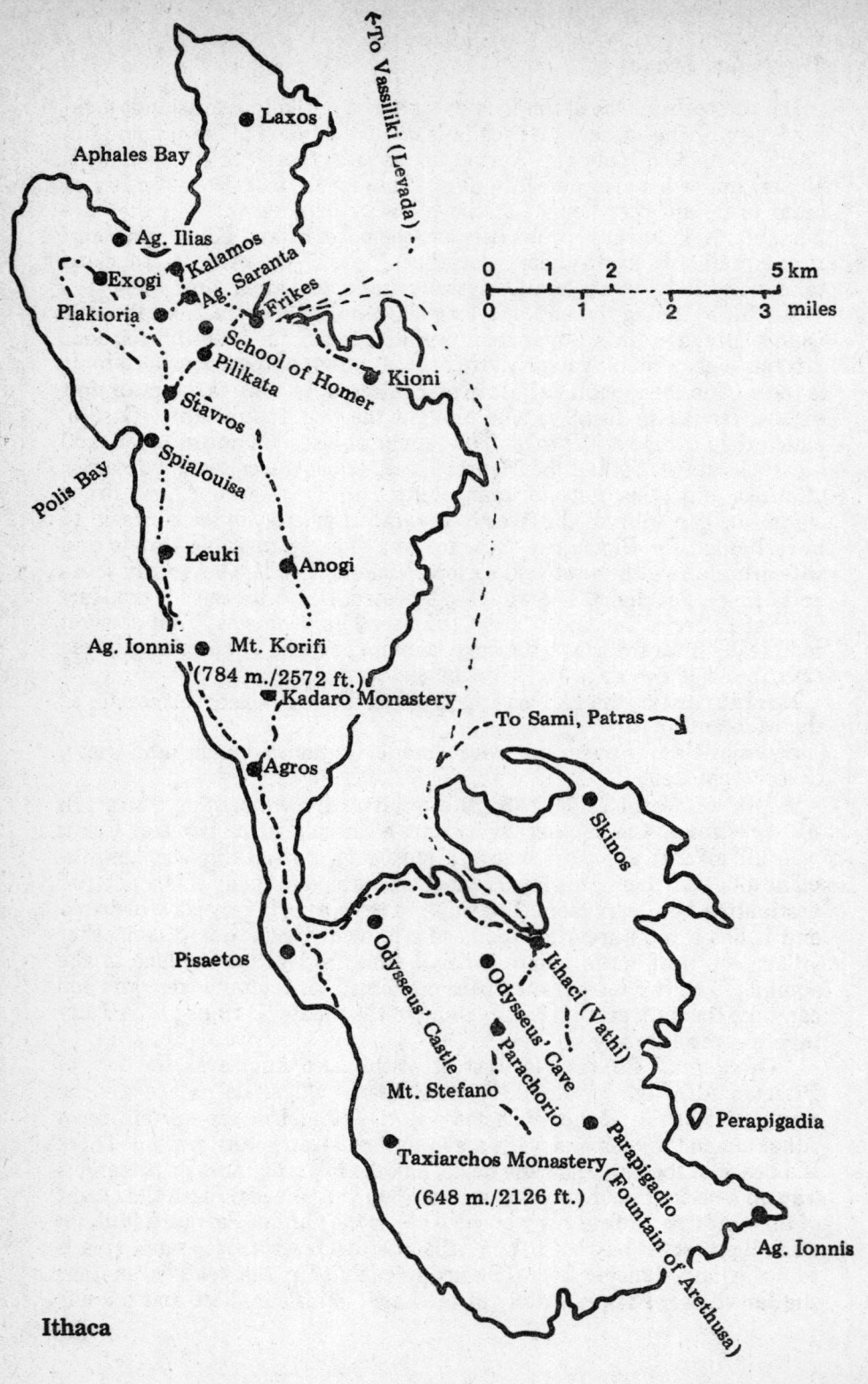

Ithaca

also an occasional connection to Vassiliki in Levkas. There are two tavernas, and buses leave twice a day for Stavros and Vathi.

Near Frikes is the so-called **"School of Homer,"** another Cylopean structure even older than the castle of Odysseus, dating from the early Bronze Age. Nearby the church Ag. Thanios was left in ruins by one of the many earthquakes which have shaken the island since ancient times, reminding one of Poseidon's wrath against Odysseus. Stavros, the largest village in the northern half of Ithaca, looks over **Polis Bay,** so named for the sunken city it contains, discovered in 1932. A bust of Odysseus in an unkept little garden surveys the scene from above. The teacher at the nearby school of Stavros, Mr. Sotiros S. Kouvaras, has the key for the small **Museum** on Pilikata hill, the probable site, at least from the information given by Homer, of the palace of Odysseus. One can see the three seas (the bays of Frikes, Polis and Aphales) from there. Mr. Kouvaras, who knows some English and is well versed in the lore of Odysseus, can explain the exhibits of the little museum, which include a very rare tripod (or should, if it ever comes back from the restorer in Athens). Other finds from "The School of Homer" date back to 2000 BC. At a cave near Stavros, **Spialouiso,** signs of an ancient cult to the mother goddess were discovered. There are beaches at Aphales and Polis Bays.

Panayiéria: 22 August-15 September, Theatre festival at Vathi; early September, wine festival at Parachorio; 8 September, at Kadaros Monastery; 24 June, Ag. Ioannes at Kioni and in the south of the island.

Hotels in Ithaca: area code 0674
in Vathi
B: Mentor, tel. 32433/32293; 3604251 in Athens
B: Odysseus (pension), tel. 32381
E: Aktaeon, 24 G. Gratsou, Petalata; tel. 32387

   Tourist police: Regular police at Vathi.

Kalamos and **Kastus,** two islands off Meganisi, near Mitikas on the mainland, are under the jurisdiction of Ithaca. Kalamos, the larger one, is connected once a week to Sami, Ithaca, the port Astakos and Meganisi, and Nidri and Vassiliki on Levkas. There is also a more frequent service from Mitikas. There are three small fishing villages on its rocky coast: Kalamos, Episkopi, and Kefali. Only two or three families live on Kastus, unable to care for all the vineyards which once produced a fine wine.

Kephallonia
Connections: Daily flights from Athens; bus three times a day from Athens; ferry boat at least twice a day from Patras; to Ithaca three times a week or by the occasional caique from Fiscardo to Stavro; once a week with Astakos, Kalamos, Mitikas, Meganisi, Vassiliki, Nidri, Frikes and Vathi.

247

History: The name of the island derives from its first legendary king, the wise Kephalos, and his sons founded the four ancient cities: Sami, Krani, Pahli and Pronnoi. These, along with Ithaca (the smallest in area, but strongest in the days of Homer) formed the ancient kingdom of Odysseus. Sami, located by the present port of the same name, was the oldest and most important of these cities in later history, dominating the frequent rivalries between them. When the Romans came, the people of Sami resisted heroically and as a result were sold as slaves when they finally surrendered after a siege of months.

Robert Guiscard took Kephallonia in the 11th century, but died there in 1085. According to his historians, this saved the throne of Alexis Comnenus by weakening the Norman threat to the Byzantine Empire.

Kephallonia, the largest of the Ionian islands, was the capital of the theme during the age of Byzantium, the governor living in the Byzantine fortress at Ag. Georgios. In 1099 it withstood a siege by the city of Pisa, and in 1194 was taken by Count Matteo Orsini, who along with his fellow pirate Vetrano, used it as a base for their operations in the Ionian islands. In 1209, however, when the Venetians crucified Vetrano, Orsini put his "possessions" under the rule of Venice, who claimed the theme of Kephallonia after the sack of Constantinople. They formed the County Palatine of Kephallonia (Kephallonia, Ithaca, and Zachynthos), but in 1483 it was captured by the Turks. The Venetians and the Spanish were determined to get it back. Leading the assault in 1500 was the Gran Capitan de Cordova, who after a fifty day siege succeeded in winning Ag. Georgios for the Christians.

After this the fortress was repaired and the town nearby became the Venetian capital. A huge earthquake caused heavy damage to Ag. Georgios, and by the 18th century it was abondoned, Argostoli becoming the island's new capital. In 1823 Lord Byron came to Kephallonia as an agent of the Greek Committee in London, where he was as ever a great inspiration to those fighting for the Independence of Greece. At the village of Metaxata he wrote *Don Juan* before going on to die at Messolongi on the mainland. During the British occupation of the Ionian Islands, the Kephalloniotes demanded Greek union there more stridently than anyone else, and many of the nationalist leaders were imprisoned there. Yoannes Metaxas, prime minister-dictator of Greece from 1936 to 1941 came from Kephallonia; and it was he who said the historic "No" to Mussolini's ultimatum during the beginning of the Second World War. Another famous son of Kephallonia was the wealthy ship owner Vergotis.

Kephallonia today: The difference between the inhabitants of Kephallonia and those of Zakynthos is that the Kephalloniotes leave home and the Zakynthiotes stay. So great is the Kephalloniote predilection for leaving their island for all the countries of the world that a local joke has Neil Armstrong making his first steps on the moon in the direction of a coffee shop called "Beautiful Kephallonia". A certain fir tree that grows in the mountainous regions of Kephallonia is named for the island; outside Kephallonia it is found only in parts of Russia. It is very aromatic, making the whole island smell good. Kephallonia is not only rich from the ambitious adventures of its sons, but it produces one of the finest wines of Greece.

Argostoli, the capital of the island since 1715, is new and modern and not all that attractive. There are two museums in town, both located near the square. The **Archaeology Museum** is open 9 am-1 pm and 4 pm-6 pm; 10.30 am-2.30pm Sundays; closed Tuesdays. It contains finds from the ancient cities and Mycenean tombs on the island. The **Historical Museum and Library** is open every day except Sunday, in the morning and after the siesta. A short walk from town brings one to the **sea mills.** These no longer work as they should because of the rise in the level of the land after the last earthquake and subsequent reduction in water volume. A restaurant and night club at nearby Katavothri make it a lively place in the evening, and there is a splendid view of the pretty lighthouse in a rotunda, the **Fanari.** Two beautiful beaches line the shore — the organized **Platis Yialos** and the free **Makris Yialos** closer to town. The port of Argostoli is an official **port of entry** and supplies berthing and over wintering for yachts.

Restaurants: Lorentszatos, Kephalos, Ainos,and Liminaki.
Specialities: Rombola wine, black currants.

Before the earthquake of 1953 there were 365 villages on Kephallonia, a number now reduced. More of a town than a village, **Lixouri** is connected by ferry boat from Argostoli five times a day. In the centre square stands a **statue of Vlaskarados,** a local man of letters of the 19th century, remembered in particular for his dislike of the church. He was a poor man with a large family to support, and he kept heckling the priests so much that they finally excommunicated him — this is aforismos, in Greek, meaning that the body will not decompose after death. Vlaskarados, in response, hurried home, collected his children's shoes and returned to the priest with the request that he should please aforismos the footwear, too, as he had no money to buy new shoes! Beside the town (which has produced the wealthiest of the Kephalloniote ship owners) is a small pebble beach.

Ag. Georgios to the south is a long stretch of golden sand, most easily reached by caique. Just south of it the famous **Kounopetra** once created the optical illusion of opening and closing; the earthquake, however, fouled up the magic, and likewise destroyed the houses on the pretty, deserted **Vardiana islet** off the coast. This large peninsula of Kephallonia, the site of ancient Pahli, is rocky and full of caves. The most interesting one, **Drakondi Spilio,** can be reached from the **Tafios monastery.** The people of the Lixouri region are said to be in an eternal state of disagreement with the Argostolians across the bay.

Argostoli is in the region of ancient **Krani,** and the remains of some of its ancient walls may be seen at the site called **Cyclopean Walls,** east of

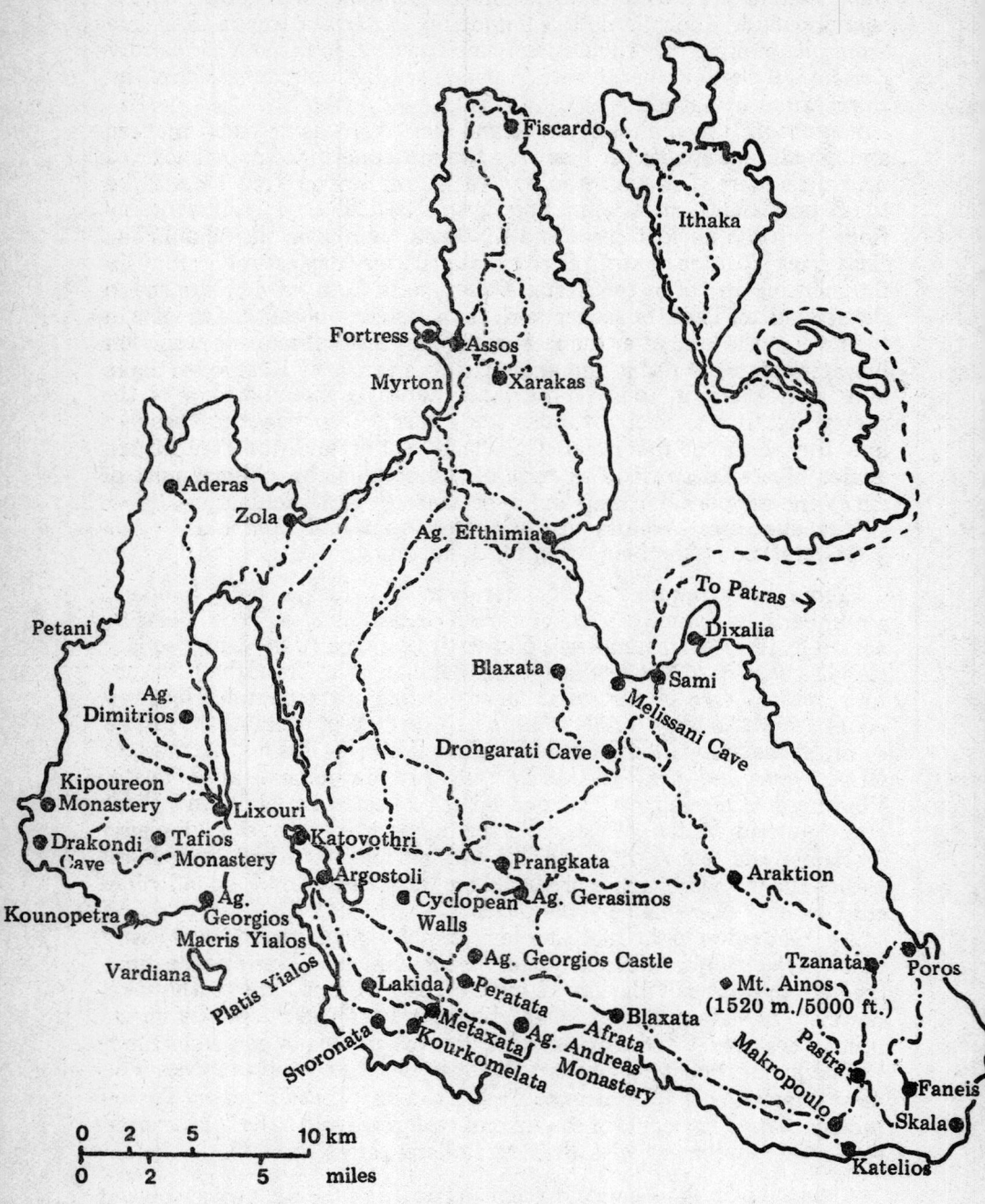

Fiscardo

Ithaka

Fortress
Assos
Myrton
Xarakas

Aderas
Zola

Ag. Efthimia

To Patras →

Petani

Dixalia

Blaxata
Sami
Ag.
Dimitrios

Melissani Cave

Drongarati Cave

Kipoureon
Monastery
Lixouri

Drakondi
Cave
Tafios
Monastery
Katovothri

Prangkata

Araktion

Argostoli

Ag. Gerasimos

Kounopetra
Ag.
Georgios
Macris Yialos
Cyclopean
Walls

Vardiana

Ag. Georgios Castle

Tzanata
Poros

Platis Yialos

Lakida
Peratata

Mt. Ainos
(1520 m./5000 ft.)

Svoronata
Metaxata
Kourkomelata
Ag.
Andreas
Monastery
Afrata
Blaxata

Makropoulo
Pastra

Faneis

Skala

Katelios

0   2   5   10 km
0   2   5   miles

Kephallonia

town. The blocks of stone in the walls are huge, and are considered an excellent example of ancient Greek defences. South-east of the walls is a fertile, rolling region, Lakidra, with many villages, including **Metaxata,** where Byron wrote *Don Juan* and **Korkomelata,** which was destroyed by an earthquake but rebuilt by Vergotis. Everything there is bright, new and very well kept, reminding one of a suburb in California. **Kallithea** restaurant affords a lovely view of the vineyards and sea below and specializes in scordalia, a fish dish with garlic sauce. Another village, **Peratata,** has a discotheque, and from there one may visit the **convent of Ag. Andreas,** which has relics of the saint. The **Castle of Ag. Georgios** is also in the region, still very impressive despite the damage it has suffered. What exists today was built by Nickolaos Tsimaras on the Byzantine fort; in Venetian times it was known simply as Kephallonia, the capital and most important stronghold of the island. From its bastions one has a privileged view of the surrounding plains and mountains.

By another fertile plain, **Omala,** the Church of **Ag. Gerasimos** contains the body of the patron saint of the island. If 50 per cent of Corfiots are named Spiros after St. Spyridon, then 50 per cent of the Kephalloniotes are named Gerasimos after their saint, who is known for curing mental disturbances, especially if one keeps an all-night vigil at his church on the night of 27 October, his feast day. High above the regions towers **Mt. Ainos,** the highest peak of Kephallonia. In 1957 a road was constructed to the TV receiver on the top, and it makes a splendid drive amidst the tall Kephallonia fir trees. The view of course, is magnificent, encompassing all of Kephallonia, Ithaca, Zakynthos and Patras.

Afrata along the south coast is a long beach, **Blaxata** being the nearest village (names ending in "ata" date from the Venetian occupation). At **Makropoulo** it is said that on the day of the Assumption of the Virgin, 15 August, little crosshead snakes "inoffensive to the Virgin Mary" make a brief annual appearance. **Skala** and **Poros** on the east coast of the island have long sandy beaches, some of the best on the island, although the road between them is a real catastrophe. Poros has hostels and restaurants, and there are also some facilities at Skala. Both are archaeological sites still under excavation.

Sami serves as the port of the island. The bus that runs from there to Argostoli is the only regular one on the island, but even then it may be necessary to spend a night in the port in order to catch an early ship out. Some of the **ancient fortifications of Sami** remain in the hills above the present little town, which is of practically no interest whatsoever. Nearby, however are two of the most splendid sites on the island — its two caves. **Drongarati Cave,** located by the village Haliotata, is open from 7 am to 7 pm daily and entrance costs 8 dr. Inside a fairy land of orange and yellow stalactites and stalagmites awaits the visitor. One of the rooms is occasionally used as a concert hall, so excellent are the acoustics. The other cave, **Melissani** (The Purple Cave) is by the village

Vlahana, half an hour's walk from Sami. Open from 7 am to 7 pm (15dr entrance) it has a salt water lake in its centre, which can be explored in the row boat provided. About 120 metres (400 ft) long and 30 (100 ft) high, Melissana is a vast play of blue and violet colours, caught in the sun which sneaks through the hole in the roof. The salt water inside supposedly came from under the island, all the way from Argostoli, where there is a sea hole by the sea mills.

Ag. Efthimia to the north has a harbour for small boats and yachts, and there is a hotel there. At the northern tip of the island, **Fiscardo** derives its name from a mispronounciation of Guiscard, the Norman prince who died there and was buried in a cairn (by the hotel). Only at Fiscardo were some of the old Venetian houses saved from the earthquake, and they give the visitor an idea of what the rest of the island looked like before 1953. In the summer a caique leaves Fiscardo for Stavros in Ithaca and by the sea a Greek American runs a small but pleasant restaurant. Also by the sea on an ugly cement block is an ugly mobile home, one of the few in Greece.

South-west of Fiscardo, on the way back to Argostoli, is the magnificent castle **Assos,** far below the mountain road on a small peninsula. Built by the ancient Greeks, it was restored by the Venetians who sent a proveditor to govern it. Two harbours are formed by the peninsula,and on one of them is the little fishing village of Assos. Just south lies the superb beach **Myrton,** one of the most picturesque in Greece, especially from the road above where it appears snow white against an incredibly blue sea. A hotel is being built in the vicinity.

The easiest way to see the island is by taxi and drivers specialize in gathering up a carload of people to make the trip less expensive. The terrain of Kephallonia is hilly and the roads are not very good, making bicycling and even scootering unpleasant. Buses for an island this size are surprisingly few. When they do go to some distant part, they usually don't return until the next day. However, buses can be rented, should a group of people decide that they all want to go to the same place.

Panayiéria: 16 and 21 October, Ag. Gerasimos; 15 August, tis Panayias at Makropoulo; 23 April, Ag. Geordios; 21 May, Ag. Konstantinos near Argostoli.

Hotels in Kephallonia

The Xenia (B) at Argostoli is located in a grove of pines at the edge of the capital, overlooking the large port. Not far from Argostoli, at the lovely beach Platis Yialos, the White Rocks (air conditioned) is at the heart of the region's nightlife, with two disco-tavernas in the area. While the large Mediterranee (A) has every luxury, the little Myrto (B) at Assos and the Panormos (B) at Fiscardo have the simple charm of pretty little fishing villages, where rest and relaxation are the order of the day.

in Ag. Efthimia: area code 0674
C: Pylaros, tel. 61210

in Argostoli: area code 0671
B: Xenia, tel. 22233
C: Aegli, 3 21st Maiou, tel. 22522
C: Aenos, 10 21st Maiou, tel. 28013; 3632196 in Athens
C: Aghios Gerassimos, 6 Ag. Gerassimou, tel. 28697
C: Armonia, 1 Geroulanou, tel. 22566
C: Dido, 3 D. Lavranga, tel. 22317
C: Phocas, 3 Gerouglanou tel. 28100
C: Tourist, 94 J. Metaxa, tel. 22510
D: Agrambeli, 34 Vyronous, tel. 28358
D: Allegro, 2 A. Hoida, tel. 22268/28684
D: Emborikon, 2 Lochagou Mitaki, tel. 22407
D: Hara, 87 Leof. Vergoti, tel. 22427
D: Paralia, 144 J. Metaxa, tel. 22627
D: Parthenon, 4 Zachynthou, tel. 22246
in Assos
B: Myrto (pension)
in Fiscardo: area code 0674
B: Panormos (pension), tel. 51340
in Lassi: area code 0671
A: Mediterranee (Messoghios), tel. 28760; 722915 in Athens
in Lixouri: area code 0671
D: Ionios Avra, 2 Valaoritou, tel. 91241
E: Horpoula, tel. 91245
in Platis Yialos: area code 0671
White Rocks (hotel and bungalows), tel. 28332; 3628216 in Athens;
teleg. Rockhotel
in Poros: area code 0674
B: Iraklis (Hercules) (pension), tel. 52351; 6710506 in Athens
C: Atros Poros, tel. 52205; 9517406 in Athens
in Sami: area code 0674
C: Ionian, 5 Chorofylakis, tel. 21235
D: Kyma, Platia Kyprou, tel. 21264
E: Krinos, 8 M. Alexandrou, tel. 21202
E: Sami, tel. 21204
in Svoronata (Ag. Pelagia): area code 0671
Irinna Hotel, tel. 41286; 3618383 in Athens

Tourist police: Regular police in Argostoli.

Kythera
Connections: Daily flight from Athens. Connections by sea — three
times a week Neapolis to Ag. Pelagias; once a week via Piraeus, Neopolis,
Ag. Pelagias, Cythion, Kestelli (Crete); Piraeus, Monemvassia, Neopolis,
Ag. Pelagias; and Piraeus, Kiparission, Monemvassia, Neopolis,
Elafonissi, Ag. Pelagias, Cythion, Kapsali, Antikytherea, Kastelli

(Crete). Frequent caique from Ag. Pelagias to Elafonissos.

History: When Zeus castrated his father, Cronus, then ruler of the world, he cast the bloody member into the sea. This gave birth to Aphrodite, the goddess of love, who rose out of the sea foam at Kythera. Later she went across to Cyprus, and was thus referred to as either the Cypriot or the Kytherian. An ancient sanctuary was dedicated to Aphrodite on Kythera, the most sacred of all such sanctuaries in Greece.

Aphrodite was known as Astarte by the first settlers of Kythera, the Phoenicians, who came to the island for a certain snail from which they extracted a purple dye to colour royal garments. The Minoans from Crete used Kythera as a trading station, for it is centrally situated between Crete and the mainland, and between the Aegean and Ionian seas. This cross-road location, while encouraging commercial activity, also encouraged raids, and Kythera was invaded no less than 80 times in known history. Particularly frightful were the visits of the Saracen Arabs from Crete: in the 10th century they caused the island to be deserted, as the people sought refuge on the mainland, returning only when Nikephoros Phokas won Crete back for Byzantium.

The rulers of Kythera during the age of Byzantium were the Eudhaemonoyannis family from Monemvasia. The Venetians occupied the island in 1204, but with the help of Emperor Michael Palaeologos, Kythera was regained for the Eudhaemonoyannis, and it served as a refuge for Byzantine nobles when the Turks took the Peloponnese, most of them living at Paliochora. However, in 1537, Barbarossa stopped at Kythera on his way home from the unsuccessful siege of Corfu and destroyed the town. The Venetians occupied the island again in the 15th century and they called it "Cerigo" the name by which it is known in the old histories. The Turks took the island early in the 18th century. In 1964 it was ceded to Greece by the British with the rest of the Ionian islands.

Kythera today: The opening of the Cornith canal doomed any commercial importance Kythera once had by virtue of its position between the two seas. Today, unless one takes the small plane from Athens, the island is rather difficult to reach. It is totally unconnected with its sister Ionian islands far to the north-west. Two or three times a week a ship leaves Piraeus, stopping at many Peloponnesian towns before calling at Ag. Pelagia and Kapsali, the two ports of the island. There is also a regular ship from Kastelli in the western part of Crete. As 100,000 people of Kytheran origin now live in Australia, the island is jokingly called a Kangaroo colony, while some call Australia "Big Kythera." All the immigrants who can, come back to Kythera in the summer, constituting its main tourist rush. With only a few rooming houses the island is hardly prepared to take on many foreigners who have no relatives to stay with. Although blessed with a good deal of fresh water, Kythera doesn't quite match the lovely painting of Antoine Watteau, "The Journey to Cythere."

Kythera, or **Chora,** the capital of Kythera, is a pretty blue and white village, 275 metres (900 ft.) above the port of Kapsali, impressively surrounded by the **Kastro,** finished by the Venetians in 1503. The location was supposedly designated by pigeons, who took the tools of the builders from a less protected site and carried them to a hill above the village of Kapsali. There are ten old **Venetian mansions** in Chora still retaining their coat of arms, and a small **museum,** generally open in the morning, which contains artifacts dating back to Minoan times. A few of the inhabitants rent rooms and the town boasts one, unlabelled restaurant. Below, a 20-minute walk down, **Kapsali** has a large rooming house owned by Emmanuel Comnenus (probably a descendant of the Byzantine nobles who fled to Kythera from Mystra), two restaurants and two beaches, along with a yacht supply station.

Buses leave Kythera about once a day for the major villages of the island. Alternatively there are taxis (notably little Tarzan or Mitata) which charge a set fee for different excursions. **Kalamos,** just east of Chora, is within walking distance. One of the churches of the village, Ag. Nikitis, has a pretty bell tower, and there is a taverna by the square. A dirt road leads across some wild landscapes to Vroulaia, a pebble beach and taverna, where many people pitch their tents. Skandeia at Paliopolis was the port of the ancient town of Kythera, mentioned by Thucydides, and ruins of the settlement may be seen at the site called **Kastri.** The ancient town itself was above Paliopolis on the **Paliokastro** mountain, and here worshippers came to the ancient temple of Urania Aphrodite to pay their respects to the goddess. The Christians, however, destroyed the renowned sanctuary to build the church of Ag. Anargyroi. Remains of the acropolis walls can still be seen at Paliokastro.

From Paliopolis the coastal road leads to **Avlemonas,** where the Minoans had a trading settlement dating from 2000 BC until the rise of the Myceneans. By the sea is a small octagonal fortress built by the Venetians, who left a coat of arms and a few rusting canon inside. There is also a small beach.

Back in the heart of the island, just north of Kapsali at **Livadio,** with its golden wheat fields run wild from a lack of labour is a pretty bridge of thirteen arches. From Livadio via Drimon a paved road leads to the most important religious establishment of Kythera, the **Monastery of the Panayia Mirtidion.** A golden icon of the Virgin and child, faces blackened with age, attracts a huge number of pilgrims to the monastery on 15 August. Situated on the rugged west coast among Gothic cyprus trees, Mirtidion is ornamented with many flowers, peacocks, and a tall, carved bell tower. Two small islets off the coast are evidently pirate ships which the Virgin turned to stone. At the monastery are many lodgings set up to house pilgrims on the panayiéri days.

North of the monastery, also attainable from Livadio, **Milopotamo** is the closest thing to Watteau's vision of Kythera. It is the island's loveliest village, crisscrossed with tiny canals of clear water (so much water, in

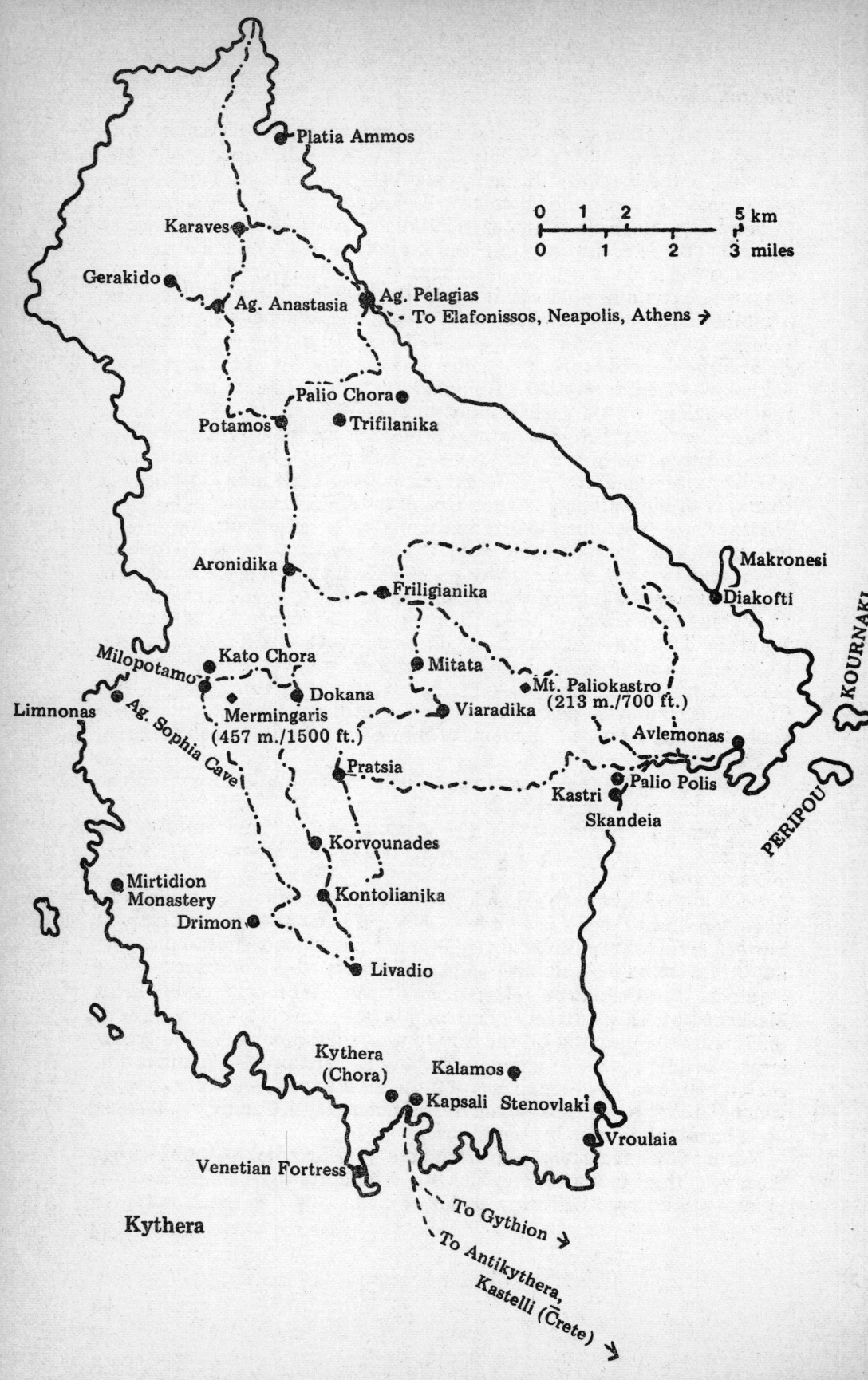

Platia Ammos

Karaves

Gerakido

Ag. Anastasia

Ag. Pelagias
To Elafonissos, Neapolis, Athens ➔

Palio Chora

Potamos

Trifilanika

0 1 2   5 km
0   1   2   3 miles

Makronesi

Aronidika

Friligianika

Diakofti

KOURNAKI

Milopotamo

Kato Chora

Mitata

Dokana

Mt. Paliokastro
(213 m./700 ft.)

Limnonas

Ag. Sophia Cave

Mermingaris
(457 m./1500 ft.)

Viaradika

Avlemonas

Pratsia

Kastri

Palio Polis

Skandeia

PERIPOU

Korvounades

Mirtidion
Monastery

Kontolianika

Drimon

Livadio

Kythera
(Chora)

Kalamos

Kapsali

Stenovlaki

Venetian Fortress

Vroulaia

Kythera

To Gythion ➔

To Antikythera,
Kastelli (Crete) ➔

fact, that the toilet in the valley is in a constant state of flush). This valley, in the middle of town, is called Neraida, or Nymph, and a good restaurant there has music and dancing at night. An old watermill lies along the path to the waterfall, very lovely amid the ancient trees, flowers, and banana plants. On quiet days, one can even hear the nightingales singing. For rooms to rent in the village, ask in the square by the bell tower.

Kato Chora lies just below Milopotamos in the walls of a Venetian fortress built in 1560. Above the gate of the deserted town a bas-relief of the lion of St. Mark accompanies a Latin inscription. Inside many of the old stone houses are open for exploration. By the sea below is the cave **Ag. Sophia,** at the end of a rugged, descending road. In the past the cave was used as a church of Ag. Sophia, and inside there are frescoes and mosaics, besides stalactites and stalagmites and small lakes. It is quite a large cave and incredibly is said to go all the way to Ag. Pelagia — where indeed a sign points down a rocky hill to a site called Ag. Sophia.

Palio Chora, also known as Ag. Dimitriou on the north-east coast of Kythera, south of Ag. Pelagias, was built by the Byzantine noble Eudhaemonoyannis in the Monemvasian style. High on the rocks it was hidden from the sea — Barbarossa found it only by capturing the inhabitants and forcing them to tell him where it was. Beside the ruins of the fort is a terrible abyss down which the mothers threw their children before leaping themselves, to avoid the Turks. Most of the island's ghost stories and legends are centered on this tragic place.

Potamos, despite its name, has no river. It is the largest village in the north part of the island, all blue and white like Chora. It has a bank and the Olympic Airways office, and the largest building at the edge of town is the island's retirement home. At **Gerakido** to the northwest one can see yet another tower, this time built by the Turks in the early 18th century. **Platia Ammos** is a fine beach just east of Karaves, and south of it another beach may be found at **Ag. Pelagias,** the northern port of the island. Two large rooming houses operate in the village, and there are numerous tavernas.

From Ag. Pelagias one can see the islet **Elafonissos,** connected by ship three times a week, or more frequently in the summer by caiques. The village, also called Elafonissos, has about 750 people, mostly fishermen and sailors. A new village, **Kata nisso,** is under construction with a hotel, for little Elafonissos has two gorgeous sandy beaches about a mile long, as yet hardly discovered by tourists.

Another islet, **Antikythera,** lies south of Kapsali. Ships call there twice a week in between Kythera and Crete. Less than 150 people live there in two settlements, Potamos and Sochoria, and it is very rocky with few trees. By Potamos are the ruins of ancient **Aigilia** with a wall dating back to Classical times.

Panayiéria: 15 August, Panayias Mirtidion; 29-30 May, Ag. Trias at Mitata.

Tourist Police: Regular police at Chora.

Levkas (Levkada)

Connections: Bus three times a day from Athens or Patras; flights from Athens via Aktion; twice a week by sea from Nidri and Vassiliki to Ithaca, Kephalonia, Mitikas, Kalamos and Astakos. Daily to Meganisi.

History: If the Corinthians, the colonizers of Levkas, had not dug a canal between it and the mainland, it would not be an island but a peninsula of Greece. To protect the new island, a fort was built at the tip of the island and mainland, around which evolved most of the history of Levkas, for taking this key position in effect meant taking the whole island.

Nirikos was the Mycenean capital of the island. In the 7th century BC the Corinthians build the town of Lefkas near the present capital. Two famous moments in the ancient history of the island are when Sappho, for the love of a man, committed suicide by leaping off the white cliffs of Levkada Cape; and the battle of Aktium, which took place off the north coast of the island and settled the claim of Octavius over Mark Antony. The Byzantines lost the island to the Franks in the 13th century, who built the original fortress of Santa Maura, a name later adopted for the whole of the island. When Constantinople fell in 1453, the mother of the last Emperor Constantinos XI, Helene Palaeologus, founded a monastery in the walls of Santa Maura, which the Turks, when they took Levkas in 1479, turned into a mosque. They also took many of the inhabitants of the island to the Turkish slave markets.

In 1500 the combined Spanish and Venetian forces under de Cordova captured Levkas and Santa Maura in the name of Christianity, but the very next year Venice made a treaty with Turkey and returned the island. Francesco Morosini, however, after losing his own fortress at Herakleon, Crete, was determined to win Levkas back for Venice in 1684, and he did, with the help of a great number of Greeks from the Ionian islands. With the fall of the Serenissima Republic of Venice, the French and then the Russians took Levkas, the latter establishing it as part of the Septinsular Republic and adding fortifications. They also widened the canal. In 1807 the Tyrant Ali Pasha of Epirus moved to take Levkas, but was held back by forces under the Secretary of State, Count John Kapodistrias, who is said to have sworn to the cause of an Independent Greece with rebellious refugees on the island, including Kolokotronis.

Levkas today: Levkas is the most rural of the Ionian islands,and geologically it has much in common with the mainland to which it once belonged. The hand-made lace and embroideries of the women on the island are famous, and many are exported to England. In almost every back room one can find the mistress of the house, dressed in the brown, full-skirted dress of the island, working a loom. It is one of the least visited islands of the group, although when Aristotle Onassis was still alive many photographers came, as his private island, Scorpios, lies just off the east coast of Levkas.

The capital of Levkas, old Santa Maura but now also called **Levkas,** is located at the northern tip of the island near the mainland. A small ferry launch operated by ropes brings cars and buses across the tiny canal every 10 minutes or so. A road then follows the long causeway to the town. An alternative and longer route winds around the cape, where five windmills line the long, pebble beaches. The **Fortress of Santa Maura,** part of it in the sea by Arkanania on the mainland, offers a noble but crumbling picture to all who set out on the island. It, however, survived the earthquakes better than the houses in town, although a few Venetian vestiges remain here and there. Three churches from the 18th century solidly built of stone, can still be seen, two by clock towers that look like oil rigs: **Ag. Minas, Pantokrator, and Ag. Nikolaos.** Many shops sell the needlework and rugs of the Levkadian ladies. Up along the cape are two tavernas which provide the town's nightlife (other tavernas are along the east shore road), and by the beach at the far end is the Byzantine **Ag. Ioannes Anzousis** more than 1000 years old, according to the local priest. In late August a huge festival of art and literature attracts participants from 14 countries of the world, who, among other things, perform native songs and dances. Anyone who plans to attend should book a hotel room in advance.

Restaurants: Kali Karthia, H. Xara and Kali Orexi.

Just above the town is the beautiful **Faneromeni monastery;** a cave on the way up has some legend connecting it with Odysseus. Supposedly founded originally by a disciple of St. Paul, the present building of the monastery is more recent (possibly 17th century) and affords a splendid view of the area below. Other notable churches in the area are the Red Church, or the **Kokkino Eklisia,** at **Alexandros** and the 15th century church at **Othigitria,** built with Byzantine and western influences. Inside are many lovely frescoes. Pigadissani and Karia are other villages in the interior, near the mountain Ag. Ylias, a name which reminds one of the ancient peak sanctuaries dedicated to Helios, the sun god. It has also been suggested that the Greek custom of building chapels to Profitis Elias on mountains is a remnant of ancient sun worship.

Nydri along the east coast is where the German archaeologist Dorpfeld placed the capital of Odysseus, much to the indignation of the Ithacians, after he found signs of an Homeric settlement there. Today Nydri is a small seaside village, built up in the last 30 years, facing the islets of **Mandouri, Sparti, Scorpion,** and **Scorpios,** all wooded and beautiful.

A taverna at Nydri, so close to the shore that one may eat, drink and put one's feet in the sea at the same time, faces Mandouri, which at twilight floats from the horizon on a magic carpet of mist to the brekakekek-skoax-skoax of the frogs. The mansion on Mandouri belongs to the family of the poet Aristelis Valaoritis, who like Angellos Sikelianos, came from Levkas. Both poets were inspired by the combina-

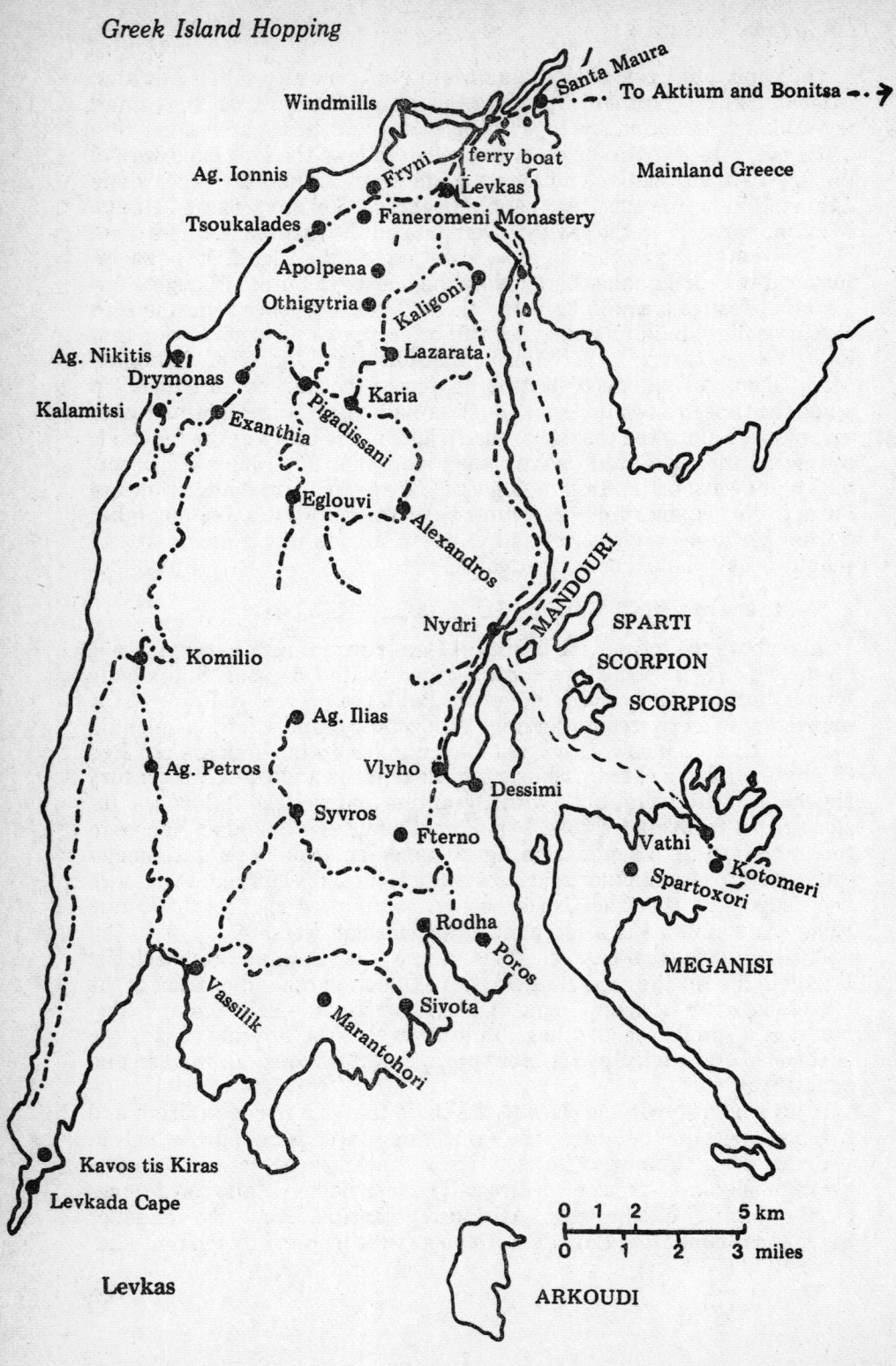

Greek Island Hopping

Windmills

Santa Maura

To Aktium and Bonitsa

Ag. Ionnis

Fryni

ferry boat

Levkas

Mainland Greece

Tsoukalades

Faneromeni Monastery

Apolpena

Kaligoni

Othigytria

Lazarata

Ag. Nikitis

Karia

Drymonas

Pigadissani

Kalamitsi

Exanthia

Eglouvi

Alexandros

Nydri

MANDOURI

SPARTI

SCORPION

SCORPIOS

Komilio

Ag. Ilias

Ag. Petros

Vlyho

Dessimi

Syvros

Fterno

Vathi

Kotomeri

Spartoxori

Rodha

MEGANISI

Poros

Vassilik

Sivota

Marantohori

Kavos tis Kiras

Levkada Cape

0 1 2   5 km

0   1   2   3 miles

Levkas

ARKOUDI

tion of mainland and island cultures there. Nydri, and Vassiliki on the south coast, are far more pleasant for an extended stay on the island than the larger capital of Levkas.

From **Vlyho** a winding road descends through the olive groves to the rocky Dessimi beach, where many people camp. From **Syvros,** a larger village, one may climb to the cave **Karouha,** the largest on the island. **Rodha** and **Sivota** (with a taverna) are popular swimming places with the natives. **Vassiliki** is a shady, charming village with rooms, restaurants and beaches. From here one may take a caique (or go by road from Komilio) to see the white cliffs of **Kavos tis Kiras,** or Levkada Cape or Lover's Leap, where Sappho, by tradition, died for Phaon. A temple once stood there dedicated to Apollo Levkada, and the priests are said to have made the leap safely as part of their cult. Later, Romans rejected by their sweethearts continued the practice begun by Sappho, but employed wings and rescue parties to save them in the waters below! Today a lighthouse marks the historic spot.

The west coast of Levkas is rocky and rugged until **Ag. Nikitis,** which has a sandy beach. **Ag. Petros** is the prettiest village on this side of the island.

Panayiéria: 11-13 August, Ag. Spyridon, at Karia, when the people bring out their old costumes; 30 May, Faneromeni monastery; 11 November, Ag. Monas in Levkas; 26 July, Ag. Paraskevi near Ag. Petros; Panayias on the west coast.

Meganisi lies off the south-east coast of Levkas. Every day except Monday a caique goes there from Levkas and Nydri and twice a week the larger ships call at **Vathi,** its port and largest settlement. It is a rocky islet, but not without beauty. The only time when many people go there is for the panayiéri of Ag. Konstantinos on 21 May at the hamlet of Kotomeri. **Arkoudi,** another islet south of Levkas is inhabited by a few fishermen and shepherds.

Hotels in Levkas: area code 0645
in Levkas
C: Santa Mavra, 2 Sp. Vianti, tel. 22342
E: Averof, tel. 22423
E: Patrae, 1 Meganissiou, tel. 22359
E: Vyzantion, tel. 22629
in Vassiliki
D: Paradise, tel. 31256
Tourist police: Regular police at Levkas.

Paxi
Connections: Daily with Corfu; twice a week with Patras, Kephallonia, and Corfu. Bus from Athens and Patras twice a week.

History: Homer mentions Paxi in regard to one of its seven sea caves,

Ipparandi, which the poet described as having brilliant rooms of gold. Another of the seven caves appears later in Paxian history, when in 1940 the hero Papanikolaos hid in it and waylaid passing Italian ships. The Germans learned the trick from him and hid their submarines in the caves. During the Venetian period a castle was built on the little islet facing Giaos.

Paxi today: What really puts tiny Paxi on the map, is its olive oil. From head to tail the island is covered with groves of silvery, writhing olive trees, set in equally winding dry stone terraces with little dwarf roads wiggling in between. There are over 300,000 trees in all, and each family on the island owns 500 or more. Since oil provides their major income, the inhabitants work very hard to keep the product top rate. It is considered the best olive oil in Greece, and has won many international prizes.

As it is very close to Corfu, many tourists visit Paxi, smallest of the Ionian islands — or rather, relatively few come, but the island is so tiny that it seems like a multitude. The boat from Corfu generally stops at Lakka, the northern port, before heading on to Gaios. From Lakka one can take the mini bus to Gaios and see the whole island (in half an hour). The people of Paxi are extremely kind and will often let people camp in their olive groves if they are very careful with fire — what the Paxians fear most.

Gaios, the pretty little village capital of the island, is named after a disciple of St. Paul, who brought Christianity to Paxi and is buried there.

On the islet facing the harbour is the well preserved **Kastro Ag. Nikolaos,** built by the Venetians in 1423, and near it is a windmill of the same period. The streets of Gaios are too narrow for automobile traffic, although the rest of the roads on the island are passable. The main road was constructed with funds given by Aristotle Onassis, who found the island charming. By the town one can swim at a small sandy beach, but the other beaches of Paxi are rocky or pebbly. There are many rooms to rent, and small restaurants, often in the middle of the trafficless streets. A shop also rents scooters.

From Gaios one may visit the islet **Panayia,** which on 15 August is crowded with pilgrims. In the evening they come back to Gaios and dance all night in the village square. **Mongonissi,** another islet, is connected by the caique of the family who owns a pretty little restaurant there, which brings customers over for dinner in the evening. Caiques may also be rented for a tour of the island, to see its seven sea caves of brilliant blue. Most are located among the sheer cliffs of the western side of Paxi, one of the more impressive being **Kastanitha,** 185 metres (600 ft.) high. Another distinctive cave, **Ortholithos,** has a sentinel-like monolith at its entrance. It is possible to penetrate about 5 metres (18ft.) inside by caique. Homer's Ipparandi does not have the golden rooms he mentions, although if often shelters numerous seals. **Grammatiko** is the largest cave of them all. When touring the

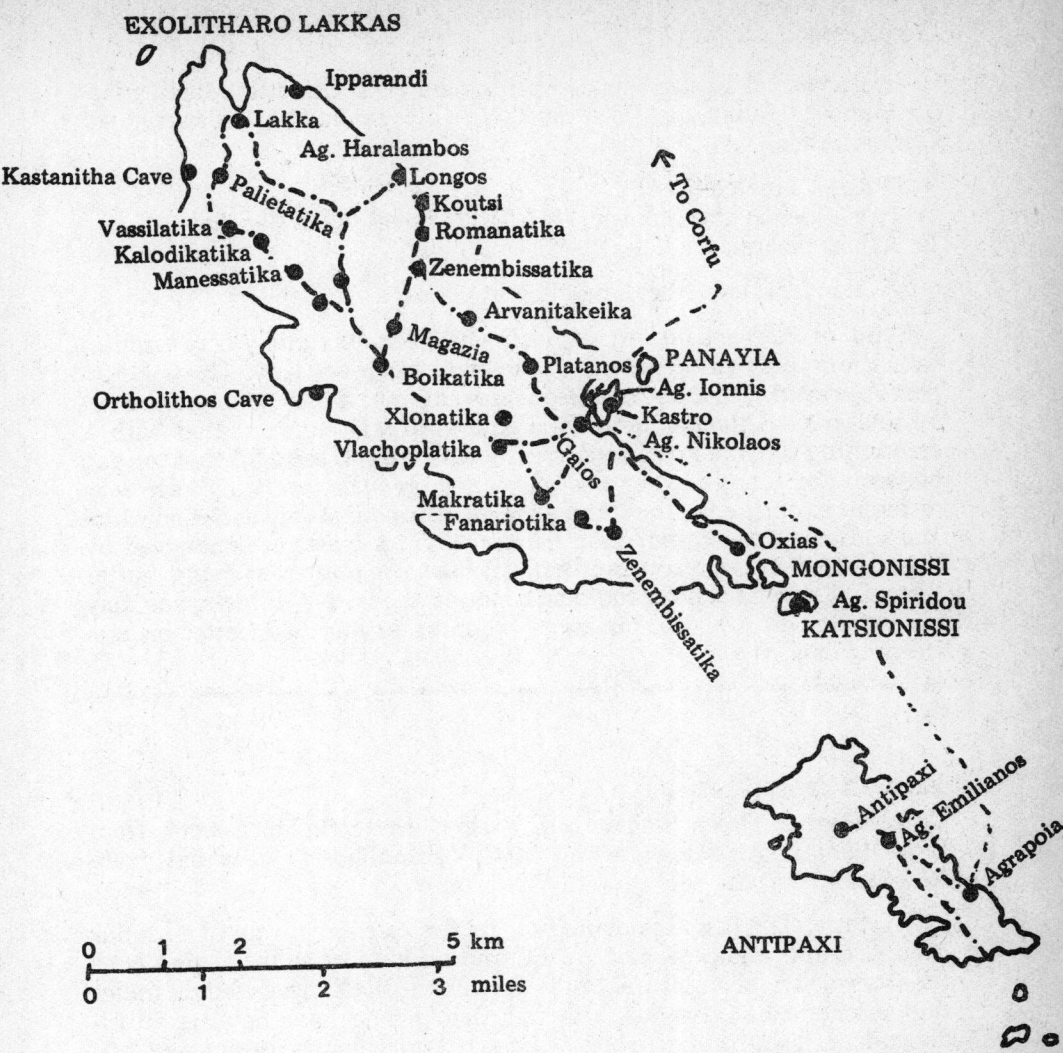

EXOLITHARO LAKKAS

Ipparandi

Lakka

Ag. Haralambos

Kastanitha Cave

Palietatika

Longos

Koutsi

Romanatika

Vassilatika

Kalodikatika

Manessatika

Zenembissatika

Arvanitakeika

Magazia

Boikatika

Platanos

PANAYIA

Ortholithos Cave

Xlonatika

Ag. Ionnis

Vlachoplatika

Kastro

Ag. Nikolaos

Gaios

Makratika

Fanariotika

Zenembissatika

Oxias

MONGONISSI

Ag. Spiridou

KATSIONISSI

To Corfu

Antipaxi

Ag. Emilianos

Agrapoia

ANTIPAXI

DASKALIA

0   1   2   5 km

0   1   2   3   miles

Paxi

perimeter of the island, you can also see the **Mousmouli Cliffs** and
their natural bridge **Tripitos**.

By **Lakka**, the charming little port in the north, is a Byzantine church
with particularly musical Russian bells. If you ask, someone in the
village will give you the key so that you can climb up in the belfry and
ring them. The **Grammatikou mansion** by Lakka dates from the 19th
century and is fortified with a tower. In **Boikatika** village the church
Ag. Charalambos contains an old icon of the Virgin, and in nearby
Magazia are two churches of interest, Ag. Spyridon and Ag. Apostoli. At
Apergatika the Papamarkou mansion dates from the 17th century.

Panayiéria: Easter Monday procession from Gaios to Velliantitika; 15 August, Panayias; 11 August, Ag. Spyridon; 10 February, Ag. Charalambos

Hotels: area code 0662
B: Paxos Beach (bungalows), tel. 31211; teleg Paxos Beach
E: Aghios Georgios

Tourist Police: Regular Police at Gaios

South of Paxi lies little **Antipaxi,** where approximately fifty families live. From June till September four or five caiques leave Gaios for its port **Agrapdia,** and out of season one may rent a boat to make the 40-minute trip. Although both Paxi and Antipaxi were created with a resounding blow of Poseidon's trident (the sea god thought that the gap between Corfu and Levkas was a bit too large), the two islands are very different in nature. Rather than olive oil, Antipaxi produces a good white and red wine, and rather than being rocky, its coasts are enhanced by fine sandy beaches. **Voutoumia** and **Vrika** are praised as being "softer than silk". There is no accommodations on the islet — if lucky one may find a room in a house, but those planning to stay had better bring a sleeping bag.

Zakynthos (Zante)

Connections: Daily flights from Athens; three flights a week from Kephallonia; four ferries a day from Kyllini; bus twice a day from Athens and Patras.

History: The island is named for its first settler, a son of Dardanus from Arcadia, who came in 1475 BC and built a fort on the same site as the later medieval structure. In the Trojan war the Zantiots fought under the command of Odysseus, although their island later became an independent, coin-minting state which set up colonies throughout the Mediterranean. One called Zakanthi was founded in Spain and later demolished by Hannibal. General Levinus took the island for Rome in 214 BC, and when the inhabitants rose up against their conqueror he burnt all the buildings on Zakynthos.

Uniting with the Aeolians, the Zantiots forced the Romans to leave, although in 150 BC Flavius finally made the troublesome island buckle under. Pliny refers to Mons Nobilis on Zakynthos (now Mt. Skopos), identifying its cavern as the entrance to the underworld.

In 844 AD the Saracens captured the island from their base in Crete, but the Byzantine forces were strong enough to expel them. The Norman-Sicilian pirate Margaritone took Zakynthos in 1182, and three years later Byzantium lost the island to the County Palatine of Kephallonia, first governed by Margaritone. One of his successors ceded the island to the Venetians in 1209. They kept the island for almost 350 years, although the Turks captured and pillaged it between 1479 and 1484. The aristocratic social system of the Venetians and wealthy Zantiots caused so much resentment among the commoners that they rose up in "the Rebellion of the Popolari" and took control of the island for four years. When the Turkish forces occupied Crete in the 17th century, many Cretan artists took refuge on the Venetian Zakynthos, initiating a great artistic movement on the island. It was the centre of the famous Ionian School of painting, which produced such artists as Doxaras, Koutouzis, and Kantorinis. The song cult of the Cantades flourished and in the 18th century two national poets Andreas Kalvos and Dionysos Solomos, were born and wrote here, the latter, the Poet of the Greek War of Independence, writing the words to the Greek National Anthem.

The Zantiots responded actively to the ideas of the French Revolution, forming their own Jacobin Club and destroying the hated rank of nobility. The Russians in 1798 forced the French garrison and the inhabitants to surrender, after a seige of months, and when the Septinsular Republic established aristocrats of its own Zakynthos rebelled again in 1801. During the War of Independence many rebels on the mainland found asylum on the island.

Zakynthos, marvellously endowed by nature, was known lovingly by the Venetians as "il Fiore di Levante", the flower of the East. Green, rolling hills and mountains, pockets of orchards and vineyards, flowers in variety of colours and beautiful beaches indeed mark it as one of the most beautiful islands in Greece. Unfortunately the earthquake of 1953 hit Zakynthos harder than any other island, devastating the Venetian buildings and masterpieces of architecture once judged the finest in Greece. However, in rebuilding their towns, the Zantiots have managed to blend a certain amount of charm in with the new anti-seismic buildings, which the other post-earthquake towns of the Ionian Islands seem to lack. Sometimes in the evenings one can still hear the cantades, songs more Italian than Greek, the inheritance of Zakynthos' once great cultural importance.

Zakynthos today: Zakynthos, the capital of the island, is situated beneath the mountain of the ancient acropolis of Zakynthos, the son of Dardanos, known as **Psophis.** Much of it fell down in the earthquake, however, and the site has now been planted with trees. To the right of town rises **Mt. Skopas** ("Look out", which someone would climb every day to scan the horizon for pirate ships). The **Vrondenero Cavern** is considered to be the entrance to hell mentioned by Pliny, down which the nobili would fall. **Platia Solomou,** on the north side of the long town, is the home of the **tourist police** and the **neo-Byzantine museum** (open 9am-1pm and 4pm-6pm; closed Tuesday. Entrance 25 dr; 2.5 dr with student card; free on Thursday and Sunday). Inside the museum are examples of art from the Ionian school, icons taken from the ruined churches dating back to the 16th and 17th centuries. The town's other

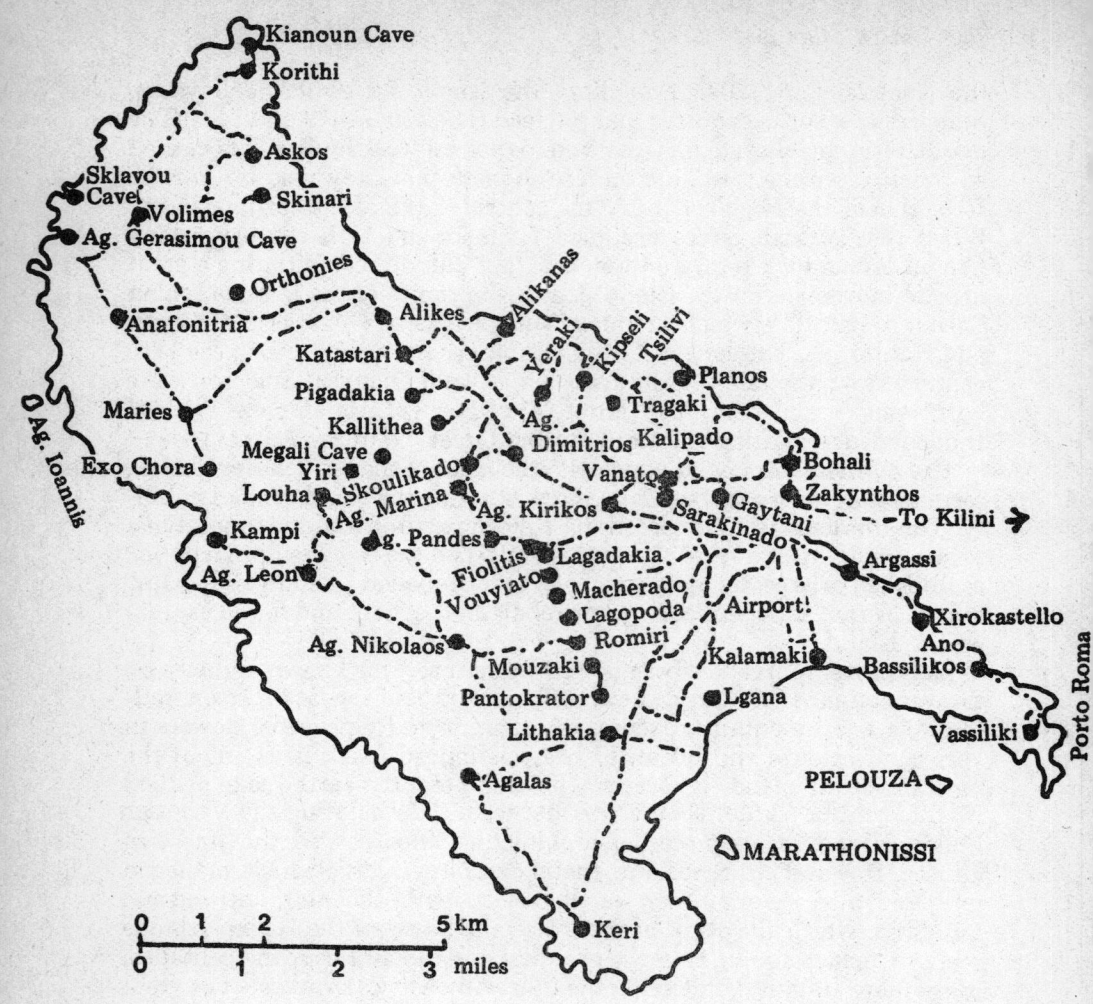

Zakynthos

museum is two blocks up at Ag. Markou Square, and it is dedicated to
Dionysos Solomos, containing that poet's mausoleum and writings and
momentoes from his life, together with those of other famous sons of
Zakynthos.

For **Ag. Dionysos,** the patron saint of the island, a huge church was
constructed on the south side of town below Mt. Skopas. The mortal
remains of the saint are inside, along with many gold and silver ex-votos,
and nearby one can see the **tomb of Andreas Kalvos.** An older church
owned by the Roma family, **Kira ton Angelous** (Our Lady of the
Angels), dating from the 17th century, is by Platia Solomou. One can
rent a canaped double-pedal vehicle or hire a horse-drawn cab to see the

town. It is an hour's walk to the **Venetian castle** above town (by road from Platia Solomou). There is a good restaurant there and a splendid view, not only of Zakynthos but of the Peloponnese and the Bay of Navarino, where the most famous naval battle of modern Greece took place.

The port of Zakynthos is an official port of entry and has a **yacht supply station**. There is also a **youth hostel** in town.

Restaurants: Very good are Boukios, Kallinikos, and Kokkinos Vrahos; less expensive are Spiros Petas and Kala Bokas; places specializing in meat are Strozas, Psiaria, Marinos, and Kefalinos Tachis.

Discotheque: Valeninto.

Specialities: Mandalato (a white nougat with peanuts, sold all over the port), Pasteli (with seasame seeds), and melons. Zakynthos also produces a fine perfume. Local wines (red and white) include Verdea, Laganas and Byzantis.

In the summer many buses run from Zakynthos town to all corners of the island. In winter travel is far more difficult, a problem easiest solved by renting two or four-wheeled transportation. A camping site is being organized at **Vassiliki** at the far end of the small eastern peninsula, close to the lovely pine-shaded beach **Porto Roma**. There are also rooms to rent in the village. The little islet **Pelouza** to the south was colonized in 1473 BC by King Zakynthos; today many come to fish there. **Kalamaki** and **Argassi** are two villages with sandy beaches on the other side of Mt. Skopos, at the beginning of currant country. **Lagana** just west of Kalamaki and at the edge of the fertile plain of the island rates as Zakynthos' resort area, with all modern tourist amenities. The sand of Lagana Beach is claimed to be the finest in all of Greece, and there are some curious rock formations by the sea.

On the south peninsula, picturesque **Keri** lies in the hills, affording a grand view of the surrounding region. Like **Exo Chora** in the west, the village is a hunting centre. Zakynthos abounds in rabbits and fowl (the hunting season is from 25 August to 15 March). Northwards in a cluster of farming villages. **Macherado** stands out with its lovely church of **Ag. Mavra,** housing a beautiful old icon of the Saint. The church bells are noted for their musical quality. In nearby Lagopoda there is also the pretty **Eleftherias monastery.** All of the villages in the Zakynthos plain are surrounded by gardens and orchards, with vineyards producing both grapes and currants. **Ag. Nikolaos** is a very pretty village, on a hill at the edge of the region. **Katastari** to the north is the second largest community on the island, lying only a mile or so from the beach Alikes, where an ancient bridge, **Pendi Kamares,** can still be crossed. The beach continues eastwards at **Alikanas.** Still further east is the fifth major beach on Zakynthos, **Tsilivi** at **Planos.**

Anafonitria, where Ag. Dionysos, patron saint of Zakynthos lived, is the site of a convent, the most important on the island. Of the various caves in the area, **Ag. Gerasimou** and **Sklavou** are the more interesting, excluding of course Kianoun Cave, also known as the **Blue**

Cave. Kianoun should be visited by caique, either from Zakynthos town or Alikes. It may be possible to reach it from the shore by Korithi, the northernmost village on the island, but the climb will not be very easy. The cave glows with every imaginable shade of blue.

Volimes to the south of Korithi is one of the largest villages of the island; to go swimming there one needs to wear swim shoes, so hot are the rocks and sand. **Ano Volimes** just above it is a pretty little mountain village.

A small islet south of Zakynthos, called **Strophades,** has a Byzantine monastery which served as a fortress for many years, until the Saracens finally overcame the defence of the monks and plundered it. Today only the building remains.

Panayiéria: The Carnival in Zakynthos lasts for two weeks prior to Lent, and is known for its masked singers and dancing among the general festivities. For the panayiéria of Ag. Dimitriou on 24 August and 17 December Zakynthos town is strewn with myrtle and there are fireworks at the church. During Holy Week the inhabitants also give themselves over to an infectious merriment. Slighty more modest is Zoodochos Pigi in town on 10 November.

Hotels in Zakynthos: area code 0695
in Alikes
C: Asteria, tel. 83203
C: Montreal, tel. 83241/83341
D: Alykae, tel. 83242
in Argassio
B: Mimosa Beach (bungalows), tel. 22588/28676/28876; teleg: Mimosa Argassi
C: Argassi Beach
C: Chryssi Akti, tel. 28679/28278
in Lagana
B: Galaxy, tel. 72271/72277; 9237467 in Athens
B: Zante Beach (hotel & bungalows), tel. 72230/78870; 7455001 in Athens; Teleg: Zantetels Zakynthos
C: Asteria
C: Atlantis, tel. 72242
C: Eugenia, tel. 72249
C: Hellinis, tel. 72264
C: Ilios
C: Ionis, 14 Kryoneriou, tel. 72241
C: Blue Coast
C: Medikas, tel. 72222
C: Panorama, tel. 72244
C: Selini, tel. 72252
C: Vezal, tel. 72255
C: Victoria, tel. 72265
C: Vyzantion, tel. 72236

D: Anatoli
in Planos
C: Cosmopolit, Tsilivi, tel. 28752
C: Orea Heleni, Tsilivi, tel. 28788
in Zakynthos town
B: Strada Marina, 16 K. Lomvardou, tel. 22761; teleg: Stradamarina
Zante
B: Xenia, 66 D. Roma, tel. 22232/22666
C: Adriana, 6 N. Kolyva, Ag. Trias, tel. 28149
C: Aegli, 1 A. Lountzi & 12 Lomvardou, tel. 28317
C: Apollon, 30 Tertseti, tel. 22838
C: Astoria, 1 Rizospaston, Platia D. Solomou, tel. 22419/22719
C: Diana, 11 Kapodistriou & Metropoleos, tel. 28547/28604
C: Phoenix (Finix), 2 Platia Solomou, tel. 22419/22719
C: Zenith, 44 Tertseti & 2 Martinegou, tel. 22134
D: Alfa, 1 Tertseti, tel. 22411
D: Avrochares, 36 Filikon, tel. 22284
D: Charavghi, 3 Xanthopoulou, tel. 22778
D: Diethnes, 102 Ag. Lazarou, tel. 22286
D: Ionion, 18 A. Roma, tel. 22511
D: Kallithea, 15 Dessylla, tel. 22323
D: Kentrikon, 25 L. Zoi, tel. 22374
D: Omonia, 4 Xanthopoulou, tel 22113
D: Ouranion, 7 Ag. Eleftheriou, tel. 22495
D: Rezenta, 36 A. Roma, tel. 22375
E: Acropolis, 13 Filikon, tel. 22373
E: Aghios Stylianos
E: Aketeon, 65 Foskolou, tel. 22685
E: Astir, 5 Ifantourigou, Ag. Georgios, tel. 22110
E: Emborikon, 5 Rizospaston & Dessylla, tel. 22373
E: Nea Zakynthos, 7 Filikon, tel. 22257
E: Oassis, 58 Koutouzi, tel. 22287
E: Olympia, 7 Ifantourgiou & Ag. Georgios, tel. 28328/28479

Tourist police: On Platia Solomou, Tel. 22550

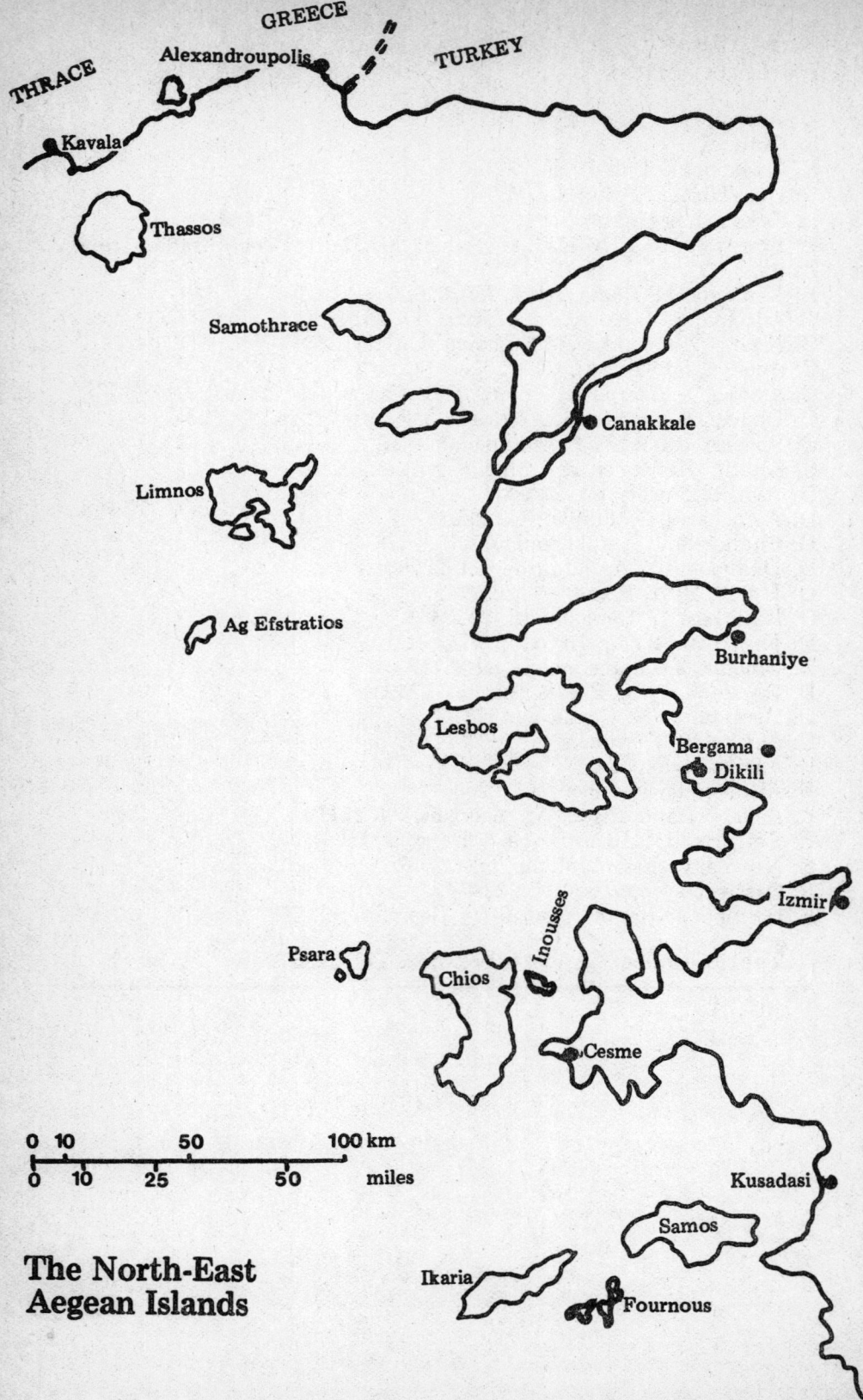

THRACE

GREECE

TURKEY

Alexandroupolis

Kavala

Thassos

Samothrace

Canakkale

Limnos

Ag Efstratios

Burhaniye

Lesbos

Bergama
Dikili

Izmir

Psara

Inousses

Chios

Cesme

Kusadasi

Samos

Ikaria

Fournous

0 10   50   100 km

0 10   25   50   miles

**The North-East
Aegean Islands**

Part 10
The North-Eastern Aegean Islands

The grouping of these seven major islands (Chios, Ikaria, Lesbos, Limnos, Samos, Samothrace, and Thassos) under one title is done nowadays for convenience rather than for any cultural or historical consideration.

What they have in common, however, is their location off the coast of Asia Minor and Northern Greece. The Ionians colonized most of them during the Dorian Invasion of the 12th century BC, when the invaders forced the earlier settlers of the mainland to seek new homes in the east. The Ionians took the coastal regions of Asia Minor and the islands, which flourished during the 7th and 6th centuries BC, producing some of the greatest geniuses of ancient Greece such as Pythagoros, Sappho, and probably Homer himself. The ancient cities on the islands were very important in early Greece, not only in commercial trade and the production of wine and olive oil (the soil is ill suited for other agriculture), but in the religious sphere as well. Samothrace is famous for its sanctuary of the gods of the underworld, Limnos was dedicated to the god Hephaestus, and on Samos, the temple of the goddess Hera was considered one of the Seven Wonders of the Ancient World.

These prosperous independent islands slipped into obscurity as they fell prey to the greater powers around them, who attacked first from Asia Minor and then from the West, and then from Asia Minor again in the form of the Ottoman Empire. They were annexed to Greece only in 1912, following the Balkan Wars.

The north-eastern Aegean islands were the last to be discovered by the summer invasions of visitors, partly due to their great distance from Athens — Ikaria, the closest island to Athens, is a 12-hour journey by ship. Almost all the islands, however, have now built airports to shorten the trip, although anyone planning to fly to one during the summer had better reserve a seat as much as two months in advance (Olympic Airways). Connections between the islands are regular if not exceptionally frequent.

Chios

Connections: Daily flights from Athens; boat five times a week from Lesbos and Piraeus; other connections — twice a week with Limnos, Lesbos, Samos, Ikaria, Patmos, Leros, Kos, and Rhodes; once a week with Thessaloniki and Kavala; daily with Inousse and Tsemai (Cyme), Turkey; twice a week with Psara.

History: Inhabited from approximately 3000 BC, Chios was later colonized by the Pelasgians who left walls near Exo Didyma and Kourounia and a temple of Zeus on top of Mt. Pelion. The Achaeans followed the Pelasgians, and they in turn were usurped by the Ionians. In the 9th century it is believed that the greatest poet of all time, Homer, was born on the island, which was then an independent kingdom with colonies abroad (notably Voroniki in Egypt). By the 7th century BC Chios reached the climax of its importance, famed for its sculpture workshop and system of government. Solon himself studied it and adapted parts of it in his Athenian reforms. In 494 BC the battle of Ladi took place, where the Chiote fleet, outnumbered six to one against the Persians, inevitably succumbed, and the island became part of Persia. Fifteen years later, however, after the battle of Plateia, Chios regained its independence, and held on to it even after Athens moved the treasury of Delos to the Acropolis, subjugating other former island allies as tribute-paying dependencies.

Later Chios allied itself with Rome and fought the enemy of the Empire, Mithridates of Pontus (8 BC) only to be defeated and destroyed, although it was liberated two years later when Mithridates in his turn was destroyed by General Sulla. A few hundred years later Chios made the mistake of siding with Likios against his brother-in-law Constantinos the Great. The latter then conquered the island and carried off to Constantinople many precious sculptures of antiquity, including, it is thought, the bronze horses which ended up in front of St. Mark's in Venice after the sack of Constantinople in 1204. In 1261 the Emperor Michael Paleologos gave Chios to the Genoese for their assistance in reconquering Byzantium. The Genoese lost the island to the Turks three hundred years later, in 1566.

The Turks favoured the island, especially for its production of mastic, which the Turks liked to chew to sweeten their breath. Despite this, Chios rebelled with the rest of Greece in 1822, and the Sultan, angered by this subversion of the island he had so favoured, ordered that the rebellion be quenched. This led to one of the worst massacres in history. In a few days 30,000 Greeks were murdered, and 45,000 others taken into slavery. All who could fled to other islands, such as Syros. The massacre deeply moved the rest of Europe; Delacroix painted his masterpiece of the tragedy and Victor Hugo wrote about it. On 6 June of the same year, the Greek Admiral Kanaris took revenge on Kara Ali, who had carried out the slaughter, by blowing up his flag ship, killing Kara Ali and 2000 soldiers. In 1840 Chios attained a certain amount of autonomy under a Christian governor, and was incorporated into the Greek state in 1912.

Mythology: Chios was supposedly named for the daughter of Poseidon and the nymph Chioni who lived on the island. A later myth suggests it was named for another daughter, this time of King Oenopion, who attracted the attentions of Orion, the handsomest man in the world and a great hunter. Oenopion had little enthusiasm for wedding his daughter to anyone, for he loved her very much himself. However, he promised her to Orion on the condition that he rid Chios of its ferocious beasts, a task the young man easily performed. But rather than give Orion his reward, Oenopion kept putting him off, and finally Orion took the matter into his own hands and violated the girl. For this the king poked out his eyes. Orion then set out blindly, but the goddess of the dawn Eos fell in love with him and persuaded Helios the sun god to restore his sight. Before he could avenge himself on Oenopion, however, Orion was killed. His foolhardy boast that he could rid the world of all harmful creatures made Mother Earth send a snake after him. Orion fled the snake, but his friend Artemis, the goddess of the hunt, killed him by mistake. In mourning, she placed his image among the stars.

Chios today: Chios is a wealthy island, not only because of the numerous ship-owning dynasties it has produced, but for its mastic trees, which grow only in Chios and nowhere else in the world. In August the sweet sap drips down the shrub-like trunks of the trees, glistening like liquid diamonds in the sun, and by September it is ripe for the mastic manufacturer. Mastic gum, sweets, and a liqueur are the major products made on Chios.

The geography of the island surprises one with its variety. While some parts are so barren that one can go for miles without seeing a touch of green, other places are thickly forested and still others are fertile agricultural plains. Byzantine and medieval monuments abound, and the International Society of Homeric studies is based on Chios, where a conference is held every summer.

Chios, the capital of the island, has both tall modern buildings and old houses dating back to the Turkish Occupation. The old town is located within the walls of the **fortress,** a Byzantine structure repaired by the Genoese under Giustiniani. The ancient Macedonian castle had stood on the same site before Mithridates destroyed it in 86 BC. During

Agiasmata

Kabia

Giossona

Ag. Gala

Nagos

Melanios

Marmaron

Kardamila

Parparia

Pirama

Pitios

Volissos

Skala
Volissos

Katavasis

Sidirounta

Anevatos

Vrontados

Karyes

Neo Moni

Chios

Lithion

Karfas

Vessa

Tholopotami

Pass Limani

Kallimassia

Mesta

Kataraktis

Armolia

Olymbai

Fanna

Pirgi

Kalamoti

Emborio

Kommi

Chios

0	2	5	10 km
0	2	5	miles

the period of Turkish rule the Greeks settled outside the walls, and the gate was closed every day at sun-down. Inside is a ruined **mosque** and the **tomb of Kara Ali,** who ordered the massacre of Chios, located in the Turkish cemetery. In a tiny **prison** by the gate Bishop Platanos and 75 leading Chiotes were incarcerated as hostages in incredibly crowded, inhumane conditions before they were all hanged by the Turks in 1822.

The **main square,** with its café and sweet shops, is a few minutes' walk away. On one side stands a statue of Bishop Platanos, and in the municipal gardens behind the square is a statue of "Incendiary" Kanaris. Also in the square is the **mosque** that once housed the **archaeology museum,** which is now located near the Chandris Hotel (open 9am-1pm and 4pm-6pm; 10am-2pm Sunday; closed Tuesday. Entrance 25 dr.; 2.5 dr. with student card. Free Thursday and Sunday). It contains many lovely finds from the island, some marked with the sphinx which was the symbol of ancient Chios. In the same area are modern swimming facilities by the sea. At **Karfas,** twenty minutes down the road, there is another beach with sand as fine as flour, and restaurants renowned for their fresh fish.

The **tourist police** are located by the shore, and on the other side of the quay the crowds take their evening volta by the mastic shops. There are many inexpensive places to eat off the main thoroughfares, and a stand by the square sells souvlaki. The road along the quay is blocked off when an inter-island steamer docks at Chios.

Restaurants: Thilina, Vyzantino, Omavoudris; Yamos at Karfas.

Bazookia: Trias Mili (at Vrontados), Psaradaki (by the airport).

Discotheques: Aquarius, Moutafi, Hotel Xenia.

Specialities: Mastic, ouzo, and other liqueurs.

The rest of the island may be visited by bus or taxi (from the square and municipal gardens). Alternatively, there are six places in Chios town which rent out cars. A trip to **Neo Moni** is perhaps the most beautiful excursion on Chios. Buses go there twice a day. Located high above the town among the pine-wooded mountains, Neo Moni was "new" in 1042, when Emperor Constantinos Monomarchos VIII had it built, to replace an older structure erected by three monks who found a miraculous icon of the Virgin in a burning bush. Constantinos built them a new monastery in gratitude for a prophesy, given by the Virgin through a monk, that he would return from exile and gain the throne of Byzantium. This new, powerful monastery ruled most of the island. Later the Empresses Zoe and Theadora donated the mosaics inside. These are still some of the most beautiful examples of Christian art, although damaged by the Turks during the Massacre, who also stole many of the treasures of the monastery. Besides the mosaics there are other interesting items on display in the church, including a large clock which keeps Byzantine time (the sun rises and sets at 12 every day). One can also visit the chapel which houses the bones of the victims of Kara Ali, and there is an ancient refectory, an underground vaulted cistern, and an old olive press besides the ruins of a settlement that surrounded the monastery. Women should wear skirts to visit Neo Moni. It is open in the morning until noon and in the afternoon from 5pm to 8pm.

A poor road leads to the monastery **Ag. Pateras,** built in honour of the three monks who founded Neo Moni. The present Ag. Pateras dates from 1890, and only men are allowed inside. Further up the road is the striking, deserted village **Anevatos,** the scene of other Turkish brutalities. Above Anevatos stands a medieval castle. By **Karyes** on the way back to Chios town is a church to **Ag. Markus,** built in 1835. Karyes is a pretty mountain village known for its healing waters.

Near **Vrontados** just north of Chios town was the church of **Ag. Isidoros,** build on the site where the first church of Chios was founded in the third century. A later church, erected by Emperor Constantinos the Great, fell in an earthquake and was succeeded by three successive structures, the last ruined by the Turks in 1822. The saint Isidoros was buried on Chios, but his relics were transferred to Venice in the 12th century, where a chapel at St. Marks was constructed to house them. In 1967 Pope Paul ordered the return of one of Isidoros' bones to Chios, and it was placed in the town cathedral. 7th century mosaics discovered at the ruined church can now be seen in the museum.

The beach at **Vrontados** is rocky, and above it are three windmills. On the far side of the harbour is the **Petra Omirous** (Homer's Stone), a rather uncomfortable natural rock throne where the poet is said to have sung and taught. A strange legend has Christopher Columbus stopping at Vrontados before going on to America! At Vrontados the International Society of Homeric studies has its base. The **Monastery of Panaya Myrtidiotissa** nearby, built in the 19th century, has the robes of Gregory V, the Patriarch of Constantinople. Klouvas is a good restaurant in the area.

Kardamila, the largest village of northern Chios, is full of philanthropic gifts from wealthy Chiote ship owners. By **Nagos beach** to the north are the ruins of a **temple of Poseidon,** and nearby **Giossona** was named for Jason of the Golden Fleece. A medieval village in the mountains, to which taxis have a monopoly on transport, is **Pitios,** which has claims to be the birthplace of Homer; one can still see his "house" and olive grove. A 12th century Aegean tower dominates the village where one can find food at the café. The landscape from Pitios towards Chios town is lunar in its burnt emptiness, but just above the village begins a lovely pine forest, filled with fire warnings.

Further to the west the **Monodoktisma Monastery** near Katavasis dates back to the 13th century. Byzantine nobles were exiled in the medieval fortress at **Volissos.** Ag. Markella came from Volissos, considered to be another possible birthplace of Homer, or at least the village where the great poet took his baths. The beach below the town has a restaurant. Another medieval tower rises above the middle of little **Pirama,** where the lovely church of Ag. Ioannes contains some very old icons. **Parparia** to the north is a medieval hamlet of shepherds, and at

Melanios many Chiotes were slain before they could flee to Psara in 1822. On the north-west shore stands the church **Ag. Gala,** by a cave which drips milk ('gala' in Greek means milk). Legend claims that it is the milk of the Virgin, and the church was built during Byzantine times.

South of Chios town towards **Vavli** the church **Panayia Krina** was built in 1287, with old frescoes of the Cretan school inside. At **Scalvia** are many 14th century Genoese villas and gardens, and a few towers remain. The name Scalvia was derived from the Greeks forced to work as slaves for the Genoese nobility. This whole region of the island, south of Chios town and including **Thymiana** and **Kambos,** is very beautiful with its orchards surrounded by tall medieval walls, the gates often inscribed with some forgotten coat of arms. Each of the large medieval houses has a water wheel, which, with the meadows, wooden bridges and ancient trees, creats a scene of rural peace unique on the Greek islands. Among the Genoese country mansions that of the **Argenti** in Kambos has been restored to the old style, including the oxen-turned "Hesiod's water wheel". Mastodon bones have been discovered at Thymiana.

South of Karfas on the coast is the **Ag. Minas** Monastery, built in 1590. In 1822 it was the site of one of the worst massacres of Chios, when women and children from the surrounding villages took refuge there, thinking to escape from the maddened Turks. A small, hopeless battle took place before Ag. Minas was overrun and all 3000 of the Greeks were slain, their bodies thrown down the well. Recently their bones have been recovered and set in an ossuary by the church (closed in the afternoon until 6pm).

Further south, **Kontari,** the beach of Kambos, may have been the site of Levkonion, although a more likely candidate is the old mastic exporting port of **Emborio** further south. Archaeologists have discovered signs of a settlement dating from 3000 BC. East of the port a 7th-century BC **temple of Athena** was found on the ancient acropolis, surrounded by ancient walls. Levkonion, mentioned by Thucydides, was an ancient city and rival of Troy. Some way from the shore are the ruins of a 6th-century **Christian basilica** with mosaics.

This southernmost region of Chios is mastic land, and the villages here were almost all built during the Middle Ages. **Pirgi** in the centre is the largest, dating from the 13th century. It was defended by a Byzantine-style fort, whose walls consisted of the thick outer walls of the houses. Pirgi is fascinating to explore in its excellently preserved medieval state, with tiny arched streets and houses decorated with *sgraffito*, designs scratched onto the stone of the walls. The 12th century **Ag. Apostoli** is decorated with frescoes from the 16th century. The inhabitants of the village preserve many of their traditional customs and dress.

Two other medieval villages, **Olymbai** and **Mesta,** are on the road from Pirgi. Near the former once stood the Great Temple of Apollo Fannas, which had an oracle that Alexander the Great is said to have consulted. Only the fountain by the temple remains today; other items excavated from the site are now in the Chios museum. Two churches in Mesta are worth visiting: the medieval **Ag. Paraskevi** and the 18th-century **Taxiarchos.** North of Pirgi ancient walls and wild rock formations, along with a 12th-century **Panayia Sicelia,** can be seen at **Tholopotami. Armolia** is the site of the castle **Oreas tis Kastro,** a Byzantine fort which was the abode of a beautiful but fatal seductress. Armolia is known for its potteries. **Nenita** and **Kalamoti** are other mastic-growing medieval villages east of Pirgi.

Panayiéria: 15 August, Panayias at Pirgi, Nenita, Kambos and Ag. Georgios; 23 August, Neo Moni; 18 July, Ag. Milianos, outside of Chios town; 22 July, Ag. Markella at Volissos; 23 April, Ag. Georgios at Ag. Georgios.

Three times a day caiques leave Chios for **Inousses** which consists of nine islets in all. On the largest is a School of Navigation, along with other buildings donated by the great ship owners who were born on these large rocks. A medieval fort is near the village, which has a hotel and restaurant with a good deal of lobster. There are a few small beaches for swimming.

Psara to the west of Chios is connected only a few times a week with the larger island. Archaeologists have discovered there signs of the 13th century BC **Achaean** settlement near **Paliokastro,** which was built by refugees who fled to Psara from the misgovernment of the Turks, for the tiny rocky islet had been generally ignored by the Sultan. During the War of Independence the Psariotes contributed many ships to the cause, and they even invented a certain weapon, the bourleta, which the captains of the revolution used to destroy the Turkish fleet. So irksome were the rebel attacks from Psara that the Sultan finally demanded vengeance on the islet.

On 20 June 1824, he sent 25,000 troops to destroy Psara. In the subsequent slaughter only 3,000 of the 30,000 men, women, and children managed to escape to Eretria. The rest were either slain with the Turks in their own explosions, or were massacred when the Turks finally swarmed into Paliokastro after the heroic battle. Thus the islet of Psara was annihilated as the Sultan had ordered. Today 500 people live on Psara, a very quiet place with an inn, a small taverna, and a bit of beach.

Hotels in Chios

The tall seaside **Chandris** in the town of **Chios** is the place to meet the wealthy ship owners of that island back home on vacation. It is ideally located, not in the noisy heart of town yet within easy walking distance of it, and one has merely to cross the street to swim in the seaside pool.

in Chios town: area code 0271
B: Chandris Chios, Prokymaea, tel. 25761; teleg. Chandrotel Chios
B: Xenia, Bella Vista, tel. 23507; teleg. Xenia Chios
C: Aktaeon, 24 Vas. Georgios, tel. 23287
C: Kyma, tel. 25551
D: Filoxenia, Voupalou-Roidou, tel. 23476
D: Palladion, El. Venizelou & 1 Roidou, tel. 22222

D: Pelineon, Prokymaea, tel. 23242
E: Apollon, 1 Zachariou Frourion, tel. 23134
in Kardamyla: area code 0272
B: Cardamyla, tel. 21378
in Inousses: area code 0272
D: Prassonissia, tel. 51313

Tourist Police: on quay at Chios town, tel. 26555

Ikaria
Connections: Four times a week with Samos and Piraeus; daily caique to Fournous; twice a week with Limnos, Lesbos, Chios, Samos, Patmos, Leros, Kalymnos, Kos and Rhodes; once a week with Kavala, Thessaloniki, Mykonos and Syros.

History: In mythology, Ikarus, when fleeing Crete with his father Daedalus, flew too near to the sun with the lovely wings his father had made him. When the wax that held the feathers together melted, the boy plumeted to his death off the south coast of an island thereafter known as Ikaria. More prosaically, its name was probably derived from the Latin word for fish. The most common name of Ikaria in ancient times was Oenoe, or wine island. So much wine was produced on ancient Ikaria that some considered it to be the birthplace of Dionysos, the god of wine. An inscription found on the acropolis describes Oenoe as being second only to Athens in sending the yearly contributions to Apollo on Delos. During the age of Byzantium it is thought that the island was a place of exile, for the ruins of a palace have been found in Kambos. Another large settlement existed at Therma.

During the Turkish Occupation the inhabitants imprisoned their Turkish rulers and for five months Ikaria was an independent state with its own flag and stamps. At the end of 1912 the island joined Greece. Later Greek governments sent political dissidents to Ikaria, who succeeded in making the population one of the most progressive in Greece.

Ikaria today: Ikaria experienced its first large influx of foreign tourists only 1977, and hardly knew what to do with them. The island is known as 'The Island of Radium' and most of the tourists come to take baths at Therma, where the hot springs are considered the most radioactive in Europe. One source, in fact, is so strong that it is a danger to public health and kept permanently closed. There are ten springs on the island, and a plentiful supply of fresh water keeps the rocky land green. The other natural phenonemon Ikaria is known for is its wind. The god of the wind himself is said to live in the mountain which divides the long island into the North Side and the South Side. The Ikarian sea is one of the roughest in Greece and the island has a very low level of humidity for six months of the year.

279

Ag. Kyrikos, the capital and largest port on the island, is in fact rather small, the trees outnumbering the buildings. By the shore there is a small beach, opposite the public toilets, and a large outdoor taverna restaurant above often has live music in the summer. The large pier for the steamers must be the least popular with captains of the high seas, for it often takes an hour or more to bring a ship in, especially on a windy day. The little pier on the other side of the town has a constant bezina taxi service to Therma, only ten minutes away (there is also a road), where most of the island's hotels and restaurants are located. Buses from the square leave once a day for the villages.

People come from far and wide to **Therma,** where the radioactive baths cure chronic rheumatism, arthritis, gout, and spondylitis; one is even reputed to make women fertile. Ruins of ancient baths have been discovered in the region. Just how powerful the baths are is illustrated in the case of two men brought to Ikaria on stretchers: after a twelve-day cure they were dancing in the street. Further up the coast at **Faros** is a well preserved, round Hellenistic tower from the 3rd century BC. This is by the ancient city of **Drakanon,** of which only a few 5th-century BC remains can be seen on the acropolis. Another ancient city of Ikaria was at **Katafyion,** where the acropolis that remains is Archaic. The name Katafyion means "shelter" and refers to an underground passageway beneath the church. One day, it is said, the Turks came to Katafyion with bad intentions, but as it was Sunday all the villagers were at church. The Turks decided to wait outside and capture the people as they came out. They waited and waited, then impatiently broke their way into the church. It was empty! The priest had opened the secret trap door in the floor, and everyone escaped the Turks in safety.

The second most popular spring on Ikaria is also on the south side of the island, called **Therma Lefkados,** or Loutra. Situated in the pine trees by the Toula Hotel and Discotheque, some of its water is so hot that locals on picnics use it to boil their eggs. Athanatos Nero (immortal water) runs between the pretty little **Evangilistria** and **Xilosirti,** where the locals can show you exactly where Ikaros fell. Like most of the villages of the island, Xilosirti is spread out among the trees, particularly apricot trees: Ikarian apricots are said to be the best in Greece. On the way up to the mountain village of **Chrissostomo** is Hartia, a lovely place to visit. All but deserted, it has innumerable raspberry bushes. **Manganitis,** the furthest west of the villages on the south side of the island, has no road as yet nor electricity. A daily caique connects it to Ag. Kyrikos. It is as steep as a stairway, and despite its isolation tends to be one of the liveliest places on Ikaria.

The north side of the island, with its vast pine forests and sandy beaches, attracts more tourists than the south side. **Evdilos,** the largest village, also serves as a steamer stop once a week on the route to Piraeus and Samos. In nearby **Kambos** are the ruins of the **Palatia,** or Palace, dating from the Byzantine settlement of Doliche, or ancient Oenoe, the capital of Ikaria in antiquity. **Ag. Irene** church in Kambos is Byzan-

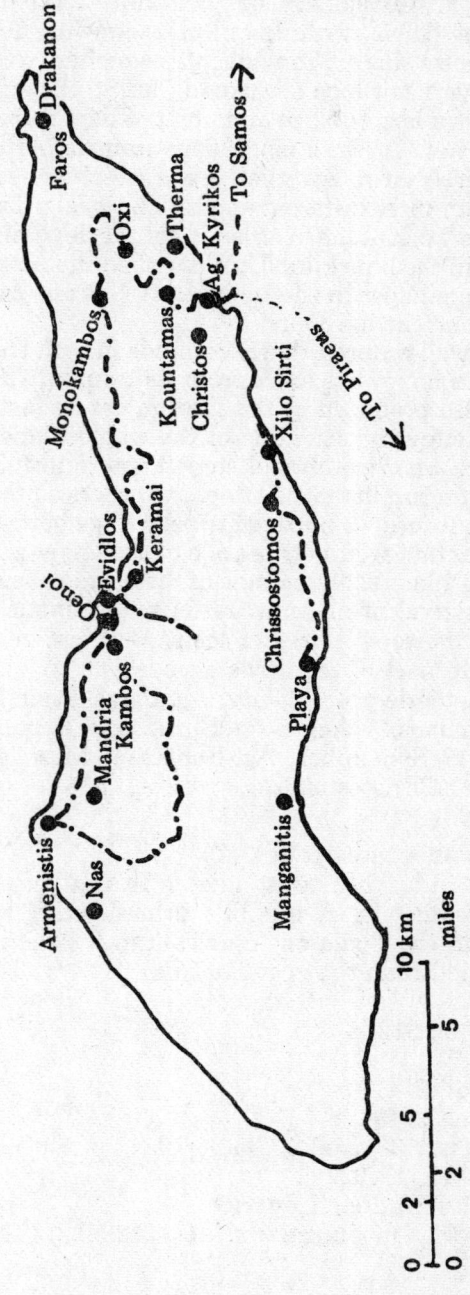

Ikaria

tine, and the local museum houses finds mostly dating from that era. Above Kambos are the ruins of the **Kastro of Koskinou,** by the village of the same name. It was built in the 10th century.

Rachis by a monastery of the same name is called the Little Switzerland of Ikaria, with its tall pines growing down from the mountain onto a sandy shore. Many people come here to camp, and there are rooms and tavernas which are usually full in the summer. Further west **Armenistis** is a large village and point of departure for **Pappas** village and ancient **Nas.** In Nas a marvellous statue of Artemis was discovered about a hundred years ago, the eyes of which are said to have followed the viewer from three different angles. The local priest, however, decided that it was the work of the heathen if not the devil himself and ordered it to be thrown in the lime kiln! Thus perished the Artemis of Ikaria, never to hold its sacred spot in the Louvre. At Nas one can still make out the ruins of the ancient harbour.

Rocky but well watered Ikaria abounds in fruit trees of all kinds. Raki and a delicious honey are made from the koumaro bush. A special canned sweet is also produced in the Ikarian candy factory. In the summer panayiéria occupy the attention of the whole island, when many of the many Ikariots who live abroad come home faithfully just to celebrate. These feasts are run in the old style: one orders a prothesi, which consists of a kilo of goat meat, a bottle of wine, a huge bowl of soup and a loaf of bread — enough to feed four. At one of the larger panayiéria at Christos (above Ag. Kyrikos) 2200 pounds of meat are consumed each year. But the biggest festival of all is on 17 July, in honour of the defeat of the Turks by the Ikariotes in 1912. Feasts, speeches, music and folk dancing in costume are part of the day's agenda.

Other Panayiéria are: 26 July, Ag. Paraskevi in Xilosirti; 27 July, at Ag. Panteleimonos; 6 August at Christos; 8 September, at Playa and Manganitis; 17 September, Ag. Sophia at Mesokambo; 15 August at Akamatra and Chrissostomo.

Hotels in Ikaria: area code 0275

The **Toula (A)** is the newest hotel in **Ikaria,** boasting the island's one and only discotheque. A minibus brings guests to and fro from Ag. Kyrikos. From the Toula one can walk to the thermal baths of Loutra (less frequented than those at Therma).

in Evdilos
E: Georgios, tel. 31218
in Therma
C: Apollon, tel. 21477
D: Ikarion, tel. 21481
D: Radion, tel. 21381; teleg. Radiopalas
D: Thermae, tel. 21432
in Therma Lefkados (Loutra)
A: Toula (hotel and bungalows), tel. 21298/21498/21348; 3622893 in Athens

C: Anna (pension)

Tourist Police: At Ag. Kyrikos, Tel. 21222

From Ag. Kyrikos a caique leaves daily for **Fournous** (known locally as Furni), situated in between Ikaria and Samos and a part of the same nomos. Actually consisting of two islets, the larger Furni is blessed with a huge circular harbour that hid a group of Algerian pirates for many a year, from where they would ambush passing ships. Today the harbour is better known for its fish, especially the much loved barbouni and lobster. Rooms and tavernas may be found in the capital **Chora,** or Furni, which is connected by the island's only road to the village of **Chrissomilia. Thymena** is the village on the smaller islet.

Panayiéria: 23 April, Ag. Georgios; 6 December, Ag. Nikolaos.

Lesbos (Mytilini)

Connections: Daily flights from Athens; connected by sea nine times a week with Piraeus; four times a week with Chios; twice a week with Limnos, Samos, Patmos, Leros, Kalymnos, Kos, and Rhodes. In summer daily connections by Turkish boat to Aivali (ancient Aeolis) in Turkey.

History: Lesbos was settled by 3000 BC; during later years it had contacts with Knossos, and was a territory of Troy. For that reason the Achaeans attacked it frequently during the Trojan war, in particular Achilleus who took the girl Brisies as his battle prize. In the 11th century Aeolians from Thessaly colonized Lesbos and the nearby coast of Turkey. The Archaic period (8th to 6th centuries BC) was the height of the island's civilization, when its capital Mytilini was a centre of Greek culture. Pittachos, one of the Seven Sages of Ancient Greece was from Lesbos, as were the poets Aesop, Alcaeus, and the immortal Sappho who held a marriage school on the island at the beginning of the 6th century BC. She invented the characters Daphnis and Cloe, and her erotic poetry was so intense that the church burnt most of her works at Constantinople in 1073.

Although Lesbos remained strong in the Classical period, the island lost most of its importance and its fortunes swayed with the rise and fall of Athens, Sparta, the Hellenistic rulers, and Rome. Like Chios, Lesbos was given by the Byzantine Emperor Michael Palaeologus to the Genoese for their help in restoring the Byzantine Empire (1261). In 1462 Mohammed the Conqueror captured the island, despite the heroic resistance led by Lady Oretta d'Oria. Lesbos remained in Turkish hands until 1912.

Mythology: Even in myth Lesbos is connected with music and poetry. The mythical-historical musician Arion was a son of the island, accredited with the invention of the dithyramb. His talents brought him great wealth. After a musical contest in Italy, where he had won all the prizes, the crew of the ship bringing him back to Lesbos decided to throw him overboard and keep his treasures for themselves. Arion was allowed to sing for the last time, after which he dived into the sea. His song, however, had charmed the dolphins, and they saved his life, carrying him safely to shore. The ship's crew were later executed for their treachery. Another myth deals with the great poet Orpheus, who was torn to pieces by furious followers of Dionysos and thrown into a river of Thrace. His beautiful head floated to Lesbos, where the inhabitants carried it to a cave. There, Orpheus' head sang and prophesied so well that no one went to Delphi any more to hear Apollo. This angered the god, who came to Lesbos to tell Orpheus' head to be quiet.

Lesbos today: Lesbos, the third largest island in Greece, glistens with the silver of its numerous olive trees, and its mountains are clothed in a thick mantle of pines. Many of the villages retain their Byzantine character, with an architectural style similar to that of northern Greece. True to its artistic heritage, a large municipal theatre hosts many musical and theatrical programmes during the year and there are summer drama festivals. The island has also produced a fine primitive painter, Theophilos (1873-1934). Theophilos, a poor villager, would earn his ouzo by painting lovely pictures on the walls of the island.

The capital of Lesbos, **Mytilini** (which is how most Greeks refer to the whole island), is a large town of magnificent old mansions, impressive public buildings, and beautiful gardens. Its two harbours are divided by what was once an islet, but today is a peninsula, with a **Byzantine-Genoese castle** on top. This was the ancient acropolis of Mytilini, where a temple of Apollo (600 BC) stood. In the area where a canal once flowed between Mytilini and the islet, the remains of an ancient trireme were found, stranded in the accumulation of sand and sediment which filled in the "Euripos of the Mytilineans". The present fortress was founded in the 6th century, and in 1373 the Genoese repaired it with any available material from various epochs. One can still see ancient pillars crammed in between the stones. Inside are numerous buildings left by the various occupants of the fortress, and a well preserved Roman cistern.

In the **north harbour,** the least picturesque side of town, are many small antique shops selling some very unexpected items. By the pine forest above the town, to the north-west, one may find the **Ancient Theatre,** built in the Hellenistic period. It was one of the largest of ancient Greece and Pompey admired it so much that he used its plans to build a theatre in Rome (55 BC). Just north of the north harbour is a wooded hill where campers pitch their tents, and there is a small beach by the shore, **Tsamakia.**

Heading towards the south harbour, the **tourist police** are to the immediate right of passengers disembarking at the pier. The **Archaeology Museum** (open 9am-1pm and 4pm-6pm; 10am-2pm Sunday, closed Tuesday. Entrance 25 dr., 2.5 dr. with student card; free Thursday and Sunday) can be found in a beautiful mansion near the tourist police. Its three small rooms contain mostly pre-historic items from Lesbos, and there are also some carved wooden chests.

Nearer to the heart of town is the **Popular Museum** with folk art and costumes, and south of town (Akrotipi) a museum houses the works of the primitive artist **Theophilos.** Dominating the town the cathedral **Ag. Athanassios** (16th-17th century) should be visited for its carved wooden iconostasis. By **Ag. Therapon** are Turkish fountains, and by **Ag. Kyriaki** are some of the walls of ancient Mytilini. Between the new **Municipal Theatre** (1968) and the post office behind it, the placards advertize films that often include some real classics, and are generally a cut above the film fare offered by the other islands (usually Bruce Lee and spaghetti westerns).

Mytilini is an official port of entry.

Restaurants: Galazia, Thalassa, and Asteria; less expensive — Choriatiki Taverna, Kosmiki, Averof, To Fanari, Gatos, Betaloudes, and Zoumbolis.

Bazookia: Dalabeki, Vrachos, Milton, Xenithes, and Paradissos.

Discotheques: Asteria, What, Space, Totem, Seven.

Specialities: Ouzo, olive oil, sardines.

One can go by bus to the beaches near the town, including **Neapolis, Achivala,** and **Kalimari,** all with tavernas nearby. Buses leave from the square at the back of the harbour. After 8am one must buy a ticket reserving a seat on a bus, unlike other places in Greece where seats are first come, first sit. There are also nine places to rent cars, scooters or bicycles for those who want to see the island under their own steam. The peninsula south of Mytilini, by the airport, is one of the loveliest regions of the large island. There are two long, sandy beaches, one at **Kratigos** with many trees, and **Ag. Ermogenis,** still relatively unknown by the summer crowds. In the region one can see the huge mansion, Villa Sifneios.

Therma to the north is the health spa of Lesbos; just before it lies **Pirgi Therma** with the 12th century Panayia Troullouti. A settlement existed at Therma before 3000 BC until Mycenean times, and its five successive levels of civilization were excavated by Winifred Lamb in 1923-33. Ancient Therma had connections with Troy, and during the Trojan War the Achaeans burnt it to the ground. A large Turkish tower stands by the baths, and there are rooms and restaurants and a beach nearby. **Mantamandos** further north is a large village with a restaurant, Mayeriou, and the interesting 18th century church Taxiarchos Michael. At nearby **Sarakena** is the medieval castle Ag. Theodoros.

On the north coast of Lesbos is the popular town **Methimna,** known also as Molyvos. It was the birthplace of Arion, and the site of the tomb of the Achaean hero Palamedes, who was buried by Achilleus and Ajax. Achilleus besieged the ancient fortress of Methimna but with little success until the daughter of the king of Methimna fell in love with him

285

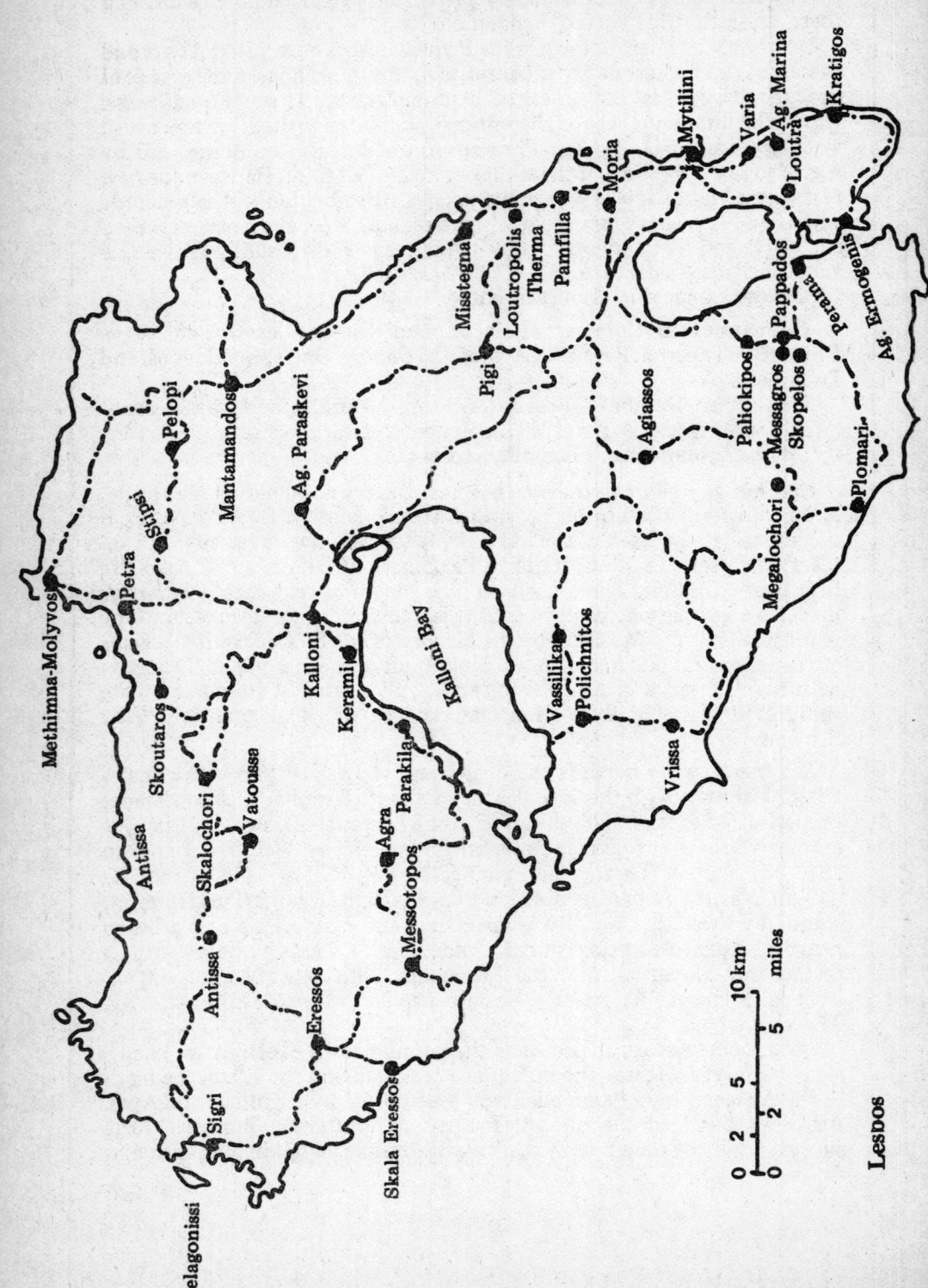

Kratigos

Ag. Marina

Varia

Loutra

Mytilini

Pappadas

Petra...

Moria

Ag. Ermogenis

Pamfilla

Therma

Loutropolis

Misstegna

Skopelos

Messagros

Paliokipos

Pigi

Agiassos

Megalochori

Plomari

Ag. Paraskevi

Mantamandos

Pelopi

Stipsi

Vassilika

Polichnitos

Petra

Kalloni

Kerami

Kalloni Bay

Methimna-Molyvos

Skoutaros

Vrissa

Parakila

Vatoussa

Skalochori

Agra

Antissa

Messotopos

Antissa

Eressos

Sigri

Eressos

Skala Eressos

Melagonissi

10 km

miles

5

5

2

2

0

0

Lesbos

and opened the city gates to him. Despite her kindness to him, Achilleus had her slain for betraying her father. As Mytilini's greatest rival, Methimna insisted on always doing the opposite to that city, and when Mytilini joined Sparta in the Peloponnesian War, Methimna remained in the Athenian confederacy. From Roman times onwards Methimna was frequently attacked. In 1373, when Lesbos belonged to the Genoese, Francesco Gattilusio repaired the old Byzantine fortress on top of the hill, but it fell to Mohammed the Conqueror in 1462.

Modern Molyvos is a very pretty red-roofed village located under the **Genoese castle.** Ruins of ancient Methimna can be seen in many places, especially at **Drapia.** A long, sandy beach has made the town one of the biggest tourist centres on Lesbos, and the night scene is very lively. In the summer classical and modern dramas are performed by different theatre companies. Three buses a day go to Molyvos from Mytilini.

Restaurants: Koxili, Ble Alegou, Nassos, Ippokambos, Ramona and the Delfina Hotel restaurant.

Petra, just south of Methimna, also has a fine beach, and a small **museum** there contains works by Theophilos. A church on a precipice, Panayias, dates from the 18th century. **Kalloni,** a large village further south, is by the ancient city of Arisbe; its acropolis was located where the medieval **Kastro of Kalloni** is today. Arisbe flourished until a few of the local young men abducted some girls from Methimna, whereupon the stronger city responded by destroying Arisbe and enslaving all its people. Also near Kalloni one may visit the **Ag. Ignatius Limonos monastery,** built in the 16th century and containing fine examples of local art. There are three tavernas by **Skala Kalloni beach** and Kalloni bay, where sardines are caught.

At **Ag. Paraskevi,** another village in the region, a rather unusual festival takes place in the second half of May when bulls are ritually sacrificed. It has been suggested that this custom dates back to the ancient rites of the Mithras cult. South of Ag. Paraskevi, at the foot of Mt. Olympos, lies the lovely village of **Agiassos.** Despite its discovery by tourists it remains one of the most interesting settlements of the island. Besides its picturesque houses, there is a medieval castle, the Kastelli nearby, and the **church of the Panayia,** founded in the 12th century by the Archbishop of Mytilini, Valerios Konstantinos, to house an old icon of Mary saved from the iconoclasts. The present church building was constructed in 1812 after a fire destroyed the older structure, and it has one of the most beautiful 19th century interiors of all Greek churches. On 15 August the village is thronged with pilgrims. From the **Kipos Panayias** taverna (up the steps from the bus stop) one has a splendid view of the village and its orchards of fruit trees that produce very good black plums. The village speciality is in ceramics, which are sold in the many shops. From Agiassos one may drive to the top of **Mt. Olympos** and have a superb view of the area.

Polichnitos to the west has a thermal spa and a beach with tavernas. On the south coast **Vrissa** was the hometown of Briseis, but only a wall remains of the ancient Trojan town which was destroyed in 1080. The modern village was built by the survivors. A Genoese tower stands west of Vrissa. **Plomari** to the east has an ouzo distillery producing Greece's best aperitif, and at the small port **Ekranto** there is a restaurant. By **Pappados** is the ruined Paliokastro, of uncertain date, and at **Perama** there is a good sandy beach.

Eressos, a large village in the south-west volcanic part of Lesbos, minted coins depicting Sappho and is thought to have been her birthplace. Ancient Eressos existed north of the present village, near the castle **Xokastro,** and some ruins remain. Nearer the sea, by the **Skala Eressos,** a Byzantine fortress rises on Vigla hill. Although it stood up to the Genoese siege in 1333, it later surrendered to Mohammed the Conqueror after the rest of the island had been captured. Nearby **Apotheka** is a ruined village still retaining a long wall and tower. The modern village of **Antissa** lies inland north of Eressos. Further north again, on the coast, is the site of the Bronze Age town of the same name. Once an islet, **ancient Antissa** was joined to Lesbos in an earthquake. Orpheus' head supposedly ended up here. The Romans later destroyed the town to punish the inhabitants for their support of the Macedonians. **Hourekastro,** a Genoese fort, faces the sea over the ruins of the ancient town, which produced another of Lesbos' great poet musicians, Terpander, inventor of choric poetry. Near Antissa is the **Ag. Ioannes Theologos Ipsilos Monastery,** high on a promontory. Founded in the 9th century and rebuilt in the 12th, there are many old ceremonial items inside. At **Sigri** and the coastal islet Megalonissi are **petrified trees,** 700,000 years to 1,000,000 years old; to see them involves a healthy hike. There is a beach at Sigri, and a Turkish castle (1757) by the shore still has its canons.

Panayiéria: 26 August, Ag. Ermolaou at Paliokipos; 8 May, Ag. Theologos at Antissa; 26 July, at Ag. Paraskevi; 2nd day of Easter and 15 August, at Agiassos; Ag. Magdalinis at Skopelos; end of September, at Plomari.

Hotels in Lesbos

The capital of Lesbos, Mytilini, is rather far from a beach, which makes the swimming pool at the Xenia (B) all the more worthy of consideration. Sappho (C) on the waterfront is nice but somewhat noisy. The increasingly popular Methimna in the north has but one hotel, Delfina (B), located by the sea. To stay there one should reserve well in advance.

in Antissa: area code 0253
E: Athina, tel. 56216
in Eressos: area code 0253
C: Sappho the Eressia, c 12 Theofrastou, Skala, tel. 233
in Kratigos: area code 0277
C: Katia (bungalows), Akti Katia, tel. 25109/28650
in Methimna-Molyvos: area code 0253
B: Delfina, tel. 71315; 22627 in Mytilini; 4121173 in Piraeus; teleg:

Telhotel
in Mytilini: area code 0277
B: Blue Sea, 91 Kountouriotou, tel. 23994/28383
B: Lesvion, Prokymaea, tel. 22037/28177
B: Lesvos Beach (furnished apartments), Neapolis, tel. 27531/24794;
712329 in Athens
B: Xenia, tel. 22713/22717; teleg: Xeniahotel Mytilini
C: Rex, 3 Cataskouli, tel. 28523
C: Sappho, Prokymaea, tel. 28415/22888/24522; teleg: Sappho
D: Lycabettus, 1 Limnou, tel. 28791
E: Kentron, tel. 25172
E: Megali Bretannia, Prokymaea, tel. 28449
in Pappados: area code 0277
E: Splendid, tel. 82217
in Petra: area code 0278
C: Petra, tel. 41257
in Plomari: area code 0252
C: Oceanis, tel. 32469/32498
in Polichnitos: area code 0252
E: Olympos, tel. 41443
in Sigri
B: Nisiopi (pension), tel. 6
in Thermi: area code 0277
B: Blue Beach, tel. 28376
B: Votsala (motel), Paralia, tel. 71231
E: Sarlitza, Paralia, tel. 71219
in Vrissa: area code 0252
E: 55 Kentriki Agora, tel. 61206

Tourist police: Customs house, tel. 22776 in Mytilini

Limnos

Connections: Daily flights from Athens and twice a week from Thessaloniki. Ferry boat twice a week from Kavala and Thessaloniki, also connected twice a week with Lesbos, Chios, Ag. Efstratos, Samos, Ikaria, Patmos, Leros, Kalymnos, Kos, Rhodes; ferry boat three times a week from Kimi, Evia.

History: A settlement on Limnos, Paliochoe, dates back to 4000 BC and is one of the oldest Neolithic settlements of the Greek islands. In the Bronze Age its inhabitants traded with Troy and spoke a language similar to Etruscan. Hesphestia was the Classical capital, and for a time the island attracted adherents of the Caberi cult until the religion was centred on Samothrace. Limnos was taken by the Venetians in the 13th century, and then retaken by Kario for Byzantium. In 1475 Mohammed the Conqueror sent Turkish troops to Limnos. They would have captured the island were it not for the leadership of the Limniote heroine Maroula, who seized her dying father's weapons and shouted the battle cry. In 1478, however, Mohammed himself came and took the island, and the Turks held it until 1912. In the First World War Moudros Bay became famous as a naval base of the Allies.

Mythology: Limnos was the island of the iron and fire god Hephaistos, for it was there that he landed when a furious Zeus hurled him from Mt. Olympus for daring to defend his rebellious mother Hera. The fall left Hephaistos crippled forever, despite all the care lavished on him by the islanders. The ancient capital of Limnos was named for the god, who was so beloved that when his wife, the goddess of love Aphrodite, betrayed him with Ares, the women of Limnos stopped worshipping her. Aphrodite retaliated by making their breath and underarms stink, which led the good men of Limnos to prefer the company of captive Thracian women to that of their own wives. This led to further incidents: the women of Limnos doctored their husbands' wine to make them sleep, and then slit their throats, throwing their bodies into the sea. Henceforth the smelly women of Limnos lived as Amazons, warlike and independent. When Jason and the Argonauts appeared on the horizon, the women would have attacked had not one of them realized that a shipload of Greek heroes was just what they needed to continue the Limniot race. So the Argonauts, rather than facing battle at Limnos, met only the kindest courtesy.

In another story the hero Philotekes was left on Limnos after a snake bit him when the Achaeans were on their way to Troy. For ten years the poor man suffered from his wound, living in a cave, with only his spear to help him hunt for his dinner. After the death of Achilleus, a prophecy declared that the Achaeans could take Troy only with the spear of Philotekes, and as Sophocles' play *Philotekes* recounts, Odysseus and Neoptolemos, the son of Achilleus, went to retrieve it.

Limnos today: Of all the Aegean islands, Limnos lies the lowest above sea level. Green and lovely in the spring, it becomes rather yellow in the summer when water is in short supply (it is turned off between 6 pm and 6 am). Besides agriculture, much of the flat land of Limnos is devoted to grazing animals. There are some very imaginative scarecrows on the farms. Limnos is in the process of asphalting its roads, perhaps in the hope that such a move will bring more tourists than the few that visit the island now, despite its many beaches.

Every morning in **Myrina** (or Kastro), the capital town of Limnos, one wakes up to the voice of the town crier: "Wake up, you tourists! Eggplants! Figs!" Like Mytilini, Myrina town is divided into two parts by its acropolis and **castle,** a very impressive structure with a classical foundation. A good road leads to the top of it from the north side of the harbour, where there is a long stretch of sandy beach and the **Archaeology Museum** (open 9 am-1 pm and 4 pm-6 pm; 10 am-2 pm Sunday; closed Tuesday. Entrance 25 dr., 2.5 dr. with student card; free Thursday and Sunday) in the mansion of the Turkish Pasha, on the other side of the bridge. Upstairs are prehistoric remains, mostly from Paliochoe, divided into four different periods by colours; the oldest, the 'Black' period, is from 4000 BC. Downstairs are more recent discoveries from Hephestia, Chloi, and Myrina.

On the cape beyond the pretty beach **Akti Myrina,** it is said that the women of Limnos hurled their hapless husbands into the sea. This north side of Myrina has most of the town's night life.

The long, main shopping street runs down to the south, commercial harbour (Limnos is an official port of entry), passing the banks, the post office, OTE, etc. Some of the old houses are built in the Turkish or Thracian style, and although Myrina isn't an exceptionally pretty town, its gardens and old houses give it a touch of charm. From the north harbour there are caiques to the **Morasiti sea cave.**

Restaurants: Papamalis, Kangouries, Platanos, Tasos Taverna.
Discotheques: Oasis, Akti Myrina.
Specialities: Thyme honey (the honey of the gods), the best peaches in Greece, wine (muscat and white).

One can rent a car in Limnos, or visit the villages by bus, although the service is rather infrequent. South of Myrina, **Platis** (with a beach, and a bazookia on Wednesday) and **Thanos** are quiet little villages frequented by the townies, although their favourite is **Tsimantria** by Moudrous bay, where there are restaurants with music at weekends. South of Tsimantria at **Vryokastro** fort are the remains of Mycenaean walls. During the First World War the large **Moudros Bay** was the Allies' naval base for their Gallipoli campaign, and on 7 September, 1912 a great naval battle took place there. To its north is the island's airport.

North of the bay, towards the north coast of the island, is the village of **Kotsinas.** A statue to the heroine Maroula stands here and a spring with good water flows down a long stairway by the church **Zoodochos Pigi.** Ancient walls remain, and there is a good beach and view of the island from the top of the village. Ancient **Hephestia,** further west along the coast, derives its name from the god who made a rather ungraceful landing there when tossed from Mt. Olympos. Part of the theatre remains together with houses, and an agora. A medieval fortress also remains at the nearby village **Kokkino.** Another ancient site, excavated by the Italian School of Archaeology (who have done almost all the work on Limnos) is **Chloi,** the site of one of the most ancient sanctuaries of the Underworld deities, the Cabeiri (associated with the earth gods of fertility). In the Archaic period women came here to pray for fertility. The Italians found a 6th-7th century BC temple of initiation, dedicated to Thracian Aphrodite; in fact, there are two buildings, the old and the more recent. The cave of Philoktetis is also at Chloi.

On the tip of the north-east peninsula lies **Plaka.** Castello Plaka is a city in the sea, fallen into the waves after an earthquake. If one goes out in a boat, the city can be seen below, especially on a calm day. Jacques Cousteau did some exploring in the area. There are two lakes on the east

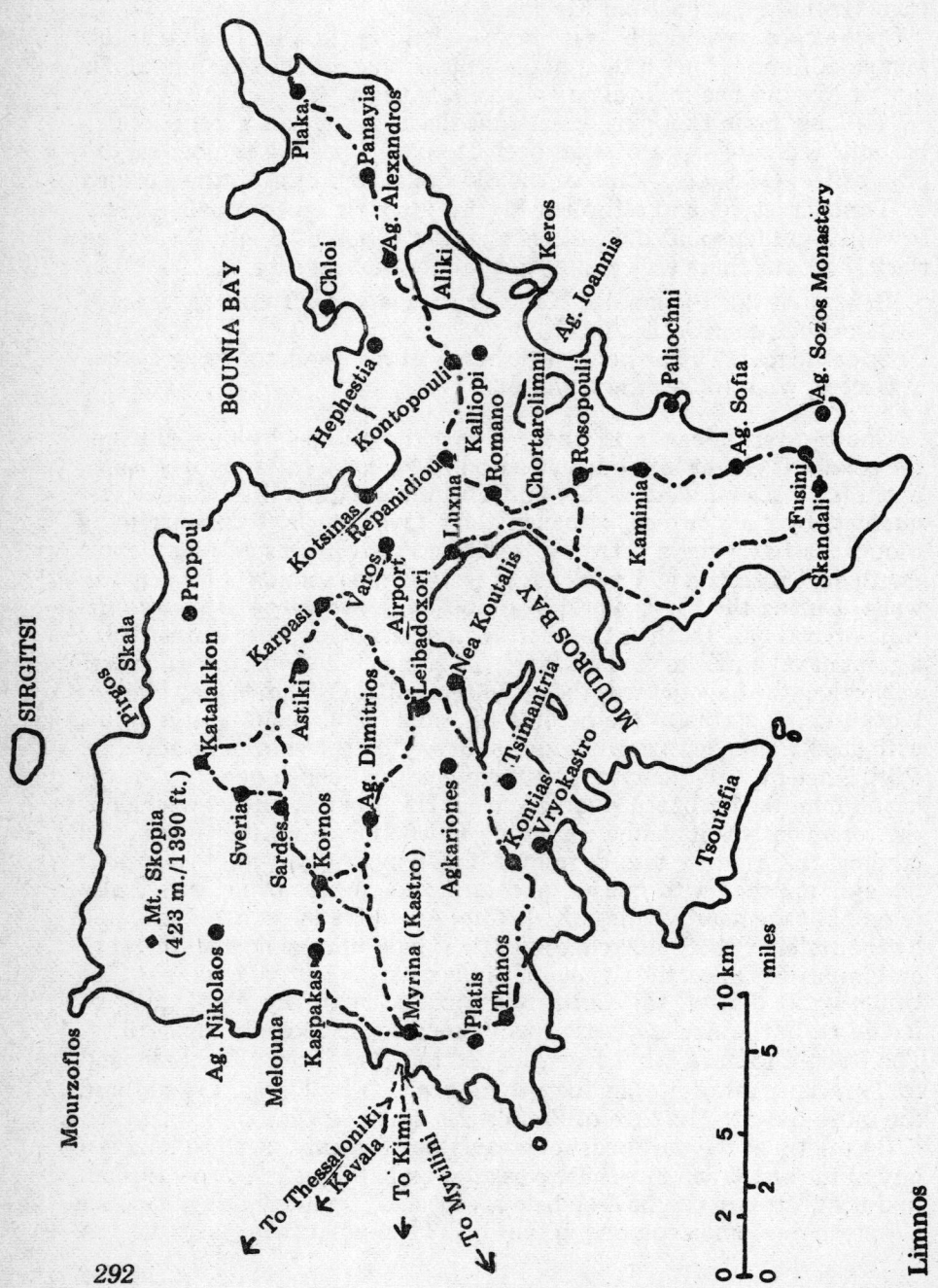

SIRGITSI

BOUNIA BAY

Plaka
Panayia
Ag. Alexandros
Chloi
Aliki
Keros
Ag. Ioannis
Paliochni
Ag. Sozos Monastery
Hephestia
Kontopouli
Chortarolimni
Rosopouli
Ag. Sofia
Kotsinas
Repanidiou
Kalliopi
Romano
Kaminia
Fusini
Luxna
Skandali
Propoul
Varos
Airport
Leibadoxori
Nea Koutalis
MOUDROS BAY
Pirgos Skala
Katalakkon
Karpasi
Ag. Dimitrios
Tsimantria
Tsoutsfia
Mt. Skopia
(423 m./1390 ft.)
Astiki
Agkariones
Kontias
Vrvokastro
Sveria
Sardes
Kornos
Myrina (Kastro)
Thanos
Ag. Nikolaos
Melouna
Kaspakas
Platis
Mourzoflos

To Thessaloniki
Kavala
To Kimi
To Mytilini

10 km
miles

Limnos

side of Limnos, **Aliki,** which has salt water, and **Chortarolimni,** which is dry in the summer and filled by river torrents in the spring. On the bay, **Moudron** village has a beach and tavernas, and from there one can visit **Paliochne,** where four periods of settlements, on top of one another, were excavated by the Italian School. The lowest, oldest settlement predates the Egyptian dynasties, the Minoan kingdoms of Crete, and even the earliest level of Troy. Walls and houses remain of the next oldest city (2000 BC) which was probably destroyed by an earthquake; the third city dates back to the early Bronze Age and the newest coincides with the Myceneans (1500 BC). **Ag. Sozos monastery** to the south looks over the sea from a high cliff. This whole south-eastern peninsula is planted with vineyards.

North of Myrina, **Mt. Skopia** is the highest point on Limnos, and can be climbed from Ag. Nikolaos where the road ends. **Pirgos** on the coast has a small fort, Mikro Kastelli, and ancient tombs have been found in the region. Nearby **Skala** has some pretty sea caves that one may see by boat from Myrina or perhaps Kotsinas. **Astiki** to the south is one of the larger villages of the island.

Panayiéria: 23 April, Ag. Georgios at Kalliopi — horse races are run by the locals, who bet goats on the outcome; 26 October, Ag. Dimitrios at Ag. Dimitrios; 15 August, at Kaminia and Tsimantria; 6 August, Sotiris at Vlaka; 7 September, Ag. Sozos; 21 May, Ag. Konstantinos at Romano.

Hotels in Limnos: area code 0276

In **Myrina,** the capital of **Limnos,** the **Akti Myrina bungalows (L)** are located on the long sandy beach on the north side of town, protected by some rather interesting rock formations. It is a short walk from the peaceful bungalows to the finest tavernas on the island, the two discotheques, the fortress, and the museum.

in Myrina
L: Akti Myrina (Myrina Beach) (bungalows), tel. 22681; 3230249 in Athens; teleg. Aktimyr Lemnos
C: Lemnos, Platia 28th Oktovriou, tel. 22153
C: Sevdalis, 6 Garofalidou, tel. 22691
D: Aktaeon, 2 Arvanitaki, tel. 22258
D: Thraki, 23 28th Okyovriou, tel. 22617

Tourist police: Regular police in Myrina.

Far off the south-west coast of Limnos lies little **Ag. Efstratios,** belonging to the same nomos. Rich in minerals (including petroleum), the islet has been inhabited from Mycenean times, and on the north coast one can see the walls and ruins of the ancient settlement, which lasted into the age of Byzantium. In 1967 an earthquake struck Ag. Efstratios, and ruined its port and major village, which has now been rebuilt higher up above the sea. Although there are some fine beaches, very few tourists visit the little island; there are no hotels and only a few rooms to rent. The 400 inhabitants make their living from sheep, goats,

and fish. There is a taverna where one can find food. Every few days a
ship from Kimi or Limnos stops at the islet.

Samos
Connections: Daily flights from Athens; almost daily ferry boats from
Piraeus and Ikaria; many daily connections with Kusadasi, Turkey (via
Epheses) in the summer but none in the winter; twice a week with Lim-
nos, Lesbos, Chios, Patmos, Leros, Kos, Kalymnos, and Rhodes, Syros
and Mykonos; once a week with Kavala and Thessaloniki.

History: By 3000 BC Samos was inhabited by Pelasgians who
worshipped Hera, the wife of Zeus, believing that she was born on the
island by the stream Imbrassos. Her first temple was built by the
mythical king Angaios, who was a member of the crew of the *Argos* on its
quest for the Golden Fleece. In the 11th century BC the Ionians invaded
Samos, and by the Archaic period the island was enjoying a great
prosperity, and producing an excellent wine. In 670 BC Samos became a
democratic state and its citizens grew wealthy from commercial activities. The swift battleship *Samaina* was designed there. The great
mathematician and philosopher Pythagoros was born on Samos in the
6th century BC. Not only did he invent the right angle theorum for which
all school children know his name, but he was the first to note the
mathematics of music and the planets and the beauty of proportions, an
idea that brought perfection to Classical architecture and sculpture.
Aristarchus, a later Samian mathematician, was the first in history to
put the sun in the centre of the universe. In the late 6th century Samos
was ruled by the famous tyrant Polycrates, probably the most powerful
man in Greece at the time. Samos then became a grand imperialistic
power, taking even Delos. Under Polycrates the grand temple of Hera
was built, one of the Seven Wonders of the Ancient World, and the
engineering miracle, the Efplinion tunnel, was dug through a mountain
to bring water to the then capital of the island, modern Pythagorion.

The Persians occupied Samos during their second invasion of Greece
and kept their fleet at the island. During the battle of Plataea (479 BC)
the Greek fleet attacked them at Mycale, the strait between Samos and
Turkey, soundly defeating them (helped by the defection of the Ionians
in the Persian navy to the Greek side). After the battle of Mycale, the
Persians no longer posed a threat to Greece from the sea. Samos allied
itself with Athens following the battle, but during the Peloponnesian
War, Lysander, commander of the Spartans, took the island. Epicurus
was born on Samos at the end of the century.

In 129 BC Rome incorporated Samos as part of her Asia Province, and
Augustus often visited the island in the winter, granting it many
privileges, despite the fact that his enemies Antony and Cleopatra had
lived there for a short time.

After the sack of Constantinople Samos was captured by the Venetians and Genoese. In 1453, when the Turks came to take their place, the inhabitants took refuge on Chios, leaving their island deserted for 80 years. Gradually the population returned, and many Turks also settled on the fertile island, although life became uncomfortable for them in 1821 when the Samiots joined the revolution. The second battle of Mycale was fought against the Turks in 1824, and again the enemy from Asia Minor was defeated at sea. Although Samos was excluded from joining Greece in 1830, it was granted semi-independence under a Christian governor appointed by the Sultan. In 1912, the Samian National Assembly took advantage of Turkey's defeats in the Balkan Wars to declare unity with Greece, under the leadership of Sophoulis, later Prime Minister of the country. The union was ratified at the end of the war.

Samos today: With its verdant hills and golden beaches, Samos has had a great surge of tourism in the past year or so which caught the inhabitants somewhat by surprise: extra food had to be imported quickly and the water commissioner stayed up many nights worrying about how to give all these people their baths. Much of the island is planted with vines, producing the wine immortalized by Lord Byron in his revolution-inspiring poem, "The Isles of .Greece". The women of Samos are also reputed to be the most beautiful in Greece, but of course such a claim is called into question by almost every other place in Greece.

When coming from Athens, ships dock at **Vathi,** the second port of the island and its capital. Although the immediate port is called Samos and the older town higher up is officially Vathi, the latter name is usually used for the whole area, which became the capital only in 1832. A **Youth Hostel** is located near the waterfront, on Sofouli and Smyrnas Streets. Behind the very colourful **Public garden** and zoo (with deer, chickens, and a monkey) is the **archaeology museum** (open 9am-1pm and 4pm-6pm; 10am-2pm Sunday; closed Tuesday. Entrance 25 dr., 2.5 dr. with student card. Free Thursday and Sunday). Most of the items inside come from Pythagorio and Hereon; the griffin, the ancient symbol of Samos decorates the pottery. The **Byzantine Museum** is behind the pier on 28th Oktovriou Street, and it contains objects used in the church services. A little way further up Sofouli Street is the **Municipal Library,** with some interesting old editions, and the **British Consulate.** Platia Pythagorio with its cafés and sweet shops attracts tourists and soldiers in large numbers. The **town hall** exhibits momentoes from Samos' fight for freedom.

Boats to Turkey leave at 8.30 in the morning and there are also day excursions to Patmos. **Buses** leave frequently for nearby **Gagou beach** and other popular places on the island.

Restaurants: Zorbas, Vassilis, Gregorios, Fagas, Koutopula Stellos (chicken), Gagou (with music at night).

Discotheques: Koukili; others at Mytilini Akoukarion and Kilamanjaro.

Bazookia: Samos by Night, Ximeromata.

Specialities: Muscat wine, Fokiano wine, and Samina (dry).

The hinterlands of Samos are very lovely, consisting of rolling green hills and valleys. There are two mountains, Kerkis and Ampelos.

The **Zoodochos Pigi Monastery** to the east was built in 1756 on a high hill overlooking the coast of Asia Minor. The village of **Possidonion** and one of the beaches called **Psili Ammos** are on the south-east coast of Samos (connected by bus from Vathi). Another, larger beach called Psili Ammos lies on the south-west coast.

Closer as the crow flies than by actual road from the eastern Psili Ammos is **Pythagorio,** the most popular village on Samos and its most ancient capital. Many relics remain from the great age of Polycrates, the most impressive being the **Efplinion tunnel** about a mile north of the town. Efplinos, the chief engineer of Polycrates, had it dug by slaves who worked on the project for years; some started on one side of Mt. Kas, some on the other, and they met each other exactly in the middle. The tunnel is more than 900 metres (1000 yards) long, and used to bring water to Pythagorio from the springs of Mt. Ampelos. A path runs along half of the tunnel and can be reached by climbing down from the **Tigani Temple**: bring a flashlight.

The **long walls** that surrounded ancient Pythagorio are also very impressive, although they were partly destroyed by Lysander when the Spartans took Samos. They were 6500 meters (7100 yds.) long, running all the way to Cape Fonias, and protected with towers and gates. The modern village of Pythagorio was built on the **ancient harbour mole,** another masterpiece of Efplinos; some of its foundations may still be seen. Little remains of the **ancient theatre** (en route to the tunnel), but above Pythagorio is **Spiliani,** the cave where the prophetess Sybilla Feto spoke of a one and true god. The cave has a lake inside, and a church, **Panayia Spiliani** built in 1836. Lycurgos Logothetis, a hero of the 1821 Revolution, built a **fort** by the town and there is also a **museum** housing local finds. Nearby beaches are at **Fonias** and **Iratis Bay.** Pythagorio is an official port of entry with a yacht supply station, and from there one can go to Patmos, Kusadasi (Turkey), Agathonissi, and **Samiopoula.** The latter lies off the south coast of Samos. It is a pretty little islet with trees, a beach, a restaurant, and a pension. There are many restaurants and a discotheque in Pythagorio.

From there the **Sacred Way,** once lined with statues, leads to the **Hereon,** or the Temple of Hera, the largest ever built in Greece and one of the Seven Ancient Wonders. One pieced-together column remains of what was once a great gallery of art; the temple itself was 107 metres (354 ft.) by 52 metres (171 ft.). Twice a year a grand celebration took place there, in honour of Hera's birth by the Imbassos stream nearby and her marriage to Zeus. In mythology Zeus had to use cunning to seduce an uninterested Hera (perhaps because he was her brother), and they spent a 300-year-long wedding night on Samos. Other curiosities at the site include the **altar, a Mycenean wall,** other small temples and buildings,

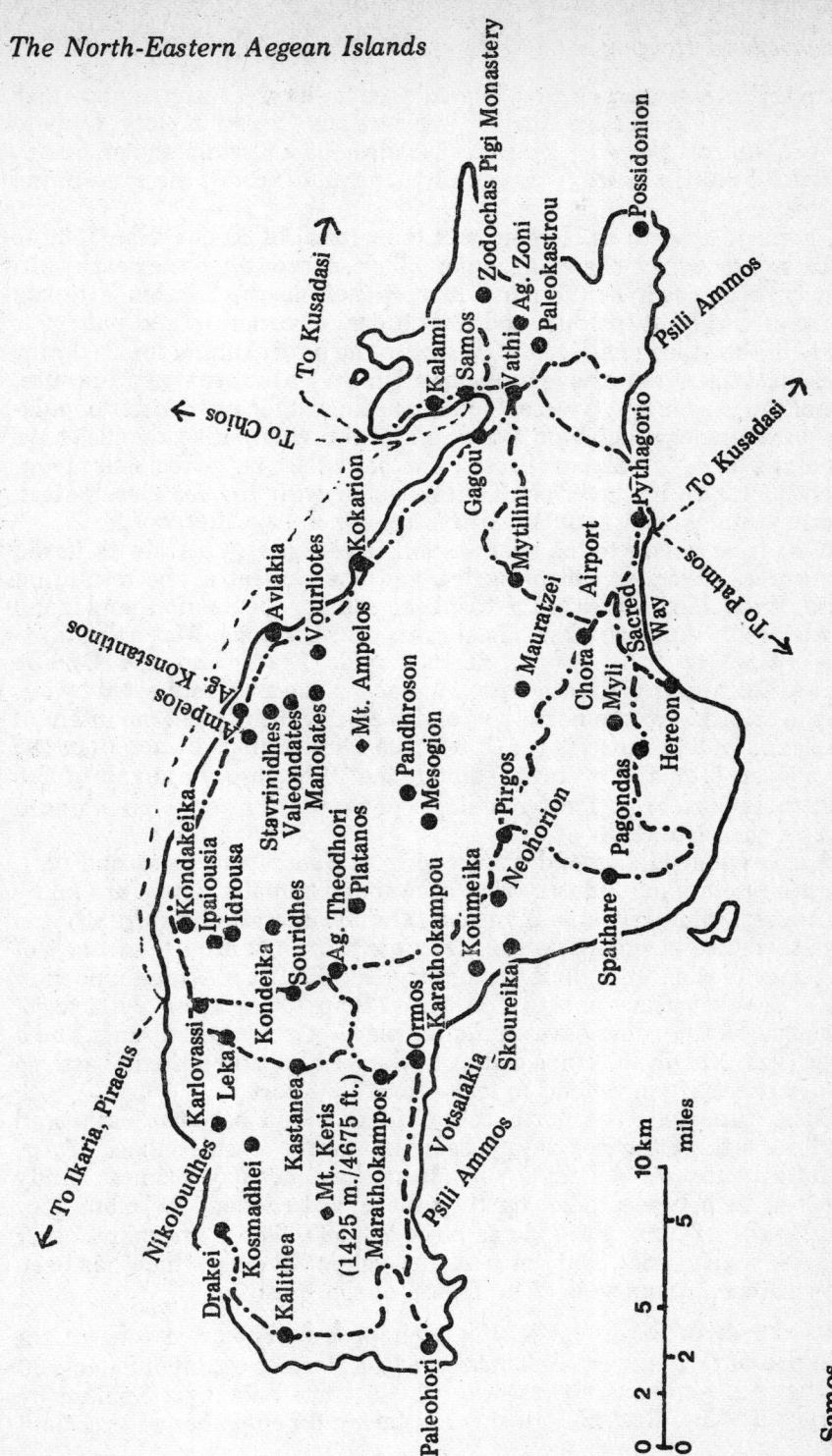

The North-Eastern Aegean Islands

Samos

Zodochas Pigi Monastery
Possidonion
Ag. Zoni
Paleokastrou
Psili Ammos
Kalami
Samos
Vathi
To Kusadasi
To Chios
Gagou
Mytilini
Pythagorio
To Kusadasi
Kokarion
Airport
To Patmos
Avlakia
Vourliotes
Mauratzei
Chora
Sacred Way
Ampelos
Mt. Ampelos
Pandhroson
Myli
Ag. Konstantinos
Stavrinidhes
Valeondates
Manolates
Mesogion
Pirgos
Pagondas
Hereon
Kondakeika
Ipaiousia
Idrousa
Souridhes
Ag. Theodhori
Platanos
Neohorion
Spathare
Kondeika
Karathokampou
Koumeika
Karlovassi
Leka
Ormos
Skoureika
Nikoloudhes
Kastanea
Votsalakia
To Ikaria, Piraeus
Kosmadhei
Marathokampos
Psili Ammos
Drakei
Kalithea
Mt. Keris
(1425 m./4675 ft.)
Paleohori

10 km
miles
5
5
2
2
0
0

Samos

and a **tribute** sent by Cicero. The damage to the great temple and other antiquities is attributed to various invaders and Christian piety. The site is open during the day; entrance 25 dr., 2.5 dr. with student card. **Sarakini castle** nearby was built by a naval officer of the same name in 1560.

Chora, just north of Hereon, was the capital of Samos from 1560 to 1855, and today is a charming, quiet village, except when the nearby airport is being used. To the north **Mavratzei** has the **Timios Stavros Monastery,** built in 1592, and a good deal of ceramics and pottery is made in the village itself. In **Mytilini** to the north animal fossils dating back 15,000,000 years have been placed in the **Paleontology Museum,** one of the very few in Greece. Samos was known for its monster population in mythology, although today in Mytilini village discotheques have taken the place of fearsome beasts. Another village in the region is mountainous **Pirgos,** by the lovely **Koutsi,** which, with its trees, clear waters, and mountains, is a popular destination for a lazy afternoon.

Platanos village to the west is another very pretty place with its old plane trees, river, and nightingales, and one can eat at the restaurant there. **Votsalakia** rates as the best beach among the Samiots, and it and nearby **Psili Ammos** have restaurants and pensions. **Marathokampos** village, a little to the north, builds boats, and the **Ormos Marathokampou** is another pretty beach in the area, connected by bus from Karlavassi to the north. On **Mt. Kerkis,** the highest mountain of the island at 1425 metres (4675 ft.) (the name Samos comes from the Phoenician "sama" for "high") stands the 10th century **church of the Annunciation.** From **Drakei** village one may visit a very high ceilinged cave in the mountain.

Karlovassi, the second largest town of Samos and its second port, has a large tanning industry that occasionally smells. There are many old houses, some veritable mansions, and an interesting bridge. By the town there are two monasteries: **Panayia tou Potamou** (Our Lady of the River) dating from the 10th century, and **Profitis Elias** founded in 1703. Less tourists come to Karlovassi than to Vathi or Pythagorio, although the town does have swimming places nearby, restaurants, and a night club. Not all the ships calling at Samos also stop at Karlovassi, so always check if you intend to leave from that port.

Buses run along the north coast of the island between Vathi and Karlovassi three times a day, passing the pretty seaside village of **Ag. Konstantinos.** At **Avlakia** and **Kokarion** one may swim at sandy beaches. In between them, by the village **Vourliotes,** the monastery **Our Lady of Vrontiani** dates back to 1560. There are many other villages, small, quiet, and verdant, throughout Samos, which has been known since antiquity as "The Island of the Blest".

Panayiéria: 27 July, Ag. Panteleimonos at Kokarion (one of the most popular); 6 August, Celebration of the Revolution, all of Samos; 29 August, Ag. Ionnes at Pythagorio; 21 November, Panayia Spiliani by Pythagorio; 26 July, Ag. Paraskevi at Vathi; 8 September at Vrontiani

Monastery; 20 July, Profitis Elias celebrated in many villages throughout the island.

Hotels in Samos: area code 0273

In Samos town, both the Xenia (B) and the Samos (C) face the huge harbour, centrally located and relatively modern. The daily boats to Turkey dock before them.

in Hereon
D: Hera (Ira), tel. 27247
in Karlovassi
B: Merope, Pefkakia-Alsos, tel. 32650/32510
D: Aktaeon, Limin, tel. 32356
D: Morpheus, tel. 32672/32262/32671; teleg Morfeus Karlovassi
D: Samion, N. Vliamou, tel. 32309; teleg Samion
in Kokarion
C: Kokkari Beach, tel. 28538/28563
C: Venus (Aphrodite), tel. 28530/28560
D: Lito, tel. 28507
In Pirgos
D: Koutsi, Koutsi, tel. 61389
in Pythagorio
C: Damo, tel. 61303.
C: Dolfin (Delfini), Paralia, tel. 61205.
C: Polycrates, tel. 61398.
C: Pythagoras.
D: Alexandra, 11 Lykourgou, tel. 61429.
in Vathi (Samos)
B: Xenia, 23 Themistokli, Sofouli, tel. 27463/28461.
C: Avlakia, Avlakia, tel. 28512.
C: Samos, 6 Themistokli Sofouli, tel. 28377.
D: Artemis, 4 Kontaxi, tel. 27792; teleg. C. Kateris.
D: Hera (Ira), 4 Kalomiri, tel. 27247.
E: Parthenon, Themostokli Sofouli, tel. 27234.
E: Poleos, tel. 27506.

Tourist Police: Regular police at Vathi or Pythagorio.

Samothrace (Samathraki)

Connections: Ferry boat twice a week from Kavala; daily boat at 9am from Alexandroupolis, which has an airport (every other day in winter).

History: Once densely inhabited and forested, Samothrace owed its importance to its location by the straits of the Dardenelles. Settled in the Neolithic period, an Iron Age population from Thrace built the first temple on the island (the rock altar beneath the Arsinoeion). In the 8th century BC Aeolians from Mytilini colonized Samothrace and mingled apparently peaceably with the earlier settlers, worshipping Athena and the

Great Gods of the Thracians. These were chthonic deities (of the earth and underworld), darker and older in origin than the twelve gods of Olympos. A great mother figure was the centre of worship in the cult, which also included Hekate — the Queen of the Night and witchcraft, and Aphrodite on the female side, and Kadmilos-Hermes, the less important spouse, on the male side, along with the Cabeiri, the demonic twins the Greeks later associated with the Dioscuri, who protected sailors and are thought to be Phoenician in origin. As in Eleusis, members were initiated, although the rites of the Great Gods were more open and cosmopolitan in nature. There were two levels of initiation, the higher stage believed to involve a confession of misdeeds. On certain summer days a grand fete took place, to which ambassadors were invited from all over the known world. Philip II of Macedon and Herodotus are among some of the famous initiates, and in mythology even the Argonauts, at Orpheus' suggestion, joined the cult for extra protection before entering Hellespont.

Samothracians colonized in Alexandroupolis and had their own navy. In the 5th century BC the island joined the Athenians which, as for all the other islands, meant a decline in importance. The Sanctuary of the Great Gods, however, attracted more and more pilgrims every year, saving the island from obscurity. The Hellenistic kings of Macedonia and the Romans were also faithful adherents to the mysteries there. Occasionally they used Samothrace as a naval base, relying on its sacred soil for protection.

In the Roman period, the island began to suffer from invasions and earthquakes. St. Paul stopped there, but failed to convert many of the locals, who continued to repair the damaged sanctuary until the 4th century AD. During the age of Byzantium Samothrace was depopulated and forgotten. Pirate raids forced the remaining inhabitants to the hills, where they settled Chora. The Genoese ruler Gattilusi fortified the castle, affording them some protection. After the fall of Byzantium to the Turks, Samothracians were sent to resettle Constantinople. Under the Turks life was very quiet, apart from a few uprisings during the War of Independence. Samothrace joined Greece in 1912.

Samothrace today, even in July and August, attracts few tourists, its relative inaccessibility probably being the main reason behind this. By September the only visitors are the archaeology lovers and a few Germans. There is only one sandy beach on Samothrace, although there are sufficient hotels and restaurants for those who come, and camping is possible almost anywhere. Samothrace today has lost most of its forests, consisting mainly of rocks and stony fields: no longer quite "the Samos of Thrace," as its name claims.

High in the hills, **Chora** remains the capital of the island. It is a scenic village, the ruins of the **Byzantine fort** standing a lonely guard on the rock above. Many of the homes are built in the Thracian style with their balconies and tiled roofs. Behind Chora looms the mountain of the moon,

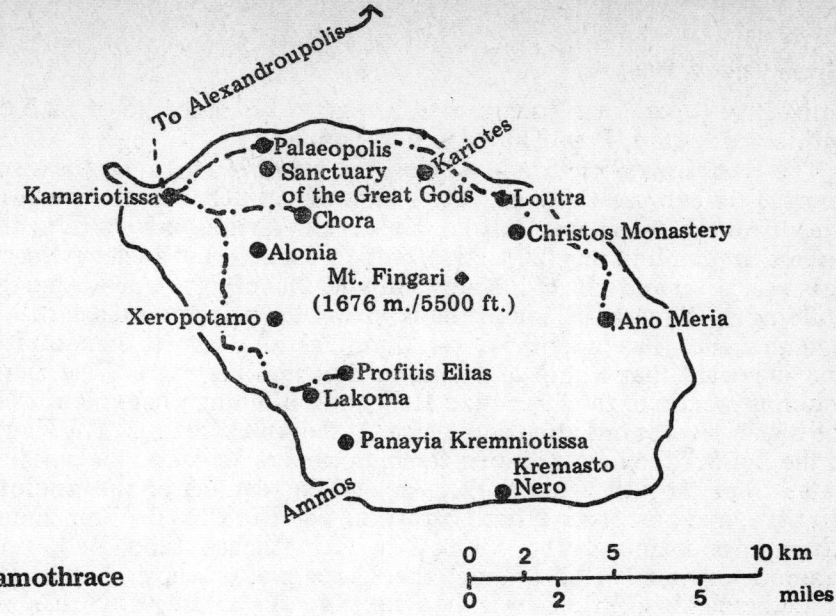

Samothrace

```
0     2      5          10 km
|-----|------|-----------|
0     2              5    miles
```

Fingari, with the tallest peaks in the North Aegean, and a snowcap nine
months of the year. From there Poseidon watched the developments of
the Trojan War, and indeed one can see Asia Minor from its summit. It is
a four-hour climb from Chora, and anyone attempting it should take a
local guide along who knows the path. The post office, banks, etc. are all
located in Chora, which is connected four times a day by bus with the
port Kamariotissa and Palaeopolis.

Restaurants: Stavraki, Yannis Chodros.

Specialities: Krikout (milk and wheat dish made in the winter), and
Psirouki (flour balls in milk).

Near Chora is the second largest settlement of Samothrace, **Alonia,**
which has the remains of a Roman bath and is near the Glosta monastery
(the locals say Samothrace had 999 churches in the past). Other villages
further inland are even smaller, including **Xeropotamo, Lakoma,** and
Profitis Elias. From Lakoma one can visit the church Panayia Krem-
niotissa above **Ammos,** the only sandy beach of Samothrace, and
Kremasto Nero, a tall waterfall. The journey is far easier by caique
from Kamariotissa, however.

Kamariotissa is the port of the island. It has no true harbour but a
long cement pier instead. Every Sunday night in the summer, the
Samothracians bring out their violins and laoutos and bazookias and
play in Kamariotissa. Edelweisse, Thio Asteria, Deliani and Galatou are
some of the restaurants there. All along the north coast of Samothrace is
a rocky beach, followed by a road that kicks up a cloud of dust when the
rural bus bounces over it. On the way to **Loutra,** the thermal baths of
Samothrace, lies **Palaeopolis,** the site of the ancient Sanctuary of the
Great Gods. In the museum of Samothrace are finds excavated at the
Sanctuary from 1938 onwards by Dr. Karl Lehmann of New York

301

University (open 7am-7pm; closed Tuesday. Entrance 25 dr.; 2.5 dr. with student card. Free Thursday and Sunday).

The **Sanctuary** itself is just below the museum and open the same hours. One can see the long, **ancient walls** which stretch from Mt. Fingari to the sea shore. Outside them is the **Arisinoe Rotunda,** the largest circular building (20 metres/66ft. in diameter) of ancient Greece. Arisinoe, sister and wife of Ptolemy Philadelphos of Egypt, dedicated the building to the Great Gods in thanksgiving for being granted fertility. The mother of Alexander the Great, Olympias, also came to Samothrace, and it is said that Philip of Macedon first met her there. Five Doric columns remain of the **Hieron,** a Hellenistic building where the rites of the higher level of initiation took place. At the **Anaktorion,** "The House of the Lords," the first initiation ceremonies were held, and the building dates from the 6th century BC. An outline remains of the **ancient theatre,** and near it the **Nike Fountain,** where in 1863 the Frenchman Champoisean found the Victory of Samothrace (258 BC), now dramatically set in the Louvre; there is a plaster copy of it in the Samothrace Museum. Below is the **Propylae of Ptolemy II** (Arisinoe's husband) and a small theatre-like area dedicated by the successors of Alexander the Great, Philip III and Alexander IV. At the museum one can purchase an excellent guide to the site and museum written by Karl Lehmann.

Five minutes' walk away are **two Genoese towers** built of materials from the Sanctuary. A small taverna is down by the sea, set among plane trees and icy cold streams. Up on the hill is the loveliest place to camp on the island.

Panayiéria: 6 August, a kilometer from Chora in a pretty setting; 26 July, Ag. Paraskevi, near Palaeopolis; 20 July, Profitis Elias at Kormbeti; 15 August, Panayias at Loutra; 8 January, Ag. Athanarsios at Alonia.

Hotels in Samothrace: Area code 0551
The Xenia (B) is in the grove by the famous Sanctuary of the Great Gods and the museum. A rocky beach is not far away, but on the whole, it is a hotel for archaeology lovers only, with little to offer the typical tourist.

B: Xenia, Palaeopolis, tel. 41230.
C: Akroyali.
E: Ilios, tel. 41245.

Tourist Police: Regular police at Chora.

Thassos

Connections: Ferry boat from Keramoti to Limenas 30 times a day; from Kavala to Limenas four times a day; from Kavala to Prinos eight times a day; from Kavala to Limenaria once a day. Daily flights from Athens to Kavala; also buses from Athens to Kavala.

History: Always a bit out of the way, Thassos wasn't settled for certain until 1500 BC. First the Phoenicians, and then the Parians, as mentioned by Thucydides, colonized the island, and they were followed by the Thracians, who at the time were considered to be non-Greek barbarians. In 750 BC the Ionians made Thassos an independent state, an outpost of Hellenic civilization which often exploited the Thracians and occasionally expelled them from the island. Their major city was at the site of the modern capital Limenas and huge walls encircled the town, as its proximity to Thrace and Macedonia made defence a primary concern. The 5th and 4th centuries BC were prosperous years for Thassos, although the island's external policies went less well. In 490 BC it was ruled by Miletus from Asia Minor, but ten years later Thassos joined the Athenian league, which did not prevent the inhabitants from assisting Sparta during the Peloponnesian War. As punishment General Kimon of Athens destroyed Limenas, but he did not succeed in subduing the wilful Thassiots, who took advantage of every Athenian setback to return to the side of Sparta.

For a brief period Thassos was independent, before admitting the sovereignty of Philip II of Macedon. In 197 BC the Romans defeated the Macedonians, and Thassos gladly became part of the Roman Province, sheltering the defeated Roman Republicans after their defeat at the battle of Philippi. Among the various marauders who troubled the island during the age of Byzantium, the Genoese took the most permanent possession of it in the 14th century. The Turks chased them out in 1460 and occupied Thassos themselves. Russia took over from 1770 to 1774, but later gave the island to the renowned Mohammed Ali, who had been raised there. In 1821 the inhabitants rebelled with little result, and were ruled by Egypt when Mohammed Ali became regent there. In 1913 the King of Greece visited Thassos, marking its inclusion in the Greek state.

Thassos today: Known for its forests and sandy beaches, Thassos has become the island of islands for camping — although the minute one steps off the boat, little notices warn that camping outside official areas is forbidden. People still manage to lay a sleeping bag or pitch a tent almost anywhere in complete tranquillity. Provisions are inexpensive, there is a lot of fresh water, and countless places for hiking and swimming. The insect world, however, also likes Thassos; those sleeping under the twinkling stars should bring mosquito lotion or light a coil. Also remember to be extra careful with fires. Thanks to a good deal of hard campaigning, with the mixed approval of the inhabitants, Thassos is becoming one of the most popular islands in Greece.

A most obvious sign of this openness to tourism is at the capital of the island, Limenas (also known as Thassos), where the whole waterfront has been lined with the flags of the world, so that everyone will feel at home. Dotted throughout the town are various excavations of ancient Limenas, including temples to Dionysos, Artemis, and Poseidon, and a shrine to foreign gods (even then

Limenas showed international courtesies). The **Roman agora** is particularly lovely, the white marble in lyrical ruins on the green grass. The ancient walls, begun by the Ionians and repaired at various times, lastly by the Genoese, encompass the acropolis and the town. Some very fine gates remain (Classical-Hellenistic), including that of Silenus, the Goddess and the Chariot, Zeus' Gate, Parmenons' Gate, and the gate of Heracles and Dionysos, restored by the Romans. On the east side of town long wide steps and a path lead to the beautiful Hellenistic theatre, situated on the hillside among the trees. Classical tragedies and comedies are performed there during the summer as part of the Phillippi and Thassos Festival presented by the Northern Greece State Theatre.

A path from the theatre leads to the **acropolis,** a wonderful place in the pine trees commanding a magnificent view of the island; on a clear day one can see Samothrace and Mt. Athos. The **fortress** was built by the Venetians and the Genoese out of ancient materials, including the Kouros Kriophoros now in the museum. One can also see the relief of a symposium stuck in one of the walls. The **temple of Athena** (5th century BC) on the next hilltop has been stripped by the builders, and only its foundation remains.

Below in the town by a pretty flower garden is the **Archaeology Museum** (open 9 am - 1 pm and 4 pm - 6 pm; 10 am - 2 pm on Sunday; closed Tuesday. Entrance 25 dr., 2.5 dr. with student card; free Thursday and Sunday). Among the many beautiful exhibits is the famous Kouros Kriophoros — a 6th century statue of a young man carrying a lamb, a relief of griffons slaying a deer, and a lovely bust of Dionysos from the 3rd century. On the other side is a generally crowded sandy beach, although a half hour's walk in either direction will bring one to prettier, emptier, and cleaner beaches. There is a healthy night life at Limenas, and the evening volta along the waterfront is well worth seeing. This is a stupendous parade in the summer months, perhaps because most of the tourists who come to Thassos are Greek. There is a yacht supply station at Limenas.

Restaurants: Palladion, Platanous, Psistaria Thessaloniki, Glyfada and George's.

Discotheques: Thea, Africa, Magic; disco-bazookia at Romeo and Samantha (disco 9 pm - 1 am, bazooki music afterwards); Stelaki for Greek and American music.

Specialities: Honey, walnut candy, wine, and octopus.

The official camping sites are off the coastal road, which circles the entire island:

Rochoni Camping, Skala Rachoni; open mid-May to mid-September.

Ioannidis Camping, Rachoni, tel: 71377/71477.

Skala Panayias Camping and Golden Beach Camping, on the east coast.

Cape Sapuni in the south is another very popular place to pitch a tent.

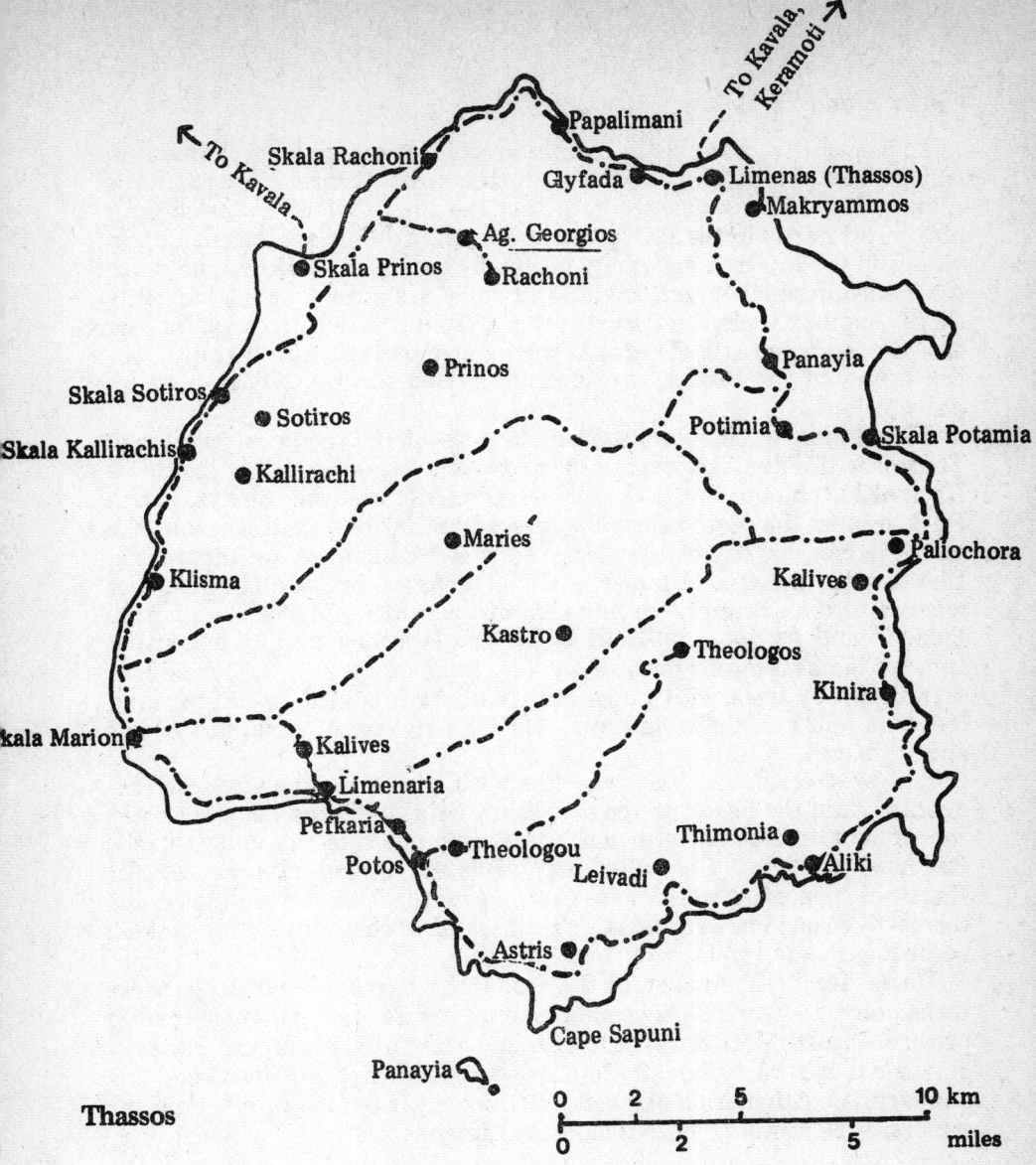

To Kavala
Skala Rachoni
Papalimani
Glyfada
To Kavala, Keramoti
Limenas (Thassos)
Makryammos
Ag. Georgios
Skala Prinos
Rachoni
Panayia
Prinos
Skala Sotiros
Potimia
Skala Potamia
Sotiros
Skala Kallirachis
Kallirachi
Maries
Kalives
Paliochora
Klisma
Kastro
Theologos
Kinira
kala Marion
Kalives
Limenaria
Pefkaria
Theologou
Thimonia
Potos
Leivadi
Aliki
Astris
Cape Sapuni
Panayia

Thassos

| 0 | 2 | 5 | 10 km |

| 0 | 2 | 5 | miles |

    Buses make the round of the island a few times a day. Of the many beaches, Kali, Pefkaria, Pharos, Panayia, Potamia, Rachoni, Alaki are considered the best; Makryammos is lovely but has become a high class tourist beach; Archangelos and Ag. Ioannis are isolated and forested. Directly south of Limenas, along a picturesque road, lies **Panayia,** the most charming village of Thassos. Its old Macedonian houses, decorated with carved wood, overlook the sea and the fine beach below. The **church Panayias** has an underground spring inside. There are many restaurants in town and by the beach below. Between Panayia and Limenas, **Makryammos** has become the luxury beach of Thassos and even has a Class A restaurant.

To the south of Panayia is another pretty mountain village, **Potamia,** which also has a beach below, lined with many tavernas. **Kastro,** in the centre of the island, was the refuge of the Limenarians in the days of piracy, primarily in the 19th century. It, and **Maries,** another mountain village in the interior, are rarely visited by outsiders. **Aliki** on the south coast was an ancient settlement, and ruins are strewn about its sandy shore. Another ancient settlement was at **Thimonia** nearby, where part of a Roman tower still stands. **Astris,** above pretty **Cape Sapuni,** was the home of the Sirens, whose singing tried to lure Odysseus to his destruction.

Theologos to the west shared the title of the medieval capital of Thassos with Panayias. In the village one may see the ruins of the castle **Kourokastro,** and in the church Ag. Dimitrios are icons 800 years old. **Pefkaria** on the coast below is a lovely beach with pine trees along the sand. It can be reached by caique from **Panorama** or Limenaria. **Limenaria,** the second largest town on Thassos, draws a fair crowd of tourists in the summer. On one side of town one may see the "**Little Palace**" and gardens, built in 1903 by a German mining executive. Limenaria has retained more of a village atmosphere than Limenas. It is surrounded by trees, with a huge stretch of shady beach. There are many rooms to rent and the restaurants Aktaeon, Hellas, Athenia, and Alex's above the sea.

The west coast of Thassos is lined with beaches, usually less frequented than the beach on the east coast. **Skala Prinos** has the closest connections to Kavala, although there isn't much to the village itself. **Rachoni** and **Ag. Georgios** are two quiet inland villages, **Skala Rachoni** sponsoring most of the camping on the island. A small islet off the north coast, **Thassopoula,** is pretty and wooded but full of snakes, according to the locals.

Panayiéria: In August, at the Samantha bazooki, a beauty contest takes place, in which both local girls and tourists are eligible for the big prize. 6 August, Metamorphos tou Sotirou at Sotiros; 15 August, Panayia at the village Panayia; 26 October, Ag. Dimitrios at Theologos; 18 January, Ag. Athanasiou at Kastro; 27 August, at Limenaria with special dances; 6 December, Ag. Nikolaos at Limenas.

Hotels in Thassos: area code 0594

The Makryammos Bungalows (A) are on the most lauded beach of sand-surrounded Thassos, perfect for the sincere sun seeker. Although rather isolated, it is only a short boat trip to Limenas, the diversion-filled capital of the island.

in Limenaria
C: Menel, 43 Omonias, tel. 51396
C: Sgouridis, 3 Megalou Alexandrou, tel. 51241
C: Theodora, 14 Olonias, tel. 51251
D: Hatzichristos, tel. 9419870 in Athens
E: Papageorgiou, tel. 51205

in Limenas
B: Timoleon, tel. 22177/22179
B: Xenia, tel. 22105
C: Angelika, Paralia, tel. 21387
C: Glyfada, Glyfada, tel. 21264
C: Lido, 12 Megalou Alexandrou, tel. 22139
C: Theano, tel. 22109
D: Acropolis, 62 Gallikis Archaeologikis Scholis, tel. 22488
D: Akti, Paralia, tel. 22326/22270
D: Astir, Paralia, tel. 22260
D: Dionyssos, tel. 22198
D: Galini, 1 Theagenous, tel. 22195
D: Palladion, 33 18th Oktovriou, tel. 22110
in Makryammos
A: Makryammos (bungalows), tel. 22101/22102; teleg: Makryammos
Thassos
in Panayia
E: Helvetia, tel. 61231
in Potamia
C: Blue Sea, Skala
in Prinos
C: Crysstal, Dassylion, tel. 71272
D: Kali Kardia, Skala
D: Leto, tel. 71229
D: Vogdanos, tel. 71223
in Rachoni
C: Hara
in Theologos
C: Gerda, tel. 51269
D: Io, Potos

Tourist Police: By the quay at Limenas, tel. 22122

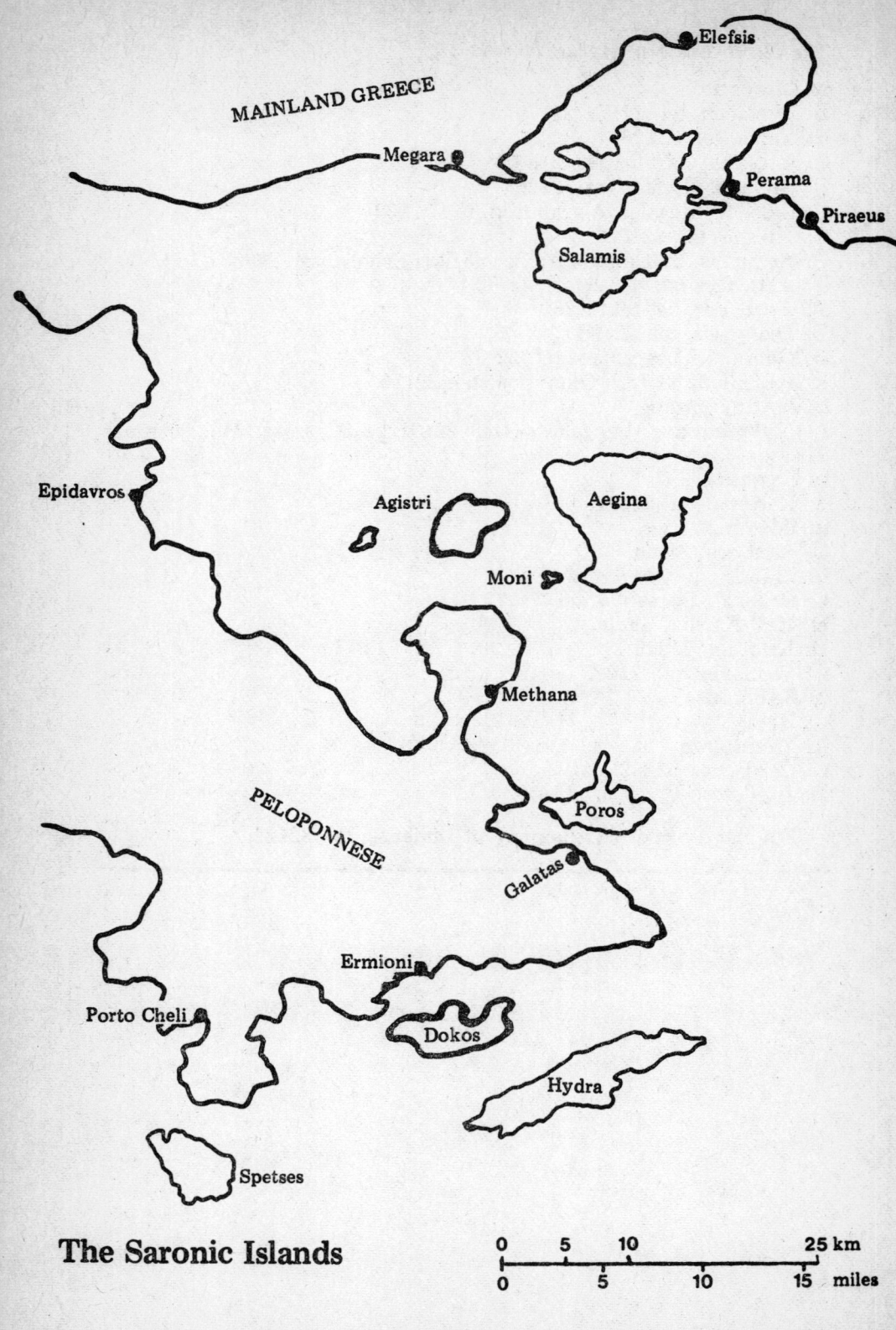

MAINLAND GREECE

Elefsis

Megara

Perama

Piraeus

Salamis

Epidavros

Agistri

Aegina

Moni

Methana

PELOPONNESE

Poros

Galatas

Ermioni

Porto Cheli

Dokos

Hydra

Spetses

The Saronic Islands

| 0 | 5 | 10 | | 25 km |
| 0 | 5 | 10 | 15 | miles |

Part 11
The Saronic Islands

Saronic Islands

The history of the five islands in the Saronic gulf is bound up with the sea. Aegina was one of the most powerful maritime states in Greece; Poros is the island of Poseidon; Salamis gave its name to one of the world's greatest sea battles; and Hydra and Spetses led the Greek fleets in the battles of the War of Independence. Other than their links with the sea and geographical location, the five small islands have little else in common. This, combined with their proximity to Athens, makes them ideal for the visitor with little time at his disposal. Connected by hydrofoil and ferry boat almost hourly with Athens and with each other, they are by far the most accessible of all the Greek islands.

From the beginning of this century tourists began to visit the Saronic Islands. First the Athenians came, buying or renting villas for the three summer months while the father of the family commuted to and fro at weekends. After the introduction 20 years ago of such conveniences as fresh water supplies, electricity and telephones, sun and fun seekers from all over the world began to arrive. Today Aegina is one of the three most visited islands of Greece, and Hydra has become a bit of a Mykonos.

Aegina

Connections: 14 times a day with Piraeus; frequent connections with Poros, Hydra and Spetses.

History: Aegina was inhabited from the 4th millennium BC by people from the Peloponnese, followed by the Minoans, the Myceneans and the Dorians.

In 950 BC Aegina joined an amphictyony of seven towns (the Heptapolis), initiating its commercial development. In 650 BC the island was the first place in Europe to mint coins and develop a banking system; money from Aegina has been discovered all over the Mediterranean world, attesting to the ancient importance of the island. Situated as it was between Corinth, Attica and centres in the east, trade made Aegina wealthy through its exports of pottery and perfumes in the holds of its powerful commercial fleet. With the fall of Samos to Persia, Aegina knew no rivals in trade in the Mediterranean sea.

This prominence lasted less than 50 years, however, with the challenge of a very close neighbour: Athens. In the first Persian war Aegina supported the Persians against Athens, but it later changed sides and sent many ships to Salamis, helping to defeat the Persians in the invasion under Xerxes. Even so, Pericles could not forgive Aegina for its prosperity and competition with Athens; he called it "a speck that blocked the view of Piraeus". In 458 BC the Athenian fleet defeated the triremes of Aegina, and three years later the city of Aegina was forced to surrender to the siege of the Athenians, who made the inhabitants destroy their fortifications and hand over their fleet.

When the Peloponnesian War broke out, the Athenians deported all the Aeginetans, who were welcomed by the Spartans and later returned to their homes by Lysander. Saracens, Venetians and Turks took the island many times, the last occupation of the Ottomans lasting from 1715 to 1821, when Aegina was one of the first places in Greece to be liberated. Many refugees came to the island from other parts of Greece. In 1828 Aegina became the capital of free Greece under Capodistria, who was elected there. The first modern drachma, the first newspaper and, less pleasant, the first prison of Greece were created on Aegina, although a year later the capital was relocated in Nauplia.

Mythology: The name Aegina comes from one of Zeus' many loves, with whom he fathered Aeacus, the first king of the island. Aeacus, to honour his mother, renamed what was then Oenone "Aegina". This was too much for the ever jealous and ever unjust Hera. She punished Aeacus for being an illegitimate son of Zeus by plaguing Aegina with poisonous serpents, polluting the water and causing all the people to perish. Aeacus begged his father Zeus for help, wishing for as many inhabitants to repopulate his island as there were ants on a nearby oak, a wish Zeus granted. Thus the new Aeginetans were known as the Myrimidons, or ant people (during the Dorian invasion Aegina was indeed inhabited by the Myrmidons of Thessaly). Aeacus, a bitter foe of Minos of Crete, went on to father Peleus and Telamon, thus becoming the grandfather of both Achilleus and Ajax. When Aeacus died, Zeus appointed him one of the three judges of the dead along with Minos and Rhadamanthys, his other sons from Crete.

Aegina today: There are so many connections between Aegina (pronounced Eggina) and the mainland that it is sometimes called a sub-urb of Athens; indeed not a few people commute daily to work in the city. Tourism, pistachios and shipping are today the major sources of income for the island, the first two very much in evidence, despite Aegina's heat and very low rainfall in the summer. Pistachios are produced commercially in only three places in the world: California, Iran and Aegina, and the Greeks claim that the Aeginetan variety is the biggest and best. At the end of August one can watch the pistachio harvest in process, when the ripe nuts are delicately knocked from the trees with sticks, to fall on to the canvas laid underneath. From there they are taken to the pistachio peeling machines and dried on roofs and terraces. After roasting in ovens, the finished product is placed in plastic sacks that sell for 200 drachmas a kilo.

It was the pistachio, however, that brought drought to Aegina. After uprooting all the fruit and olive trees to make room for the more profitable pistachio, the farmers realized that they demanded far more water than the trees they had destroyed. Deeper and deeper they dug the wells to slacken the pistachios' thirst, until the wells ran dry or turned into salt water. So now Aegina must import its water from the mainland, and large water ships can be seen every day in the harbour.

Aegina capital also serves as the main port of the island, its harbour having been constructed in 1826 by Samuel Greenly Howle, an American philanthropist and Hellenophile. Right on the harbour, and built at the same time, is a small chapel of Ag. Nikolaos, patron of sailors. On the north side of town stands a column from the **temple of Aphrodite** (or Apollo) built in the early 5th century BC. A great deal of material from the temple was used by Capodistria to construct the quay. German excavations of the site have uncovered signs of a Neolithic settlement. Towards the other side of town, by the cathedral, is the **museum of Aegina** (open 9 am - 1 pm and 4 pm - 6 pm; 10.30 am - 2.30 pm Sunday; closed Tuesday. Entrance 25 dr., 2.5 dr. with student card). It contains various items excavated from the temples of Aphrodite and Aphaia and others from the Neolithic to Classical age. Some of the older houses in town have had famous occupants, including Capodistria, Kanaris, Trikoupis and Kazantzakis. On the south side of town, towards the house of the great statesman Trikoupis, is the orphanage built by Capodistria.

An evening stroll at Aegina is particularly pleasant for the lovely sunsets (probably due to the dirty atmosphere emanating from Athens) which bathe the town in a gentle light far different to the daytime glare. Colourful fishing boats solidly line the waterfront. They no longer fish for the famous katsoulas, once a speciality of Aegina but today almost extinct, nor do the sponge boats operate any more, having been pushed out of business by synthetics. Now the small marida comprises most of the catch, which one can try with Aegina-produced retsina in one of the

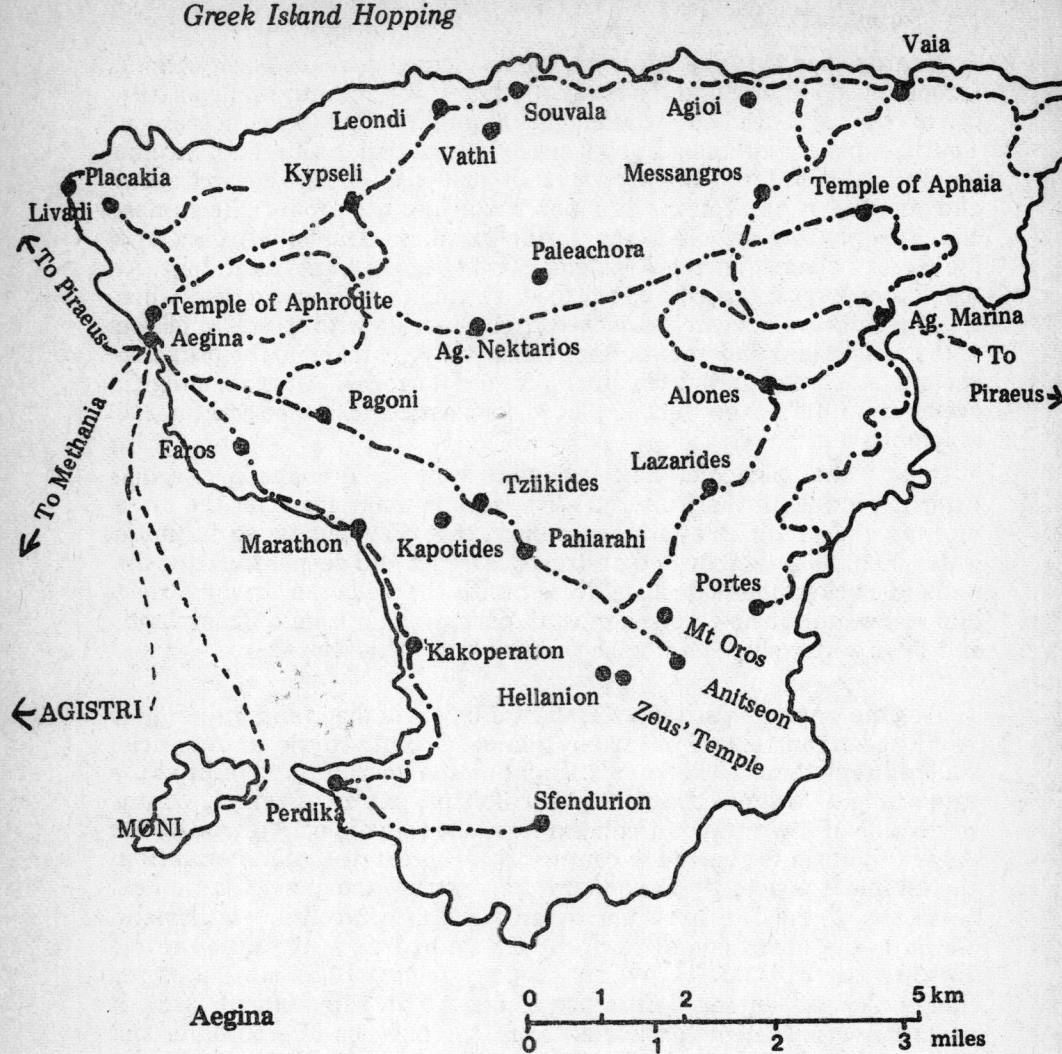

Aegina

many tavernas along the port. Aegina has a yacht supply station.

Restaurants: Alexiou, the House of the Fisherman; cheap souvlaki at Bergos, Anasis and Pantezis.

Discotheques: Noah, Elpiana, and Enoi.

Bazookia: Sketos (20 minute walk from town).

Renting a bicycle is one of the popular ways to see the rest of Aegina, or one may rent a car or scooter or simply use the buses, which leave Aegina town by the temple of Aphrodite (where there is also a camping area). On the north coast **Souvala** has radioactive thermal baths, recommended for rheumatism and arthritis, and there is also a beach and hotels. A road south from Souvala leads to ruined **Paleachora,** the Byzantine and medieval capital of the island, founded in the 9th century during the raids of the Saracens. Here Ag. Dionysos came from Zakynthos after his brother's death to live at the **Episkopi cathedral.** The town was destroyed twice, first by Barbarossa in 1538 and then by Morosini in his siege of 1654. At Paleachora are the remains of twenty or so 13th century churches; it is said that there were once 365, but most were torn down to build new houses. Many of those remaining have frescoes inside. Above the crumbling old village is the crumbling **Venetian castle** of 1654.

A bit to the east of Paleachora is the **convent of Ag. Nektarios,** who was canonized in 1967, the most recent of Greek Orthodox saints. His remains are in the church, and he is considered the protector of Aegina. On 9 November, a large pilgrimage is made to the convent to commemorate the date of the saint's death in 1920. To the east of the convent lies the pretty village **Messangros,** surrounded by the vineyards that produce Aegina's retsina.

On the pine-covered hill above Messangros is the prize attraction of the island, the beautiful **temple of Aphaia.** Like Apollo and Artemis, Aphaia was a child of Leto. She often went hunting with her sister and followed her cult of virginity. Minos of Crete fell in love with her, but she would have nothing to do with him; he chased her, and she fled him for nine whole months. Unable to bear it any longer, Aphaia threw herself into the sea, but was rescued by kindly fisherfolk. Artemis later made her a goddess, although she was hardly known outside of Aegina.

The temple of Aphaia (7am-7pm; entrance 25 dr., 5 dr. with student card) was built in the Doric order in the early years of the 5th century BC, and today it is the best preserved temple on the Greek islands. Of the 32 original columns, 25 still stand (some reconstructed). The bas-reliefs of the Trojan War it once contained were bought by Ludwig of Bavaria in 1812 and can now be seen in the Munich Glyptotheque. In the great hall of the temple, where a statue of the goddess once stood, examples of 19th century graffiti can now be seen. Outside the temple are the ruins of an ancient wall, the altars, a cistern, and some of the houses of the priest. There is a café across the road from the temple, offering a splendid view of the east coast of Aegina, including **Ag. Marina,** the seaside resort of the island with a long sandy beach. Ag. Marina is the final destination of the bus from Aegina, which leaves every half-hour.

One of the most popular excursions on Aegina is to cycle to **Perdika** in the south. Still relatively untouched by tourism, Perdika is a pretty fishing village and the best place to find fresh fish on the island. One can also swim at its small beach. Inland on **Mt. Oros** is the third temple of Aegina, dedicated to Zeus. The hike there from Marathon village takes about two hours. Its reward is a magnificent view from the summit, although little remains of the sanctuary of Zeus, called Hellanion for the ancient name of the mountain.

Panayiéria: 9 November, Ag. Nektarios; 6 December, Ag. Nikolaos at Aegina; September, Ag. Sorsti in Perdika; 14 September, Stavros in Paleachora.

From Aegina a boat leaves three times a day for **Agistri,** or Hook islet, which has many pine trees, some beaches, and tourist facilities. The streets of the village are narrow, lined with white houses with red tiled roofs. A club, **Agistri,** has music at night to entertain the 1500 inhabitants and visitors, and there is a beach beside it. Another islet, facing Perdika, is **Moni,** once owned by a monastery but today run by the National Tourist Organization, who have set up a **camping site** there, open from the end of June until September. During this period, a boat runs to the pretty wooded islet three times a day from Aegina. For more information see the National Tourist Organization, or telephone 61242 on Aegina, or 548602 in Athens.

Hotels in Aegina: area code 0297
in Ag. Marina
B: Apollo, tel. 32271/32281; teleg: Apollotel
C: Aegki (motel), 199 Aphaeas, tel. 32221
C: Akti, tel. 32249/32288
C: Ammoudia, tel. 32313/32204
C: Aphaea, tel. 32227; teleg: Lalaouni
C: Argo, tel. 32266/32331; teleg: Hotel Argo
C: Blue Horizon, tel. 32303
C: Galini, tel. 32203; teleg: Lalaouni
C: Kalliopi, tel. 32225
C: Karyatides, tel. 32391
C: Kyriakakis, tel. 32222
C: Magda, tel. 32325
C: Marina, tel. 32301
C: Nuremberg (Nyremvergi), tel. 32438
C: Oassis, tel. 32312
C: Saronis, tel. 32386

in Agistri
C: Kekryfalia, Skala, tel. 23895
D: Dina, tel. 23885

in Aegina
B: Nausica (Nafsika) (bungalows), 55 Leof. N. Kazantzaki, tel. 22333; teleg: Nafsikahotel
B: Pavlou (pension), 21 P. Aeginitou, tel. 22795
C: Areti, tel. 22806/23917
C: Avra, 2 N. Kazantzaki, Paralia, tel. 22303/239681
C: Brown, 4 Toti Hatzi, tel. 22271
C: Danae, tel. 22424
C: Faros, tel. 22218/22543
C: Klonos, tel. 22640/22597; teleg: L Klonotel

D: Aktaeon, tel. 22241
D: Artemis, 20 Kanari, Ag. Nikolaos, tel. 22523
D: Marmarinos
in Messangros
C: Possidon, tel. 32392
in Perdika
B: Moondy Bay (bungalows), Profitis Elias, tel. 61241/61228j/729402 in Athens; teleg: Moondy Aegina
in Souvala
C: Ephi (Efi), tel. 52214/52045
D: Saronikos, tel. 52224
in Vaia
C: Xeni, tel. 52435

Tourist police: Georgios St. Tel. 22391 in Aegina

Hydra

Connections: Three boats and five hydrofoils a day from Piraeus; daily connections with Aegina, Poros, and Spetses; also caique from Hydra Beach on the mainland; other connections with Methana, Porto Heli and Ermioni.

History: In the 6th century BC the Tyrant Polycrates of Samos bought dry, rocky Hydra with the tribute he captured in Sifnos. However, no permanent settlers moved to the island until the 15th century, when Greeks and Albanians from Epirus escaped there from the Turks. By the late 18th century, Hydra became the major refuge for rebels, many fleeing the tyranny of Ali Pasha. Shipbuilding and piracy were the two sources of income, as the island could not otherwise support its population of 20,000. The Hydriots soon grew wealthy from their adopted trade, the Albanians in particular making their fortunes by their daring in running Napoleon's blockade.

Hydra was one of the major centres of insurgency, and in 1821 it sprung into the revolution with enthusiasm. A merchant and pirate fleet of 150 ships was fitted out for war with funds given by the wealthy merchants and pirates, most notably the Koundoriotis family, who owned the largest mansion in town. Under such famous leaders as Miaoulis and Tombazis, the Hydriots terrorized the Turkish fleets, especially with their fire ships. Under the cover of night, a few brave Greeks would row a decrepit vessel full of explosives alongside the Turkish ships, ignite it and swim for their lives. The Turks, should they notice it in time, could only do the same, as they had little defence against a lighted bomb. After the war, sponge fishing became the islander's major occupation, but then that, too, declined through lack of demand. In the 1950s life on Hydra was very quiet indeed, until it began to attract artists who painted the island, thus paving the path for the many tourists who visit Hydra today.

Hydra today: The name Hydra seems a euphemism for the barren island — the Hydriots are jokingly known as the Hydrophiles, and the nickname "Little England" (given by Ibrahim Pasha) was provoked more by the mansions of the sea captains than by anything very green or pleasant. But Hydra is extremely and uniquely picturesque, and for that reason people come from all over the world, sunbathing off its rocks and few beaches, and shopping in its numerous establishments which sell everything from the simplest junk to beautiful paintings and custom-made jewellery. There is, however, a note of sadness behind this bustling cosmopolitanism which hit Hydra so suddenly. "What happened to our kafeníons?" ask the fishermen, looking down the rows of pastel-coloured armchairs in front of the new tourist establishments. "Where can we meet in the evening?" Indeed that austere bulwark of Greek social life is nowhere to be seen. The fishermen shrug and add: "No one wants to work any more. It is so much easier peddling postcards."

There is only one real settlement on the island, called **Hydra,** which serves as both capital and port. On entering its harbour one is struck by the houses, seemingly piled on top of one another along the steep winding lanes. This immediate and vivid impression has brought artists, beginning with Hadjikyriakos Ghikas, from Greece and from all over the world. Although many fled before the cruise boats packed with tourists, a **School of Fine Arts,** in the mansion of Tombazis, still operates. Another school in town is in the Tsamados mansion: **Skoli Borakis Naftilios,** the oldest school for merchant sea captains in Greece. The loveliest mansion in town is that of Koundouriotis, a family which produced two very important leaders in Greek history, Georgios and Pavlos. In the centre of town is the church **Panayia Mitropoulis,** built in the 18th century, which has some pretty things inside including a silver chandelier. There is also a statue of Miaoulis, the famous fighter for the revolution on the high seas. It is said that Nelson once captured Miaoulis on one of his adventures, but Miaoulis in turn captured Nelson with his charm. In his honour the **Miaoulia celebrations** are held in the town on 20 June, complete with mock re-enactments of the Hydriot admiral's battles.

Of course the main thing to do in Hydra is to walk around and soak up local colour. A climb up to **Kalo Pigadi** is an easy and worthwhile excursion just above the town (go by Miaoulis Street). There are some old 18th century mansions on top and two deep wells with fresh water, and from there one can walk to the south side of Hydra. There is a yacht supply station in the harbour.

Restaurants: Grigorios Moriates, Mavromatis in Kaminia.

Discotheques: Thalassopoula, Lagoudera, Kavos, Sirocos.

The beach of the island is at **Mandraki,** an hour's walk to the east of town. It was the site of the old shipbuilding docks of the Hydriots, and there are some recent fortifications there. One may also swim at **Kaminia** (Italian for 'whitewash', which was once made there) although

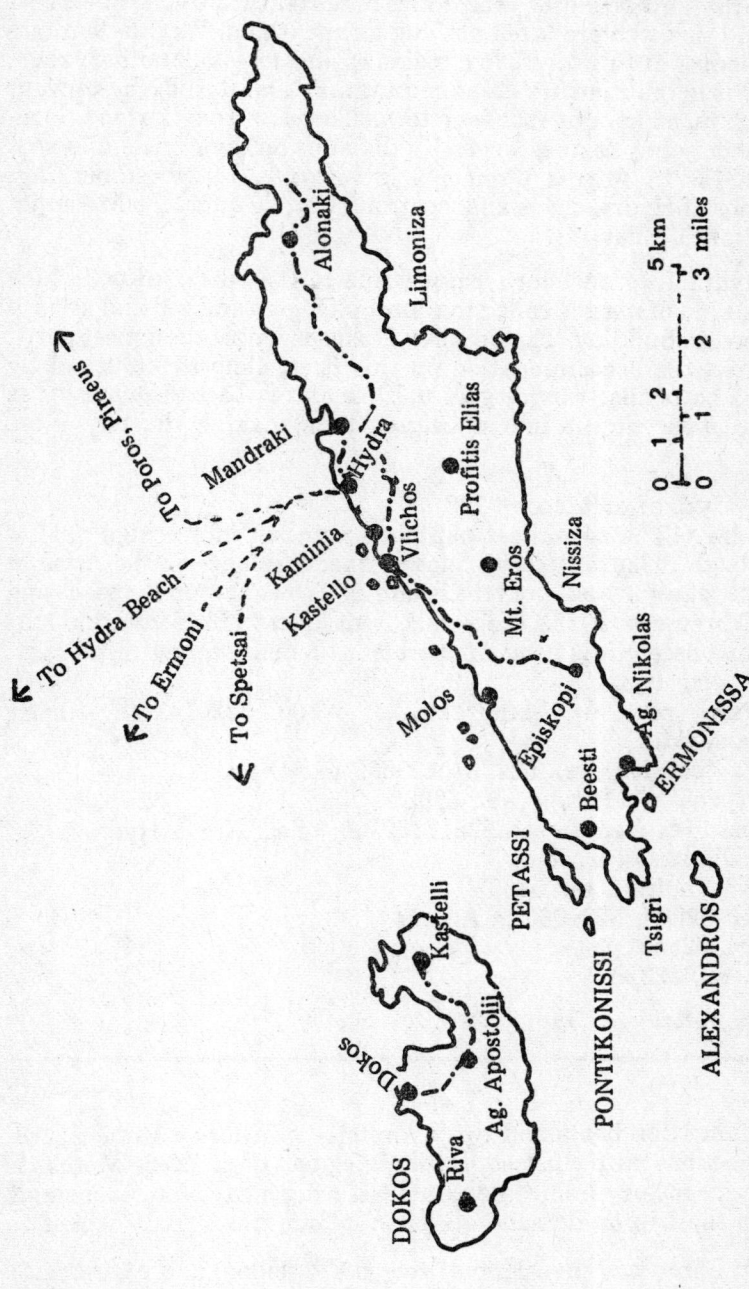

5 km

3 miles

0 1 2

0 1 2

0 1 2

Alonaki

Limoniza

To Poros, Piraeus

Mandraki

Hydra

Profitis Elias

Vlichos

Nissiza

Kaminia

To Hydra Beach

Kastello

Mt. Eros

Ag. Nikolas

To Ermoni

To Spetsai

ERMONISSA

Molos

Episkopi

Beesti

Tsigri

PETASSI

ALEXANDROS

PONTIKONISSI

Kastelli

Ag. Apostoli

Dokos

DOKOS

Riva

Hydra

the beach is mostly rocks. At **Kastello** are the ruins of a thick-walled castle, down near the shore. Further on, **Vlichos** has a good taverna. A pine forest and cove for swimming make **Molos** a popular place for outings; a nearby cliff was used, according to ancient tradition, to toss off the aged and sick who produced nothing for the island. Wealthy hunters have their lodges at **Episkopi**, in a region of pine forests. Another excursion inland is to the **Profitis Elias monastery** and the nearby convent **Ag. Eypraxia,** an hour by foot from town. The view from the top is lovely, and one may buy textiles woven by the nuns on their ancient looms.

Panayiéria: 15 August, Panayias in town; 13-14 November, Ag. Konstantinos of Hydra, the island's patron saint; 20 June, the Miaoulia; 20 July, Profitis Elias.

From Hydra it is an hour's caique ride to the islet **Dokos**, which produced a kind of marble called marmaropita, grey and red and as hard as steel, used in building. The beach at Dokos is longer than most ports, but there is little accommodation on this islet, almost untouched by tourism. As no regular service goes to Dokos, it is best to round up as many people as can fit into a caique, thus making the trip more reasonable.

Hotels in Hydra: area code 0298

The Hydra (C) is an old sea captain's mansion in the high narrow town, although it lacks luxury. Another inconvenience is the noise at night, as the jet set has adopted the island as its own. For more peace and quiet, the Miramare (A) is a short walk from town on the Mandraki harbour. Unfortunately it is pension operated; there are many restaurants on Hydra worth trying.

A: Miramare (pension), Mandraki, tel. 52300; 3220142 in Athens; teleg: Miramaridra

A: Miranda (pension), tel. 52230/5229686 in Athens

B: Delfin (pension), Paralia, tel. 52082

B: Hydroussa (ex Xenia), tel. 52217/52400; teleg: Xenia Hydra

B: Xenon Dimitras (pension)

C: Hydra, 8 Voulgari, tel. 52597

C: Leto, tel. 52280; 5229686 in Athens

D: Argo, tel. 52452

D: Sophia, tel. 52313

Tourist police: At Hydra town, tel. 52205

Poros

Connections: Nine boats and two hydrofoils a day from Piraeus; frequent connections with Spetses, Hydra, Aegina, Porto Heli, Methana, and Ermioni; car ferry from Galatas at least twice a day, and other small boats make the trip on demand (Galatas is four hours from Athens).

History: Poros was the island of the god Poseidon, and a sanctuary

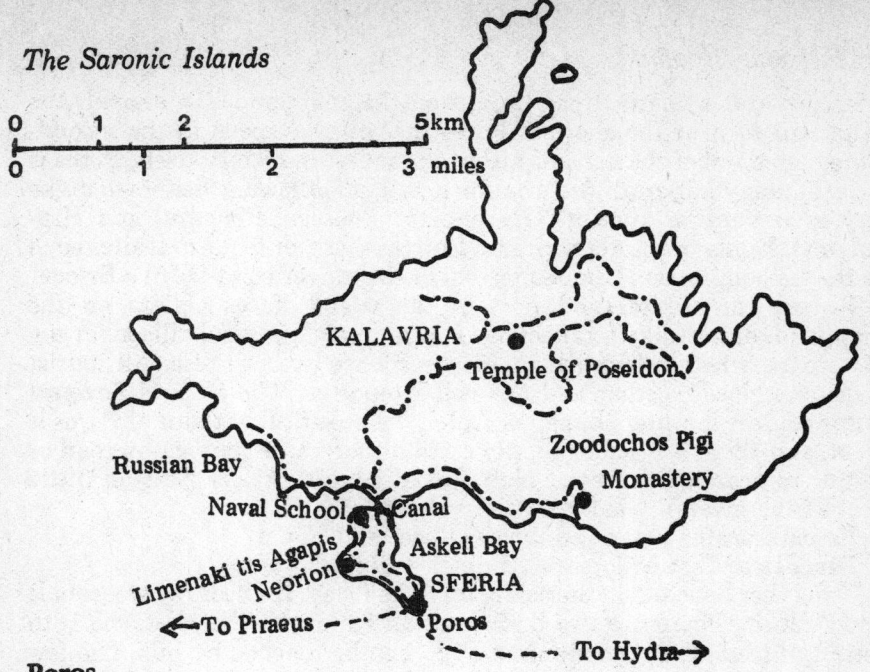

The Saronic Islands

KALAVRIA
Temple of Poseidon
Zoodochos Pigi
Monastery
Russian Bay
Naval School   Canal
Limenaki tis Agapis   Askeli Bay
Neorion   SFERIA
←To Piraeus - - -   Poros
- - - - To Hydra→

Poros

dedicated to him was the centre of the ancient Heptapolis (the amphityony which included Athens, Aegina, Epidavros, Nauplia, Ermioni, Orchomenos and Pasiai). Not much remains of the temple today, except for the memory of the great orator Demosthenes, who fled there in 322 BC from the troops of Antipater and poisoned himself. In the 19th century the Russians built a naval base on Poros, at a place still known as Russian Bay.

Mythology explains the name of the other bay, Askeli, which was named after Skylla, a princess of the island whose father, the king, had a magic lock of hair that made him immortal. When Minos of Crete besieged her father's castle, Skylla fell in love with the handsome Cretan king as she watched the battle. To prove her love for him, she cut off her father's magic lock of hair while he slept and brought it to Minos proclaiming her affection. By killing the king, Minos succeeded in taking Poros the next day. But rather than thank and love Skylla for her help, he was revolted by what she had done and left for Crete without her. Desperately Skylla swam after him, but she was attacked by her father's spirit in the form of an eagle, and drowned in the bay which still bears her name.

Poros today: Both Russian Bay and Askeli Bay lie between the two islands which make up Poros: Sferia with most of the population, and Kalavria with most of the land. The islands are quite different in character: Kalvaria is pine-forested with many quiet, sandy coves, while Sferia is a volcanic titbit that popped out of the sea when the volcano at Methana erupted. The two islands are connected by a bridge. A narrow

319

strait separates Sferia from Galata on the mainland. On arrival, the ships sail so near the shore of Poros that one can peek in the second-storey windows of the houses. Although modest in history itself, Poros is close to many important sites on the mainland, allowing visitors to make day excursions to ancient Troezene (of Theseus, Phaedra, and Hippolytos), Epidavros and the drama festival there, or to natural sites such as the Lemon Forest (Lemonodassos) or the magnificent Devil's Bridge.

Poros, the capital and port of the island, faces Galata on the mainland, almost like a reflection. It is a pretty, peaceful village for the most part, where relaxation takes precedence over all else. All tourist needs are close together and are well signposted. The **School Zannou** offers courses in water skiing, for which the beautiful harbour of Poros is ideal, and there is a yacht supply station there. One may go by road or caique to nearby beaches at **Neorion** or **Limenaki tis Agapis** (little port of the lovers). Nearby is a naval school.

Restaurants: Asteria, Sotiris, Lukas, and Fotis.

Discotheques: Milopetras, Xenias's Club.

Two other beaches on Sferia are on Askeli Bay, **Kanali** (by the canal) and **Askeli.** There are two basic sites on Kalavria. The first, the 18th century **monastery Zoodochos Pigi,** can be reached by bus. The few monks who live there now will show visitors round their church with its gilt iconostasis. Further north are the few blocks that remain from the **Temple of Poseidon,** which was built in the 6th century BC. Along the road one can eat at the pretty taverna Ag. Nektarios, or by the canal at the Platanos taverna.

Panayiéria: 15 August; Easter Friday at the Monastery.

Hotels in Poros: area code 0298

Little Angyra (C) is not far from the bustling town, yet located in the pretty pine-clad cove of Neorion, popular with yachtsmen. It is a simple hotel, in one of the most serene places on the touristy island.

B: Anessis (pension), tel. 22111/22239/22257

B: Latsi, 74 I. Papadopoulou, tel. 22392

B: Neon Aegli, Askeli, tel. 22372

B: Poros (ex Xenia), tel. 22216; 3227334 in Athens; teleg: Poroshotel

B: Paralia, tel. 22279; teleg: Saron Poros

B: Sirene, Moastiri, tel. 22741; teleg: Sirene Poros

C: Aktaeon, 6 Platia Heroon, tel. 22281

C: Angyra, Neorion, tel. 22432/22368

C: Chryssi Abgi, Askeli, tel. 22277; teleg: Chrysavgi

C: Manessi, Paralia, tel. 22273; teleg: Xenmanessi

Tourist police: In Poros town, tel. 22462

Salamis (Salamina)

Connections: Ferry frequently from Perama to Paloukia, or from a point south of N. Peramos to Faneromeni (less frequently). Small boats all through the day from Piraeus to Paloukia, Ambelaki, Selinia or Kamateron.

History: Salamis was the Mycenean kingdom of Telemon, the father of the famous hero Ajax of the *Iliad*. Megara and Athena quibbled over the island in 632 BC, and twenty years later Solon made it an Athenian colony, in order to protect Piraeus. During this time Kamatero was the capital of Salamis, and on Mt. Patsi there are remains of towers which were used to communicate with the mainland. The island was also defended to the west against possible Megarian aggression.

In September of 480 BC a massive Persian fleet under Xerxes, the King of Kings, moved into Faliron Bay, 1200 ships in all, according to Herodotus. The Athenian fleet, which with their allies numbered only 378 ships, fled before them and anchored off Salamis' Ambelaki Bay. In the middle of the night Xerxes ordered his best ships to positions north of Ambelaki, and sent the rest to surround the Greek fleet in the south. Then, as the story goes, he went to the top of Mt. Aegalion to watch his certain victory.

But Themostocles, the leader of the Greeks, was warned of the Persian manoeuvres. In the morning he moved his triremes up against the strongest Persian vessels, which began the attack. At first the Greeks fell back — then quickly spun their swift ships around and drove the bulkier craft of the Persians into the dangerous shallows that the defenders knew so well. Helpless, Xerxes' fleet foundered and his ships in the south fled back to Faliron Bay. The King of Kings watched his incredible defeat in anguish and was eventually forced to create a diversion in order to escape back to Persia with his 300 remaining ships. The army he left behind was defeated later at Plataea, thus ending the Persian threat.

The victory at Salamis gave the Athenians a moral boost which brought about their golden age. It also demonstrated the might of their navy, leading them to form the Delian league and control the fate of so many islands. As for Salamis, it gave birth to the tragedian Euripides and then fell back into obscurity.

Salamis today: The proximity of Salamis to the mainland has made it lose much of its island identity. Excepting the frescoes in the Faneromeni convent, neither nature's nor man's creations are particularly inspiring. The southeast side of Salamis is the prettiest part of the island with its pine forests and beaches, although only accessible by private car and foot. The villages of Salamis are connected by an efficient bus system. Moulki, also called Eantion, and Selinia are popular seaside villages among families from Athens and Piraeus.

Salamis, the rather uninteresting capital of the island, is nicknamed Koulouri ('croissant') for its shape. There are no hotels, although one may find a room to rent. There is a small beach by the town.

Restaurants: Lathouris.

Discotheques: Faro, Serais at the nearby Ag. Georgios.

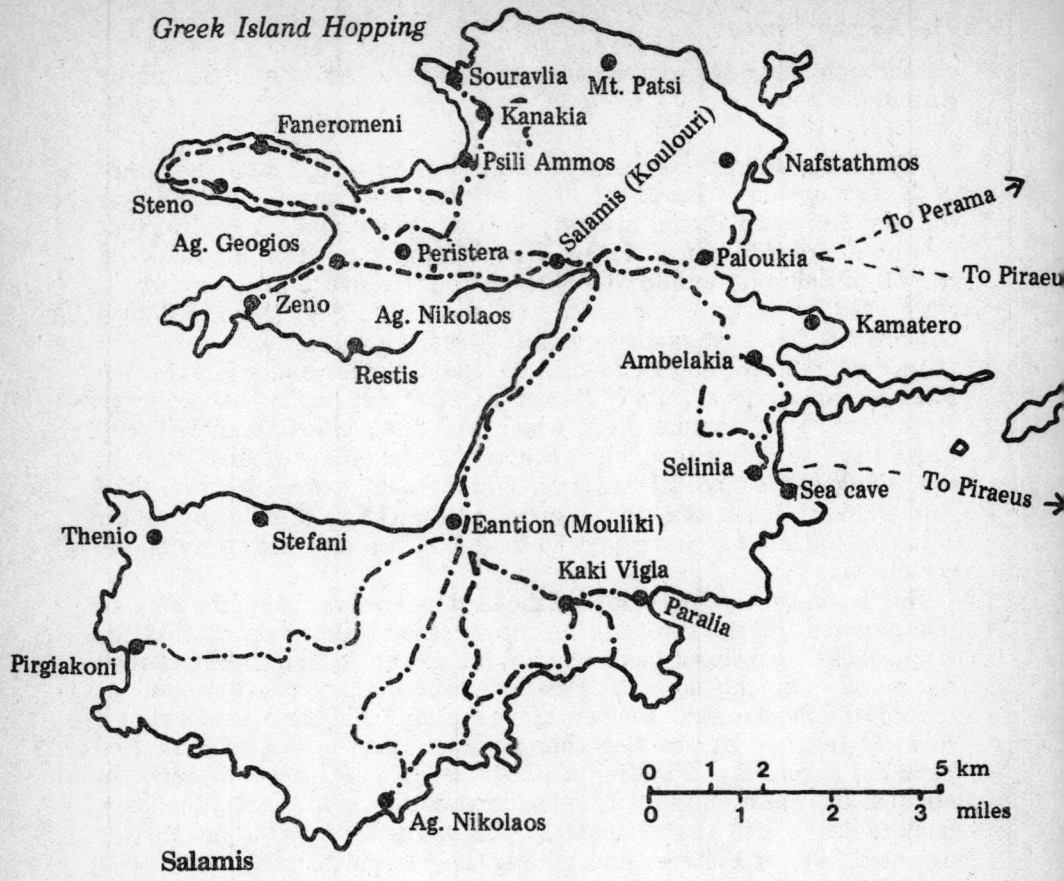

Salamis

Above Koulouri is **Mt. Profitis Elias,** from which one can see the whole island. From Koulouri a bus leaves every hour for **Faneromeni,** the convent and ferry-boat landing stage. Situated in a large pine forest popular with picknickers and campers, Faneromeni dates from 1661, although the stones of its foundation are from an ancient temple. In the convent's church Metomorphosis are huge fascinating frescoes of the Last Judgement, containing more than 3000 figures. These were painted in the 18th century by Georgios of Argos and his pupils, and they have been restored to their original state. The best time to find the convent open is in mid-morning or around 5pm. Across the road by the sea is a fine, open air taverna, and there are many places to swim all along the shore. To the east is the beach **Psili Ammos** (village and taverna) which unfortunately smells of petrol a lot of the time.

South of Kououri is the pleasant village **Moulki,** also with a beach. One can find accommodation there, or sleep out under the pine trees nearby. There is a discotheque, Zodiac. From Moulki a bus goes to **Kaki Vigla,** and a rough road from there leads to **Ag. Nikolaos,** a monastery with a 15th century chapel. Between Ag

Nikolaos and Kaki Vigli one can find excellent isolated camping sites, and the beaches are often sandy. On the east coast of Salamis, **Paloukia,** the ferry-boat landing stage, has a naval festival at the end of August. The boats are met by buses which leave for the villages.

South of Paloukia is **Ambelakia,** which, despite its part in the Battle of Salamis, has become a ship rubbish dump and often smells bad. Should members of the Ugly Art Movement search for an ideal setting for a colony in Greece, Ambelakia awaits them. **Selinia,** a couple miles south of Ambelakia, is a collection of summer houses. The beach is nothing special but the food at the tavernas is good, among them Vassilou, Kalavamos, and Papamichelis. Victoria is the local discotheque.

Panayiéria: 5 June, at Metamorphosis; last Sunday of carnival and Clean Monday at Kouloura when the fishermen dance the trata.

Hotels in Salamis: area code 01 (same as Athens)
in Eantion (Moulki)
C: Gabriel, tel. 4662275/4662223
in Selinia
C: Selinia, tel. 4663424/4663464
D: Votsalakia, 64 Akti Themistocleous, tel. 4653494
E: Akroyali

Tourist Police: In Koulouri, tel. 4651100

Spetses
Connections: Twice a day with Piraeus, Hydra, Poros; less often with Aegina; three hydrofoils a day. Boats from Porto Heli, Ermioni and all day from Kosta.

History: Archaeologists have found evidence at Ag. Marina proving that Spetses (ancient Pityoussa) has been inhabited since 2500 BC. However, Spetses' days of glory came only in 1821, when the island was the very first to rebel on 3 April, 1821. A hundred ships were sent against the Turks and fought very actively with the Hydriot and Psariot fleets. The great local hero of Spetses was a woman, Luscarina Bouboulina, a capitana who inspired patriotic Greek writers and artists.

Spetses today: The furthest Saronic island from Athens, Spetses is a pretty island covered with pine forests. Its climate is very healthy, and the beaches are safe for children, facts which have made it a popular family holiday destination since the Second World War. Every 8 September the whole island celebrates the anniversary of the Battle of the Straits of Spetses, when local revolutionaries destroyed the Turkish vessels in their harbour with a fire boat. This great scene is re-enacted with fireworks instead of dynamite, and a good deal of dancing and feasting follows.

The streets by **Dapias,** the port and capital of Spetses, are paved with black and white pebble mosaics commemorating the island's history, and on a tall, white wall the **canons from the war of 1821** serve as memorials by the cafés. Up the street is the large yellow mansion of the island philanthropist Sotiris Anargyro, and in front of it stands a bust of Bouboulina. The **Spetses museum** has been located in the large mansion of Hatziyannis Mexis (open 10am-2pm). Besides a box holding Bouboulina's remains, one can see the flag (Freedom or Death) raised in the Spetses rebellion, some ancient coins, paintings, and costumes. As the only cars on Spetses are the official vehicles of the doctor and policeman, and the municipal bus, one travels about by horse-drawn fiacre (three street cleaners are employed by the town to keep things sweet and fresh) and boat-taxi. The latter are always on hand at the port, to make the trip to near-by Kosta on the mainland and to other places on the island. The **old harbour,** however, is only a short walk away, by **Ag. Mamas** which serves as the town beach. A story is told that when the Turks came to occupy the island, the inhabitants created mannikins with bright red fezes and Turkish-appearing uniforms and set them up along the shore. Seeing them from a distance, the Turkish commander thought that the island had already been taken and sailed on! The old harbour is a serene place, with its large white houses. In the new harbour is a yacht supply station and agencies offering excursions on the mainland.

Restaurants: Karalambos, Terassa, Lyrachis, Chovitsas (wine barrels and songs), Tzortzis (live music).

Discotheques: Karnayo, Zozo, Old Harbour, Delfini, and Twins.

Bazookia: Aloni, Paradisos, and George's.

Specialities: Almond cookies, fish á la Spetiosa, and Svingi (hot honey sweet).

The entire uneven coastline of the island is decorated with beaches, whose access depends on the strength of one's tennis shoes. Every morning a boat leaves for Ag. Anargyroi, stopping at various other beaches along the way. The captain of this vessel is a bit of a Casanova, a happy soul, always the first to dance and entertain the ladies by carrying a table between his teeth. One can walk, however, to the lighthouse to see the church **Panayia Armata,** built after the victory on 8 September 1822. Inside a large painting by Koutzis commemorates the heroic scene. One may also walk to **Ag. Marina,** a beach and night centre on the island in the summer. Further south along the coast one sees the idyllic islet **Spetsopoula,** circled by a paved road; it is the private island of the wealthy shipowner Niarchos.

Ag. Anargyroi with its shady beach and good taverna is the most popular destination on the island. From there it is a short walk to **Bekiris' cave.** This Turkish name is derived from 1770, when Moslems from Albania came to take revenge on the Spetsiots for siding with Russia in the war. They burnt the houses, and the women and children of the island took refuge in the cave. It is said that one mother killed her

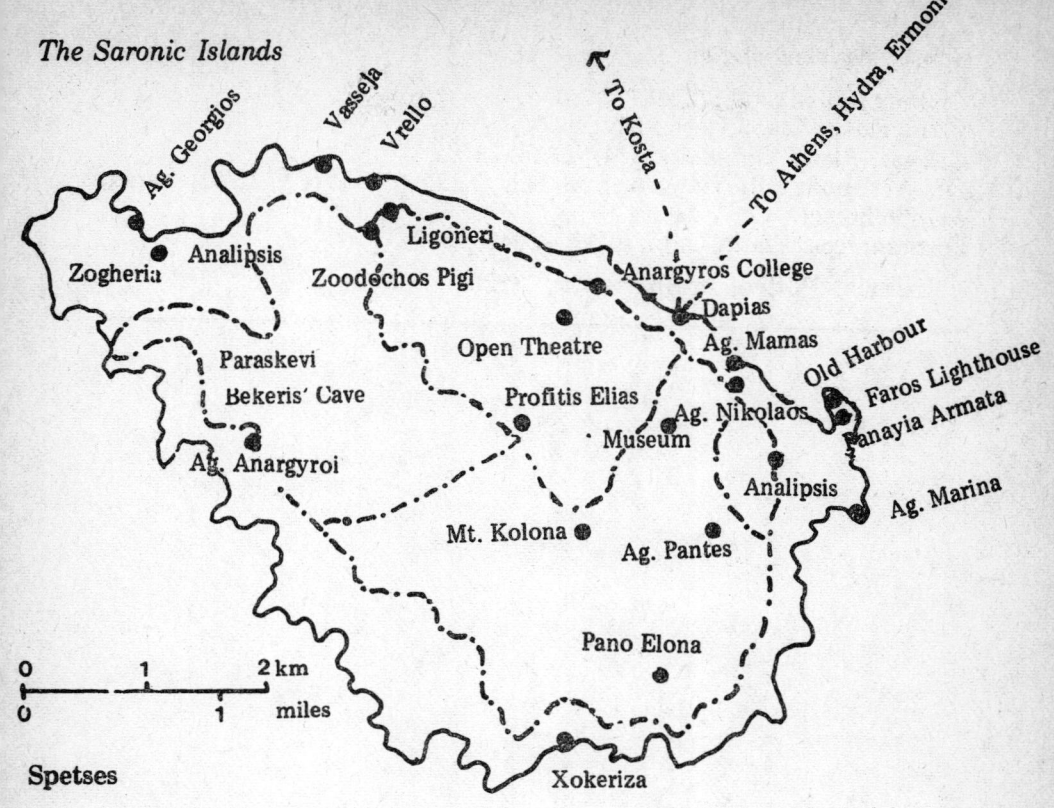

Spetses

whining baby to prevent discovery, but just as many other stories say that the refugees were eventually discovered and slain. One can enter from the sea or there is a low entrance by land (be sure to duck). The best time of day to go is in the afternoon, when the sun shines inside. One can see the beginning of an underground road said to have run to Profitis Elias monastery until blocked up by an earthquake. There are also a few stalactites.

From **Vrello** in the north one can hike up to Profitis Elias, although it is far more pleasant just to stay in Vrello, which is in that region of Spetses called **Paradise** for its beauty. To the east is the well-known **Anargyros College** and its outdoor theatre, and the **house of Bouboulina.**

Panayiéria: 26 July, Ag. Paraskevi at Zogheria; 1 July and 1 November, Anargyroi; 23 April, Ag. Georgios at Zogheria; Easter Friday, Zoodochos Pigi; 40 days after Easter, Analipsis.

Hotels in Spetses: area code 0298
A: Kasteli (hotel & bungalows), tel. 72311; 732191 in Athens
A: Possidonion, tel. 72208/72308
A: Spetses, tel. 72602; teleg: Spetseshotel
B: Roumanis, tel. 72244/72344
C: Faros, Kentriki Platia

C: Ilios (Soleil), tel. 72268/72488
C: myrtoon, 72555; teleg. Myrtotel
C: Star, Platia Dapias, 72214/72314/72462
D: Acropole, Platia Dapias, tel. 72219/720178/72970; teleg. Acropolhotel
D: Saronicos, Platia Dapias, tel. 72646/72464

Tourist Police: In Spetses, tel. 72205

Part 12
The Sporades and Evia

The Sporades (the "sporadic" or "scattered" islands), lying off the coasts of Evia and Thessaly, are thought to have been settled by Thracians in misty prehistoric times. In the 16th century BC the Cretans colonized the islands, introducing the cultivation of olives and grapes. When the Minoan civilization fell, Myceneans from Thessaly, known as the Dolopians (of the same race as the Achaeans), settled the Sporades, using them as bases for their enterprises at sea, for they were great sailors. Much of the rich mythology of the islands had its historical roots during this period: Achilleus himself was raised on Skyros.

The Chalkidians in the 8th century BC captured the Sporades as stepping stones to further their ambitions in Macedonia. These new invaders continued the sea traditions of the Dolopians, inciting hostility from Athens. In the 5th century, she sent General Kimon to crush the rival fleets of the Sporades. The Athenians then colonized the islands, and their culture dominated and was accepted by the inhabitants. Thus, of all the islands of Greece, the Sporades had the closest ties and friendship with the Athenians, who managed to present themselves as liberators rather than conquerors. The government of the islands was run on the model of Athenian democracy, and Athena became a prominent goddess in the local pantheon.

When the Spartans defeated Athens in the Peloponnesian War, the Sporades were part of their spoils, although their reign on the islands was short. A greater threat to Athenian influence came in the person of Philip II of Macedon. His dispute with Athens over the possession of the

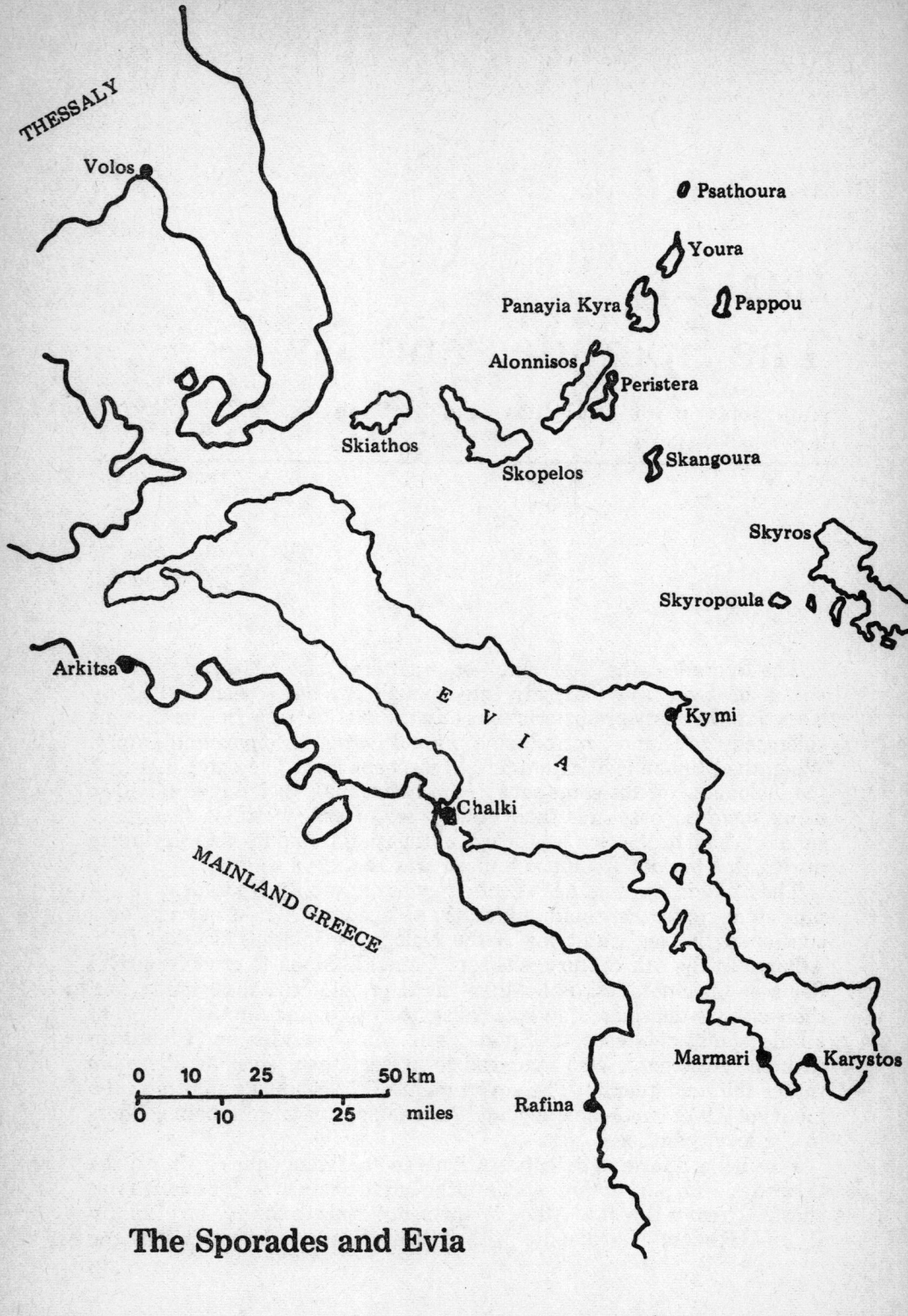

THESSALY

Volos

Psathoura

Youra

Panayia Kyra

Pappou

Alonnisos

Peristera

Skiathos

Skopelos

Skangoura

Skyros

Skyropoula

Arkitsa

Kymi

E V I A

Chalki

MAINLAND GREECE

Marmari

Karystos

Rafina

0   10   25   50 km
0   10   25   miles

The Sporades and Evia

islands attracted the attentions of the entire Greek world, as suspicions began to surface — later proved correct — that the Macedonian king intended to unite all of Greece against Persia. Philip eventually took the islands and Athens itself, although the conquest of Persia was left to his son Alexander.

Even during the Roman occupation (beginning in the 2nd century BC), the Sporades retained their connections with Athens, who still, even after its own fall to General Sulla in 88 BC, nominally held sway over some of the Sporades. Christianity, with a good helping of pagan rites, spread on the islands in the 2nd and 3rd centuries. The Byzantines sent many of their exiles there, who formed the local aristocracy. In 1207 the Venetian Gizi family made their claim on the Sporades. Philip, the most notorious of the dynasty, usurped authority from a senior relative and ruled the area as a pirate king, claiming no one could stop him. His pride, however, was forced into submission when Likarios, the admiral of Emperor Michael Palaeologos, took him in chains to Constantinople, where he only gained his liberty by handing the islands over to the restored Byzantine Empire. Afterwards possession of the islands changed hands a few more times between Greeks and Franks, until Constantinople fell to Mohammed the Conqueror in 1453. The islanders quickly invited the Venetians to reoccupy their lands, which the Venetians willingly did, although they, too, were forced out when their agreements with the Ottoman Empire crumbled before the violent attacks of the Terror of the Aegean, Barbarossa.

After taking the Sporades, however, the Turks manifested little interest in them, sending only a Cadi to assure the payment of taxes; the islands were so subject to raids that a permanent Turkish population never settled there. In the 1821 revolution, Thessalian insurgents found refuge on the islands, which also helped the cause financially. In 1830 the Treaty of London included them in the original kingdom of Greece.

Today the thickly forested mountains and superb sandy beaches of the Sporades seem to have been invented just for summer holidays. Shell fish abound in their waters, and the climate, cooled by the meltemi in the summer, is one of the best in Greece. Although these beautiful islands have definitely been discovered by tourists (especially Greek), their comparative inaccessibility means that they do not swarm oppressively with foreign hordes. Most of the inhabitants still make their living in traditional ways, and hope that they will continue to do so. Of the four, Skiathos with its airport, is the most visited; Alonnisos with its rural charm, the least; Skopelos has the most striking beauty; and Skyros, lovely Skyros, is one of the most marvellously original islands in Greece.

Unless one flies to Skiathos, the trip to the Sporades from Athens involves either a bus or train ride to Volos, or a bus ride to Ag. Konstantinos, both followed by a ferry trip; or a bus to Oropou, a ferry to Eretria on Evia (every hour), a further bus ride to Kymi and a ferry boat from there. If times coincide, this latter is the shortest journey, and the only way of getting to Skyros, which nowadays is connected only to Kymi and not to its sister islands. The other three Sporades, however, are connected frequently with one another by ferry boat and tourist caique.

Alonnisos

Connections: Twice a day in summer with Skopelos; three times a week with Kymi, Volos, Ag. Konstantinos and Skiathos.

History: A notable confusion in the history of Alonnisos is the fact that ancient Alonnisos was not modern Alonnisos, but an island known today as Kyra Panayia. Modern Alonnisos was ancient Ikos. This confusion resulted from the Greek government's enthusiasm for restoring the ancient names of the islands (Liadromia was the name of the island pre-1836). Alonnisos was a case of a leap before a look, but a lucky leap as Alonnisos is a far more musical name than Ikos.

Inhabited from Neolithic times, Ikos, as it was known then, was part of the Cretan colony of Prince Stapylos, who began the cultivation of the vine which was later to make Ikos famous. In the 14th century BC the Mycenaeans took over the affairs of the island. The most famous of the Ikian settlers was Peleus, the father of Achilleus, who died on the island. In Classical times two cities thrived on Ikos, exporting wine. The Athenians established a naval base there in the 4th century, and later in Roman times, General Antonius gave Ikos to Athens (42 BC).

During the Middle Ages Ikos, gradually known as Achilliodromia and later Liadromia or simply Dromos (road), was subjected to Skopelos. Barbarossa wrecked havoc on the island in 1538 when it was added to the Ottoman Empire. In 1965 an earthquake left many of the homes of Alonnissos in ruins.

As for Kyra Panayia, or ancient Alonnissos, inhabited from 5000 BC, as discoveries at Ag. Petros suggest, it had the earliest settlement in the Aegean. In Classical times it belonged to Athens, although in the 4th century BC the pirate Sostratos governed it de facto. Philip of Macedon took it from him, sparking the famous speech of Demosthenes "Concerning Alonnisos", which initiated the troubles between Athens and Macedonia Skopelos took the island in 341 BC when Philip offered to return it to Athens; Philip, however, crushed these opportunists and the island lost all its importance. In Byzantine times it was given to Mt. Athos, and the monks built a monastery on what was then known as Pelagos.

Alonnisos today is the centre of nine other more or less deserted islets to the north and east, including Kyra Panayia. It once produced a healthy crop of grapefruit, but the trees on the island all perished from disease. The earthquake of 1965 brought the population who stayed down from the lovely village of Chora to the coast; many immigrated to Germany. A road has recently been built to replace the time-worn paths, but as it hardly covers a tenth of the island, seekers of tranquillity and beautiful, isolated beaches have only to put on their hiking shoes or catch one of the many caiques.

Patitiri is the modern capital and port of the island. In the mayor's office one can see the foot-long key which once locked the massive gate at Chora every sundown. Most of the buildings in Patitiri were built in the last twenty years, and are decorated with polychromic gardens. A whole series of practically identical restaurants specializing in fish and lobster face the beach. Tourists on the island stay in Patitiri or nearby **Votsi**, which is a short walk away and by another beach. There are many rooms to rent in private houses. A museum will be opened in the future.

Restaurants: Amoria, Alonnisos, Flisbos.
Discotheques: Rock.

South of Patitiri are two beaches, **Vithisma** and **Marpounta.** The remains of a round temple of Asklepeios, the god of healing, can be seen in the sea at the latter. A 5th century BC settlement existed at the beach **Kokkino Kastro,** but it too sank into the sea, although one can still see the fortress and the town hall. It is a two-hour walk from Patitiri, or one may go by boat. A shorter walk or even shorter drive should be made to the old capital of the island, **Chora,** situated above Patitiri. Walkers can choose between two delicious routes: the mule path is hedged with raspberry bushes, while the road is lined with pear and nut trees. Only thirty families live in Chora today, for the earthquake ruined many of the old houses there; many Germans, however, have now begun buying and repairing these houses for summer use. The walls of the town were built by the Byzantines and repaired by the Venetians, and ghosts are said to dance around the 17th century church **Christos.** The women of Chora, distaff in hand, wear their traditional pale blue and white dresses and scarves, their long braids hanging before them. Two of the oldest churches on the island are in Chora, **Ag. Athanasios** and **Ag. Georgios.**

Other walks can be made from Chora to the shepherds' villages of **Milia, Gerakis,** and **Diaselo.** Camping is officially prohibited but this is often ignored, especially in the hinter lands. Lobster and other fish are most plentiful along the north coast, by **Kopelousako** beach and Gerakis. At **Ag. Dimitrios** beach on the east coast are the remains of a Byzantine fountain. Ancient pottery was discovered at **Tsikalia** to the north-east and fossils of prehistoric animals were found at **Megaliamos.** The average cost of a caique trip from Patitiri to these sites and the many other beaches that line the rectangular island is 50 drachmas, varying according to weather conditions and distance.

Panayiéria: 1 July, Ag. Anargaroi; 26 July, Ag. Paraskevi; 15 August, Panayias; 17 July, Ag. Marina; 40 days after Easter, Analipsos.

Peristera (Dove) islet, following the east coast of Alonnisos, was part of the island until separated by a natural upheaval. Also known as Xiro, the island is also endowed with many sandy beaches. There are three villages, Mnimata, Livadhia, and Xilos, the latter having the ruins of a castle nearby. Every ten days a caique goes to **Psathoura,** where one of the most powerful lighthouses in Greece lights the way of passing ships. It is another candidate for the island of the Sirens. A sunken city may be seen in the sea by the lighthouse, as well as a sunken volcano.

Panayia Kyra is two or three hours by caique from Alonnisos. Ag. Petros is the port of the islet, where an 11th century Byzantine ship was found, its hold full of ceramics. On the islet one can visit the old monastery founded by monks on Mt. Athos, and the new one on the east coast. Besides the monks, the only inhabitants of Panayia Kyra are shepherds. There is another monastery on **Skangoura,** connected with that on Mt. Athos, which offers excellent fishing in its many sea coves and caves. On little **Vrachos** signs of a stone age settlement have been found. **Pappou** swarms with hares, while on **Youra** (ancient Geronta) a special breed of goat skips about the rocks. A large empty house is said to have belonged to King Konstantine, should he ever desire to come to Youra to visit the goats! A few Classical and Roman remains have been discovered there; the most spectacular is the Cyclops cave with its stalactites (bring a light).

Hotels in Alonnisos: area code 0424
Marpounta Bungalows (C) are over the hill from the town, bordered by one of the more accessible beaches on the island.
C: Galaxy (bungalows), Patitiri, tel. 65251/65363
C: Marpounta (bungalows), tel. 65219/65212
D: Alonissos, Patitiri, tel. 65210

Tourist Police: Regular police in Patitiri.

Skiathos
Connections: Daily flights from Athens, boats two or three times a day from Volos and Ag. Konstantinos (buy tickets early in the summer) and daily from Skopelos, Alonnisos, and Kymi.

History: The Chalkidians developed the two ancient cities on Skiathos which played a minor part in the later Persian wars. Xerxes, who has a bay on the island named in his honour, built one of the first lighthouses in the world on the nearby islet Kyrminx, now a reef called Lepheteris and still dangerous to sailors. A few vestiges of the lighthouse remain. The rest of Skiathiot history follows that of the other Sporades: the Gizis took the island and built the fort on Bourtzi islet by the present-day town, which was settled in 1790 by refugees from Limni on Evia. The Skiathiot navy assisted the Russians in the campaign at Tsesme, when they defeated the Turkish fleet. In 1805 the island began to revolt against the Ottomans, and sent her ships to aid the Greek cause so enthusiastically that Skiathos itself was left unprotected and prey to marauders. It was one of the first places to be touched by the Orthodox reformist movement, Kollivades, emanating from Mt. Athos (although the name Skiathos means "shadow of Athos" it was derived from a pre-Hellenic source). A homegrown writer, Alexandros Papadiamantis (1851-1911) immortalized Skiathos by setting the scenes of his novels there, although the books have yet to be translated into English.

Skiathos today: Little Skiathos, with its 62 beaches (Koukounaries, one of them, is considered one of the best in the country), forests, and a happy attitude towards tourism draws thousands of Greek and foreign visitors. This has made it a bit more expensive than the other Sporades. It also has the most nightlife of the four islands, and people intending to sleep out will have to go far afield to avoid the lively strains of bazooki or discotheque music.

The modern capital of the island, also called **Skiathos,** was built in

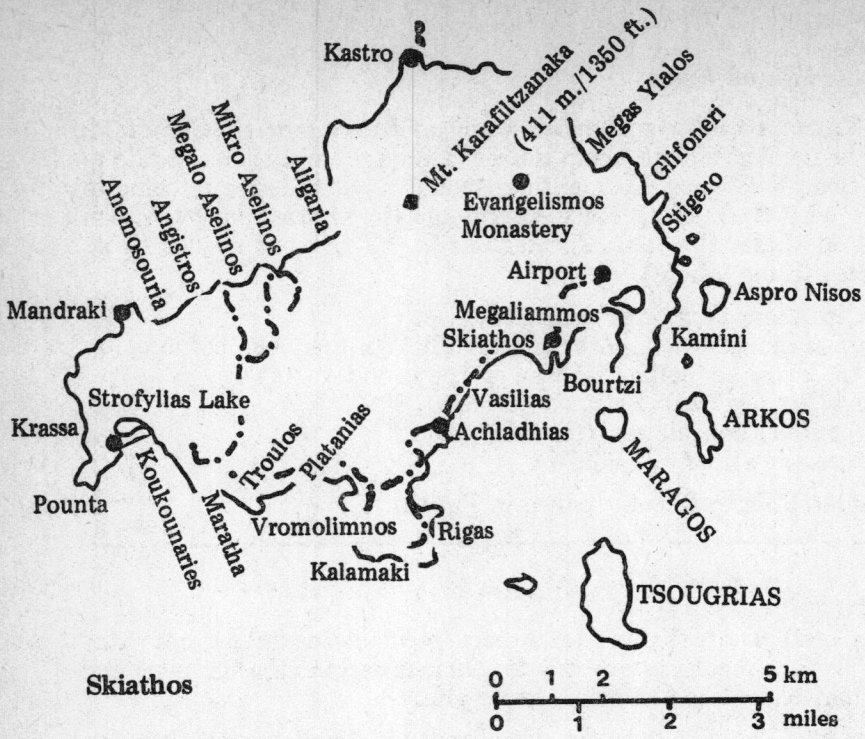

Skiathos

0 1 2   5 km
0   1   2   3 miles

1830, after union with Greece. A bridge connects the islet Bourtzi to the town, with its medieval fortress turned discotheque. In the little harbour to the right of Bourtzi are the many small caiques eager to take visitors to the beach of their choice; larger ones make the same excursion daily and post their times of departure. The island bus leaves from the other side of the waterfront, in the shade by the ugly statue. There is a waterskiing school, and in the summer theatre groups perform in town. One can visit the **home of Alexandros Papadiamantis.** Of the many restaurants the ones furthest from the waterfront are the less expensive.

Restaurants: Canapicia (the best), Karnaio, Limenakia, Mandraki, Yiannis', and Kipos (excellent moussaka).

Bazookia: Thelta, Skuna.

Discotheques: Bourtzi, Scorpio, Galaxy.

Specialities: Skiathiki tiropita (Skiathos cheese pies), chamali (like baklava).

Of the 62 beaches of Skiathos, the ones connected by the island's single road are first **Megaliammos** (with a restaurant), **Achladhias** (with tavernas and restaurants), **Vromolimnos, Platanias,** and **Troulos** (with a restaurant), facing the islets Troulonisia; further on are **Maratha** and the famous **Koukounaries,** a long sandy stretch shaded by pines with restaurants and water skiing. **Krassa** is a walk away and the largest nude beach on Skiathos. **Mandraki,** on the north-west coast, has lovely sand but is not connected by road; neither is **Aselinos** where one may also see the 17th-century church **Panayia Kounistra.** The

334

icon of the Virgin for which the church is named was discovered by a monk as it dangled from a tree. **Kastro,** in the middle of the north coast, is one of the less frequented of the major beaches. Two of the nine islets surrounding Skiathos also have attractive shorelines: **Tsougrias** with its beach **Lalarias,** a marvel with its silvery pebbles; and **Arkos islet.** There are many, many others. There are also three caves which can be reached by caique: **Skotini** (the dark cave — bring a flash), **Galazia,** the blue (by Lalarias), and **Chalkini,** the copper.

In the interior of the island, one may hike to the medieval capital **Paliokastro,** where inhabitants would take refuge in case of attack. Its ruins are interesting, including Byzantine churches and Turkish baths, and the view from the walls is worth the three-hour trip from Skiathos town. A two-hour walk takes one to the monastery **Panayia Kechia,** dating from the 15th century and the oldest on the island. It has some fine 17th century icons inside. **Evangelismos monastery,** built in 1797, attracted monks from Mt. Athos during the Kollivades movement. In 1827 the Skiathiots raised the Greek flag there for the first time. It has a small museum.

Panayiéria: 15 August, at Evangelismos; 27 August, Ag. Fanourios; 26 July, Ag. Paraskevi; 27 July, Ag. Panteleimonos.

Hotels in Skiathos: area code 0424

Nostos (A) has the unique feature of a small golf course besides its beach. The most luxurious hotel on the island, however, is the **Skiathos Palace** (L), on **Koukounaries** beach, the ideal starting point for the beach connoisseur.

L: Skiathos Palace, Koukounaries, tel. 42544/42242/42259 60; 3245963 in Athens; teleg. Dervenis Skiathos
A: Esperides, Achladhias, tel. 42245/42535; 323833 in Athens; teleg. Hotelesprides
A: Nostos, Tzaneria, tel. 4250/ (0421) 26133; teleg. Nostoshotel
B: Xenia, Koukounariesk, tel. 42041/42544; 3245963 in Athens; teleg. Dervenis Skiathos
C: Akti, 26 F. Georgiadou, tel. 42024
C: Koukounaries, 47 F. Georgiadou, tel. 42048/42021; 3243667 in Athens; teleg. Dervenis Skiathos
D: Avra, tel. 42044
D: Sporades, tel. 42165

Tourist Police: In Skiathos, tel. 42392

Skopelos

Connections: four times a week with Kymi; twice a day with Volos, Skiathos, and Alonnisos in the summer; frequently with Ag. Konstantinos.

History: Known in ancient times as Perparethos, Skopelos was another part of the Cretan Staphylos' colony in the Sporades. Recently his tomb was found there with royal Minoan trophies from the 16th century BC. In the 13th century King Pelias, usurper of the Iokan kingdom in Thessaly, settled the island; Pelias is known in history for ordering his rival Jason to undertake the quest for the Golden Fleece. Under Athens Skopelos retained a certain amount of autonomy and minted its own coins. Dionysos and Demeter were the most popular gods on the island. During Roman times it was given its present name, which means "cliff". The first bishop of Skopelos in the 4th century, Reginos, became the island's patron saint. When Philip Gizi played pirate he used Skopelos as his headquarters; his capture meant a decline in local excitement, enabling the inhabitants to return to a peaceful way of life until the Byzantine renegade's son Barbarossa decimated their island, leaving it deserted. The island gradually regained a population, including many refugees from the Turks. Skopeliot sailors fought with the Russians at Tsesmes, and the Russian admiral gave the islanders a larger church bell in thanks for their help. A British consul on Skopelos, Stephan Dapondes, founded an academy there. After assisting the Thessalian mountaineers in the Revolution, Skopelos joined Greece in 1830.

Skopelos today: Although not a few Greeks consider Skopelos as the most beautiful island in their country, the Skopeliots are the least enthusiastic in Greece with regards to the tourist industry. They give no encouragement to promoters. There is very little night life on the island, and most of the tourists so far have been Greek families. The entire 104 sq. km. (40 sq. miles) that make up Skopelos are covered with forests, giving the whole island a gentle pine fragrance. The waters by the beaches are generally shallow and safe for children. Some of the Sporades' best architecture is in the island's two major towns, and the women, as in Alonnisos, often wear their traditional blue and white dress.

Skopelos capital is considered one of the prettiest towns in Greece. The houses, rising up on the hill between the shore and the castle, are very colourful, incorporating many different styles. The older building have a definite Venetian touch, such as the Fragomacholas house; newer ones are built in a sturdy Thessalian style, while others seem Macedonian. The newer houses have been harmonized by incorporating older features such as balconies in their structure, and the Greek national instinct for planting a seed wherever it might have half a chance to grow manifests itself in the house gardens. Above the town is the **Venetian castle** of Gizi, which was so strong that Skopelos was left untouched during the War of Independence. Nearby at a site called **Ampeliki** are the ruins of an Asklepeion, half in the sea; a temple of Athena once stood where the castle is today, now replaced by the 9th century **Ag. Athanasios** with frescoes dating from the 16th century. On the other side of the town stands the fortified monastery **Episkopi,** where the patron saint Bishop Reginus lived. By **Ag. Konstantinos beach** a little

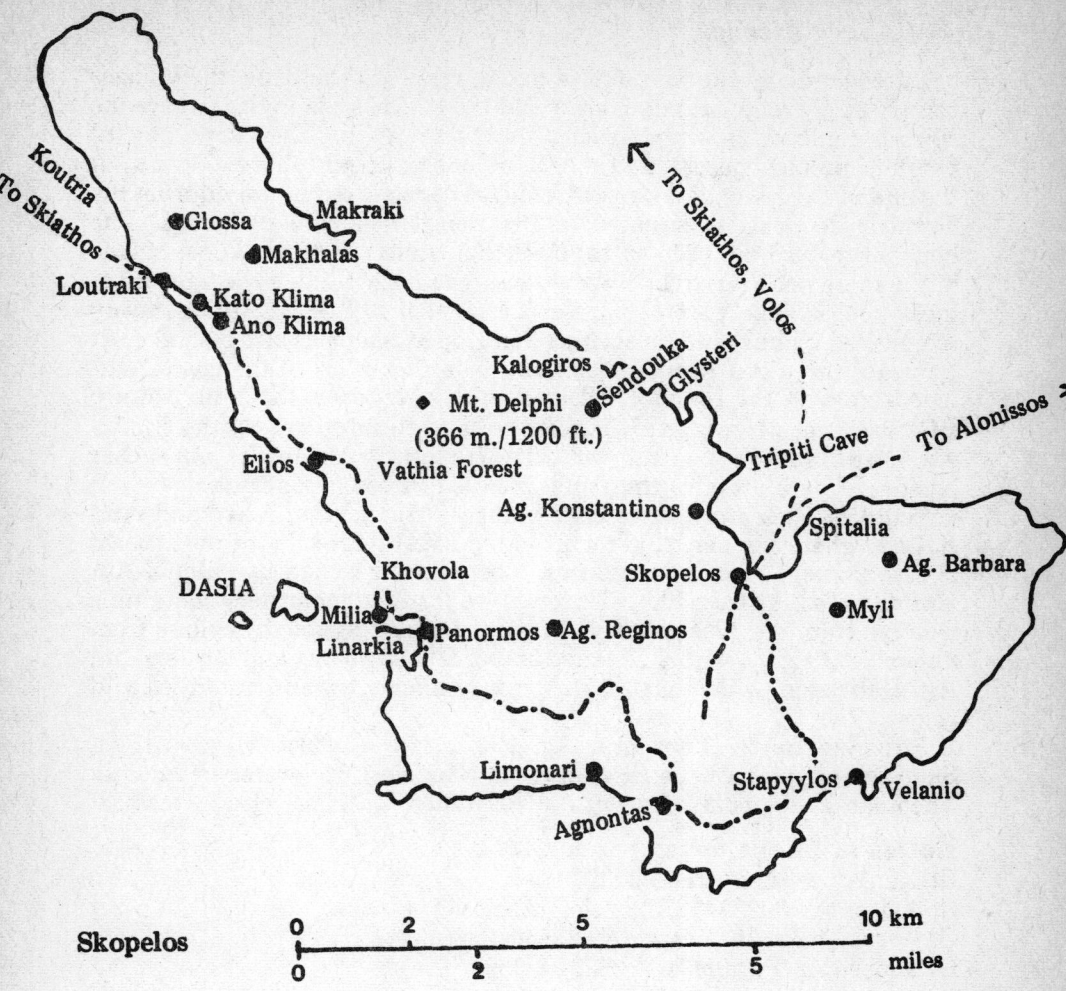

Skopelos

0	2	5	10 km
0	2	5	miles

to the north is a Hellenistic watch tower. Two nearby monasteries, **Evangelismos** and **Transfiguration** (now abandoned) were founded by monks from the Xenophon monastery on Mt. Athos.

In the vicinity of Skopelos one may also visit the **Fourno Damaskinon,** or the prune oven, which is in action during August.

There is a long beach right beside the town faced by a line of sweet shops specializing in loukoumades (hot honey pastries). Most of the Greek visitors stay here in the evening, while rucksackers pitch their tents (unofficially) on **Staphylos beach** in the south and listen to music in the evening.

Restaurants: Grippiotes, Lemonis Ioannes, Kosmos Kristos, Zorbas, Georgaki, Terpsi, and Tifiraki.

Specialities: Plums and prunes (the best in Greece), almonds, retsina.

Buses leave by the harbour (a yacht supply station) for the villages connected by road, mainly Glossa and the beaches Staphylos (where the Minoan tomb was found), Agnontas, Linarkia, Milia, Elios (by an awful patch of prefab houses), and other stretches of sandy shore. **Glossa,** at the end of the route, is a beautiful village constructed mainly during the Turkish Occupation, situated in the woods high above the sea. The houses survived the 1965 earthquake that ruined parts of Skopelos. One of the more peculiar architectural features is the toilet on the balcony of most houses. The port of Glossa, **Loutraki,** is 3 km (2 miles) away (connected by bus) and most ships that stop at Skopelos also call here. At Loutraki there is a pebble beach and tavernas. Most of the island's almonds grow in the region of Glossa, which also boasts three 4th century BC towers, at **Mavragani, Helliniko,** and **Sendouka.** By the church **Ag. Nikolaos** in Loutraki are the 7th century ruins of an earlier basilica. There are also the remains of a fortress at **Selinus.**

South of Glossa are three little villages, **Makhalas, Kato** and **Ano Klima,** where one may find rooms to rent. **Kalogiros** on the north coast is a settlement of country houses, most easily reached by caique. **Ag. Barbara,** a hike from Skopelos town, is a fortified monastery containing frescoes from the 15th century. Two islets are accessible by caique from Skopelos: **Tripiti,** with a sea cave and excellent fishing and lobsters and **Ag. Georgios,** which has a 17th century monastery and a herd of wild goats.

Panayiéria: 25 February, Ag. Reginos; 6 August, Megosotiri on Skopelos bay; 15 August, Panayias in Skopelos; 9 November, Esothia Theotoko at the edge of town; 25 November, Christos, also in town.

Hotels in Skopelos: area code 0424
B: Xenia (pension), tel. 32232
C: Aelos, tel. 32233/32132; teleg. Aeolos
C: Avra, Loutraki Glossa, tel. 33550/33681
D: American, Paralia, tel. 32231/32363

Tourist Police: In Skopelos, regular police.

Skyros
Connections: Daily with Kymi; four times a week with Volos.

History: Long ago the two distinct parts of Skyros were two islands: present-day southern Skyros was wild stone, while the north was fertile and pine-forested. A type of native Shetland pony, the Pikermies, ruled the southern part unopposed except at harvest time, when they were rounded up to assist the farmers in the north. This state of affairs went back countless years, perhaps even to the time of the Achaeans, when Achilleus was hidden on the island by his mother Thetis, in order to avoid the Trojan War. In the 6th century, the Athenian fleet came to Skyros, to destroy the island's sea power and to take possession of the relics of the hero Theseus, who had died on Skyros. Because so many Athenians eventually settled on Skyros, it was treated on equal terms with the city and paid no tribute. The Dionysia, in honour of the god of wine, was the biggest festival on the island.

Skyros remained part of Athens until 86 BC when General Sulla captured the city. During the Byzantine period, many important people were exiled to Skyros, marking the beginnings of a rather tyrannical upper class. Barbarossa took Skyros for the Sultan in 1538, and it is thought there was a small Turkish settlement on the island. During the First World War, the British built a naval base at Tris Boukies, and the English poet Rupert Brooke is buried there.

Mythology: Skyros was the home of Atlanta, a princess who refused to marry anyone who could not outrun her. This challenge brought young men from all over Greece but all failed to defeat the swift Atlanta, paying for their failure with their lives. The numerous tombs surrounding the stadium did not deter Melanios, however, who was determined to win her. Obtaining three golden apples from the Garden of the Hesperides, he challenged her to a race, and then won it by tossing the apples into Atlanta's path, forcing her to waste precious time in retrieving the treasures. Later, Atlanta was the only woman to accompany the Argonauts on their quest for the Golden Fleece. She also attended the great boar hunt, as Ovid relates, where she helped to take the prize, sparking off a show of ancient Greek male chauvinism.

Another famous personage associated with Skyros is Theseus, hero of Athens for his unification of Attica. In his later life, however, it appears that Theseus met a decline in popularity. He was exiled or retired to Skyros where he was the guest of the king, Lycomedes, who betrayed the ancient obligations of a host when he pushed Theseus off the Skyros acropolis. Another famous guest of King Lycomedes was Achilleus, who lived disguised in the women's quarters, a situation he profited from by fathering a son, Neoptolemis. A prophecy, however, declared that the Achaeans would never win the Trojan war without Achilleus, and so Odysseus went in search of the young hero. He suspected the trick of Achilleus' mother, Thetis, who had hidden her son in this way because she knew that he would die if he went to the war. In order to make Achilleus reveal himself, Odysseus brought a chest full of treasures when he called on King Lycomedes. These included perfumes, jewellery, finery — and a sword, which the young transvestite in the crowd of women seized joyfully for his own, just as Odysseus had anticipated. Thus Achilleus joined the Achaeans. When an arrow in his heel ended his life, Odysseus returned to Skyros to fetch his son Neoptolemis to Troy, and the war was eventually won.

Skyros today: Old customs and traditions on Skyros are still much in evidence. The men of the island still don their baggy blue breeches, flat leather shoes, and straw hats, and the women may often be seen in their long skirts and yellow scarves. The interiors of Skyriot houses are often adorned with carved wood and painted plates, the latter a local mania dating from the days of the wealthy Byzantine exiles.

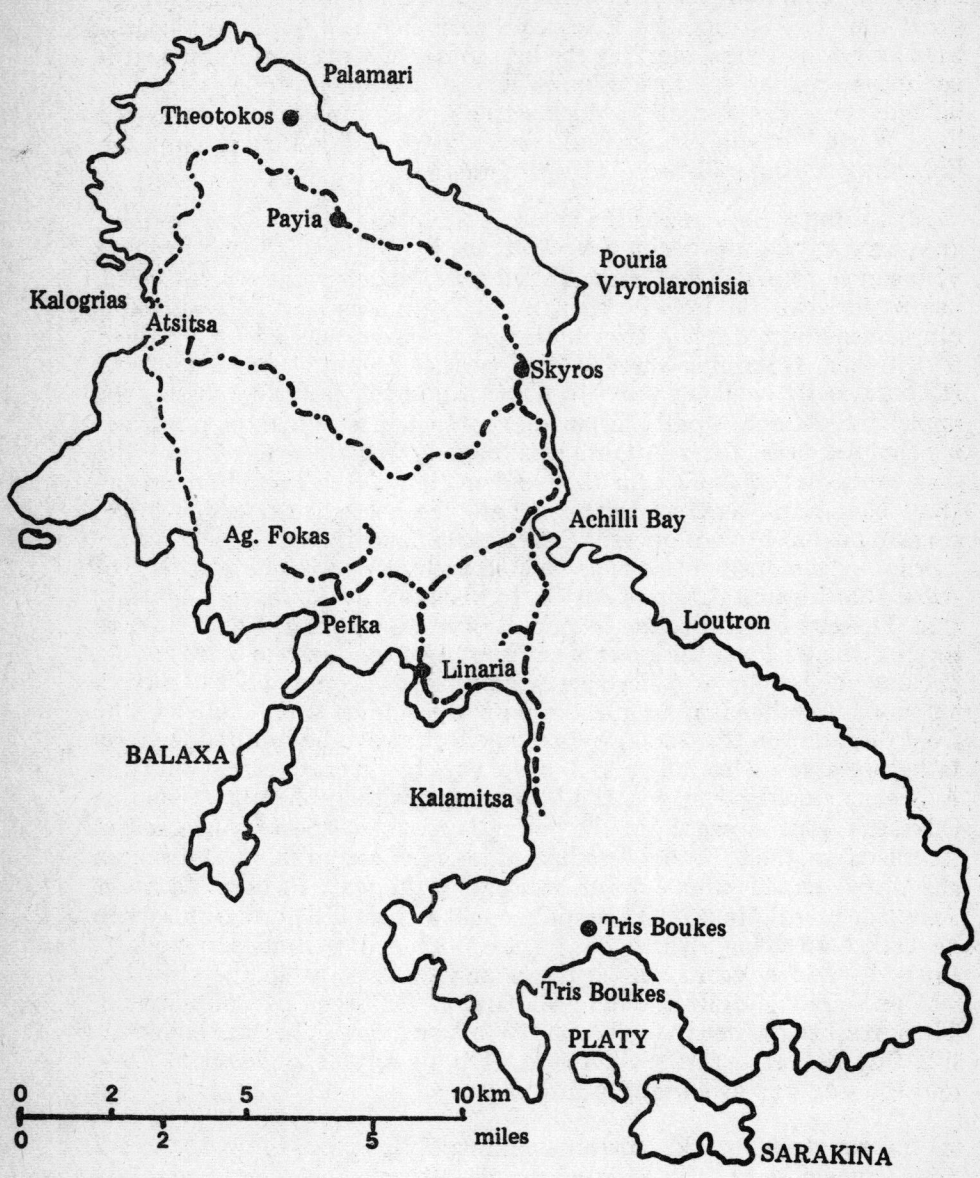

Palamari

Theotokos ●

Payia ●

Pouria
Vryrolaronisia

Kalogrias

Atsitsa

● Skyros

Ag. Fokas

Achilli Bay

Loutron

Pefka

Linaria

BALAXA

Kalamitsa

● Tris Boukes

Tris Boukes

PLATY

| 0 | 2 | 5 | 10 km |
| 0 | 2 | 5 | miles |

SARAKINA

Skyros

When these nobles lost their power, which had been so resented by the locals, they sold their dinner ware, creating the Skyriot status symbol which the women have since bought, traded, and displayed with great enthusiasm. Thus a Skyriot sailor in a distant land knows exactly what gift to bring his wife or mother: a plate. Some in Skyros are from as far away as China.

The very ancient inhabitants of the island are said to have worshipped goats and cattle, and vestiges of this cult remain even on modern Skyros. During Carnival, three characters dance down the street, led by a man in a goat skin costume and sheep bells called the Old Man, followed by the Frangos (the European) and the Korela (a man dressed up as a woman). These perform the Horos tou Tragoun, or the Goat Dance, an ancient rite that gave us the word "tragedy" ("goat song"). Every day during the carnival the Old Man, the Frangos, and the Korela make their way up to the monastery of Ag. Georgios, the patron saint of Skyros. Satires are produced, making fun of almost everything, along with other, more traditional festivities.

The capital village of **Skyros** is reminiscent of a Cycladic town with its hilly, narrow streets and white houses. Making hand-carved wooden furniture is the major occupation, and on 1-10 August there is an annual exhibition of local handicrafts. One may buy chairs and tables in the town, but bringing them home is about as easy as shipping an elephant to Alaska. There is an **archaeology museum** and the **Phaltaitch Folklore Museum** located by the **monument to Immortal Poetry** by Tombros (both open 9am-1pm and 4pm-6pm. Entrance 20 dr. free on Sundays). Each morning a towncrier still announces what is for sale in the greengrocers and when the ferry boat leaves. Because soldiers and restaurants get first option to buy bread in town, there is often a shortage in the summer.

A long path leads to **Magazia,** the nice, sandy beach below town; along the way are fine, open-air tavernas. Above town is the soufflé-like **acropolis** where Theseus met his doom. Part of the ancient wall remains along with the Byzantine-Venetian structure, built by the Duke of Naxos, Dalle Carcerio. The **church of Ag. Georgios** above town was founded by Nikephoros Phokas after his victory in Crete, and given to his friend Athanassios, who later incorporated it with the monastery Ag. Lavra on Mt. Athos. Scholars believe the church was built over a temple of Dionysos. Below the church is another one dedicated to **Ag. Athanassios.** Although there are not many hotels in town, the little widows in black have a grand old time trading tourists around their rented rooms.

Restaurants: Emmanuel Phergardi, Kampanera, Manolis Satholis; at Magazia Xenia, Stepahes Stephanideis, Yialos.

Discotheque: Skyropoula and On the Rocks.

Specialities: Graviera cheese, honey, all kinds of handicrafts.

The famous ponies of south Skyros have mostly been transferred to the islet **Skyropoula** in between Skyros and Kymi. There are two beaches on little Skyropoula, and a cave, **Kavos Spilia.** On Skyros itself the most popular beaches are **Atsitsa** (with a restaurant but no bus) **Pefka** (with a taverna), **Kalamitsa** (with a restaurant), **Agalipa, Kalogrias, Markesi** (with an ancient town nearby, dating back to 1000 BC), **Ormos Achilli** (where Achilleus embarked for Troy) and **Linaria,** the port of Skyros. One bus route connects Skyros to Linaria, while the other heads out in the direction of the beach Kalamitsa. From Linaria, a fishing village with colourful houses, one may take a caique to the sea caves **Pentekali, Gerania Spilies,** and **Spilies.** Caique is also the easiest transport to **Tris Boukes,** where one may visit the **grave of Rupert Brooke.**

Sites of the ancient, rival cities on Skyros have been found near Skyros capital, **Markessi, Vokolinas,** and **Chrission,** near the lovely beach Kalamitsa, where an ancient tomb is popularly known as "the tomb of Homer". Signs of an early Christian temple have also been excavated here.

Panayiéria: Carnival; 23 April, Ag. Georgios; 2 September, Ag. Mamon by Kalikri (Ag. Mamon is the patron of shepherds, and their festival also includes traces of ancient rites); 12 March, in town.

Hotel in Skyros: area code 222

The very popular Xenia (B) overlooks the lovely Magazia beach, only a kilometer from the pretty white village of Skyros itself. There are fine tavernas and night places in the vicinity.

B: Xenia, Magazia, tel. 91209; teleg: Xenia Skyros
E: Aegeon

Tourist police: Regular police in Skopelos

Evia (Euboea)

Connections: Athens and Chalki are connected by train nine times a day, and by bus 20 times a day. Bus connections from Athens to Kymi seven times a day, to Edipsos ten times a day, to Limni three times a day. Ferry boats between Oropou and Eretria, Rafina and Karystos, Rafina and Marmara, Rafina and N. Styra, Arkitsa and Edipsos, Glyfa and Kampos Agiou. Boats between Kymi and the Sporades, Limnos and northern Greece.

History: Inhabited from prehistoric times, Evia is first mentioned in Homer for its participation in the Trojan War. The island's two major cities, Chalki and Eretria, set up many colonies, the best known today being modern Chalkidiki. In the Archaic period the Ionians predominated on Evia. Chalki, which means copper, produced a great amount of that metal in this period and grew wealthy from its trade, and it and Eretria were among the most important cities before the domination of Athens. Only Eretria, along with Athens, dared to assist the Io-

nian uprising against powerful Darius, the King of Kings in Persia. This
sparked off Darius' attack on Greece in 490 BC, when he announced he
had come to castigate Athens and Eretria, although he was more interested in making their harbours his own.

In 338 BC Macedonia took Evia, and the Romans who followed them
used the name of an Eviot tribe, the Graeci, to refer to the entire Hellenic
people, an error which Europeans have perpetuated. Venice gained Evia
after the sack of Constantinople, placing the various feudal barons who
divided and ruled the fertile island between them under the King of
Thessalonika, Boniface de Montferrat. The main rulers were three lords
from Verona, who called the island Negroponte. When the Turks took
the island in 1470, they did not even allow a puppet Frankish governor to
remain, but occupied the island themselves, settling more permanently
then they did elsewhere in the Aegean. In 1830 Evia became part of the
original Greek kingdom.

Mythology: Evia, split from the nearby mainland with a blow of
earth-shaker Poseidon's trident, was the sea god's favourite island. He
lived in the Evian gulf in a fantastic palace with his wife Amphitrite.
South of this gulf is the Myrtoan Sea, named for a son of Hermes who
was a charioteer of King Oenomaus. Oenomaus had a beautiful daughter
and a team of divine horses. Anyone who desired his daughter's hand was
required to race the chariot of the king, which was invincible. Myrtilus,
the king's charioteer, himself wished to marry the princess, a fact that
the hero Pelops, a challenger in Oenomaus' race, took advantage of. If,
Pelops suggested, Myrtilus would replace the lynch pins in the axles of
the chariot with wax (thus enabling Pelops to win the race and the
princess), then Pelops would allow Myrtilus to share the girl. The
charioteer eagerly agreed, and events unrolled as predicted: Oenomaus'
chariot collapsed in the heat of the race. The king was killed and Pelops
was given his daughter. He and Myrtilus left with her in the direction of
Evia, but Pelops, never intending to keep his bargain with Myrtilus,
pushed him into the sea where he drowned. His father Hermes then named the sea in his son's honour.

Evia today: The second largest island in Greece after Crete, Evia is
separated from Boetia on the mainland by the famous Euripos strait,
now crossed by a short bridge. The currents of the Euripos strait or canal
change every six hours, a phenonemon that so puzzled the great Aristotle
that it drove him to his death, according to tradition. Despite its great
size and proximity to Athens, touristically Evia is one of the most
neglected islands in Greece, although efforts are being made to correct
this summertime deficiency. Evia has some of the best farmland in
Greece, which was the reason for its long Turkish settlement. Although
almost every hill of the island is crowned with some Frankish or Byzantine fortification, there are relatively very few Classical remains, coin-
ciding with Evia's relative lack of importance in ancient history. Quiet
rural farming has been the Eviot's way of life for centuries, and it

remains so today.

Chalki, the capital of Evia, lies at the narrowest point of the strait between the island and the mainland, a position which led to its early importance, for should Chalki wish, it could seriously block trade between Athens and the north of Greece. Next to nothing remains of its fortifications, however, except for the remains of a **Turkish fortress** across from the city, built on the ancient acropolis. An **archaeology museum** houses a few finds discovered in Eretria (open 9am-1pm and 4pm-6pm; 10am-2pm Sunday; closed Tuesday. Entrance 25 dr.; free Sunday and Thursday); and there is a **Byzantine Museum** on El. Venizelou, located in the old Turkish mosque. **Ag. Paraskevi,** the most interesting church in Chalki, was used by the Crusaders in the 13th century and is in the south of the town. Every year a market, "the panayieri of Ag. Paraskevi", livens up Chalki for ten days in late July, and people from all over the island and mainland swarm the stalls looking for bargains.

Chalki is a large industrial centre and not very pretty; smoky trucks chase pedestrians on the streets like bulls in the streets of Spain. Almost all of the summer visitors are Greek, and they spend their evenings lazing about the waterfront over a glass of ouzo and a bit of octopus. Nearby beaches include **Asteria,** which has been equipped with facilities and restaurants, **Likni, Ag. Minos,** and **Kourenti.** Boats also leave Chalki daily for the islet **Tonnoiron,** where there is a hotel and beach. A good bus service connects Chalki with all the major villages of the island and towns on the mainland such as Thebes. There is a yacht supply station.

Restaurants: Paliria, Samaras, Moukritsas, Stathis (3 km. (2 miles) away, specialising in chicken), Sofronis.
Discotheques: Top Hat, Asteria, Haros, Andrutsos.
Specialities: Meats, retsina.

If one has the time and energy, there is no better way of seeing Evia than by bicycle, for the terrain is not mountainous and there are innumerable springs and places to camp out. Beginning with the southern tip of the island, where poor Myrtilus drowned, **Karystos** is the largest village and the most popular with tourists, boasting a youth hostel. The modern town is near a Mycenean settlement, one of the defensive points of Evia. Ruins may be seen of the famous **Castel Rossa,** a huge fortification that the Turks occupied with 400 families. Turkish rule in the town was particularly harsh, and many Christians who refused to become Moslems were dealt a blow of the sword. Far more intact than the Castel Rossa is the coastal fort of the 14th century called **Bourdzi.** A long sandy beach stretches to one side of Karystos, excellent for a good night's sleep and known as Psili Ammos. Karystos is connected twice a day with Rafina on the mainland and has an active night life.

In the region of Karystos is another beach, 13 km. (8 miles) away at the **Borou Hotel.** Above the town is a large cave called **Ag. Triada,** which can be explored by torchlight. **Myli,** a village near Karystos, has ancient marble mines and a castle dating back to 1030. One may also visit the monastery Ag. Mavra. The **Katochi cave** by Kastanas seems to have been used as a small hotel in the past. At **Platanistos** there are large plane trees and a stream; visitors can stay overnight in rooms in the houses. At **Cape Kafateus,** the notorious Cavo Doro where tempests are all too common, are a few ruins of a Byzantine fortress, repaired by Admiral Likarios, the right hand man of the Emperor Michael Paleologus who restored the Byzantine Empire, beginning in Evia at this ruined fort.

Along the west coast are two small port resorts, **Marmari** and Nea Styra, connected by ferry from Rafina. By **Nea Styra** are the homes of the Dragons, which is actually a Venetian fortress. Ancient **Styra** lies above the modern town. Nearby are also the ruins of the Mycenean **Dryopes.**

Further north, by Evia's largest lake, are the walls of the acropolis of ancient **Dystos,** built during the Classical period and very well preserved. Homes and streets of the ancient lakeside city may also be explored. At **Lepoura** a branch of the good road heads north to **Kymi,** the point of embarkation for the Sporades. It is a very green village high above the sea, surrounded by forests. Many Greeks have built summer villas in the hills, some of quite ambitious design. While there are many restaurants and rooms to rent, Kymi has no night life except for the Psikas discotheque a few kilometres from town. Below the pretty village is the port **Paralia Kymi,** with yacht supply station and an average beach, generally crowded. Not far from Kymi at Cheili are the ruins of a Mycenean fort, and to the north, on a sheer rock, rises the Byzantine castle Apokledi. Above the town is the castle of Ag. Georgios, built during the Turkish Occupation, and just below it is the monastery Metamorphosis. At Avlonari, a village south of Kymi, one may visit a small fortress with a Venetian church inside. The tallest mountain of Evia towers to the west of Kymi, **Mt. Dirfys.** The Hellenic Alpine Club has built a mountain refuge at 1100 meters (3608 ft.) with 36 beds — for further information telephone (0221) 25230 in Chalki.

Aliveri, back on the road from Karystos to Chalki, is an old red-roofed village inhabited mainly by miners and men working in the nearby power station. There is a beach just below it and restaurants and pensions in town. Near Aliveri are the ruins of three ancient towns: **Amarinthos,** where the tall Venetian tower stands by the bay of Aliveri; **Tamynae,** above Aliveri; and **Porthmos,** near the beach.

Eretria, connected by ferry from Oropou, has been dubbed **Nea Psara,** although the ancient name is far more common. After Edipsou it is the largest resort on Evia, and has the best preserved antiquities on the island. In ancient days it rivalled Chalki, and the two cities did battle in that the combatants agreed not to use weapons of any sort, solving their dispute through wrestling contests and general fisticuffs. At the ancient

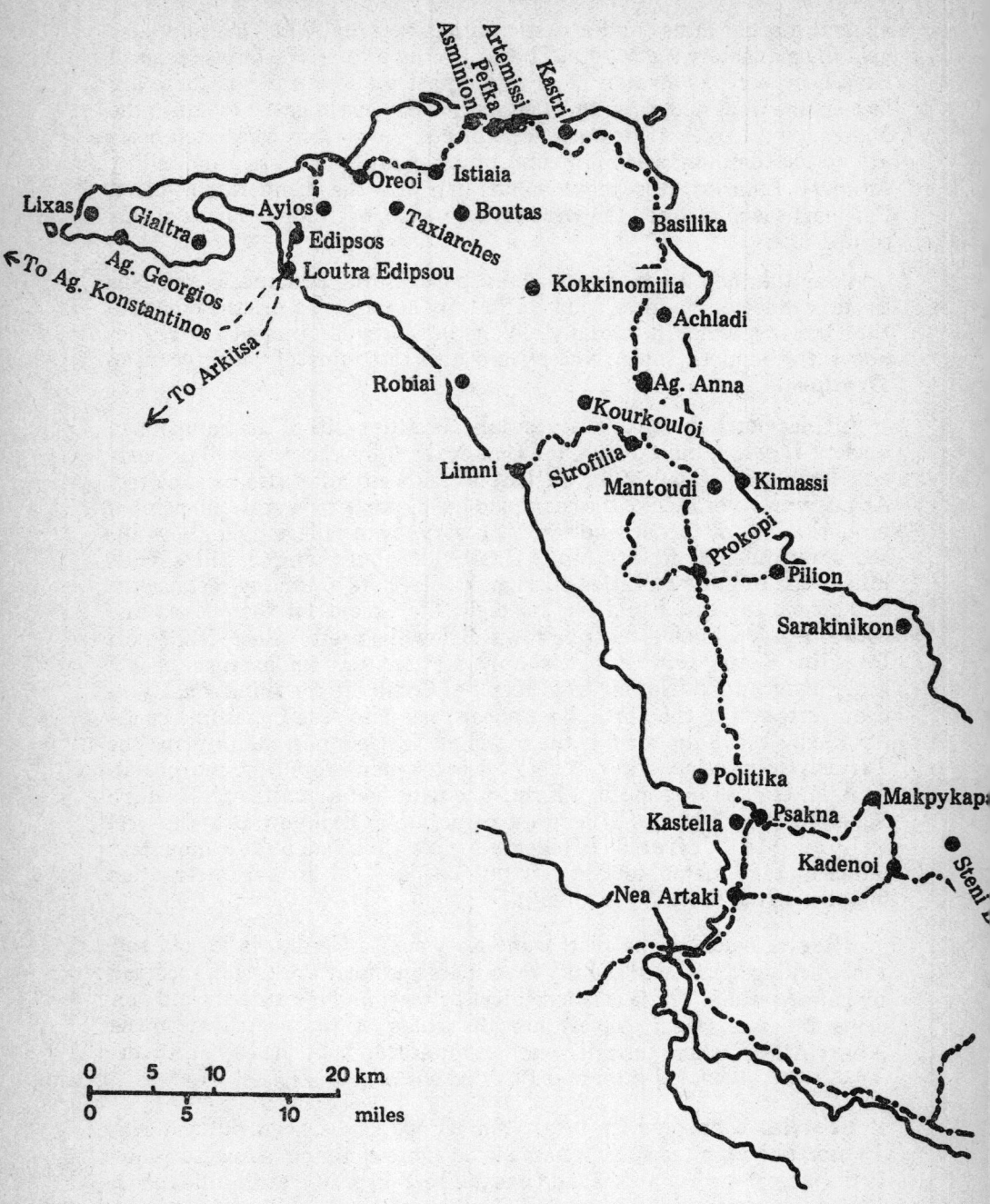

North Evia

The Sporades and Evia

Limnlonas

Lamari

Pyrgos

Konistrai

Kymi
Paralia
Oxilithos

To Skyros, Limnos

Chalki
Afration
Vasilikon
Lefkanty

Tharounia

Monodru

Oxdonia

Avlonari

Gymno

Nea Psara
(Eretria)

Amarynthos

Ag. Loukas

Aliveri

Lepoura

Dystos

Krieza

Argyro

Zarakes

Almyropotamos

Nea Styra
Kouvelas

Pyrgi

Kalergo

Kafireus

Antia

Marmari

Myli
Karystos

Psili Ammos

Platanistos

Potami

Kastri

0   5   10   20 km
0   5   10   miles

South Evia

theatre of Eretria are vestiges of the ancient mechanism which has saved the plots of many a play, the Deus ex Machina. On its acropolis are ruins of the citadel and a temple to Apollo Daphnephoros, who enjoyed a popular following throughout Evia. Although the city once had two harbours, one has since been filled in; by the other are remains of the ancient mole. A small museum in the town, open in the morning, houses local discoveries. There are many restaurants and rooms.

At both **Psakna** and **Politika,** north of Chalkis, are ancient fortifications; the most beautiful castle on the island, however, is on the road to the charming village Ahmet Agha, now known as **Prokopi.** **Kleisoura** is the name of the ancient fortress, built on a wild precipice that is almost impossible to climb. The Prokopi region of Evia, with its rich soil, trees and mountains, will enchant any visitor. The church Ag. Ioannes contains the relics of St. John the Russian, and to the north of the village stands the medieval tower **Beza Pyrgos.** From **Kimassi,** a port on the north-west coast, one may occasionally find a boat to Skiathos. **Limni,** on the opposite shore of Evia, is a fishing port turned tourist resort, surrounded by forests and boasting sandy beaches.

From Limni the road avoids the challenge of the mountains, taking a diversion across the width of the island and back again to the south-east coast, to the major tourist draw on Evia, Loutra Edipsou. One passes the village of **Artemissi** along the way, where a naval battle took place between the Greeks and the Persians in 480 BC. Here also, the statue of Zeus (or Poseidon), one of the prizes of the National Archaeological Museum in Athens, was discovered. Below Artemissi is a pretty beach, **Pefka,** with rooms available. This entire north coast of the island is spotted with beaches, popular with people from the big city Chalki.

Istiaia is the largest village on the way to Edipsou, but not very impressive in itself, although it was founded in ancient times by a people from Thessaly. They defied Athens so often that Pericles took the town and exiled the inhabitants, repopulating Istiaia with Athenians, who actually formed the nearby settlement of **Oreoi**, which dominated Istiaia for a time. The entire population of Evia rebuilt or renovated the fortress of the town, and there are other medieval fortifications at Oreoi.

Edipsos owes part of its popularity to its thermal, sulpherous waters, reputed for curing rheumatism, arthritis and gallstones, and a good many other problems, including depression. It has been famed since ancient times; Aristotle referred to Edipsos, and Augustus, Hadrian, and General Sulla visited the baths. It is connected frequently with Arkitsa on the mainland, on the major route from Athens to Thessalonika. Signs of the spa's long past can be seen, and there is a long, lovely beach. A seaside village on the peninsula facing Edipsos, **Lixas,** is connected with Ag. Konstantinos on the mainland. There are tourist facilities in the village, and a beach at **Ag. Georgios.**

Panayiéria: 15 August, at Kymi Oxilithos, Haito, Satsaroni, and Koupeios; 26 July, Ag. Paraskevi, long celebrations at Chalki, Myli, and Rukia; 17 July, Ag. Marinas near Karystos; 21 May, Ag. Konstantinos at

Vitalakimis.

Hotels in Evia

Lucy (A) is the finest hotel in the city of Chalkis. It faces the famous Euripos straits, and there is a fine view of the mainland from the garden on the roof. Ag. Minas beach is easily reached on the other side of the bridge. At the ancient bathing spa at Edipsos in northern Evia, the remodelled Aegli (A) is the most frequently recommended hotel in the area, not far from the famous baths. For more privacy, the resort Gregolimano (A) is not too far away, and has the added blessing of air conditioning.

in Ag. Anna (Chalkis): area code 0227
D: Aegli, d tel. 61277
in Ag. Minos (Drossia): area code 0221
A: Saint Minas Beach, a tel. 8241113/82357; teleg. Minas Beach
in Aliveri: area code 0223
D: Kentrikon, d 6 Platia Kriezotou, tel. 22222/22527
D: Kypros, d tel. 22221; teleg; Nicolaou
in Almyropotamos (Karystia)
C: Galazio Delfini, c
in Amarynthos: area code 0221
B: Blue Beach, b tel. 22467; 723057 in Chalkis; teleg. Blue beach
B: Stefania, b tel. 72485/72175/72176
C: Amarynthos, c 3 Karaiskaki, tel. 72241
D: Artemis, d 4 Ellispondou, tel. 72255

in Chalkis: area code 0221
A: Lucy, 10 L. Voudouri, tel. 23831; teleg. Lucy-Chalkis
B: Hilda, Angeli Goviou & Favierou, Paralia, tel. 28111; teleg. Hildatel Chalkis
B: John's, 9 Angeli Goviou, tel. 24996
B: Palirria, Leof. Voudouri-El. Venizelou, tel. 28001; teleg. Paliria-Chalkis
C: Hara, 21 L. Karoni, tel. 25541
C: Kentrikon, 5 Angeli Goviou, tel. 22375/27260
C: Manica, Panagitsa-Leof. Artakis, tel. 28922/28000
D: Ekali, 2 K. Varatassi, tel. 22670
D. Evripos, 5 Stef. Callia, tel. 22956
D: Morfeus, 3 Possidonos, tel. 24703
E: Iris, 3 Platia Athenaton, tel. 22246
E: Kymata, 21 Liaska
in Edipsos: area code 0226
A: Aegli, 16 Paraliakis, tel. 22215; teleg. Aeglotel
A: Avra, tel. 22226/22457
A: Petit Palace (pension), tel. 22206
B: Adonis (pension), 23 Philhellion, tel. 22257
B: Galaxias (pension), 5 Hermou, tel. 22184
B: Hara (pension), 2 M. Alexandrou, tel. 22236/22966

B: Hermes, 12 Hermou, tel. 22233
B: Heracleion, 7 Remvis, tel. 22247
B: Kentrikon, 14 25th Martiou, tel. 22302/22502
B: Thermae Syla, 2 Possidonos, tel. 22459, teleg. Thermesyla
C: Anessis Batis, Philhellinon & Vyzantinon Aftokratoron, tel. 22248;
teleg. Anessis
C: Artemission, 5 Philhellinon, tel. 22251
C: Atlantis, 31a Philhellinon, tel. 22627/22677
C: Galini, Ag. Nicolaou, tel. 22448
C: Ilion, 33 Philhellinon, tel. 22390/22690
C: Irene, 34 Vyzantinon Aftokratoron, tel. 22634
C: Istiaea, tel. 22049
C: Knossos, 16 Vyzantinon Aftokratoron, tel. 22460/22560; 7774026 in
Athens
C: Leto, 13 Hermou, tel. 22081/22204
C: Mikra Epavlis (pension), tel. 22579
C: Minos, 30 Vyzantinon Aftokratoron, tel. 22294/22720
C: Mitho, Thermopigon, tel. 22780/22370
C: Nefeli, 48 25th Martiou, tel. 22243
D: Achillion, Heracleous & Possidonos, tel. 22318
D: Aktaeon, 16 28th Oktovriou, tel. 22353
D: Asklipios, 56 25th Martiou, tel. 22241
D: Avrilia, 12 25th Martiou, tel. 22307
D: Diethnes, 10 Heracleous, tel. 22510
D: Crete (Kriti), 50 1st Odou Platania, tel. 22244
D: Lioutzi, 30 25th Martiou, tel. 22268/22301
D: Neon, 15 Vyzantinon Aftokrtoron, tel. 22319
D: Palladion, 32 1st Odou, tel. 22265
D: Panathinea, tel. 22267/22271
D: Pelasghia, 9 Vyzantinon Aftokratoron, tel. 22239
E: Megas Alexandros, 14 Thermopotamou, tel. 22353
E: Piraeus, 7 Vyantinon Aftokratoron, tel. 22238
Stadion, tel. 22246
in Eretria: area code 0221
B: Perighiali Eretrias, tel. 62439/62135/62113
C: Delfis, tel. 62380; 3625524 in Athens; teleg. Delfishotel
in Gregolimano (Lixas, Edipsos): area code 0226
A: Gregolimono-Roi Soleil (hotel & bungalows), tel. 33281; 3639119 in
Athens
in Istiaia: area code 0226
D: Hermes, 97a 4th Avgoustou, tel. 52245
E: Neon, 9 Angeli Goviou, tel. 52222
in Karystos: area code 0224
B: Apollon Resort, Psili Ammos, tel. 22045/5245427 in Athen
C: Als, Kriezotou, tel. 22202
C: Galaxy, tel. 22600
C: Karystion, Kriezotou, tel. 22391

C: Louloudi, tel. 22238; 5907206 in Athens
C: Plaza, 9 Loannou Kotsica, tel. 22337
in Kymi: area code 0222
C: Beis, Paralia, tel. 22604/22870
D: Aktaeon, Paralia, tel. 22604
E: Krinion, Platia G. Papanicolaou, tel. 22287
in Lefkanti (Chalkis): area code 0220
C: Lefkanti, tel. 52853
in Limni: area code 0227
C: Avra, tel. 31220
C: Plaza, tel. 31235
E: Ilion, 2 Ossiou Christodoulou, tel. 31768
in Magoula (Eretria): area code 0221
Holidays in Evia (hotel & bungalows), tel. 62611; 3246128 in Athens;
teleg. Holidevia
in Malakonta (Eretria): area code 0221
A: Eretria Beach, tel. 62411; 3222694 in Athens
B: Malakonta Beach (hotel & bungalows), tel. 6251; 3229185 in Athens;
teleg. Crowntrav (Athens)
in Marmari: area code 0224
C: Delfini, tel. 31296
C: Marmari, tel. 31301/31320
in Nea Artaki (Chalkis): area code 0221
B: Bel-Air (motel), tel. 42263
C: Angela, tel. 42330/42770
C: Telemachus, 3 Ag. Nikolaou, tel. 42111
in Nea Styra: area code 0224
C: Aegilion, tel. 41204/41254
C: Aktaeon, Paralia, tel. 41261
C: Delphini, tel. 41210; teleg. Delfini
C: Venus Beach (Akti Afroditis) (bungalows), tel. 41226
in Neos Pyrgos (Istiaia): area code 0226
D: Akroyali, tel. 71375
D: Oassis,
in Oreoi: area code 0226
Evia, tel. 71263/71214; teleg. Evia
Corali, tel. 71217
at Prokopion: area code 0227
Anessis, tel. 41277
at Steni (Chalkis): area code 0228
Dirphys, tel. 51217
Steni, tel. 51221
at Velos (Aliveri): area code 0223
Gerakina, tel. 22333, teleg. Gerakina

Tourist police: In Chalkis, 2 Kotsou St., tel. 24662; in Edipsos, tel. 23355

Index to Islands